UNITED STATES IMMIGRATION LAWS:
Working, Living, and Studying in America

SECOND EDITION

AF697096

BARST & MUKAMAL LLP

STEVEN S. MUKAMAL
AND
MARTIN L. ROTHSTEIN

DO NOT REMOVE FROM
LAW LIBRARY

AUG - 2 2000

GOLDEN GATE UNIVERSITY

William S. HEIN & Co., Inc.

Copyright 1999 by Barst & Mukamal LLP, all rights reserved

2 Park Avenue
New York, NY 10016
212-686-3838
fax 212-481-9362
email: bandm@barstmukamal.com
website: http://www.barstmukamal.com

ISBN 1-57588-531-X

Printed in the United States of America

Distributed exclusively by:
William S. Hein & Co., Inc.
1285 Main Street
Buffalo, New York 14209-1987
Telephone 1-800-828-7571
Facsimile 1-716-883-8100
http://www.wshein.com

AUTHOR'S NOTE

The internationalization of the world has greatly increased the flow of people entering the United States each year. Additionally, recent global, political, and economic changes have caused the United States to greatly adjust and revise its immigration and nationality laws and policies. Given the complexities and intricacies of the current law, it is more important than ever to master and understand the immigration process in order to deal with the increasingly bureaucratic nature of our immigration systems and procedures.

This handbook is being written during a period of great change in United States immigration law following the implementation of the Immigration Act of 1990 and the Illegal Immigration Reform and Immigrant Responsibility Act of 1996. As we go to press, many of the regulations embodying changes in the law still have not been published in final form. This handbook is designed as a comprehensive introduction to immigration law in the United States in order to endow business people and corporate managers and executives with an overall broad-based knowledge of this complex area of the law. However, this handbook should not be used as a substitute for legal counsel.

The authors wish to acknowledge the numerous individuals who contributed to the writing of this handbook, especially the research and writing provided by Alexis S. Axelrad, an associate at Barst & Mukamal LLP. We also acknowledge the numerous dedicated and knowledgeable staff members of the firm who provided invaluable assistance in the preparation of this handbook. Although much of the material reproduced in this book has been taken from the actual files of Barst & Mukamal LLP, all names of individuals and companies have been changed, and job descriptions have been modified, so that no example contained in this book relates to an actual individual, company, position or family relationship. However, the general content and format used represent time-tested models for approval of immigration applications.

Steven S. Mukamal
Martin L. Rothstein

New York, New York
June, 1999

TABLE OF CONTENTS

CHAPTER THREE - THE H VISA CATEGORY

CHAPTER SIX - O & P NONIMMIGRANT VISAS

CHAPTER SEVEN - A, C, D, F, G, I, J, K, M, Q AND R VISAS

CHAPTER NINE - LABOR CERTIFICATION

CHAPTER TEN - FAMILY-BASED IMMIGRATION

INTRODUCTION AND OVERVIEW OF UNITED STATES IMMIGRATION LAW AND POLICY

The United States has changed dramatically since it was established more than 200 years ago. In line with these changes, United States immigration policy has evolved and changed to reflect the economic and political state of the country as well as the world as a whole. The dominant trend in United States immigration policy in recent years has been one of complexity, selectivity and restriction.

Given the increasing restrictiveness and selectiveness of United States immigration policy in the latter half of the 20th Century, it has become more critical than ever to have a firm understanding of the United States immigration laws and regulations in order to effectively achieve one's goals.

Immigration law is concerned with controlling the entry of foreign nationals, known as "aliens." Like virtually every other nation, the United States, from its inception, has asserted the right to control the entry and presence of aliens. Basic immigration law is legislated by Congress with the concurrence of the President. By statute, the Attorney General is designated as the responsible officer for determining the admissibility of and regulating the terms of entry of aliens, and for expelling aliens not entitled to remain in the country. The Attorney General discharges these responsibilities through the Immigration and Naturalization Service (INS) and the Executive Office for Immigration Review (EOIR), which are both divisions of the Department of Justice. The Department of State is also directly involved in immigration enforcement in that it interprets the laws created by Congress and has the power to issue visas. Additional governmental agencies which play a part in the immigration decision making process include the Public Health Service, the Department of Labor, the Department of Health and Human Services, the Department of Commerce, the United States Customs Service, the Internal Revenue Service and the United States Information Agency.

United States immigration policy is largely reflective of the country's foreign policy. During the nineteenth century, immigration policy was very open, in light of the fact that the country was sparsely populated, and needed an expanding work force to develop the country. In the last quarter of this century, faced with unemployment and cyclical economic recession, United States immigration policy has taken on a more selective and restrictive aspect.

Chapter One
INTRODUCTION AND OVERVIEW OF UNITED STATES IMMIGRATION LAW POLICY

A. ROLE OF UNITED STATES GOVERNMENT AGENCIES IN THE IMMIGRATION PROCESS

Congress

Congress has broad powers to regulate immigration, and may set standards and distinctions regarding aliens which would be constitutionally suspect or impermissible in the context of domestic policy. Congress acts by passing legislation, which must be signed by the President.

Immigration & Naturalization Service (INS)

The Attorney General is responsible for the major administration and enforcement of the immigration and nationality laws. It is the Attorney General's duty to guard the frontiers of the United States, to determine the admissibility of those who seek to enter, to regulate the terms under which foreign nationals may enter and remain, and to expel those individuals not entitled to remain in the United States. The Attorney General has delegated the majority of these duties to the INS, and to the Executive Office for Immigration Review (EOIR), which is not part of the INS.

The Central Headquarters of the INS is based in Washington, D.C. and is headed by a Commissioner, who is an appointee of the President. The responsibility for the administration and enforcement of all laws relating to immigration, nationality and naturalization are handled through the three regional offices of the INS. The three regions are divided into Eastern, Central, and Western regions of the United States. The regional offices are headed by Regional Directors, who are responsible for the administration of the INS local offices located in their assigned geographic area.

The INS is further divided into district offices, located in over 30 major cities in the United States, as well as a number of key locations abroad. The district offices are headed by District Directors, who have broad powers to carry out the day-to-day operations of implementing and enforcing the immigration laws. District Directors have the authority to grant or deny applications and petitions submitted to the district office as well as the authority to initiate proceedings against foreign nationals. Formerly, the district office was the primary place applications and petitions were filed, now most of that responsibility has been delegated to the four INS Service Centers arranged by geographic area.

The four Service Centers are responsible for adjudicating the majority of petitions submitted to the INS. The INS Service Centers are located in Vermont, Nebraska, California, and Texas. Each Service Center is responsible for adjudicating the petitions of a particular jurisdiction made up of various states and territories. The Service Centers utilize a highly automated system of processing which is designed to settle pending petitions quickly and efficiently. In practice, each Service Center has its own procedures for filing and possible waiting times for application processing.

Department of State

The Department of State acts through the Visa Office in Washington, D.C. and United States consuls stationed around the world. The Department of State includes all offices within the State Department in Washington, D.C., its domestic field offices in the United States, all foreign service posts throughout the world and United States missions to international organizations.

The Secretary of State, as head of the Department of State, is charged with the administration and enforcement of many provisions of the immigration and nationality laws. The Secretary acts mainly through the U.S diplomatic and consular officers stationed throughout the world. The primary functions of the Department of State relate to the issuance of immigrant and nonimmigrant visas and United States Passports.

The Secretary of State is responsible for establishing regulations, prescribing forms and reports, entries and other papers, issuing instructions and performing other acts as he or she deems necessary for the carrying out of the immigration laws.

The Department of State is responsible for the preliminary screening and issuing of visas for persons seeking to come to the United States. This generally involves a dual review system. The State Department initially comes in contact with an individual when assessing their visa application, and later INS Inspection Officers at U.S. points of entry also inspect the individual. The Immigration and Naturalization Service and the Department of State attempt to coordinate their activities so that they work in harmony. However, in reality, this is not always the case. Consular officers or the Secretary of State may revoke a visa after it is issued.

Department of Labor

The Department of Labor acts in immigration matters through the Employment and Training Administration. In general, any foreign national who seeks admission as an immigrant based upon an employment petition is presumptively inadmissible. An immigrant may only be admitted based on employment after the Secretary of Labor has determined and certified to the Secretary of State and the Attorney General that there are no U.S. workers who are able, willing and qualified to fill the position. In addition, the Department of Labor must certify that the employment of the foreign national will not adversely affect the wages and working conditions of U.S. workers. For immigration purposes, U.S. workers include both U.S. citizens and lawful permanent residents.

The Secretary of Labor must certify that workers are unavailable in the locality of the alien's intended place of employment and that the employment of the alien will not adversely affect the wages and working conditions of American workers. When making these determinations, the Department of Labor will analyze the description of the job in the labor certification application and the conditions of the job market as a whole and within the particular profession in question. This process is known as "Labor Certification." Labor certification is required in some, but not all of the employment based immigrant categories.

B. IMMIGRATION STATUS IN THE UNITED STATES

Every individual who is present in the United States has a status under the immigration and nationality laws. Place of birth, parentage, employment or other factors may determine status. The following is a list of the different types of immigration status individuals may possess in the United States:

United States citizenship is the premier immigration status in the United States. United States citizens are individuals who were born in the United States, have obtained citizenship through United States citizen parents or who have become naturalized citizens. United States citizens enjoy the right to vote and may never be subject to deportation. Further, a United States citizen may petition for immigration benefits for many different types of relatives. All individuals born or naturalized in the United States are citizens under the Fourteenth Amendment of the Constitution.

Naturalized citizens enjoy the same rights as individuals born in the United States except the right to be elected president. The United States has a liberal naturalization policy. A foreign born individual who has been a permanent resident for five years may apply to become naturalized as a U.S. citizen. The Attorney General and the courts have the authority to naturalize citizens. Special expeditious naturalization benefits are granted to many classes of individuals such as the spouses of United States citizens.

Aliens are all individuals who are not citizens or nationals of the United States. Even long-term permanent residents are considered aliens under the immigration laws.

Permanent residents, also known as immigrants or "green card holders," are entitled to live and work in the United States permanently while maintaining their foreign citizenship. Lawful permanent residents can forfeit their right to residency if they do not maintain status and may be subject to the grounds of removal (formerly known as deportation).

Nonimmigrants are individuals who are authorized to come to the United States for a specific purpose and for a temporary period of time. Nonimmigrants may come to the United States to study, obtain specific employment, participate in authorized training programs, and participate in other types of activities that will be discussed in detail in this volume. Generally speaking, nonimmigrants are expected to leave the United States when they have completed their temporary authorized activity or employment.

A **refugee** is any person who is outside of the country of their nationality or habitual residence, and is unable or unwilling to return to that country because of persecution or a well-founded fear of persecution on account of race, religion, nationality, membership in a particular social group, or political opinion. An individual may also be considered a refugee even if he or she is still in the country of nationality or habitual residence, but is being persecuted or has a well founded fear that persecution on account of race, religion, nationality, membership in a particular social group or political opinion will occur. Refugees are paroled into the United States under quotas set by the President, and may apply for permanent residence one year after being granted refugee status.

An **asylee** is a person who has been granted political asylum <u>in the United States</u> but who has not yet been granted permanent residence. In order to be eligible for permanent residence, the alien must have been granted political asylum for at least one year prior to his or her application for permanent residence.

Temporary Protected Status is granted to natives of countries that are designated by the Attorney General as entitled to special consideration due to extraordinary circumstances of a temporary duration, such as armed conflict, civil war or natural disaster.

The final class of individual status is that of the **undocumented alien**. An undocumented alien, often referred to as an "illegal alien", is an individual who has entered the United States without entry documentation or without inspection, or who has overstayed their authorized period of admission, or has violated the terms of authorized status. Such aliens are subject to removal from the United States.

C. <u>FOREIGN NATIONALS (ALIENS)</u>

There are two broad categories of foreign nationals who may enter the United States: <u>nonimmigrants</u> and <u>immigrants</u>. Both of these categories have undergone great change over the years, the most recent and sweeping enactments came under the Immigration Reform and Control Act of 1986, the Immigration Act of 1990, and the Illegal Immigration Reform and Immigrant Responsibility Act of 1996.

<u>Nonimmigrants</u>

Nonimmigrants are admitted temporarily for a limited time and purpose, while immigrants are admitted for permanent residence. While immigrants enjoy many of the same rights as United States citizens, nonimmigrants have no right to remain in the United States beyond the period of stay authorized by the INS. Further, a nonimmigrant cannot engage in activities that are inconsistent with the purposes and conditions of the particular category he or she was granted approval for, such as accepting unauthorized employment. The Illegal Immigration Reform and Immigrant Responsibility Act of

1996 (IIRAIRA) created many new penalties for nonimmigrants who violate conditions of admission. These new provisions will be discussed in more detail in Chapter Eleven.

Many nonimmigrant categories require filing a petition at one of the four Immigration and Naturalization Service Centers. At the petitioner's request, the INS will forward the approved petition to a designated American Consulate, that will then issue a visa to the applicant. Other categories require the visa application to be submitted directly to an American Consulate.

Foreign nationals who seek to enter the United States are presumed to be immigrants unless it can be established to the satisfaction of the consular officer at the time of application for a visa that they are entitled to nonimmigrant status. When an applicant goes to the American Consulate to obtain a nonimmigrant visa the application must generally include documentary proof that the applicant intends to return to their home country and that the applicant's ties to their home country, either business, social, cultural or familial are sufficiently strong to assure his or her return after the expiration of authorized stay. If the consular officer is satisfied of the intent of the applicant to return, then a nonimmigrant visa will be issued. The consular officer cannot issue the visa unless satisfied that the foreign national is admissible to the United States and not subject to any ground of inadmissibility, such as a criminal conviction or a communicable disease.

The alien's admissibility is subject to further scrutiny when the individual arrives at a U.S. port of entry. Immigration Inspectors at United States ports of entry may not admit a visaholder if they believe that the individual does not intend to return to their home country or that the individual is inadmissible, by operation of law, to the United States. The most significant restriction imposed upon visaholders in many nonimmigrant categories is the prohibition against employment, in general, or employment that is not authorized under the specific visa that was issued.

Nonimmigrants may remain in the United States until the expiration or termination of the period of authorized stay, and may engage in activities compatible with the particular nonimmigrant classification that they used for admission. Employment that is not otherwise authorized by the particular visa classification is strictly prohibited.

Aliens who are admitted to the United States in one nonimmigrant classification and desire to engage in activities appropriate to a different nonimmigrant classification may apply to the INS for a change of nonimmigrant status. For example, if an individual is authorized under L-1 classification to work for a specific multinational corporation, the individual may not be employed by any other organization without first securing authorization from the INS. Any unauthorized activity by the individual may result in measures to enforce the individual's departure from the United States, or actual removal following formal proceedings.

Although (with a few exceptions) there are no limits on the number of nonimmigrants that may be admitted to the United States, nonimmigrant status is considered temporary and may not be prolonged indefinitely. Unlike permanent residents, nonimmigrant status alone can not be converted into naturalized citizenship.

Nonimmigrant Visa Categories

The following are the nonimmigrant visa categories available for temporary entry into the United States:

A-1 **Ambassador, Public Minister, Career Diplomatic or Consular Officer, and members of their immediate family.**
A-2 **Other Foreign Government Official or employee, and members of their immediate family.**
A-3 **Attendant, servant or personal employee of A-1 and A-2 visaholders, and members of their immediate family**
B-1 **Temporary Visitor for Business**
B-2 **Temporary Visitor for Pleasure**
C-1 **Alien in Continuous Transit**
C-2 **Alien Qualified to pass in transit to and from UN Headquarters District and Foreign Country.**
C-3 **Foreign Government Official, members of immediate family, attendant, servant and personal employee in transit.**
D **Crew members**
E-1 **Treaty Trader, spouse and minor children**
E-2 **Treaty Investor, spouse and minor children**
F-1 **Full-time Academic Students attending approved schools**
F-2 **Spouse and minor children of student**
G-1 **Principal resident representative of recognized foreign member government to international organization, staff and members of immediate family.**
G-2 **Other representatives of recogized foreign member government**
G-3 **Representative of non-recognized or non-member foreign government to international organization and members of immediate family**
G-4 **International organization officer or employee, and members of immediate family**
G-5 **Attendant, servant or personal employee of G-1, G-2, G-3 and G-4 visaholders and members of immediate family**
H-1A **Professional Nurses (no longer available)**
H-1B **Professional Temporary Workers within designated Specialty Occupations**
H-2A **Temporary Agricultural Workers performing work of temporary or seasonal nature**
H-2B **Skilled or unskilled workers performing temporary services or labor.**
H-3 **Trainees**
H-4 **Spouse and minor children of H-1, H-2 and H-3 visaholders**
I **Representative of Foreign Media, spouse and children**
J-1 **Exchange Visitors in approved programs**
J-2 **Spouse and children of J-1 exchange visitor**
K-1 **Fiance(e)s of U.S. citizens immigrating to the United States**
K-2 **Children of K-1 fiancé(e)s**
L-1A **Intracompany Transferees: Executives and Managers**
L-1B **Specialized Knowledge Employee**
L-2 **Spouse and children of L-1 intracompany transferee**
M **Students in approved Vocational Study Programs**
N-8 **Parent of an alien child designated as a special immigrant**

N-9 Child of a parent designated as a special immigrant

NATO-1 Principal Permanent Representative of Member State to NATO, and members of immediate family

NATO-2 Other Representatives of Member States to NATO, and members of immediate family

NATO-3 Official Clerical Staff accompanying a represenative of Member State to NATO, and members of immediate family

NATO-4 Other Officials of NATO, and members of immediate family

NATO-5 Experts, not eligible for NATO-4, employed on missions on behalf of NATO and their dependants

NATO-6 Civilian members of accompanying force entering under NATO provisions, and their dependants

NATO-7 Attendant, servant, or personal employee of NATO-1, NATO-2, NATO-3, NATO-4, NATO-5, and NATO-6, and members of immediate family

O-1 Persons with Extraordinary Ability in the Sciences, Arts, Education, Business or Athletics

O-2 Certain Aliens Accompanying O-1 visaholders

O-3 Family members of O-1 visaholders

P-1 International Athlete or member of internationally recognized Entertainment Group

P-2 Artist or Entertainer in a reciprocal exchange program

P-3 Artist or Entertainer in a culturally unique program

P-4 Spouse or children of P-1, P-2,and P-3 visaholders

Q-1 International Cultural Exchange Program Participants

Q-2 Irish Peace Process Cultural and Training Program Participants

R-1 Religious Workers

R-2 Spouse or children of R-1 visaholders

S-5 Individual supplying critical information concerning a criminal organization or enterprise

S-6 Individual supplying critical information relating to terrorism

TN North American Free Trade Act (NAFTA) professionals

TD Spouse or child of NAFTA professional

General Overview of Nonimmigrant Visa Categories

The **A-1 Visa** is issued to designated diplomatic officials and personnel of foreign nations who are coming to the United States to perform duties and services on behalf of their governments.

The **B-1 Visa** is a visitor's visa designed to enable foreign business people to travel to the United States on behalf of their foreign employers. B visaholders may only engage in activities which are incidental to their employment overseas and does not involve domestic employment or payment other than reimbursement for expenses. B-1 nonimmigrants may not be paid from a source within the United States.

The **B-2 Visa** is a visitor's visa which allows individuals to enter the United States, usually for an initial period of six months, to engage in leisure and tourist activities.

Since 1990, the United States government has conducted the **Visa Waiver Program** which allows individuals of specific countries to enter the United States as temporary visitors without having to first obtain a B-1 or B-2 visitor's visa, provided that they meet all the necessary requirements. Individuals admitted to the U.S. pursuant to the visa waiver program are limited to a ninety-day period of authorized stay. The requirements of this program will be examined in more depth in Chapter Two.

The **C-1 Visa** is a transit visa which enables travelers to make transportation carrier connections in the United States in order to reach their final destinations. The C-1 visa is not a commonly issued visa. Under no circumstances may a C-1 visaholder be employed in the United States. A C-1 visaholder's period of admission may not exceed 29 days.

The **D-1 Visa** is for crewmen, i.e. captains and stewards of ships, airplane crew, etc... The D-1 visaholder may not work or change status in the United States. A D-1 visaholder's initial period of admission may not exceed 29 days. In addition, even though a crewman has been permitted to enter the United States, he is not "admitted" for purposes of the immigration laws.

The **E Visa** is a very useful visa category for foreign-owned companies. An E visaholder may be able to enjoy a long-term period of stay in the United States. The initial authorization period of the visa is five years with unlimited extensions granted in increments not to exceed two years. The E-1 Visa is designed for companies and individuals engaged in substantial trade between their home country and the United States. An E-2 visa is available where a substantial foreign investment has been made in a United States enterprise. The issuance of an E visa depends upon the existence of an appropriate treaty between the United States and the investor or trader's home country.

E-1 and E-2 visaholders are not required to maintain a foreign residence during their temporary stay but must maintain an intention to depart the United States once the E visa has expired. E-1 and E-2 visaholders are permitted to apply for extensions of stay, changes of status, and may apply for lawful permanent residence.

The **F-1** visa is a student visa that enables foreign nationals to study in the United States at accredited academic institutions. A foreign student who wishes to study in the U.S. must obtain prior approval from a prospective school that has permission from the INS to enroll foreign students. If the student meets the admission criteria of the prospective school, the school is authorized to issue Form I-20A, the Certificate of Eligibility. Although an F-1 visa is valid for a specific period of time, an F-1 visaholder may remain in the United States for as long as the student remains in status and keeps moving towards the approved educational goal. This is referred to as Duration of Status (D/S). Under certain circumstances, F-1 visaholders may work while enrolled in school, if they secure the appropriate approval from the Designated School Official (DSO). In some cases the INS and the Department of Labor must also grant approval for work authorization. Prior to or upon graduation, the student may engage in practical training for up to twelve months, provided that the student gets authorization from the foreign student advisor at their school. Twelve months is the maximum time for practical training, regardless of whether it was performed during the student's academic career or post-graduation.

"The McDonald's Law" was a statutory provision enacted as a result of lobbying by the McDonald's fast food organization. It paved the way for American companies to hire foreign students. A foreign student may work for 20 hours a week, provided that a labor attestation is filed with the Department of Labor after a 60 day recruitment period that certifies there are no U.S. workers available.

Participating in practical training after graduation is beneficial because it provides an employer with a convenient way to hire a foreign student without the need to go through an immediate petition process with the INS. However, such employment is limited and must be within the student's academic area.

F-1 visas may no longer be issued to foreign students who seek to enroll in public elementary schools. In addition, F visas may only be issued for one year to foreign students who seek admission to public secondary schools. Foreign students who wish to enroll in public secondary schools must now reimburse local school districts for the full cost of attendance.

The **G Visa** is designed for employees of international organizations such as the United Nations, World Health Organization, and the International Labor Organization. A G visaholder is admitted for an initial period not to exceed three years and may be granted extensions of temporary stay for not more than two years. G employees and their spouses and dependants may not work outside of their organizations unless specifically authorized to do so by the Immigration and Naturalization Service.

The **H-1A Visa** was for temporary workers performing services as registered nurses. This classification expired on September 1, 1995, but certain foreign nurses already in H-1A status were eligible to obtain an extension of stay until September 30, 1997. The H-1A program has not been extended. Under limited circumstances a foreign nurse may petition for H-1B status.

The **H-1B Visa** is for members of the professions, known as "specialty occupations." These individuals must generally have a minimum of a Bachelor's Degree or equivalent education and experience. Congress has also included High Fashion Photographic Models in this category. A labor condition application certified by the department of labor and an approved nonimmigrant petition by the INS are prerequisites for H-1B visa issuance. The employer must pay the foreign national the higher of the actual wage or the prevailing wage for the position, according to the best information available at the time of filing a labor condition application. The maximum period of time an individual may remain in H-1B status, including any extensions of stay, is six years. An H-1B visaholder does not have to retain a foreign residence during the period of temporary stay. H-1B employers are liable for the reasonable costs of the individual's transportation costs at the end of authorized stay. The Immigration Act of 1990 created a binding annual limit on the total number of H-1B visas that may be issued during each fiscal year. Congress determines the annual limit.

The **H-2A Visa** is designed for temporary agricultural workers to perform service or labor of a temporary or seasonal nature. The prospective employer of an H-2A worker must first file an application with the Department of Labor. The H-2A visaholder's duration of stay is limited to the term of the approved petition, however, the worker may obtain an extension of stay. Once an alien has been in H-2A status for a total period of three years, the alien is not eligible to be considered for another H-2A visa until the alien has remained outside of the United States for at least six months.

The **H-2B Visa** is designed for skilled or unskilled workers who will perform other temporary services or labor for which no United States citizens or lawful permanent residents are available. An H-2B visa also requires prior approval by the Department of Labor. The period of authorized stay and employment should not exceed one year. The employer may petition for an H-2B worker for employment caused by a one-time occurrence, seasonal needs, peakload need or intermittent need. There is also an annual limit per fiscal year for this visa category.

Both the H-2A and H-2B visa categories require the employer to demonstrate there are no United States workers who are available to perform the temporary services or labor. In addition, H-2 visaholders must maintain a residence in a foreign country that they have no intention of abandoning during temporary stay in the United States. H-2A and H-2B visaholders total period of stay may not exceed three years.

The **H-3 Visa** is designed for nonimmigrants who are coming temporarily to the United States to receive training in any field or endeavor at a particular organization. An H-3 visaholder is prohibited from doing productive work in the United States. To be approved the training program must be designed for on the job training or learning and observing in a classroom type environment. When determining if the H-3 visa category is appropriate for a specific individual it is important to fully investigate the background, degree and salary of the candidate. An H-3 visa may be valid for up to two years. H-3 trainees must maintain a residence in a foreign country that they have no intention of abandoning during temporary stay in H-3 status.

The **H-4 visa** is a derivative category for spouses and unmarried minor children of H visaholders. H-4 visaholders are not entitled to work in the United States. H-4 visaholders are often qualified to change to another status such as H-1B, if they wish to work in the United States.

It is common to have nonimmigrant visaholders travel to the United States with their families. In the instance of an older child who is accompanying his parents in H-4 status, it may be beneficial for the child to change to F-1 status. This change will enable a child of college age to enjoy the benefits of F-1 status, including practical training authorization and the ability to work for up to twelve months prior to and post graduation. Although a change to F-1 status may be beneficial, it is not required, and derivative children and spouses may attend universities with H-4 visas. In addition, F-1 students may only attend public schools under very limited circumstances.

The **I Visa** is designed for members of the International Information Media, especially journalists and foreign correspondents. The I visaholder's authorized stay is limited to the duration of authorized employment.

The **J Visa** is designed for exchange visitors who are participating in a program approved by the United States Information Agency (USIA). In many instances, J visaholders may face a two-year foreign residence requirement after completion of the approved program before they are eligible for any other nonimmigrant categories or for permanent residence. The spouse and children of a J-1 exchange visitor may only accept employment authorized by the INS.

The **K Visa** is designed for fiancées of United States citizens who intend to marry and apply for permanent residence within ninety days of admission. An approved K visa petition remains valid for a period of four months and may be revalidated for another four months by a district director or a consular officer.

The **L-1 Visa** is designed for intracompany transferees in managerial, executive, or specialized knowledge positions, employed by multinational companies doing business both in the United States and abroad. The L visa is a very valuable tool for foreign businesses because it allows employees to be transferred between parent and subsidiary organizations, from subsidiary to parent companies, between different joint ventures, between sibling organizations and to new offices. To qualify, the foreign organization and the U.S. employing entity must be under common ownership and control.

Three criteria must be met to be eligible for an L-1 visa. The organization employing or that will be employing the foreign national must be a qualifying organization in accordance with INS regulations. In addition, intracompany transferee must be performing in an executive, managerial, or specialized knowledge capacity. And the intracompany transferee must have been employed abroad for at least one year, over the last three years, with the same international organization in a position that was managerial, executive, or involved specialized knowledge. Finally, the foreign national's prior education, training, and employment must qualify the individual to perform the prospective job in the United States.

There is a fair amount of overlap between the H, L and E visa categories, which are the most frequently used visas for international business personnel. When choosing which visa category to apply under, it is best to analyze and compare the individual alien's qualifications and needs against the requirements and characteristics of each visa option. Therefore, if an alien is performing in a managerial or executive role, and has been employed by the foreign employer for one of the past three years, he might apply for an L-1 visa, as opposed to applying for an H-1B visa. If the alien's experience and qualifications are more suited to an H-1B visa and this option is chosen, a labor condition application must be filed with the Department of Labor. This extra step may take more time and also gives the DOL an opportunity to review and dispute the wage being paid the employee. In comparison, if the corporate relationship between the United States and the foreign employer is quite complex, it might be easier to file for an H-1B. The best strategy is always determined on a case-by-case basis.

An L-1 Manager or Executive may stay in the United States for a cumulative period of seven years, and a Specialized Knowledge Employee may remain for a total of five years. Further, an individual who originally comes to the United States as an L-1 specialized knowledge employee, but then assumes a managerial role, may also be eligible to stay for a maximum period of seven years. An L-1 visaholder is usually granted an initial stay of three years with extensions granted in two-year increments until the maximum period of stay is reached.

Multinational companies who regularly petition the INS for L-1 visas may use the Blanket L petition to expedite and streamline the petitioning process. The L-1 visa is one of the most useful visas for international business personnel.

The **M Visa** is designed for individuals who seek to enter the United States temporarily and solely to pursue a full course of study at an established vocational or other recognized nonacademic institution approved by the Attorney General. Like the F-1 visa, a foreign student who wishes to study in the U.S. at a vocational school must also obtain prior approval from the prospective school. If the student meets the admission criteria of the prospective school, the school is authorized to issue Form I-20M, the Certificate of Eligibility. A M visaholder must maintain a foreign residence abroad during the period of temporary stay in the United States. This visa enables the visaholder to be accompanied to the United States by his or her spouse and children.

The **O Visa** is designed for individuals, and their family members, as well as aliens accompanying the primary O visaholder, who have extraordinary ability in the sciences, arts, education, business or athletics. Extraordinary ability must be demonstrated by sustained national or international acclaim. Extraordinary ability in the field of motion picture and television production must be demonstrated by proof of extraordinary achievement.

The primary O visaholder does not have to maintain a foreign residence abroad during the period of temporary stay in the United States. An individual granted O-2 classification to accompany and assist the primary O visaholder must maintain a foreign residence abroad that they have no intention of abandoning during the period of temporary stay in the United States.

A petition for an O visa must be supported by a consultation letter from an individual or peer group in the alien's field that testifies to the alien's ability and accomplishments. For support personnel of the primary O visaholder, the consultation letter must contain a no objection statement to the employment by the appropriate entity.

An O visa petition may be approved for an initial period of stay of up to three years. O visaholders may apply for extensions of stay in one-year increments. Although there is no overall limit on the total period of stay in O status, an O visaholder is expected to depart when the approved activity is completed.

The **P Visa** is designed for individuals who perform as athletes, individually or as part of a group or team, at an internationally recognized level of performance, or for individuals of an internationally recognized entertainment group who are coming to perform as artists or entertainers under a reciprocal exchange program, or individuals who are coming solely to perform, teach, or coach under a program that is culturally unique. A P visaholder must maintain a foreign residence abroad during the period of temporary stay in the United States.

Approval of a P visa requires consultation with labor organizations having expertise in the specific area of athletics or entertainment of the foreign national. An individual P athlete may be admitted for an initial period of up to five years, and may apply for an extension of stay for up to five years, for an overall limit of ten years. All other P visaholders may be admitted for up to one year and may be granted extensions of stay in one-year increments.

The **Q Visa** is designed for individuals who are coming temporarily to the United States (for a period not to exceed 15 months) to participate in international cultural exchange programs approved by the Attorney General for the purpose of providing practical training, employment and the sharing of the history, culture and traditions of the country of the alien's nationality and who will be employed under the same wages and working conditions of domestic workers.

An international cultural exchange program must meet three requirements to be considered for approval. First, the cultural exchange program must take place in a school, museum, business or other establishment where the public is exposed to aspects of a foreign culture as part of a structured program. Second, the cultural component must be an essential and integral part of the Q nonimmigrant alien's employment or training. Third, the alien's employment or training may not be independent of the cultural component.

Q visaholders must maintain a foreign residence abroad that they have no intention of abandoning. In addition, a Q visaholder must spend at least one-year out of the United States prior to reapplying for a new Q visa.

The **R Visa** is designed for individuals and their spouses and children, who for the two years immediately prior to the petition, have been a member of a religious denomination having a bona fide non-profit, religious organization in the United States and who seek to enter for a period not exceeding five years to perform religious work. At the end of authorized stay, R visaholders must spend one year outside of the United States before reapplying for a new R visa.

Religious workers include:

1) Ministers of Religion
2) Professional workers in religious vocations and occupations
3) Other religious personnel who work for a religious non-profit organization or tax-exempt entity.

The **S** visa is designed for individuals and their spouses and children who participate as witnesses or informants in criminal matters. There are two different types of S visas. An S-5 visa is available to individuals who possess critical, reliable information concerning a criminal organization or enterprise, and who are willing to supply or has supplied information to Federal or State law enforcement authorities or Federal or State courts. An S-6 visa is available to individuals who possess critical reliable information concerning a terrorist organization, enterprise, or operation, who are willing to supply or has supplied information to Federal law enforcement authorities or Federal court, and will be or has been placed in danger as a result of providing that information. The Attorney General and the Secretary of State must certify that the alien has met all the statutory requirements of the visa category. This visa is very limited and is rarely utilized.

The **TN** nonimmigrant category was introduced as a result of the North American Free Trade Act (NAFTA) which went into effect on January 1, 1994. The TN nonimmigrant category is available to Mexican and Canadian citizens who seek temporary entry as business people to engage in activities at a professional level. Although similar in many respects to the H-1B visa category, TN nonimmigrants are subject to different requirements and procedures for admission to the United States. In order to qualify as a TN nonimmigrant, the individual must be engaged at a professional level in one of the occupations or professions enumerated in the regulations and meet the educational and/or experience requirements for the specific occupation. There are over forty different occupations that are enumerated in the regulations. For example, accountants, computer systems analysts, engineers, lawyers, and university teachers are eligible for TN classification.

Additionally, TN nonimmigrants must maintain nonimmigrant intent during their temporary stay in the United States. INS regulations provide for different procedures for Canadian and Mexican citizens who wish to enter the United States as TN nonimmigrants.

Canadian citizens may directly apply for admission as a TN nonimmigrants at U.S. ports of entry and are visa exempt. Mexican citizens are not exempt from the visa requirement and are required to file a pre-petition with the INS' Northern Service Center before proceeding abroad to a U.S. Consulate for visa issuance. In addition, only 5,500 Mexican citizens may be admitted to the U.S. as TN nonimmigrants each fiscal year. There is no numerical limit on the number of Canadian citizens who may enter the U.S. as TN nonimmigrants. TN nonimmigrants may be initially admitted to the United States for a period of one year and may apply for extensions of stay in increments of up to one year. Unlike the H-1B category, TN nonimmigrants may apply for extensions of stay indefinitely, as long as they continue to meet the qualifications for TN visa issuance.

The spouses and unmarried children of TN nonimmigrants may be admitted to the United States as **TD (Trade Dependent)** nonimmigrants. TD nonimmigrants may attend schools in the United States but may not accept employment unless they independently qualify for a different nonimmigrant or immigrant category.

ADMISSION OF NONIMMIGRANTS

Nonimmigrant Visa Requirements

In general, each nonimmigrant must be inspected upon arrival by presenting a valid unexpired visa and an unexpired passport, valid for a minimum period of six months.

The exception to the requirement of a valid entry visa is limited to citizens of countries who are included in the Visa Waiver Pilot Program, who are allowed to enter the United States without a visa for a 90 day period, provided that they are coming for temporary business or pleasure and meet all the necessary requirements. The Visa Waiver Program is discussed in more depth in Chapter Two.

The Department of State issues visas through American Consulates located in foreign territories. Consular officers are responsible for interpreting laws for immigrants and nonimmigrants. Nonimmigrant visas are obtained in one of two ways, depending on the specific nonimmigrant category. Certain nonimmigrant visas require prior filing of a petition with the appropriate INS Service Center, that forwards the approved petition to the local American Embassy or Consulate. The Embassy or Consulate is responsible for processing the visa application and, upon approval of the visa application places a visa stamp in the applicant's passport. Embassies are located in capital cities, while Consulates are located in other major cities. In other instances, a visa application may be filed directly at an American Consulate without first obtaining INS approval. Statute and regulation govern the difference in procedure. Pre-petition categories include the H, L, O, P and Q nonimmigrant classifications. Direct applications are permitted in the B, C, D, E, G, and I categories. Certain categories such as the F and M (Student) and J (Exchange Visitor) require pre-acceptance by an approved program entity, such as a university, and require the applicant to present the certified acceptance form to a consular officer for visa approval.

Since the United States government does not currently have diplomatic relations with the government of Taiwan, commercial and other relations with the people of Taiwan are conducted through an unofficial instrumentality, the American Institute in Taiwan (AIT), which acts as a private liaison with the American Consulate in Hong Kong. Although the AIT is not technically a Consulate, it exercises de facto visa issuance authority in Taiwan.

When submitting a petition to the INS, the burden of proof to establish eligibility rests upon the person or organization petitioning. Further, in order to board a plane or any other common carrier to the United States, the carrier is required to ascertain that the foreign national travelling has a valid visa or is otherwise entitled to enter the United States. Otherwise, the carrier may be subject to fines or other penalties.

Admission to the United States by foreign nationals is a privilege, not a right. The issuance of a visa does not automatically entitle a foreign national admittance to the United States. If upon arrival at a port of entry in the United States, the foreign national is found to be inadmissible under the Immigration and Nationality Act or any other provision of law, the individual will not be admitted. Further, a nonresident alien who is not admitted has no constitutional right to entry into the United Sates, or to issuance of a visa.

Foreign nationals who seek to enter the United States must be "inspected" by INS Inspectors who are given the power to determine whether the foreign national is admissible to the U.S. and under what conditions the individual may be admitted. In order for an alien to be admitted there must be more than a physical entry. Admission is defined in the Immigration and Nationality Act as the lawful entry of an alien into the United States after inspection and authorization by an immigration officer. Once an individual has been admitted to the United States, it is possible to extend status, change status, or adjust status to permanent residence provided that the necessary requirements for each category are met. Most foreign nationals entering the United States are subject to a dual system of inspection. First, at the American Consulate which issues the visa, and second, by an Immigration Inspector at an U.S. port of entry (e.g. airport). The 1996 Act enhanced the power of Immigration Inspectors at airports, and other ports of entry. Immigration Inspectors have the right to decline admission, detain applicants, and refer matters for removal hearings before an Immigration Judge. The 1996 Act gave Inspectors the power to actually remove aliens from the United States. This is the legal and functional equivalent of deportation.

SAMPLE NONIMMIGRANT VISA

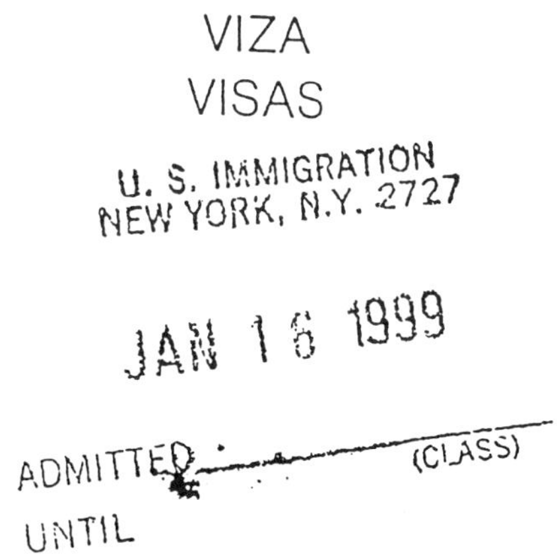

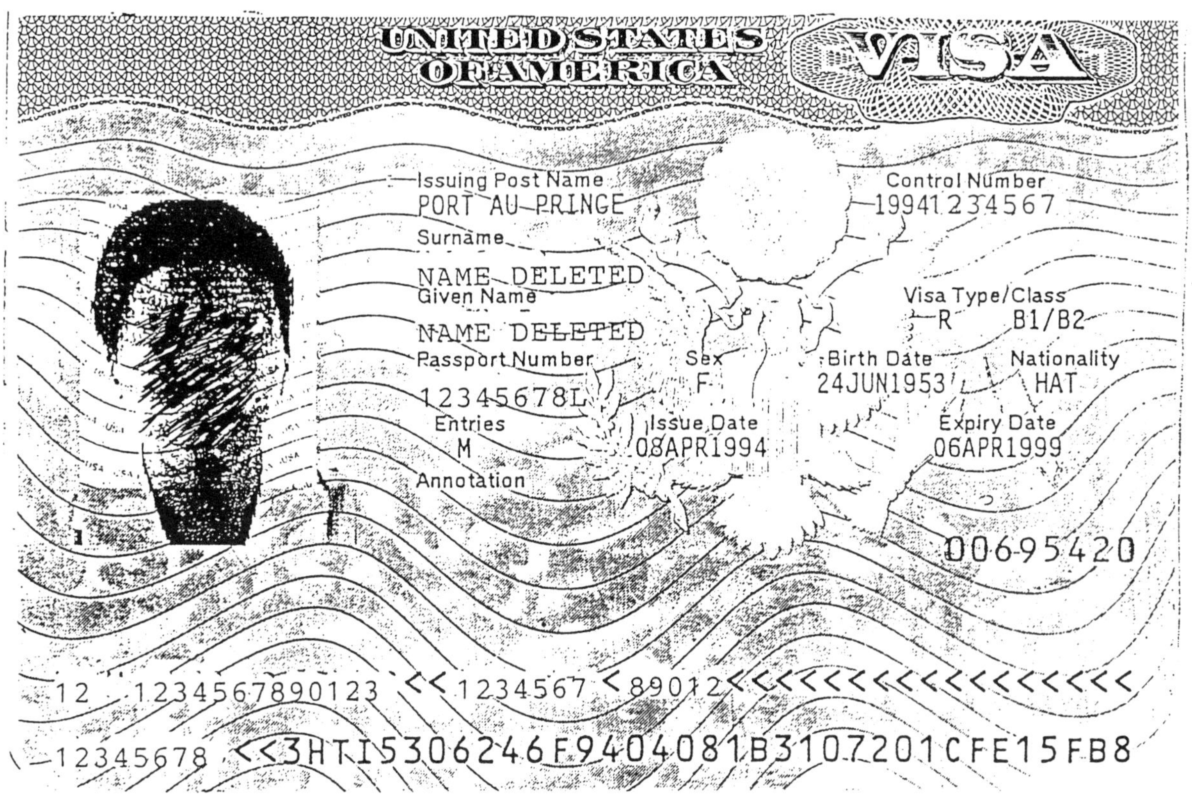

UNITED STATES OF AMERICA VISA

Issuing Post Name
PORT AU PRINCE

Control Number
19941234567

Surname
NAME DELETED

Given Name
NAME DELETED

Visa Type/Class
R B1/B2

Passport Number
12345678L

Sex
F

Birth Date
24JUN1953

Nationality
HAT

Entries
M

Issue Date
08APR1994

Expiry Date
06APR1999

Annotation

00695420

12 1234567890123 <<1234567<89012<<<<<<<<<<<<<<<<<<<<

12345678 <<3HTI5306246F9404081B3107201CFE15FB8

The I-94 Form

In order to enter the United States, a foreign national must fill out a I-94 Form (Arrival/Departure Record). This form is generally filled out while on the plane, and presented to an Immigration Inspector at the time of admission. The INS retains the first half of the form for record keeping, and the second half of the form is returned and stapled into the foreign national's passport. The Immigration Inspector fills out the I-94 to reflect the nonimmigrant category and period of admission. The same I-94 form must be surrendered upon the foreign national's departure.

The I-94 represents permission for the foreign national to be in the United States and to engage in activities consistent with the status indicated on the face of the form.

It is important to bear in mind that the I-94 is the document that authorizes and defines an individual's status in the United States. A visa stamped in a foreign national's passport by itself is not sufficient to gain legal entry into the United States. The foreign national must also be inspected and admitted. Inspection is the mechanism used to authorize a foreign national's stay in the United States. The period of time authorized upon inspection governs the foreign national's stay in the United States, and not the validity period of the underlying visa. For example, a visitor may have a B-1/B-2 multiple entry visa stamped in his or her passport valid for five years. However, if the individual's I-94 Form reflects a six month authorization period, the individual may only remain in the United States for six months and not five years. It is common to confuse the difference between visa validity and status. It is important to understand that the I-94 determines status and duration of stay, and that the I-94 often provides for a shorter period of stay than the visa.

The upper right hand part of the I-94 form indicates what category of status the individual has been granted. If a person is entering the United States pursuant to an E visa, then this designation will be indicated on the I-94 form, as "E-1" or "E-2" status. The designation will normally conform to the visa stamp in the passport.

Since the I-94 is such an important document, the traveler should check the form as soon as it is stamped and make sure that it reflects the appropriate category and duration of stay. Given the large volume of people going through the arrival process each day, Immigration Inspectors may make inadvertent mistakes that can be problematic for the foreign national in the future.

The back of the I-94 form is used to indicate subsequent extensions or changes of nonimmigrant status authorized by the INS. However with the advent of large computerized service centers, the initial I-94 is often replaced by a computer generated I-94 that supersedes the I-94 issued at the time of last entry. In such circumstances, the original I-94 should be retained in order to prove continuity of status.

Immigration Inspectors subject all foreign nationals who enter the United States (both immigrant and nonimmigrant) to primary inspection at United States ports of entry. Primary inspection usually entails a brief one or two minute interview by the Immigration Inspector. If the Immigration Inspector is satisfied during this quick inspection, he or she will stamp the individual's I-94 card and officially admit the person to the United States.

However, in certain instances the Immigration Inspector may not be satisfied with the answers he or she receives during primary inspection. The inspector may suspect the individual has misrepresented their intention to gain entry. The Immigration Inspector may also suspect that the individual is an imposter using fraudulent documents. In these cases, the Inspector can subject the foreign national to secondary inspection.

Secondary inspection normally involves detention at the place of entry. The foreign national will be required to go into a separate room and undergo detailed questioning. During secondary inspection, the foreign national will be interrogated at length and the inspector may also search any documents the foreign national is carrying. Pockets and luggage may be searched, and the individual may be asked to sign a sworn statement.

If the Inspector is satisfied upon completion of secondary inspection, the foreign national will be admitted to the United States. If the Inspector is not satisfied after secondary inspection, a deferred inspection may be conducted at the INS office that has jurisdiction over the place of entry.

At this stage, the Inspector will make a final decision concerning the foreign national's application for admission. Once it is clear that the Inspector is going to make an adverse decision the individual may be permitted to withdraw the application and immediately return to his or her country of origin. In such cases, the visa is usually canceled and a notation to this effect will be placed on the passport. If the individual is not permitted to withdraw the application for admission and the Inspector makes a determination of inadmissibility, the individual may be subject to expedited removal proceedings.

Created by the 1996 Act, expedited removal is the process by which an alien may be removed from U.S. without a hearing. A full discussion of the new provisions of the INA concerning removal of aliens from the United States is beyond the scope of this text. However, a foreign national arriving at a U.S. port of entry, making an application for admission, should be aware of the possibility of expedited removal if an Immigration Inspector believes the foreign national is inadmissible. An Immigration Inspector, under the auspices of the Attorney General, now has the power to remove a foreign national from the U.S. point of entry without a hearing or review unless the individual indicates either an intention to apply for asylum or a fear of persecution. Once a foreign national has requested asylum, an asylum officer will conduct an interview. If the asylum officer finds a "credible fear" of persecution, the applicant will be scheduled for a full hearing on the merits of the asylum claim. However, if the asylum officer does not believe the individual presents a "credible fear" of persecution, the applicant will be ordered removed without a hearing. In addition to the obvious negative associations with this process, removal from the United States may adversely affect a person's future ability to enter the United States either as a nonimmigrant or immigrant. It is advisable to avoid removal at all costs.

Generally, it is not beneficial to engage in lengthy arguments with Immigration Inspectors at the airport. A traveler's best course of action is to be fully aware of the specific requirements for their visa category and the contents of their visa petition when arriving at a United States port of entry. An individual armed with the appropriate knowledge concerning their visa category and application will be better able to adequately answer the questions of the Inspector and escape the devastating effects of expedited removal.

Preinspection

The United States has agreements with certain jurisdictions such as Canada and Bermuda, which provide for a preinspection process in lieu of the inspection that would normally occur at the point of admission in the United States. These agreements provide for the presence of United States Immigration personnel at an airport located in the foreign country to perform the inspection the traveler would otherwise undergo upon arrival in the United States.

One example of an airport with preinspection is Dorval International Airport in Montreal, Canada. U.S. Immigration Inspectors are based at this airport to conduct preinspection. Once an individual has undergone pre-inspection, he or she will not have to go through the inspection process again when entering the United States.

SAMPLE FORM I-94

Numéro du Départ

211863282 05

U. S. IMMIGRATION
NEW YORK, N.Y. 2727

Service de l'Immigration
et de la Naturalisation

I-94
Régistre de Départ

JAN 1? 1999

ADMITTED ______ (CLASS)

UNTIL JUL 15 1999

14. Nom de Famille

NAME DELETED

15. Prénom

NAME DELETED

16. Date de Naissance (J/M/An)

12 4 06 53

17. Pays de Nationalité

HAITI

Voir au Verso

STAPLE HERE

Avertissement - Une personne non immigrante qui accepte un emploi non autorisé est passible d expulsion.

Avis Important - Gardez ce permis en votre possession et rendez le en quittant les Etats-Unis. Défaut de conformité pourrait retarder votre admission aux E.U. à une date ulterieure.

Vous avez été autorisé à rester aux E.U. jusqu'à la date écrite sur ce permis. Tout séjour au delà de cette date sans permission des autorités d'immigration sera une infraction à la loi.

Retournez ce permis en quittant les E.U.:

- Par mer ou par air, à la compagnie de transport;
- Par la frontière canadienne, à un agent officiel canadien;
- Par la frontière mexicaine, à un agent officiel des E.U..

Les étudiants projetant de regagner leurs écoles aux Etats-Unis dans les 30 jours doivent se référer à la section "Arrival-Departure" en page 2 du Formulaire I-20 avant de rendre ce permis.

Record of Changes

Port:
Date:
Carrier:
Flight #/Ship Name:

Departure Record

FRENCH

Immigrants: U.S. Lawful Permanent Residents

Lawful permanent residents of the United States enjoy most of the same rights as United States citizens, namely, they are permitted to remain in the United States indefinitely, may be employed and may travel in and out of the country. Lawful permanent residents hold "green cards." Lawful permanent residents may derive their status based upon a family or employment relationship or from any of the special immigration programs that the United States government administers, such as its diversity visa program (the so-called "Lottery Program") as well as various political asylum and amnesty programs. Most immigrant categories are subject to quotas and significant time delays. However, immediate relatives of United States citizens (spouses, minor children, and parents of adult children) are not subject to quota delays. Certain other limited categories are not subject to quotas.

General Overview of Immigrant Categories

The Immigration Act of 1990 provided for 700,000 immigrant visas to be granted for the fiscal years of 1992-94 and 675,00 for every fiscal thereafter. 480,000 of these visas are allocated to family-sponsored immigrants according to the following schedule:

Immediate Relatives

There is no limit to the number of immediate relatives on whose behalf immigrant petitions may be submitted. The category of immediate relative includes the spouse and children of United States citizens and parents of United States citizens over 21 years of age. Widows and widowers of United States citizens who had been married for two years prior to the time of their U.S. spouse's death are also included in the immediate relative category.

Immediate relatives are not subject to the quotas detailed below. However, among the 480,000 visas, which are set aside for family sponsored immigration, 226,000 of these visas are set aside for the four family preference categories. The remaining visas are to be allocated to individuals who qualify as immediate relatives. Although there is no limit on the number of immediate relatives who may acquire visas, the initial number of visas for immediate relatives are to be obtained from the overall family-sponsored set aside.

It is important to note that the two allocations of visas mentioned above are merely an accounting mechanism designed to fulfill the intentions of Congress in standardizing United States immigration policy. Even if these visas are exhausted, immediate relatives will not be effected, since there is no limit on the number of immediate relatives who may immigrate to the United States based on a valid immigrant petition.

Family Preference Categories - 226,000 visas allocated on an annual basis for this category.

First Preference - Unmarried adult sons and daughters of United States citizens. 23,400 Visas allocated per year in addition to any unused visas from the Fourth Family Preference Category.

Second Preference - Spouses, and minor unmarried children of lawful permanent residents.

Adult unmarried sons and daughters of lawful permanent residents.

114,200 Visas allocated per year plus any unused visas from First Family Preference Category.

Third Preference - Married sons and daughters of United States citizens 23,400 allocated per year plus any unused visas from the top two preference categories.

Fourth Preference - Brothers and sisters of United States citizens 65,000 visas allocated per year plus any unused visas from the top three preference categories.

Employment-Based Immigration - 140,000 Visas allocated per year.

The 1990 Act made major changes to the employment-based immigration categories.

Congress believed that it would be beneficial to the United States economy to increase the quota for skilled professional individuals. Therefore, it created the following five categories for employment based immigrant visas:

First Employment-Based Category

Priority Workers - Allotted 40,000 visas per year plus any left over from the Fourth and Fifth Employment Categories.

This category includes:

- Persons of Extraordinary Ability
- Outstanding Professors and Researchers
- Multinational executives and managers of international companies

Second Employment-Based Category

Members of the Professions Holding Advanced Degrees or Persons of Exceptional Ability in the Sciences, Arts, or Business

40,000 Visas granted per year plus any unused visas from the first Employment Category. Individuals in this category are subject to the Labor Certification process, see infra Chapter Nine for a full discussion of this process.

Third Employment-Based Category

Skilled Workers, Professionals and other Workers

40,000 Visas granted per year plus any unused visas from the first and second Employment Category. Aliens in this category are subject the Labor Certification Process, see infra Chapter Nine for a full discussion of this process.

Fourth Employment-Based Category

Special Immigrants - 10,000 Visas (no leftover visas from other immigrant categories.)

Religious Workers

Fifth Employment-Based Category

Limited to 10,000 visas annually, no overlap from other categories.

This category is designed for Investors who make a substantial investment in the United States and create jobs for at least 10 United States workers (citizens and lawful permanent residents).

The goal underlying this category is to create new jobs for United States workers and infuse new capital into the economy. To qualify for this category, the investing alien must have "established" and "engaged" in a "new commercial enterprise." The foreign national must have invested or be in the process of investing no less than a specific sum ($500,000 - $1,000,000). The investment must benefit the United States economy and create full-time employment for at least ten United States citizens or employment-authorized immigrants, excluding the principal alien and his or her spouse, sons or daughters.

Diversity Immigrants

The 1990 Act created a third category of immigrants referred to as "diversity" immigrants. This category was created to facilitate the admission of individuals for permanent residence who are not eligible for the family-based or employment-based categories. First implemented in 1991, as a three-year transitional program, the diversity visa program became a permanent feature of the INA beginning in fiscal year 1995. 50,000 visas are available each year to aliens who participate in the DV visa program. To be eligible for a diversity visa, an applicant must be from a country designated by the Attorney General, have at least a high school education or its equivalent, or have worked at least two years in an occupation that requires two years of training or experience. To apply for a DV visa an applicant is required to submit an application and a specified fee at a place and time designated by the Secretary of State. A certain number of applicants and their immediate relatives are selected for the available diversity visas by formula and specific country limits. More applicants are selected than the 50,000 visas allotted, requiring the diversity visas to be awarded on a first-come, first-served basis.

Many have criticized the diversity visa allocation system as no more or less than a lottery. Allocating visas based upon a game of chance seems wholly inconsistent with a qualitative and selective immigration system based on family unity and needed skills. However, Congress for its own reasons saw fit to create the program.

Country Limitations and Priority Dates

In addition to the overall quotas for worldwide immigration, there are also per-country limits on the number of applicants that may be admitted from each country, per fiscal year. Per-country limits are calculated each fiscal year according to a specific formula. The total number of applicants that may be admitted for permanent residence based on approved family or employment petitions is 7% for an independent foreign state and 2% for a dependent foreign state of the total worldwide limit. These percentages add up to approximately 25,620 and 7,320 per year. However, the specific per country numbers of visas can not be calculated before the fiscal year in question because the final number is dependent on the number of immediate relatives that were admitted in the previous year.

Once the per country limit has been reached for a given year, applicants for visas from that country will still be allotted visas, but the visas given over the per country limit will be charged to the following years limit, thus reducing the number available during the next year. If there are no visas available for a beneficiary with an approved family-based or employment-based petition, the applicant will have to wait until their assigned priority date becomes current.

Priority dates are a method designed by regulation to allot visas per preference group and per country. The priority date is the date of filing with the INS for a family based petition or an employment-based petition that does not require labor certification. The priority date for a petition requiring labor certification is the date of filing of the labor certification application with the Department of Labor. Each month the Visa Office of the Department of State publishes the priority dates that are currently being processed in the Visa Office Bulletin. An applicant can not file an adjustment of status application in the United States or complete visa processing until that applicant's priority date becomes current for his category and country of birth.

Although the process of developing the quota numbers contained in the visa bulletin is highly mathematical with formulas applied by statisticians in the Department of State, the actual allocation of immigrant visas among countries and categories within countries is far from an exact science. The numerical decisions made by functionaries at the Department of State are not always devoid of policy considerations. It is not unusual to have quotas backlogged and retrogressed in anticipation of demand. Many believe that predicating quota backlogs and time frames for immigrant visa processing is often analogous to predicating the weather months in advance. Because the quotas are complicated, hard to predict, and based on unknowable policy considerations, the seasoned practitioner's best policy is to adopt a wait and see attitude as opposed to trying to guess exactly when a particular applicant's priority date will become current. However, it is well known that certain categories including the Second Family Preference (spouses and adult sons and daughters of permanent residents), the Fourth Family Preference (brothers and sisters of U.S. citizens) and unskilled workers have significant and growing backlogs in the range of 4-10 years.

SAMPLE VISA BULLETIN

IMMIGRANT VISA PREFERENCE NUMBERS FOR MARCH 1999
(Based on State Dept. information released February 1999)

	All Chargeability Areas Except Those Listed	CHINA-mainland born	INDIA	MEXICO	PHILIPPINES
FAMILY PREFERENCES					
1st	15OCT97	15OCT97	15OCT97	01AUG93	08JUN87
2A*	22AUG94	22AUG94	22AUG94	22JUL93	22AUG94
2B	22APR92	22APR92	22APR92	15JUL91	22APR92
3rd	08JUL95	08JUL95	08JUL95	22JUL90	22APR87
4th	08JUN88	08JUN88	01JUN86	08JAN88	08OCT78
EMPLOYMENT PREFERENCES					
1st	C	22JAN98	C	C	C
2nd	C	08SEP96	08SEP97	C	C
3rd	C	01JAN95	08FEB96	C	C
Other Workers	01JUL92	01JUL92	01JUL92	01JUL92	01JUL92
4th	C	C	C	C	C
Certain Religious Workers	C	C	C	C	C
5th	C	15JAN98	C	C	C
Targeted Employment Areas/Regional Ctrs	C	15JAN98	C	C	C

DIVERSITY IMMIGRANT (DV) CATEGORY: For MARCH, immigrant visa numbers in the DV category are available to qualified DV-99 applicants chargeable to all regions and eligible countries as follows: AFRICA (17,048); ASIA (4,661); EUROPE (14,490, EXCEPT ALBANIA: 8,876); NORTH AMERICA (BAHAMAS) (24); OCEANIA (543); SOUTH AMERICA, CENTRAL AMERICA, and the CARIBBEAN (1,850). *NOTE: For MARCH, 2A numbers EXEMPT from per-country limit are available to applicants from all countries with priority dates earlier than 22JUL93. 2A numbers SUBJECT to per-country limit are available to applicants chargeable to all countries EXCEPT MEXICO with priority dates beginning 22JUL93 and earlier than 22AUG94. (All 2A numbers provided for MEXICO are exempt from the per-country limit; there are no 2A numbers for MEXICO subject to per-country limit.)

Who Qualifies for the First Employment-Based Category?

Persons of Extraordinary Ability

To qualify as a Person of Extraordinary Ability under the first employment-based category, the individual must have extraordinary ability in the sciences, arts, education, business or athletics which has been demonstrated by sustained national or international acclaim and whose achievements have been recognized in the field through extensive documentation. Further, the individual must seek to enter the United States to continue his endeavors in the specific area of extraordinary ability and the entry must be anticipated as substantially benefiting the United States.

Two other classes of individuals may qualify under the First Employment Category, they are:

Outstanding Researchers and Professors

In order to qualify for this category the individual must:

- be internationally recognized as outstanding in a specific academic area;
- have at least three years of experience in teaching or researching in that area; and
- be entering the U.S. to accept a tenured or tenure track teaching position in a university, or a comparable position to conduct research in a university or for a private employer.

Employer sponsorship is required in this category.

Multinational Executives and Managers

Individuals who have been employed abroad by a multinational company or an affiliate or subsidiary for at least one year of the three years preceding the immigrant visa petition are qualified for this classification. The employment abroad and the employment in the United States must be in a managerial or executive capacity. The employer must submit a job offer describing the job duties to be performed by the alien. The statutory definition and regulations for this category substantially track the requirements for L-1 nonimmigrant executive and managerial transferees. See Chapter Four a discussion of the L nonimmigrant visa category.

Who Qualifies for the Second Employment-Based Category?

40,000 visas are allocated for this category plus any unused visas from the first employment category. This category is available to professionals who hold advanced degrees, or to persons with exceptional ability in the sciences, arts or business. A certified labor certification application from the Department of Labor is required.

Members of the Professions Holding Advanced Degrees

An advanced degree is defined in the regulations as a U.S. academic or professional degree or a foreign equivalent degree that is higher than the baccalaureate. If an applicant has an U.S. baccalaureate degree or foreign equivalent degree plus five years of experience in the specified field then the applicant will be deemed to have the equivalent of a Master's Degree.

Persons of Exceptional Ability

To qualify for this category, a foreign national must have exceptional ability in the sciences, arts or business. Although not specifically included, athletes may apply under this category.

Who Qualifies for the Third Employment-Based Category?

Skilled Workers

Employer sponsorship and labor certification is required in this category. The qualifying job must require at least two years of training or experience and cannot be of a temporary or a seasonal nature.

Professionals

To qualify as a professional, the prospective immigrant must hold a U.S. baccalaureate degree or a foreign equivalent degree, and have an approved labor certification. There is no provision that allows an individual to combine a period of working experience and education as the equivalent of a Bachelor's degree. Therefore, an individual who does not hold a minimum of a baccalaureate degree does not qualify as a professional in this category, but may nonetheless qualify as a skilled worker.

Other/Unskilled Workers - 10,000 Visas per year

This category includes all individuals who have an approved labor certification application and are employed in jobs that require less than two years experience. This category has traditionally experienced a backlog of several years. Therefore, if possible, it is preferable to apply as a skilled worker if the open position usually requires at least two years of experience.

Unlike the first employment category, the second and third employment categories require labor certification. The practical effect is that it will take more time to process a second or third employment-based immigrant petition since the labor certification process almost always takes a significant amount of time to complete, often more than two years. In certain cases, labor certification can be waived in the second employment-based category.

National Interest Waiver of Labor Certification Requirement

The Labor Certification requirement can be waived in the second employment category, if, in the opinion of the Attorney General, it is in the "national interest" of the United States that the applicant be admitted for permanent residence. The term "national interest" has no statutory definition, nor is it defined in regulations. The INS decides requests for national interest waivers on a case-by-case basis. Generally, an applicant who requests a national interest waiver must show evidence that their employment will pose a great public benefit to the United States. National interest waivers have been granted in the past to applicants who have shown they will provide economic, medical or legal services to needy communities. If an applicant is granted a national interest waiver, the time it takes to become a permanent resident in the second employment preference category will be significantly reduced.

Admission of Permanent Residents

Once an employment or family-based petition has been filed and approved, the individual may commence the process necessary to obtain permanent residence. One option is to "Adjust Status" while in the United States by filing an application with the INS Service Center covering the intended place of residence. Alternatively, a foreign national may opt for "Visa Processing" at an American Embassy or Consulate.

Adjustment of Status

Adjustment of Status is a convenient way to apply for permanent resident status because it eliminates the cost and inconvenience of travelling abroad to a United States consulate to undergo visa processing. In order to obtain permanent residence in this fashion, the individual must have been properly admitted to the United States and must not have engaged in any unauthorized employment, or otherwise violated or overstayed their status. Note that the bar against employment will not serve to bar immediate relatives of United States citizens from adjusting their status.

The adjustment of status process is viewed as a privilege since it allows the individual to change status from within the United States. Approval of an adjustment of status application is subject to the discretion of the INS and is not automatic. If the individual has a history of immigration violations or abuse, this may be construed against him when deciding whether or not to grant adjustment of status. Further, the alien must be admissible to the United States and not be subject to any grounds of inadmissability.

If the individual has consistently maintained lawful status, and is not otherwise inadmissible, an application for adjustment of status may be sent to the Immigration and Naturalization Service Center having jurisdiction over the applicant's place of residence. The application for adjustment of status may not be filed until an immigrant visa is available to the applicant; i.e. the priority date is current. This will depend on the particular category of immigrant visa being sought, the individual's country of origin and the quotas and backlogs involved.

In 1994, Congress enacted a special provision in the INA to benefit those individuals who were otherwise barred from adjusting their status because they either entered without inspection, worked without authorization, or in other enumerated ways failed to maintain lawful status in the United States. The provision referred to as "Section 245(i)" became an important tool for those individuals who were ineligible to adjust their status. Section 245(i) created a "super fee" or fine (five times the normal fee) for those individuals who would normally be ineligible to adjust their status in the United States. Section 245(i) was originally set to expire on September 30, 1997. In 1996, under IIRAIRA, Congress made significant changes to the adjustment of status provisions of the INA. The super fine was increased to $1,000 and other classes of applicants were statutorily prohibited from adjusting their status. IIRAIRA also made no provision for the extension of 245(i) past the September 30, 1997 expiration date.

After considerable debate and a few temporary extensions, 245(i) was permitted to "sunset" on January 14, 1998. However, a compromise was reached by lawmakers that allows applicants who had a pending family-based or employment-based petition filed by January 14, 1998 to be "grandfathered" in under 245(i) and continue to be allowed to adjust their status. "Grandfather" benefits were also granted to those whose labor certifications were filed on or before January 14, 1998. Congress created an important class of immigrants present in the United states who appear to have continuing eligibility for adjustment of status notwithstanding illegal entry, unlawful presence, or violation of status.

While the adjustment application is pending, the applicant may not travel outside the United States. If the applicant does travel, the application for adjustment of status will be considered abandoned and the individual will be required to secure an entirely new visa should he or she desire to return to the United States. However, permission to travel is generally granted upon special application. This is known as Advance Parole.

Visa Processing

If an individual chooses to Visa Process it is important to remember that even when an immigrant visa petition has been approved, the immigrant visa is not automatically available to foreign nationals, but is subject to category and country quotas and backlogs. Assuming that the alien's petition is approved, and the particular visa category has no backlogs, the alien still must be admissible to the United States, meaning that the alien must not fall into any of the categories of inadmissibility contained in the INA.

When an individual's immigrant petition is approved, the approval notice will generally be sent to the Consulate located in the same jurisdiction as the individual's last place of residence and/or citizenship. However, the alien may process his immigrant visa application at any Consulate if he is residing within that Consulate's jurisdiction and intends to remain in that jurisdiction during the entire period of visa processing.

Additionally, an individual may obtain immigrant visa processing at any other consular post that will accept his case if he is currently residing in the United States and can demonstrate that he would experience hardship if forced to return to his last country of residence. Whether or not the Consulate will accept these cases is discretionary and based upon each Consulate's particular workload. However, in cases where an American Consulate no longer exists in a foreign territory, a third country may be designated by thc Dcpartment of State to accept the cases of nationals of that territory.

In many instances, countries where American Consulates process immigrant visas for third country nationals will not readily allow visa applicants to enter their country to attend an immigrant visa interview without assurance of readmission to the United States.

To proceed through Visa Processing, an individual must complete what's known as "Packet III" sent by the National Visa Center. Packet III informs the individual of the documentation required to complete the process and also includes detailed biographic data forms. Once the individual has obtained all of the necessary documentation, which normally includes original birth certificates, police certificates, marriage certificates, and other biographical data, the completed forms are sent to the Consulate. Packet IV will then be sent to the individual. "Packet IV" includes a date for an appointment and instructions for a medical examination. Before scheduling an appointment, the Consulate will have completed appropriate FBI, Consular and Interpol "clearances", and the individual's priority date (numerical place in the quota based on the date of filing of the initial petition) will have been reached, and a visa number will have been obtained from the Department of State in Washington, D.C.

The visa appointment with the Consular Officer should be perfunctory assuming that the individual has maintained proper status and is not otherwise inadmissible. If the consular officer has any doubts about the alien's admissibility, he may seek an advisory opinion from the State Department, which will be binding upon the consular officer if it concerns a legal matter. Factual determinations are in the discretion of the consular officer. Generally if the alien is not inadmissible, and the basis for the petition remains valid, the visa will be issued. However, it is not unusual for cases to be delayed for consular investigations.

The Consular Officer does not have the authority to deny an immigrant visa merely because of the applicant's prior status violations, or because of unauthorized employment in the United Sates. Further, conduct which the consular officer may deem undesirable may not lead to a visa denial, unless the conduct would place the alien within one of the statutory bases of inadmissibility to the United States. One important ground of inadmissibility, however, is prior visa or entry fraud. Any prior misrepresentation by the applicant to the consulate or to the INS may result in denial of an immigrant visa under a statutory provision excluding from the United States those aliens who have obtained a visa or prior entry by committing fraud. Furthermore, a new ground of inadmissibility created by the 1996 Act is the accrual of certain periods of "unlawful presence," which triggers three and ten year bars.

"Homeless" Immigrant Visa Beneficiaries

The United States State Department has issued instructions regarding the issuance of immigrant visas to "homeless" visa applicants. A homeless beneficiary is one who is a national of one of certain designated countries where no American Embassy or Consulate is present. Such countries have included Afghanistan, Bosnia, Iran, Iraq, Lebanon, Libya, Somalia, and the Sudan. Different procedures apply for homeless immigrant visa processing that depend on where the beneficiary is located at the time of visa processing, with particular consular posts designated to receive cases from particular homeless nationalities.

The policy concerning homeless beneficiaries residing in the United States is constantly evolving and the current policy should be ascertained before a "homeless" individual attempts to visa process at a particular Consulate.

Consular Absolutism

Although Consular Officers are subject to the law, the Federal Courts have thus far preserved the doctrine of Consular nonreviewability. Many commentators believe that arbitrary and unreviewable consular decisions in visa matters are an aberration in today's world, and that Congress should provide for reviewability. So far, Congress has not been responsive to these demands.

Practical Considerations: Adjust Status or Visa Process?

A number of factors should be considered when determining which option best suits a particular individual. One of the primary considerations is the person's need to travel. Once an individual submits an application for adjustment of status with the INS, the individual limits his or her right to travel out of the United States. When choosing the Adjustment of Status option, travel is prohibited unless special permission is obtained from INS, referred to as "Advance Parole." Advance Parole is supposed to be granted liberally and expeditiously, but often is not. Furthermore, when Advance Parole is granted, it is usually granted for a limited period of time. For some time the INS has been considering dispensing with the Advance Parole requirement, especially for H, L, & E visaholders. However, travel without Advance Parole has historically been considered as "abandonment" of the adjustment of status application.

Visa processing provides other benefits not available in the adjustment of status option. For example, a Consulate is less likely to be as backlogged as the INS, and is more likely to have easy access to the individual's file. Furthermore, the first steps of consular processing can normally be commenced as soon as the petition is approved, but to file adjustment of status the priority date must be current. On the other hand, the individual has no right to have an attorney with him at a consular interview, and a consular officer's decision can at times be abrupt and arbitrary, with no direct rights of appeal to a higher authority. In the United States, there is a right to have an attorney present at the adjustment of status interview, and in the event that the application is denied, there is opportunity to present the case to an Immigration Judge. In visa processing as in adjustment of status, the application will be denied if the individual is found to be inadmissible to the United States. Additionally, adjustment of status applications may be denied as a matter of discretion.

The general advantage of visa processing, as opposed to adjustment of status through the INS, is that it gives the individual the ability to travel without being trapped in the United States while waiting for the INS to process the application.

When visa processing, it is also important to bear in mind, that unless an alien has a proper and valid nonimmigrant visa, the individual cannot leave the U.S. and return until he has obtained his immigrant visa. Therefore it is critical to have all the necessary documentation for a visa interview since prompt return to the United States may be contingent upon the individual's success in obtaining an immigrant visa.

PENALTIES, BARS & RESTRICTIONS

The Illegal Immigration Reform and Immigrant Responsibility Act of 1996 greatly enhanced the penalties for violations of the immigration laws and provides many new bars and exclusions for aliens who have no legal status. Important among them is Section 222(g) of the INA that penalizes those who overstay their nonimmigrant status, even by one day, by automatically invalidating their nonimmigrant visa. Except in circumstances of exceptional hardship, a new nonimmigrant visa can only be obtained in the country of nationality.

Another significant bar created in the 1996 Act penalizes those who are unlawfully present in the United States. An individual may be unlawfully present by overstaying the period of admission or entering without inspection. If an alien is unlawfully present in the U.S. for more than 180 days but less than one year, the alien will be inadmissible for 3 years from the date of departure. If an alien is unlawfully present for one year or more, following departure from the U.S., the alien is inadmissible for 10 years from the date of departure. Note that the bar on re-admission is only triggered after the alien has departed the U.S.

These and other severe penalties and sanctions tions will be discussed in greater detail in Chapter Eleven.

EDITOR'S FINAL NOTE

In the upcoming chapters, we will describe in greater detail the particular characteristics of the most important and widely used visa categories for business people and travelers. These include the E, H and L categories. We will also discuss some popular categories such as the B visitor visa, the F student visa, and the relatively new O, P and Q visas, which deal with performing artists, entertainers and exchange visitors in different programs.

In each chapter we will devote a considerable amount of attention to an overall explanation of the visa category, as well as numerous practical guidelines, sample letters and forms designed to familiarize the person seeking to enter the United States with requirements, procedures and possible problems.

Because the focus of this work is primarily the legal immigration process, we will not deal extensively with the removal process (exclusion and deportation), which, with the exception of expedited removal at airports and borders, is determined by Immigration Judges and the Board of Immigration Appeals. The consequences of removal from the United States can be devastating to members of the business community so that compliance with immigration regulations and procedures must be given the highest priority.

Chapter Two

THE B VISA FOR TEMPORARY BUSINESS OR PLEASURE

A. INTRODUCTION

Who is classifiable within the B category?

Foreign nationals may be granted visitors' visas to enter the United States for the purposes of a temporary visit for either business or pleasure. American consular officers issue B visas for single or multiple entries depending on individual cases and reciprocal policies between the applicant's home country and the United States. Generally, if the applicant's home country has a policy of granting multiple entry tourist visas to Americans, then the American Consulate will normally extend the same policy to that country's nationals visiting the United States. For example, the policy of the People's Republic of China is to grant visas for single entries only, therefore Chinese nationals are normally only eligible for single entry U.S. visitors visas.

B visas are granted in furtherance of the United States policy of facilitating and promoting international travel and the free movement of people of all nationalities to the United States. This policy is based on both cultural and economic considerations. However, as will be discussed later, certain very important restrictions apply in this visa category.

B visas are issued for limited periods of time in the discretion of consular officers. The maximum amount of time a B visa may issued at one time is ten years. The practice of issuing multiple entry B visas for an <u>indefinite</u> period has been discontinued.

The validity period of a B visa depends on the time period U.S. citizens are afforded when entering a particular foreign nation. B visa issuance is based on the theory of reciprocity between foreign nations and the United States. For example, B visas issued to citizens of Japan and Taiwan may be made valid for a total of 60 months. B visas issued to nationals of the People's Republic of China are normally valid for up to three months and for one application for admission, however, for an enhanced fee a B-1 multiple visa may be issued for a six-month period.

The authorized period of stay for a B visa will be determined by the INS at the time of admission and will not usually be for more than a six-month period. The B visa category offers no derivative status to spouses or children. At the time of B visa issuance each individual must present an application and qualify independently.

The B nonimmigrant visa is granted to those individuals who are visiting the United States temporarily for business or pleasure and who continue to maintain a residence in a foreign country which they have no intention of abandoning.

The term "<u>business</u>" refers to legitimate commercial or professional activities conducted in the United States on behalf of a foreign employer, and does not include purely local employment or labor for hire.

The term "<u>pleasure</u>" includes any legitimate personal or recreational activities such as touring, visiting family or friends, obtaining medical treatment, and other activities of a social nature.

B Visas Obtained Directly Through American Consulates

In comparison to some of the other nonimmigrant visa categories, the B visa category does not require that a petition be filed with the INS prior to applying for a visa at a U.S. Consulate. Instead the visa application is filed directly at the American Consulate in the jurisdiction where the applicant resides. Each Consulate has individual procedures for issuing B visas. Applicants should check with the American Consulate in his or her jurisdiction before applying for a tourist visa. For example, a post may only processes B visas on Tuesdays and Fridays before 11:00 a.m.

General Requirements for B Classification

In order to establish eligibility for a B visa, an applicant must show:

- That the visit is of a temporary nature.
- That the applicant intends to depart from the United States at the expiration of the temporary stay.
- That the applicant maintains a residence in a foreign country to which he or she will return and that there is no present intention of abandoning the foreign residence.
- That the applicant seeks admission for the sole purpose of engaging in legitimate activities relating to business or pleasure.
- That adequate financial arrangements have been made to enable the applicant to travel to and depart from the United States, and to carry out the purpose of the visit while in the United States.
- That the applicant will not engage in any criminal or unlawful activities while in the United States.

A foreign national who wishes to enter the United States as a visitor for business or pleasure, but does not hold a B visa, may still be admitted to the U.S. through the Visa Waiver Pilot Program. The Visa Waiver Pilot Program allows nationals of certain designated countries to be admitted to the U.S. without visas under specific statutory provisions. The Visa Waiver Pilot Program will be discussed in greater detail later in this chapter.

If an individual's home country is not one of the designated countries eligible to participate in the Visa Waiver Program, the regular course of action in obtaining a B visa is to proceed through the American Consulate. Note that this option may be preferable even in the event that a national is eligible for the Visa Waiver Program.

A consular officer may consider the following factors when evaluating whether an applicant is eligible for a B visa:

- Whether the arrangements that the applicant has made for defraying the expenses of the visit and return passage are adequate to obviate the need for obtaining employment in the United States.
- If financial arrangements depend on assurances that relatives or friends in the United States will provide all or part of the applicant's support, whether there are forceful and compelling ties between the applicant and the sponsor that lend credibility to the sponsor's guarantee.
- Whether the applicant has specific and realistic plans for the course of the contemplated visit.
- Whether the period of time for which the applicant is planning to stay is consistent with the stated purpose of the trip, and whether the applicant has established with reasonable certainty that he or she will leave the United States upon completion of the temporary visit.
- Whether the applicant has given conscious consideration to the proposed period of stay, or whether the applicant's intentions are expressed in terms of remaining in the United States for the maximum time allowable or for the period that the applicant has been invited by friends and relatives.
- If the applicant is the principal wage earner in the family, and the family is not accompanying the applicant, the manner in which the family will be supported during the applicant's absence.
- Whether the applicant has reason able permanent employment or business connections or family, social, cultural, or other associations that would impel the applicant to return to the home country.

The applicant must demonstrate sufficient ties to the home country, such as employment, business or financial connections, close family ties, or other commitments that indicate a strong inducement to return home. Additionally, the individual's prior visa and immigration history is relevant in the consular officer's determination to issue the requested visa.

The consular officer will also consider the amount of time requested for the visit by the applicant when determining eligibility. Even though the maximum time period allowed for any authorized stay is six months, it is generally recommended that the maximum time period not be requested unless actually required.

Bona fide Nonimmigrant Intent

Under United States immigration law every individual is presumed to be an immigrant until it can be demonstrated to the satisfaction of the consular officer at the time of application for a visa that the applicant is entitled to nonimmigrant status. If the visa application is denied, the applicant may submit additional evidence in an effort to establish his or her eligibility for a visitor' visa, and overcome the presumption of immigrant intent.

NOTE:

In order to obtain a B Visa, it is essential for the applicant to demonstrate that he or she has no intention of immigrating to the United States. The applicant must overcome the presumption of immigrant intent by the presentation of detailed evidence. The type of documentation necessary to prove lack of intent to immigrate will vary with the nature of the trip, the nature of the applicant's employment and the applicant's personal ties to the foreign residence, the standard of living in the country of origin, the level of fraudulent applications received in the past, and fraud profiles.

B. B-1 TEMPORARY VISITOR FOR BUSINESS

The B-1 visa is one of the most frequently used visas by individuals who wish to visit the United States for a variety of business related reasons. The underlying U.S. policy in this visa category is to facilitate and promote international travel and the free movement of people of all nationalities to the United States, both for the cultural and social value to the world as well as for economic purposes. Therefore, an applicant need not be a "business person" in order to qualify for a B-1 visa if it can be shown that his or her role is to perform a necessary function to international trade and commerce.

In order to be eligible for a B-1 visa, the applicant must not intend to engage in gainful employment in the United States, but rather must be doing something directly related to the applicant's job overseas. Further, the visaholder must be paid from a source outside the United States and not from a United States employer. However, an applicant may generally have expenses paid by a United States entity without violating B-1 status.

Although an individual may be theoretically eligible to gain admittance as a B-1 visitor, the immigration inspector may deny admission if he or she believes that the applicant is misrepresenting the reasons for entering the United States. Therefore, in the interests of avoiding confusion and uncertainty at the point of admission, it may be advisable to seek other appropriate working categories if the intentions of the applicant do not necessarily match the requirements of the B visa.

For individuals who travel a great deal for business, it may be advantageous to secure a different nonimmigrant visa. Although a B visaholder is technically entitled to be admitted to the United States, there may be some resistance from the immigration inspector who feels that the visaholder is being admitted to the United States too frequently, and the applicant may encounter rigorous secondary inspection by immigration officials.

Requirements for B-1 Classification

An applicant entering the United States is classifiable as a B-1 visitor for business, provided all other eligibility requirements are met and the visit is to:

- Engage in commercial transactions that do not involve gainful employment in the United States;
- Negotiate contracts;
- Consult with business associates, clients or customers;
- Litigate a legal case;
- Participate in scientific, educational, professional, or business conventions, conferences, or seminars; or
- Undertake independent research.

For the purposes of B-1 visa classification business is defined as legitimate activities of a commercial or a professional character and does not include purely local employment or labor for hire.

As long as the applicant maintains nonimmigrant intent upon admission and during participation in B-1 activities, the applicant may generally enter as a business visitor, even if an H or L visa petition or E visa application is pending. If some other type of visa petition is approved while the individual is present in the United States in B-1 status, the individual must still comply with the terms of B-1 status and return to their country of residence on or before the expiration of authorized stay, or apply to change status in the United States. A preconceived intent to circumvent normal visa procedures reflects implicit bad faith on the applicant's part and will be construed against him in consideration of his or her request to change status.

With regard to speakers coming to the United States to make a speech or presentation for which they will receive an honorarium, the determination of whether this fee constitutes direct remuneration or payment of incidental expenses will be assessed by considering the reasonableness of the fee and the nature of expenses incurred by an individual in similar circumstances.

In addition, the following individuals may be classified as B-1 temporary visitors for business if no salary or other remuneration is received from a United States source (other than an expense allowance or reimbursement for expenses which are incidental to the temporary stay):

- Individuals who qualify for professional H-1B visas (other than entertainment professionals) or H-3 visas (trainees) who come to the United States to perform services or to participate in a training program, provided that remuneration for services performed in the United States is from a foreign entity abroad;

- An individual coming to install, service or repair commercial or industrial equipment or machinery purchased from a company outside the United States or to train United States workers to perform such service, provided: the contract of sale specifically requires the seller to perform such services or training, the individual possesses specialized knowledge essential to the seller's contractual obligation to provide services or training, the individual will receive no remuneration from a United States source, and the trip is to take place within the first year following commencement of the contract;

- Members of religious or charitable organizations coming to the United States temporarily to perform missionary work, provided that the work does not involve the selling of articles or solicitation or acceptance of donations;

- A minister who will temporarily exchange pulpits with an American counterpart, but will only be reimbursed by the foreign church;

- Professional athletes who receive no salary other than prize money for their participation in a sporting event;

- An individual coming to the United States to open a new branch, subsidiary or affiliate of a foreign employer, if the individual will become eligible for status as an L-1 securing the evidence regarding proof of acquisition of physical premises.

- Personal or domestic servants accompanying, returning or following United States citizens who are temporarily assigned to the United States for no more than four years, or who permanently reside in a foreign country. Provided the employee has a residence abroad which they have no intention of abandoning, they have worked for the current employer for at least six months prior to the employer's admission to the U.S., and have at least one year of experience as a personal or domestic servant. Additionally, a signed employment contract between the parties must guarantee that the employee will receive the prevailing or minimum wage for the job and the U. S. citizen must be subject to frequent international transfers lasting at least two years;

- A personal or domestic servant of a foreign national in nonimmigrant status.

It is not uncommon for foreign nationals in nonimmigrant status such as H or L to bring domestic staff with them when coming to the United States on assignment. These individuals are eligible for B-1 business visitor status provided that they meet certain requirements.

Personal or domestic servants who accompany or follow to join employers who seek admission into or are already in the United States in B, E, F, H, I, J, L status may obtain B-1 nonimmigrant visas provided:

- The employee has a residence abroad which he or she has no intention of abandoning (notwithstanding the fact that the employer may be in a nonimmigrant status which does not require a showing that a foreign residence is maintained, such as L visaholders);

- The employee can demonstrate at least one year's experience as a personal or domestic servant; and

- The employee has been employed abroad by the employer as a personal or domestic servant, for at least one year prior to the date of the employer's admission to the United States; or

- If the employee-employer relationship arose immediately prior to the time of the visa application, the employer can demonstrate that he or she has regularly employed (either year-round or seasonal) personal or domestic servants over a period of several years preceding the domestic servant's visa application for a nonimmigrant B-1 visa; and

- The employer and employee have signed an employment contract which contains statements that the employer guarantees the employee the minimum or prevailing wages, whichever is greater, and free room and board and will be the only provider of employment to the servant.

This is an exception to the general rule that the B-1 visa cannot be used purely for domestic employment.

Note:

Permanent resident aliens cannot use the B-1 visa for their domestic employees. Since lawful permanent residents reside in the United States permanently it is clear that their employee's stay is not temporary, and such employment is pure domestic employment.

Additional Requirements for the B-1 Visa

- The principal place of business and the actual accrual of profits must be predominantly in a foreign country.

- Services in the United States must be incidental to international trade and commerce and profits must accrue abroad.

- The employment must be in furtherance of international trade or commerce.

Other individuals who may fall within the B-1 visa classification:

Members of Board of Directors of United States corporations coming to the United States to attend board meetings:

An individual who is a member of the Board of Directors of a United States corporation seeking to enter the United States to attend a meeting of the Board or to perform other functions resulting from membership on the Board may enter the United States under B-1 status.

A director of a company who sets the general policy of an organization or performs a ceremonial role may enter the United States under B-1 authorization. An officer of a company who is responsible for day-to-day operations is not authorized to enter as a B-1 business visitor.

Potential Treaty Investors (E-2):

An individual seeking to invest in the United States may qualify for B-1 classification if his investments would qualify for E-2 status. E-2 status may normally be obtained by showing that a national of one of the member treaty countries will undertake substantial investment in furtherance of international trade.

The business visitor eligible for E-2 status might be coming to the United States to explore investment opportunities, to purchase property that will constitute part of the investment or may be purchasing inventory. These are all authorized B-1 activities.

Additionally, individuals seeking to make purely passive investments who will take no part in their management may qualify for a B-1 visa.

Foreign Airline Employees:

A foreign airline employee who would otherwise qualify for an E visa but there is no qualifying treaty in existence between the United States and the airline's home country, or the employee is not a national of the airline's home country.

B-1 Visas under the North American Free Trade Act (NAFTA)

In effect since January 1, 1994, the North American Free Trade Act (NAFTA) provides for the admission of certain business people between Canada, Mexico and the United States. Under NAFTA, business people from Canada and Mexico may enter the United States in B-1 status for activities other than those already covered under the B visa, in the following seven categories:

- **Research and Design:** Technical scientific and statistical researchers conducting independent research or research for an enterprise located in the territory of another party;

- **Growth, manufacture, and production:** Harvester owner supervising a harvesting crew under applicable law. This applies only to harvesting of agricultural crops. Purchasing and production management personnel conducting commercial transactions for an enterprise located in the territory of another Party;

- **Marketing:** Market researchers and analysts conducting independent research or analysis, or research and analysis for an enterprise located in the territory of another party. Trade fair and promotional personnel attending a trade convention;

- **Sales:** Sales representatives and agents taking orders or negotiating contracts for goods or services for an enterprise located in the territory of another Party. Buyers purchasing for an enterprise located in the territory of another Party;

- **Distribution:** Transportation operators transporting goods or passengers to the U.S. from the territory of another Party or loading and transporting goods or passengers from the U.S. to the territory of another Party, with no unloading in the U.S. or in the other territory. Custom brokers performing brokerage duties associated with the export of goods from the U.S. to or through Canada;

- **After-sales service:** Installers, repair and maintenance personnel, and supervisors possessing specialized knowledge essential to the seller's contractual obligation.

- **General service:** Professionals, management and supervisory personnel, financial services personnel, public relations and advertising personnel, tourism personnel, tour bus operators, and translators.

Canadian and Mexican business people must meet the requirements of the general B visa and be paid from a source outside the U.S., the business activity must be international in scope, and the business person may not enter the local labor market.

One important distinction between the general B visa and the B visa under NAFTA is the ability of a foreign company to perform services pursuant to an after-sales contract in the United States. Normally, individuals from a foreign company can only perform services pursuant to an after-sales service contract for one year after commencement of the contract. Under NAFTA, an individual from the foreign company can utilize a B visa to perform after-sales service during the life of the warranty or service agreement. Additionally, the B visa under NAFTA allows self-employed individuals to work in the U.S. as long as there is no U.S. salary or compensation, accrual of profits is abroad, the location of the principal business site is abroad, and the work product is mostly created abroad.

To apply for admission as a B visitor under NAFTA, nationals from Canada do not have to procure a visa but must present their case for admission directly to Immigration Inspectors at the port of entry. The Canadian business person must present proof of citizenship, describe the purpose of entry, and provide evidence the individual is engaged in one of the occupations or professionals included in the agreement. The procedure for Mexican nationals is slightly different. A Mexican business person is required to show a B-1 visa and passport at the port of entry unless they possess a Mexican border-crossing card. In addition, the Mexican business person must also present evidence that describes the purpose of the entry and proves that the individual is engaged in one of the designated occupations or professions in the agreement. The period of admission and conditions of stay for B-1 visaholders under NAFTA are the same as for other B-1 visaholders.

Visa and Passport Waiver for Canadians and Other Nationals

Although all nonimmigrants applying for admission to the United States are normally required to present a valid passport and nonimmigrant visa, the Attorney General, acting jointly with the Secretary of State has the authority to waive these documentation requirements. Canadian nationals and alien residents ("landed immigrants") in Canada or Bermuda having a common nationality with Canada are exempt from these documentation requirements. Canadian nationals do not have to obtain a visa prior to seeking admission to the United States and do not have to present a valid passport unless they have made a visit outside of the Western Hemisphere.

However, Canadian nationals who seek to enter the U.S. as E nonimmigrants under NAFTA are not exempt from the visa requirement and must apply for an E visa at an American Consulate in Canada. Canadian nationals who wish to enter the U.S. under the other nonimmigrant categories may make an application for admission directly at the U.S. port of entry. However, because the H, L, K, O, Q, and P categories require pre-approval by the INS a Canadian national wishing to enter under these categories must present an approved petition to the immigration inspector at the port of entry at the time of application for admission. Similarly, Canadian nationals wishing to enter as F, J, or M nonimmigrants must present the certificate of eligibility issued by the school or sponsoring institution.

Canadian nationals must also present evidence of nationality at the time of admission such as a Canadian citizenship card or similar identification material. Canadian landed immigrants that do not have common nationality with Canada are not eligible to enter the U.S. without a visa but may be eligible for a border crossing card to facilitate frequent travel to the United States. Countries deemed to have common nationality with Canada or with British subjects in Bermuda are all commonwealth countries and citizens of Ireland including: Antigua, Australia, Bahamas, Bangladesh, Barbados, Belize, Botswana, Brunei, Canada, Cyprus, Dominica, Fiji, Gambia, Ghana, Grenada, Guyana, India, Ireland, Jamaica, Kenya, Kiribati, Lesotho, Malawi, Malaysia, Maldives, Malta, Mauritius, Nauru, New Zealand, Nigeria, Pakistan, Papua New Guinea, St. Kitts and Nevis, St. Lucia, St. Vincent, Seychelles, Sierra Leone, Singapore, Solomon Islands, Sri Lanka (Ceylon), Swaziland, Tanzania, Tonga, Trinidad and Tobago, Tuvalu, Uganda, United Kingdom (including colonies, territories, and dependencies, such as Bermuda), Vanuatu, Western Samoa, Zambia, and Zimbabwe.

Mexican nationals are also exempt from the visa and passport requirements if they possess a border-crossing card and are applying for admission as a temporary visitor for business or pleasure and are coming from Canada or Mexico. If a Mexican national is arriving from a territory other than Canada or Mexico, presentation of a passport and a visa is required.

Procedure for Obtaining a B-1 Visa

Required Documentation

1) Employer's Letter in Support (if applicable)
2) Form OF-156
3) Passport
4) Photographs
5) Filing Fee

Spouses and children of B-1 executives generally receive B-2 tourist visas, although visa issuance is not automatic. Dependents must show intent to return to the home country, but this usually does not present a problem when dealing with Western European and industrialized countries.

When gathering evidence to prove eligibility for a B-1 visa, providing detailed documentation is important. This may include copies of preliminary contract negotiations or inquiries, and prior correspondence between companies. Generally, more documentation will be needed for an international business person to show eligibility for a B-1 visa.

It is recommended that applicants show, whenever possible, airline tickets, hotel reservations and dates of planned travel and a detailed agenda of meetings and conferences planned. If the applicant's spouse and children will be travelling to the U.S., it is also advisable to include evidence of the family's means of support for the duration of the visit to the United States.

The usual practice with regard to a B-1 visa is to specify on the Form OF-156, the exact time needed for the trip, usually up to six months. Further, a B-1 visitor for business who intends to remain in the United States temporarily as a visitor for pleasure during the period of authorized admission need not request a change of status or apply for a new visa.

The amount of proof required for B-1 purposes will vary according to the particular application. Generally, more supporting documentation will be necessary for an independent business person than for an employee of a large well-known corporation. Further, for multiple entry long term B-1 visas, there is the need to show a continuing need for the individual to make periodic visits.

SAMPLE EMPLOYER LETTER OF SUPPORT FOR NONIMMIGRANT B-1 VISA APPLICATION

Dear Sir/Madam:

This letter is written on behalf of Mr. Yan Chen, a Vice President in our Asset Trading Department. We respectfully request that he be granted a B-1 nonimmigrant visa so that he may visit our United States branch of Taipei Bank located in Chicago, as well as finalize negotiations that he has been conducting with Deutsche Bank in San Francisco.

Taipei Bank is one of the top three banks in Taiwan and one of the largest banks worldwide. It enjoys annual revenues in excess of $100 billion and has subsidiary and affiliate branches in 450 locations around the world.

Taipei Bank specializes in structuring deals to purchase debt instruments of less developed countries, which are then sold in the thriving secondary international market.

In conjunction with Mr. Chen's activities as Vice President of Emerging Markets Assets, Placement and Syndication, he is currently being sent to the United States so that he may ascertain the current progress of our newly organized Chicago department as well as meet with executives of the Deutsche Bank in San Francisco, with whom he has been conducting extensive preliminary negotiations.

Mr. Chen's trip is expected to last four weeks, after which time he will return to Taipei to continue to perform his responsibilities as Vice President. However, given the nature of our business, Mr. Chen will be required to make future periodic business visits to the United States to conduct and conclude negotiations.

We respectfully request that Mr. Chen be granted B-1 visa classification for the purposes of this business trip.

Very truly yours,

Mei Xiao Li
General Manager
Asset Trading Department

SAMPLE FORM OF-156 FOR B-1 TEMPORARY VISITOR FOR BUSINESS

PLEASE TYPE OR PRINT YOUR ANSWERS IN THE SPACE PROVIDED BELOW EACH ITEM.

1. SURNAMES OR FAMILY NAMES *(Exactly as in Passport)*
Chen

2. FIRST NAME AND MIDDLE NAME *(Exactly as in Passport)*
Yan

3. OTHER NAMES *(Maiden, Religious, Professional, Aliases)*

4. DATE OF BIRTH *(Day, Month, Year)*
29/1/52

8. PASSPORT NUMBER
0000018

5. PLACE OF BIRTH
City, Province: Taipei
Country: Taiwan

DATE PASSPORT ISSUED *(Day, Month, Year)*
18/8/98

6. NATIONALITY
Taiwanese

7. SEX
☒ Male
☐ Female

DATE PASSPORT EXPIRES *(Day, Month, Year)*
18/8/03

9. HOME ADDRESS *(Include apartment no., street, city, province, and postal zone)*
1 Main Street, Taipei, Taiwan

10. NAME AND STREET ADDRESS OF PRESENT EMPLOYER OR SCHOOL *(Postal box number unacceptable)*
Taipei Bank, 3 Maple Street, Taipei

11. HOME TELEPHONE NO.
(886) 555-5555

12. BUSINESS TELEPHONE NO.
(886) 431-1344

13. COLOR OF HAIR
Black

14. COLOR OF EYES
Brown

15. COMPLEXION
Fair

16. HEIGHT
165 cm

17. MARKS OF IDENTIFICATION
N/A

18. MARITAL STATUS
☒ Married ☐ Single ☐ Widowed ☐ Divorced ☐ Separated
If married, give name and nationality of spouse.
Ming Chen Taiwanese

19. NAMES AND RELATIONSHIPS OF PERSONS TRAVELING WITH YOU(NOTE: *A separate application must be made for a visa for each traveler, regardless of age.)*
N/A

20. HAVE YOU EVER APPLIED FOR A U.S. VISA BEFORE, WHETHER IMMIGRANT OR NONIMMIGRANT?
☒ No
☐ Yes Where? ______
When? ______ Type of visa? ______
☐ Visa was issued ☐ Visa was refused

21. HAS YOUR U.S. VISA EVER BEEN CANCELED?
☒ No
☐ Yes Where? ______
When? ______ By whom? ______

22. Bearers of visitors visas may generally not work or study in the U.S.
DO YOU INTEND TO WORK IN THE U.S.? ☒ No ☐ Yes
If YES, explain.

23. DO YOU INTEND TO STUDY IN THE U.S.? ☒ No ☐ Yes
If YES, write name and address of school as it appears on form I-20.

DO NOT WRITE IN THIS SPACE

B-1/B-2 MAX B-1 MAX B-2 MAX

OTHER ______ MAX
Visa Classification

MULT OR ______
Number Applications

MONTHS ______
Validity

L.O. CHECKED ______

ISSUED /REFUSED
ON ______ BY ______

UNDER SEC. ______ INA

REFUSAL REVIEWED BY ______

MRV#

24. PRESENT OCCUPATION *(If retired, state past occupation)*
Banker

25. WHO WILL FURNISH FINANCIAL SUPPORT INCLUDING TICKETS?
Employer

26. AT WHAT ADDRESS WILL YOU STAY IN THE U.S.A.? *(City and State)*
Grand Hyatt; San Francisco, CA.
Hilton; Chicago, IL.

27. WHAT IS THE PURPOSE OF YOUR TRIP?
Business

28. WHEN DO YOU INTEND TO ARRIVE IN THE U.S.A.?
5/5/99

29. HOW LONG DO YOU PLAN TO STAY IN THE U.S.A.?
4 weeks

30. HAVE YOU EVER BEEN IN THE U.S.A.?
☒ No
☐ Yes When? ______
For how long? ______

NONIMMIGRANT VISA APPLICATION

COMPLETE ALL QUESTIONS ON REVERSE OF FORM

OPTIONAL FORM 156 (REV. 6/96) PAGE 1 50156-106
Department of State

SAMPLE FORM OF-156 FOR B-1 TEMPORARY VISITOR FOR BUSINESS(CONTINUED)

31. (a) HAVE YOU OR ANYONE ACTING FOR YOU EVER INDICATED TO A U.S. CONSULAR OR IMMIGRATION EMPLOYEE A DESIRE TO IMMIGRATE TO THE U.S.? (b)HAS ANYONE EVER FILED AN IMMIGRANT VISA PETITION ON YOUR BEHALF?(c) HAS LABOR CERTIFICATION FOR EMPLOYMENT IN THE U.S. EVER BEEN REQUESTED BY YOU OR ON YOUR BEHALF?

(a) ☒ No ☐ Yes (b) ☒ No ☐ Yes (c) ☒ No ☐ Yes

32. ARE ANY OF THE FOLLOWING IN THE U.S.? (X) NO ( ) YES (If YES, circle appropriate relationship and indicate that person's status in the U.S., i.e., studying, working, U.S. permanent resident, U.S. citizen, etc.)

HUSBAND/WIFE__________ FIANCE/FIANCEE __________ BROTHER/SISTER __________

FATHER/MOTHER__________ SON/DAUGHTER __________

33. PLEASE LIST THE COUNTRIES WHERE YOU HAVE LIVED FOR MORE THAN 6 MONTHS DURING THE PAST 5 YEARS BEGIN WITH YOUR PRESENT RESIDENCE.

Countries	Cities	Approximate Dates
Taiwan	Tapei	Birth - Pres

34. IMPORTANT: ALL APPLICANTS MUST READ AND CHECK THE APPROPRIATE BOX FOR EACH ITEM.

A visa may not be issued to persons who are within specific categories defined by law as inadmissible to the United States (except when a waiver is obtained in advance). Are any of the following applicable to you?

- Have you ever been afflicted with a communicable disease of public health significance, a dangerous physical or mental disorder, or been a drug abuser or addict? . . . . ☐ Yes ☒ No
- Have you ever been arrested or convicted for any offense or crime, even though subject of a pardon, amnesty, or other such legal action? . . . . ☐ Yes ☒ No
- Have You ever been a controlled substance (drug) trafficker, or a prostitute or procurer? . . . . . . ☐ Yes ☒ No
- Have you ever sought to obtain or assist others to obtain a visa, entry into the U.S., or any U.S. Immigration benefit by fraud or willful misrepresentation? . . . . ☐ Yes ☒ No
- Were you deported from the U.S.A. within the last 5 years? . . . . ☐ Yes ☒ No
- Do you seek to enter the United States to engage in export control violations, subversive or terrorist activities, or any unlawful purpose? . . . . ☐ Yes ☒ No
- Have you ever ordered, incited, assisted, or otherwise participated in the persecution of any person because of race, religion, national origin, or political opinion under the control, direct or indirect, of the Nazi Government of Germany, or of the government of any area occupied by, or allied with, the Nazi Government of Germany; or have you ever participated in genocide? . . . . ☐ Yes ☒ No
- Have you ever voted in the U.S.A. in violation of law? ☐ Yes ☒ No
- Are you a former U.S. Citizen who renounced citizenship after 09/30/1996 to avoid taxation? ☐ Yes ☒ No
- Are you a member or representative of a terrorist organization? ☐ Yes ☒ No

A YES answer does not automatically signify ineligibility for a visa, but if you answered YES to any of the above, or if you have any question in this regard, personal appearance at this office is recommended. If appearance is not possible at this time, attach a statement of facts in your case to this application.

35. I certify that I have read and understood all the questions set forth in this application and the answers I have furnished on this form are true and correct to the best of my knowledge and belief. I understand that any false or misleading statement may result in the permanent refusal of a visa or denial of entry into the United States. I understand that possession of a visa does not entitle the bearer to enter the United States of America upon arrival at port of entry if he or she is found inadmissible.

DATE OF APPLICATION __________

APPLICANT'S SIGNATURE__________

If this application has been prepared by a travel agency or another person on your behalf, the agent should indicate name and address of agency or person with appropriate signature of individual preparing form.

SIGNATURE OF PERSON PREPARING FORM
(if other than applicant) __________

DO NOT WRITE IN THIS SPACE

37 mm x 37 mm

PHOTO

Glue photo here

PRACTICAL CONSIDERATIONS FOR COMPLETING FORM OF-156

1. Item 8 - The passport expiration date must be at least six months past the expiration date of the requested period of stay.

2. Item 9 - The foreign address should be used.

3. Item 20 - Every United States visa the applicant has ever applied for must be included, whether it was issued or not.

4. Item 29 - If the applicant is applying for a nonimmigrant visa, it is important that there be nothing on the Form OF-156 incorrectly suggesting the possibility that the applicant is intending to immigrate to the United States. Therefore, only request a period of stay that corresponds with the visa category for which you are applying.

5. Item 30 - Every stay in the U.S. should be included to the extent practicable.

6. Item 31 - A "yes" answer to any of these questions will open the door to a thorough inquiry as to whether the applicant has immigrant intent which may be inconsistent with the visa category sought (especially for B, C, D, F and J categories).

7. Item 32 - Be aware that the presence of close relatives of the applicant in the United States may be interpreted as evidence of immigrant intent. The consular officer will also consider the immigration status of the close relatives relevant.

8. Item 34 - These questions all relate to possible grounds of inadmissability under United States law.

9. The attached photograph must be a "passport" photo, of the size indicated.

Applicants should be aware that statements contained on Form OF-156 and supporting documents that are later determined to constitute misrepresentations may provide the basis for permanent inadmissibility from the United States upon application for a subsequent immigrant or nonimmigrant visa.

What Constitutes Legitimate Business Activity for B-1 Purposes?

It is impossible to draw a precise line between consultation and provision of services for B visa purposes and it is often not clear what constitutes legitimate business activity for B-1 business visitor purposes. The general rule is that consultation is an authorized activity for B visa purposes while provision of services is not.

For example, a parent company may send a management executive to a subsidiary in the United States to assure that the subsidiary is conforming to the standards of the overall organization. This would be considered a valid B-1 activity. However, if the executive remains in the United States for long periods of time, providing day-to-day advice on the running of the company, this might be considered rendering services to the United States company and therefore, de facto employment, which is not authorized under the B visa category.

Impermissible and Permissible Consultation and Business Solicitation

An employee of a foreign firm who comes to the United States several times a year for short periods to sell goods to United States customers is eligible for admission as a B-1 visitor if his employer's principal place of business is in the foreign country, his commissions from sales in the United States are a minor part of his overall income, and each of his entries is plainly of a temporary nature and is in furtherance of international trade or commerce. If a business visitor enters the United States frequently, for long periods of time, and earns all income from sales in the United States, he or she would be engaging in unauthorized activity under the B-1 category.

It is not advisable to use the B visa category to gain admission and then attempt to change status from within the United States. In some instances, the improper use of the B category may be considered fraudulent. The proper approach is to make disclosures of any intent to work or study at the time the application is being made before the consular officer. Attempts to use B status as a pretext for later changing nonimmigrant status once in the United States are strongly discouraged and may jeopardize future admission to the United States.

C. B-2 TEMPORARY VISITOR FOR PLEASURE

The B-2 visa category is designed for visitors for "pleasure." "Pleasure" for the purposes of the B-2 category is defined as legitimate activities of a recreational character including tourism, amusement, visits with friends or relatives, rest, medical treatment, and activities of fraternal, social or service organizations.

A B-2 visitor who is found otherwise admissible and is issued Form I-94 will generally be admitted for a maximum period of six months, regardless of whether less time is requested, provided that the visitor's passport is valid.

The INS does not require that an applicant maintain a six month stay, but the applicant must demonstrate that he or she has access to sufficient resources for the duration of stay in the United States. Credit cards may often suffice.

The B-2 visitor's visa is one of the most frequently used visas and facilitates the flow of millions of visitors to the United States each year.

Requirements for B-2 Classification

An applicant entering the United States is classifiable as a B-2 temporary visitor for pleasure if the individual is:

- a tourist;
- making social visits to relatives or friends;
- coming for health purposes;
- coming to participate in conventions, confer-

ences or social organizations;

- a participant in an amateur musical or sporting event;

- dependent of an alien nonimmigrant coming to the United States solely for the purpose of accompanying the principal alien; <u>or</u>

- coming to the United States primarily for tourism, who, during the visit will incidentally engage in a short course of study.

Study under the B-2 visa category is specifically prohibited unless it is brief and incidental to the visit. If the individual intends to study in the United States he or she should inform the consular officer of their incidental study plans and a notation will be placed in the passport underneath the visa stamp, which reads "Study Incidental to visit: I-20 not required."

Any plans to study for a longer period of time should be made pursuant to an approved F-1 student visa petition. Plans to look for a school in which to enroll should be disclosed to the consular officer when making the visa application. The consular officer may then make a notation that the individual is a prospective student and in this case change of status will normally be authorized.

However, if it is later discovered that the applicant had a premeditated plan to change status which was not disclosed to the consular officer at the time of application, the time frame of the foreign national's actions will be strictly scrutinized to determine their true intentions and the change of status is likely to be denied.

<u>Procedure for Obtaining a B-2 Visa</u>

1) Form OF-156
2) Photographs
3) Letter of Invitation
4) Affidavit of Support
5) Filing Fee

The procedure for obtaining a B-2 visa is similar to the procedures for B-1 visa issuance. An OF-156 Form must be filed along with any required supporting documentation. The applicant will also undergo a brief interview with a consular officer.

A consular officer's decision is highly subjective and not generally appealable. Therefore, it is incumbent upon the individual to properly determine the requirements of the B visa in advance of their interview so as not to mistakenly convey to the consular officer any intentions which might be misconstrued as either unauthorized or unlawful.

It is important to note that although an individual may harbor a generalized intent to live in the United States in the future or has long term plans to do so, the individual is not barred from entering the United States as a B-2 visitor. The applicant must simply show that in spite of the generalized intent to immigrate, the individual has a clear intention to leave the United States upon the expiration of authorized stay.

The intention to leave the United States after the temporary trip is based in part on the individual being able to enter another country at the end of their stay in the United States. Therefore, when applying for the B-2 visa, the individual's passport must generally be valid for at least six months after the date of the proposed authorized B-2 stay will end.

Additionally, the B-2 visaholder must show that adequate financial arrangements have been made to carry out the purpose of the visit. Documents that may be attached include tax returns, job letters, bank statements and an Affidavit of Support (INS Form I-134).

SAMPLE LETTER OF INVITATION IN SUPPORT OF B-2 APPLICATION

U.S. Consulate
Tel Aviv, Israel

Re: Irit Mizrahi - Application for B-2 Temporary Visitor Visa

Dear Sir/Madam:

I am writing this letter on behalf of my niece, Irit Mizrahi, to express my invitation to her to visit my family for a period of two months.

Currently, Irit is a graduate student in business administration at Tel Aviv University in Tel Aviv. She intends to return to this program after her trip to the United States.

During her stay in the U.S., Irit will be staying at my home in San Francisco as well as taking brief trips around the United States.

I am a stockbroker employed by Nomura Securities in San Francisco and currently earn $350,000 per year. I agree to provide Irit with any funds she may require while in the U.S.

Thank you for your assistance in granting this visa.

Sincerely yours,

Ethan Cohen

SAMPLE FORM OF-156 FOR B-2 TEMPORARY VISITOR FOR PLEASURE

PLEASE TYPE OR PRINT YOUR ANSWERS IN THE SPACE PROVIDED BELOW EACH ITEM.

1. SURNAMES OR FAMILY NAMES *(Exactly as in Passport)*
Mizrahi

2. FIRST NAME AND MIDDLE NAME *(Exactly as in Passport)*
Irit

3. OTHER NAMES *(Maiden, Religious, Professional, Aliases)*
N/A

4. DATE OF BIRTH *(Day, Month, Year)*
4/4/72

8. PASSPORT NUMBER
10101XY

5. PLACE OF BIRTH
City, Province: Tel Aviv
Country: Israel

DATE PASSPORT ISSUED *(Day, Month, Year)*
10/8/95

6. NATIONALITY
Israeli

7. SEX
☐ Male
☒ Female

DATE PASSPORT EXPIRES *(Day, Month, Year)*
10/8/00

9. HOME ADDRESS *(Include apartment no., street, city, province, and postal zone)*
1 High Street, Tel Aviv, Israel

10. NAME AND STREET ADDRESS OF PRESENT EMPLOYER OR SCHOOL *(Postal box number unacceptable)*
Tel Aviv University

11. HOME TELEPHONE NO.
(972) 225-2222

12. BUSINESS TELEPHONE NO.
N/A

13. COLOR OF HAIR
Brown

14. COLOR OF EYES
Hazel

15. COMPLEXION
Fair

16. HEIGHT
5'4"

17. MARKS OF IDENTIFICATION
Birth mark on left hand

18. MARITAL STATUS
☐ Married ☒ Single ☐ Widowed ☐ Divorced ☐ Separated
If married, give name and nationality of spouse.

19. NAMES AND RELATIONSHIPS OF PERSONS TRAVELING WITH YOU(NOTE: *A separate application must be made for a visa for each traveler, regardless of age.)*
N/A

20. HAVE YOU EVER APPLIED FOR A U.S. VISA BEFORE, WHETHER IMMIGRANT OR NONIMMIGRANT?
☐ No
☒ Yes Where? Tel Aviv, Israel
When? 12/11/95 Type of visa? B-2
☒ Visa was issued ☐ Visa was refused

21. HAS YOUR U.S. VISA EVER BEEN CANCELED?
☒ No
☐ Yes Where? ______
When? ______ By whom? ______

22. Bearers of visitors visas may generally not work or study in the U.S.
DO YOU INTEND TO WORK IN THE U.S.? ☒ No ☐ Yes
If YES, explain.

23. DO YOU INTEND TO STUDY IN THE U.S.? ☒ No ☐ Yes
If YES, write name and address of school as it appears on form I-20.

DO NOT WRITE IN THIS SPACE

B-1/B-2 MAX B-1 MAX B-2 MAX

OTHER__________MAX
Visa Classification

MULT OR __________
Number Applications

MONTHS__________
Validity

L.O. CHECKED __________

ISSUED /REFUSED

ON______ BY ______

UNDER SEC.__________ INA

REFUSAL REVIEWED BY ______

MRV#

24. PRESENT OCCUPATION *(If retired, state past occupation)*
Student

25. WHO WILL FURNISH FINANCIAL SUPPORT INCLUDING TICKETS?
Parents, Uncle

26. AT WHAT ADDRESS WILL YOU STAY IN THE U.S.A.? *(City and State)*
3 Low Street, San Francisco, CA

27. WHAT IS THE PURPOSE OF YOUR TRIP?
Visit relatives

28. WHEN DO YOU INTEND TO ARRIVE IN THE U.S.A.?
8/17/99

29. HOW LONG DO YOU PLAN TO STAY IN THE U.S.A.?
2 months

30. HAVE YOU EVER BEEN IN THE U.S.A.?
☐ No
☒ Yes When? 12/18/95 until
For how long? 1/15/96

NONIMMIGRANT VISA APPLICATION

COMPLETE ALL QUESTIONS ON REVERSE OF FORM

OPTIONAL FORM 156 (REV. 6/96) PAGE 1 50156-106
Department of State

SAMPLE FORM OF-156 FOR B-2 TEMPORARY VISITOR FOR PLEASURE (CONTINUED)

31. (a) HAVE YOU OR ANYONE ACTING FOR YOU EVER INDICATED TO A U.S. CONSULAR OR IMMIGRATION EMPLOYEE A DESIRE TO IMMIGRATE TO THE U.S.? (b)HAS ANYONE EVER FILED AN IMMIGRANT VISA PETITION ON YOUR BEHALF?(c) HAS LABOR CERTIFICATION FOR EMPLOYMENT IN THE U.S. EVER BEEN REQUESTED BY YOU OR ON YOUR BEHALF?

(a) ☒ No ☐ Yes (b) ☒ No ☐ Yes (c) ☒ No ☐ Yes

32. ARE ANY OF THE FOLLOWING IN THE U.S.? ( ) NO ( ) YES (If YES, circle appropriate relationship and indicate that person's status in the U.S., i.e., studying, working, U.S. permanent resident, U.S. citizen, etc.)

HUSBAND/WIFE________ FIANCE/FIANCEE ________ BROTHER/SISTER ________

FATHER/MOTHER________ SON/DAUGHTER ________

33. PLEASE LIST THE COUNTRIES WHERE YOU HAVE LIVED FOR MORE THAN 6 MONTHS DURING THE PAST 5 YEARS BEGIN WITH YOUR PRESENT RESIDENCE.

Countries	Cities	Approximate Dates
Israel	Tel Aviv	1972-Present

34. IMPORTANT: ALL APPLICANTS MUST READ AND CHECK THE APPROPRIATE BOX FOR EACH ITEM.

A visa may not be issued to persons who are within specific categories defined by law as inadmissible to the United States (except when a waiver is obtained in advance). Are any of the following applicable to you?

- Have you ever been afflicted with a communicable disease of public health significance, a dangerous physical or mental disorder, or been a drug abuser or addict? . . . . ☐ Yes ☒ No
- Have you ever been arrested or convicted for any offense or crime, even though subject of a pardon, amnesty, or other such legal action? . . . . ☐ Yes ☒ No
- Have You ever been a controlled substance (drug) trafficker, or a prostitute or procurer? . . . . . . ☐ Yes ☒ No
- Have you ever sought to obtain or assist others to obtain a visa, entry into the U.S., or any U.S. Immigration benefit by fraud or willful misrepresentation? . . . . ☐ Yes ☒ No
- Were you deported from the U.S.A. within the last 5 years? . . . . ☐ Yes ☒ No
- Do you seek to enter the United States to engage in export control violations, subversive or terrorist activities, or any unlawful purpose? . . . . ☐ Yes ☒ No
- Have you ever ordered, incited, assisted, or otherwise participated in the persecution of any person because of race, religion, national origin, or political opinion under the control, direct or indirect, of the Nazi Government of Germany, or of the government of any area occupied by, or allied with, the Nazi Government of Germany; or have you ever participated in genocide? . . . . ☐ Yes ☒ No
- Have you ever voted in the U.S.A. in violation of law? ☐ Yes ☒ No
- Are you a former U.S. Citizen who renounced citizenship after 09/30/1996 to avoid taxation? ☐ Yes ☒ No
- Are you a member or representative of a terrorist organization? ☐ Yes ☒ No

A YES answer does not automatically signify ineligibility for a visa, but if you answered YES to any of the above, or if you have any question in this regard, personal appearance at this office is recommended. If appearance is not possible at this time, attach a statement of facts in your case to this application.

35. I certify that I have read and understood all the questions set forth in this application and the answers I have furnished on this form are true and correct to the best of my knowledge and belief. I understand that any false or misleading statement may result in the permanent refusal of a visa or denial of entry into the United States. I understand that possession of a visa does not entitle the bearer to enter the United States of America upon arrival at port of entry if he or she is found inadmissible.

DATE OF APPLICATION ________

APPLICANT'S SIGNATURE________

If this application has been prepared by a travel agency or another person on your behalf, the agent should indicate name and address of agency or person with appropriate signature of individual preparing form.

SIGNATURE OF PERSON PREPARING FORM
(if other than applicant) ________

DO NOT WRITE IN THIS SPACE

37 mm x 37 mm

PHOTO

Glue photo here

SAMPLE AFFIDAVIT OF SUPPORT: B-2 VISITOR FOR PLEASURE

OMB No. 1115-00

U.S. Department of Justice
Immigration and Naturalization Service

Affidavit of Support

(ANSWER ALL ITEMS: FILL IN WITH TYPEWRITER OR PRINT IN BLOCK LETTERS IN INK.)

I, Ethan Cohen (Name), residing at 3 Low Street (Street and Number)

San Francisco (City) California (State) 94101 (ZIP Code if in U.S.) USA (Country)

BEING DULY SWORN DEPOSE AND SAY:

1. I was born on 2/26/50 (Date) at Tehran (City) Iraq (Country)

   If you are ***not*** a native born United States citizen, answer the following as appropriate:

   a. If a United States citizen through naturalization, give certificate of naturalization number 123456780123

   b. If a United States citizen through parent(s) or marriage, give citizen certificate number ______

   c. If United States citizenship was derived by some other method, attach a statement of explanation.

   d. If lawfully admitted permanent resident of the United States, give "A" number ______

2. That I am 49 years of age and have resided in the United States since (date) June 4, 1981

3. That this affidavit is executed in behalf of the following person:

Name		Sex	Age
Mizrahi	Irit	F	27

Citizen of--(Country)	Marital Status	Relationship to Deponent
Israel	Single	Niece

Presently resides at--(Street and Number)	(City)	(State)	(Country)
1 High Street	Tel Aviv		Israel

Name of spouse and children accompanying or following to join person:

Spouse	Sex	Age	Child	Sex	Age
N/A					
Child	Sex	Age	Child	Sex	Age
Child	Sex	Age	Child	Sex	Age

4. That this affidavit is made by me for the purpose of assuring the United States Government that the person(s) named in item 3 will not become a public charge in the United States.

5. That I am willing and able to receive, maintain and support the person(s) named in item 3. That I am ready and willing to deposit a bond, if necessary, to guarantee that such person(s) will not become a public charge during his or her stay in the United States, or to guarantee that the above named will maintain his or her nonimmigrant status if admitted temporarily and will depart prior to the expiration of his or her authorized stay in the United States.

6. That I understand this affidavit will be binding upon me for a period of three (3) years after entry of the person(s) named in item 3 and that the information and documentation provided by me may be made available to the Secretary of Health and Human Services and the Secretary of Agriculture, who may make it available to a public assistance agency.

7. That I am employed as, or engaged in the business of Stockbroker (Type of Business) with Nomura Securities (Name of Concern)

   at 3 West Bridge Road (Street and Number) San Francisco, CA (City) (State) 94109 (Zip Code)

   I derive an annual income of *(if self-employed, I have attached a copy of my last income tax return or report of commercial rating concern which I certify to be true and correct to the best of my knowledge and belief. See instruction for nature of evidence of net worth to be submitted.)* $ 350,000.00

   I have on deposit in savings banks in the United States $ 425,000.00

   I have other personal property, the reasonable value of which is $ 1,000,000.00

Form I-134(Rev.12-1-84) Y

OVER

I have stocks and bonds with the following market value, as indicated on the attached list which I certify to be true and correct to the best of my knowledge and belief $ 700,000.00

I have life insurance in the sum of $ 2,000,000.00

With a cash surrender value of $ ______

I own real estate valued at $ 3,000,000.00

With mortgage or other encumbrances thereon amounting to $ 1,500,000

Which is located at 3 Low Street (Street and Number) San Francisco (City) California (State) 94101 (Zip Code)

8. That the following persons are dependent upon me for support: *(Place an "X"* in the appropriate column to indicate whether the person named is ***wholly*** or ***partially*** dependent upon you for support.)

Name of Person	Wholly Dependent	Partially Dependent	Age	Relationship to Me
Kaleen Cohen		X	49	Wife
Andrew Cohen		X	23	Son
Joshua Cohen	X		16	Son

9. That I have previously submitted affidavit(s) of support for the following person(s). If none, state ***"None"***

Name	Date submitted
None	

10. That I have submitted visa petition(s) to the Immigration and Naturalization Service on behalf of the following person(s). If none, state none.

Name	Relationship	Date submitted
None		

11. ***(Complete this block only if the person named in item 3 will be in the United States temporarily.)***
That I ☒ do intend ☐ do not intend, to make specific contributions to the support of the person named in item 3. *(If you check "do intend", indicate the exact nature and duration of the contributions. For example, if you intend to furnish room and board, state for how long and, if money, state the amount in United States dollars and state whether it is to be given in a lump sum, weekly, or monthly, or for how long.)*

My niece will stay at my home during her temporary visit to the United States and will be provided meals, spending money and any medical care she might require during her stay.

OATH OR AFFIRMATION OF DEPONENT

I acknowledge at that I have read Part III of the instructions, Sponsor and Alien Liability, and am aware of my responsibilities as an immigrant sponsor under the Social Security Act, as amended, and the Food Stamp Act, as amended.

I swear (affirm) that I know the contents of this affidavit signed by me and the statements are true and correct.

Signature of deponent ______

Subscribed and sworn to (affirmed) before me this ______ ***day of*** ______ ***,19*** ______

at ______ . ***My commission expires on*** ______

Signature of Officer Administering Oath ______ ***Title*** ______

If affidavit prepared by other than deponent, please complete the following: I declare that this document was prepared by me at the request of the deponent and is based on all information of which I have knowledge.

(Signature) ***(Address)*** ***(Date)***

Other Authorized Uses of the B-2 Visa

Alien Fiance(e)s

Generally, in the case of an alien fiance(e), a K-1 visa is the appropriate visa to obtain if the couple intends to remain in the United States after marriage. However, a B-2 visa may be issued to the alien fiance(e) if it is evident that the couple intends to depart the United States shortly after their marriage.

Other possibilities that may exist concerning alien fiancées and the B-2 visa category occur in cases where:

- The individual is entering the United States for the purpose of meeting the family of his or her fiance(e).
- When the individual is entering the United States for the purposes of becoming engaged (but not to remain).
- Where the individual is entering the United States in order to make arrangements for the wedding.
- Where the individual is entering the United States to renew the relationship with his or her prospective spouse.

In addition to these special circumstances with regard to fiance(e)s, an individual may also enter the United States under B-2 authorization to marry a nonimmigrant worker, employed in the United States (such as H, L or E nonimmigrants) provided that after the marriage he or she files an application to obtain the derivative status to the nonimmigrant spouse.

It should be noted, however, that all of the above purposes are sometimes considered by immigration officials as "red flags" of visa fraud, and the applicant may be required to overcome an especially heavy burden of proof regarding nonimmigrant intent.

Accompanying Spouse and Children

B-2 visitor visas may be issued when spouses and children are accompanying a family member on a temporary visit to the United States. In addition, with regard to elderly parents who would not otherwise qualify for other visa categories, one-year admissions under B visa authorization may be requested from the Immigration and Naturalization when derivative status is unavailable.

D. VISA WAIVER PROGRAM

In 1986, Congress created the Visa Waiver Pilot Program (VWPP). Initially the program was to be conducted by the Attorney General in conjunction with the Department of State for a three-year period. The visa waiver program permits nationals of designated countries to apply for admission to the United States as visitors for business (B-1) or pleasure (B-2) for ninety days, without having to first obtain a visa at United States consular posts overseas. Eligible nationals are able to board a plane without securing a visa or appear at a land border and apply for admission directly at the United States port of entry. The primary goal of the program was to promote international travel and tourism and reduce U.S. government personnel costs.

The Illegal Immigration Reform and Immigrant Responsibility Act of 1996 (IIRAIRA) made a few modifications to the program. The Attorney General now has sole authority over the program and probationary status for some participating countries was eliminated. Initially the program was set to sunset on September 30, 1997. Congress, for the foreseeable future, seems to have no intention of ending the visa waiver program, and it can be expected that the program will continue to be available.

Currently, the following countries are designated under the program:

Andorra, Argentina, Austria, Australia, Belgium, Brunei, Denmark, Finland, France, Germany, Iceland, Ireland, Italy, Japan, Liechtenstein, Luxembourg, Monaco, the Netherlands, New Zealand, Norway, San Marino, Slovenia, Spain, Sweden, Switzerland, and the United Kingdom.

To be eligible to participate in the program applicants must be nationals of the designated country and be traveling on the passport of that country. Applicants may arrive by air, sea or land. Applicants arriving by air or sea must be in possession of a nontransferable, nonrefundable return trip ticket valid for one year. The trip must not terminate in a contiguous territory on an adjacent island unless the traveler is a resident of the country of destination. Applicants arriving at land border ports must provide evidence to the immigration officer of financial solvency and a permanent residence abroad.

Individuals entering the United States under the Visa Waiver Program must fill out and present Form I-94W Nonimmigrant Visa Waiver Arrival/Departure record. The form is usually handed out on the plane and must be completed and signed before inspection.

The Visa Waiver Program is advantageous in that it allows a traveler the spontaneity of being able to travel on short notice without the inconvenience or expense involved in obtaining a visa. However, under certain circumstances it may be more advantageous to obtain a visa at a United States consular post abroad rather than proceed under the conditions and limitations of the Visa Waiver Program. The most notable limitation of the program is that admission into the United States is only authorized for a maximum period of ninety days, without the possibility of extension or change of status.

In the alternative, if entering with a B-1 or B-2 visa issued by a United States consular post, a traveler may be granted an authorized stay of up to six months after which time they may request an extension of stay under certain circumstances. Furthermore, if a change of status is sought the individual in some circumstances may be able to obtain this change of status while in the United States. Individuals who are in the United States under the Visa Waiver Program must return to the home country in order to change status.

Finally, because the traveler is under the visa waiver program he or she is only examined upon arrival at the point of admission, as opposed to prior review by a consular officer, the individual's is admission is subject to the sole discretion of the Immigration Inspector. If an Immigration Inspector believes the individual is ineligible for admission under the program, is inadmissible to the U.S. on other enumerated grounds, or that the individual has presented fraudulent documents, the inspector may deny admission. The traveler will be summarily expelled and put on the first available means of transportation back to the point of embarkation without any recourse in law. The only exception is when a traveler presents himself or herself as an applicant for asylum.

Therefore, in a situation where an individual's background might lend an Immigration Inspector to doubt their nonimmigrant intent, it is advisable for the individual to proceed through the Consulate for a visa rather than opt for the Visa Waiver Program. The consular option permits the individual to submit more documentation and evidence supporting the traveler's proposed trip. Although in theory an individual may submit all of this information to the immigration inspector at the time of inspection, it is unlikely that an individual will want to travel with all his or her original documentation. Moreover, the consular officer is in a better position to judge all of the documents and the applicant's intentions based upon the presentation of evidence, rather than the immigration inspector, who may conduct a more cursory questioning of the indi-

SAMPLE FORM I-94W

Departure Number
523795077 06

U.S. IMMIGRATION
NEW YORK, N.Y. 2780

MAY 06 1998

Immigration and Naturalization Service
Form I-94W (05-29-91) - Departure Record
VISA WAIVER

ADMITTED
UNTIL Aug 05 98
CLASS

14. Family Name
NAME DELETED

15. First (Given) Name
NAME DELETED

16. Birth Date (day/mo/yr)
150273

17. Country of Citizenship
AUSTRALIA

See Other Side

Staple Here

T/S 42065 (JUN. 97)

Departure Number
446607783 03

U. S. IMMIGRATION
NEW YORK, N.Y. 2256

SEP 19

移民帰化局
I-94W (05-29-91) 出発記録
査証免除

ADMITTED
UNTIL

14. 姓
NAME DELETED

15. 名
NAME DELETED

16. 生年月日（日/月/年）
7/4/62

17. 国籍（国名）
JAPAN

裏面を見て下さい

Staple Here

I94W (JAPANESE)

Departure Number
575867097 06

U. S. IMMIGRATION
NEW YORK, N.Y. 2638

MAY 23

Einwanderungs- und Einbürgerungsdienst
Formular I-94W (05-29-91) - Ausreise
AUFHEBUNG DER VISUMSPFLICHT

ADMITTED
UNTIL AUG 22 1998
(CLASS)

Sichtvermerke/Visas/Visas

14. Familienname
NAME DELETED

15. Vorname
NAME DELETED

16. Geburtsdatum (Tag/Monat/Jahr)
150670

17. Staatsbürger von (Land)
GERMANY

Siehe Rückseite

Staple Here

I-94W (German)

Designated employers are not required to make the displacement and recruitment attestations until the Department of Labor and the INS issue final regulations implementing these changes to the LCA process. The new attestation requirements will sunset on October 1, 2001, unless Congress acts to extend this provision.

Posting Notices

At the time of filing the labor condition application, both H-1B dependent and exempt employers must have either:

1) Provided notice of the filing of the labor condition application to the bargaining representative of the employer's employees in the occupational classification in the area of intended employment for which the H-1B nonimmigrants are sought; or

2) If there is no such bargaining representative, has posted notice of the filing of the labor condition application in conspicuous locations in the employer's establishment. The LCA may also be posted through electronic notification to employees in the occupational classification in which H-1B nonimmigrants are sought.

Prevailing or Actual Wage

The "Wage Obligation" portion of the labor condition application requires employers to attest they will pay H-1B nonimmigrants the actual wage for the occupation at the place of employment or the prevailing wage for the occupation in the area of employment, whichever is higher.

The wage the employer must pay is to be based on the best information available at the time of filing of the labor condition application.

The Actual Wage must be determined on the basis of what the employer pays to all other H-1B aliens with similar experience and qualifications for the specific employment in question.

The factors to consider with regard to the actual wage include: experience, qualifications, education, job responsibility and function, specialized knowledge and "other legitimate business factors."

To determine the actual wage level for an H-1B worker, the employer must consider only the wage level paid to all other H-1B aliens with similar experience and qualifications who are in the same specific position, in that they perform the actual set of duties and responsibilities as the H-1B nonimmigrant. If no one else performs the same duties, then the actual wage will be considered to be the wage paid to the H-1B worker. Since the comparison is only among other H-1B nonimmigrants, it is less likely that the employer will have to adjust the individual's salary to the actual wage. The wage however, must conform to the "prevailing wage" in the industry and geographic area.

Prevailing Wage Determination

The determination of what is the prevailing wage may be done using any of the methods listed below:

1) A wage rate established by the Department of Labor under the Davis-Bacon Act or the McNamara-O'Hara Service Contract Act.

2) A collectively bargained wage rate contained in a union contract to which the employer is a part.

3) A prevailing wage determination provided in writing from the State Employment Security Agency that accesses the Occupational Employment Statistics from the Bureau of Labor Statistics.

4) A prevailing wage obtained from an independent authoritative source.

5) A prevailing wage obtained from another legitimate source of wage.

The advantage in using the first three means of determining the prevailing wage is that the employer will be protected in the event of a complaint alleging an inaccuracy in the determination of the prevailing wage.

Similarly, the use of an independent authoritative legitimate source means that in the event of a complaint, the employer will only be required to demonstrate that the source complies with the standards for prevailing wage set forth in the pertinent regulations.

If the employer later discovers the H-1B nonimmigrant's rate of pay was below the prevailing wage, the employer will not suffer penalty if the pay differential is rectified by retroactively paying the alien the difference within 30 days of obtaining the State Employment Security Agency prevailing wage determination.

The prevailing wage must be updated every three years and adjusted upwardly in the event that the prevailing wage is greater than the actual wage.

In addition to offering the H-1B nonimmigrant the prevailing or actual wage, the 1998 Act requires employers to offer H-1B nonimmigrants benefits and eligibility for benefits (including participation in health, life, disability, and other insurance plans, retirement and savings plans, bonuses and stock options) on the same basis, and accordance with the same criteria as offered to U.S. workers. Violations of this provision are considered to be violations of the wage requirement and are subject to the same penalties discussed below.

Penalties

The 1998 Act enhanced the penalties for employers who fail to comply with the LCA requirements of the H-1B program. Employers who violate the provisions of the H-1B program are subject to the following penalties:

Basic Penalties: A $1,000 fine and not less than one year debarment from use of the H-1B program for failure to meet the no strike or lockout or layoff attestations, a substantial failure to meet the working conditions, posting or recruitment attestations or misrepresentation of a material fact in the application.

Willful Penalties: A $5,000 fine and not less than two year debarment from use of the H-1B program for failure to meet any attestation condition, or willful misrepresentation of a material fact, or violation of the whistleblower clause.

Severe Violations: A $35,000 fine and no less than three year debarment from use of the H-1B program for willful failure or willful misrepresentation of a material fact in the course of which an employer displaced a U.S. worker within the 90 days before and 90 days after the filing of an H-1B visa petition based on the application.

Unconscionable Contract Provisions: A $1,000 fine per violation for requiring an H-1B nonimmigrant to pay a penalty for leaving the employer's employ prior to a date agreed to by the nonimmigrant and the employer.

The 1998 Act created "whistleblower" protection for H-1B nonimmigrants who disclose information or cooperate in investigations concerning employer violations of the H-1B program. Employers are prohibited from intimidating, threatening, restraining, coercing, blacklisting, discharging or otherwise discriminating against employees who are involved in investigations or proceedings concerning employer misconduct.

In order to be eligible to file a labor condition application as an H-1B employer, the employer must have an Internal Revenue Service employer tax identification number and make a copy of the labor condition application and all supporting documentation available for public examination at the employer's principal place of business in the United States or at the beneficiary's intended place of employment.

H-1B nonimmigrants may be employed by more than one employer, provided that a valid labor condition application has been filed for each employer, and a separate petition is filed and approved by the INS for each employer. The labor condition application is filed with Department of Labor regional office that has geographical jurisdiction over the place of employment. Labor condition applications can not be filed more than six months prior to the start date of employment.

In light of the changes made to the H-1B program by the 1998 Act, the DOL is in the process of revising the labor condition application (Form ETA-9035). The LCA form may undergo many revisions, it is therefore prudent for an employer to check with the DOL before filing and obtain the most current version of the labor condition application.

SAMPLE LABOR CONDITION APPLICATION (Prior to 1998 Act)

1. Full Legal Name of Employer International Printing (America) Inc.	5. Employer's Address (No., Street, City, State, and ZIP Code) 222 Park Avenue New York, New York 10001 OMB Approval No.: 1205-0310 Expiration Date: 11-30-97
2. Federal Employer I.D. Number 13-1111111	
3. Employer's Telephone No. 212-555-5555	6. Address Where Documentation is Kept (if different than item 5)
4. Employer's FAX No. 212-555-5554	

7. OCCUPATIONAL INFORMATION (Use attachment if additional space is needed)

(a) Three-digit Occupational Group Code (From Appendix 2): 161 (b) Job Title (Check Box if Part-Time): International Marketing Analyst ☐

(c) No. of H-1B Nonimmigrants	(d) Rate of Pay	(e) Prevailing Wage Rate and its Source (see instructions)		(f) Period of Employment From	To	(g) Location(s) Where H-1B Nonimmigrants Will Work (see instructions)
1	$ 70,000	$ 62,500	☐SESA ☒Other: Watson Wyatt Survey	5/1/99	4/30/02	222 Park Avenue
	$ per year	$ per year	☐SESA ☐Other: 1998-1999			New York, NY 10001

8. EMPLOYER LABOR CONDITION STATEMENTS (Employers are required to develop and maintain documentation supporting labor conditic statements 8(a) and 8(d). Employers are further required to make available for public examination a copy of the labor condition application anc necessary supporting documentation within one (1) working day after the date on which the application is filed with DOL. Check each box t indicate that the employer will comply with each statement.)

☒ (a) H-1B nonimmigrants will be paid at least the actual wage level paid by the employer to all other individuals with similar experience an qualifications for the specific employment in question or the prevailing wage level for the occupation in the area of employme whichever is higher.

☒ (b) The employment of H-1B nonimmigrants will not adversely affect the working conditions of workers similarly employed in the area c intended employment.

☒ (c) On the date this application is signed and submitted, there is not a strike, lockout or work stoppage in the course of a labor dispute in th occupation in which H-1B nonimmigrants will be employed at the place of employment. If such a strike or lockout occurs after th application is submitted, I will notify ETA within 3 days of the occurrence of such a strike or lockout and the application will not be used support of petition filings with INS for H-1B nonimmigrants to work in the same occupation at the place of employment until ETA determine the strike or lockout has ceased.

☒ (d) A copy of this application has been, or will be, provided to each H-1B nonimmigrant employed pursuant to this application, and, as of th date, notice of this application has been provided to workers employed in the occupation in which H-1B nonimmigrants will be employ (check appropriate box)

☐ (i) Notice of this filing has been provided to bargaining representative of workers in the occupation in which H-1B nonimmigrant will be employed; or

☒ (ii) There is no such bargaining representative; therefore, a notice of this filing has been posted and was, or will remain, posted f 10 days in at least two conspicuous locations where H-1B nonimmigrants will be employed.

9. DECLARATION OF EMPLOYER. Pursuant to 28 U.S.C. 1746. I declare under penalty of perjury that the information provided on this form is tru and correct. In addition, I declare that I will comply with the Department of Labor regulations governing this program, and, in particular, that I w make this application, supporting documentation, and other records, files and documents available to officials of the Department of Labor, upon suc official's request, during any investigation under this application or the Immigration and Nationality Act.

Name and Title of Hiring or Other Designated Official ____ Signature ____ Date ____

Complaints alleging misrepresentation of material facts in the labor condition application and/or failure to comply with the term of the labor condition application may be filed with any office of the Wage and Hour Division of the United States Department c Labor.

AN APPLICATION CERTIFIED BY DOL MUST BE FILED IN SUPPORT OF AN H-1B VISA PETITION WITH THE INS.

FOR U.S. GOVERNMENT AGENCY USE ONLY: By virtue of my signature below, I acknowledge that this application is hereby certified and will be valid from ____ through ____.

Signature and Title of Authorized DOL Official ____ ETA Case No. ____ Date ____

Subsequent DOL Action: Suspended ____ (date) Invalidated ____ (date) Withdrawn ____ (date)

The Department of Labor is not the guarantor of the accuracy, truthfulness or adequacy of a certified labor condition application.

Public reporting burden for this collection of information is estimated to average 1 1/4 hour per response, including the time for reviewing instructio searching existing data sources, gathering and maintaining the data needed, and completing and reviewing the collection of information. Sen comments regarding this burden estimate or any other aspect of this collection of information, including suggestions for reducing this burden, to th Office of U.S. Employment Service, Department of Labor, Room N-4470 and/or the Office of IRM Policy, DOL, Room N-1301, 200 Constitution Aven N.W., Washington, DC 20210. (1205-0310).

DO NOT SEND THE COMPLETED FORM TO EITHER OF THESE OFFICES ETA 9035 (Rev. Dec 19

SAMPLE PROPOSED LABOR CONDITION APPLICATION

Labor Condition Application for H-1B Nonimmigrants

U.S. Department of Labor
Employment and Training Administration
U.S. Employment Service

ETA Form 9035
OMB Approval:
Expiration Date:

It is preferred that this form be completed using the form fill program available from the U.S. Department of Labor. If you cannot use the program, please follow the guidelines below.

Circles must be filled completely.

When using a **typewriter**, use a sans serif font equivalent to 12-14 point. Center each letter in each box. DO NOT put more than one character per box. Use only CAPITAL LETTERS.

If you need to **hand write** the form, for optimum accuracy, use a medium to thick pen with black ink. Print in CAPITAL LETTERS and avoid contact with the edge of the box.
The following will serve as an example:

A	B	C	D	E	F	G	H	I	J	K	L	M
N	O	P	Q	R	S	T	U	V	W	X	Y	Z

0	1	2	3	4	5	6	7	8	9

1. Employer's Information

Full Legal Name of Employer

Federal Employer I.D. Number (9 digits) (EIN from IRS) -

Employer's Telephone Number -

Return FAX Number -

Contact Telephone Number (Optional) -

Contact's Name (Optional) (This may be an attorney or an employer's contact other than hiring official.)

Employer's Address (Number / Street)

City State Zip Code

Address Where Public Disclosure File is Kept (* ONLY If Different than Employer's Address – If the address is the same leave this BLANK *)

City State Zip Code

NOTE: See OMB notice on page 3 of this form.

Employer's Control Number

Page - 1 of 4

Draft

SAMPLE PROPOSED LABOR CONDITION APPLICATION (CONTINUED)

Labor Condition Application for H-1B Nonimmigrants

U.S. Department of Labor
Employment and Training Administration
U.S. Employment Service

ETA Form 9035
OMB Approval:
Expiration Date:

2. Occupational Information

Three-Digit Occupational Code ☐☐☐ Number of H-1B Nonimmigrants ☐☐☐

Job Title

3. Rate of Pay

$ ☐☐☐☐☐☐☐.☐☐ PER Fill Only ONE Circle: Year ○ Month ○ 2 Weeks ○ Week ○ Hour ○

Mark (X) If Part Time ☐

4. Period of Intended Employment

Begin Date: MM / DD / YYYY End Date: MM / DD / YYYY

5. Location Where H-1B Nonimmigrants Will Work and Related Information

5(a) Initial Work Location Information – REQUIRED -- Do not write 'Same as above' et al.

City ☐ State ☐☐

Prevailing Wage $ ☐☐☐☐☐☐☐.☐☐ PER Fill Only ONE Circle: Year ○ Month ○ 2 Weeks ○ Week ○ Hour ○ Source: SESA ☐ Other ☐

Source of Other

5(b) Additional or Subsequent Work Location Information – IF Applicable

City ☐ State ☐☐

Prevailing Wage $ ☐☐☐☐☐☐☐.☐☐ PER Fill Only ONE Circle: Year ○ Month ○ 2 Weeks ○ Week ○ Hour ○ Source: SESA ☐ Other ☐

Source of Other

5(c) Additional or Subsequent Work Location Information – IF Applicable

City ☐ State ☐☐

Prevailing Wage $ ☐☐☐☐☐☐☐.☐☐ PER Fill Only ONE Circle: Year ○ Month ○ 2 Weeks ○ Week ○ Hour ○ Source: SESA ☐ Other ☐

Source of Other

NOTE: See OMB notice on page 3 of this form.

Employer's Control Number ☐☐☐☐☐☐

Page - 2 of 4

Draft

Labor Condition Application for H-1B Nonimmigrants

U.S. Department of Labor
Employment and Training Administration
U.S. Employment Service

ETA Form 9035
OMB Approval:
Expiration Date:

5(d) Additional or Subsequent Work Location Information — IF Applicable

City ☐☐☐☐☐☐☐☐☐☐☐☐☐☐☐☐☐☐☐☐☐☐☐☐☐ State ☐☐

Prevailing Wage $ ☐☐☐☐☐☐☐ . ☐☐ PER Fill Only ONE Circle: Year ◯ Month ◯ 2 Weeks ◯ Week ◯ Hour ◯ Source: SESA ☐ Other ☐

Source of Other ☐☐☐☐☐☐☐☐☐☐☐☐☐☐☐☐☐☐☐☐☐☐☐☐☐☐☐

5(e) Additional or Subsequent Work Location Information — IF Applicable

City ☐☐☐☐☐☐☐☐☐☐☐☐☐☐☐☐☐☐☐☐☐☐☐☐☐ State ☐☐

Prevailing Wage $ ☐☐☐☐☐☐☐ . ☐☐ PER Fill Only ONE Circle: Year ◯ Month ◯ 2 Weeks ◯ Week ◯ Hour ◯ Source: SESA ☐ Other ☐

Source of Other ☐☐☐☐☐☐☐☐☐☐☐☐☐☐☐☐☐☐☐☐☐☐☐☐☐☐☐

6. Employer Labor Condition Statements

All applicants are required to develop and maintain documentation supporting labor condition statements 6(a), (b), and (d). Employers are also required to make available for public examination a copy of the labor condition application and necessary supporting documentation within one (1) working day after the date on which the application is filed with DOL. Mark (X) each box to indicate that the employer will comply with each statement.

☐ (a) H-1B nonimmigrants will be paid at least the actual wage level paid by the employer to all other individuals with similar experience and qualifications for the specific employment in question or the prevailing wage level for the occupation in the area of employment, *whichever is higher*.

☐ (b) The employment of H-1B nonimmigrants will not adversely affect the working conditions of workers similarly employed. H-1B nonimmigrants will be offered benefits and eligibility for benefits on the same basis, and in accordance with the same criteria, as offered to similarly employed U.S. workers.

☐ (c) On the date of this application there is not a strike, lockout, or work stoppage in the course of a labor dispute in the occupation in which H-1B nonimmigrants will be employed at the place of employment. If such a strike, lockout, or work stoppage occurs after this application is submitted, I will notify ETA within 3 days of such occurrence and the application will not be used in support of a petition filing with INS for H-1B nonimmigrants to work in the same occupation at the place of employment until ETA determines the strike, lockout, or work stoppage has ceased.

☐ (d) A copy of this application has been, or will be, provided to each H-1B nonimmigrant employed pursuant to this application, and, as of this date, notice of this application has been provided to workers employed in the occupation in which H-1B nonimmigrants will be employed, either by:

- Providing notice of this filing to the bargaining representative of workers in the occupation in which H-1B nonimmigrants will be employed; OR
- There is no such bargaining representative, therefore, providing notice of this filing either through physical posting for 10 consecutive days in the locations where H-1B nonimmigrants will be employed, or through electronic notification to employees in the occupational classification for which H-1B nonimmigrants are sought.

7. Notice to Employers

☐ Every employer who, as of the date of this application, (a) is H-1B dependent or (b) has been found to have commited a willful violation or misrepresentation during the five (5) year period preceding the date of this application, is required to check this box and complete the attestations in item 8 on page 4 of this form. NOTE: See item 7 of the instructions for the definition of 'H-1B dependent employer'. NOTE: If an employer is or becomes H-1B dependent, or is found to have committed a willful violation or misrepresentation, any labor condition application for H-1B nonimmigrants which was certified by the Department of Labor prior to [insert effective date of interim final rule], will be demed invalid, and may not be used in support of a petition or an extention of a petition for an H-1B nonimmigrant.

Persons are not required to respond to this collection of information unless it displays a currently valid OMB control number. Respondents obligation to reply to these reporting requirements are mandatory (INA Act, Section 205). Public reporting burden for this collection of information is estimated to average 1 1/4 hour per response, including the time for reviewing instructions, searching existing data sources, gathering and maintaining the data needed, and completing and reviewing the collection of information. Send comments regarding this burden estimate or any other aspect of this collection of information, including suggestions for reducing this burden, to the U.S. Employment Service, Department of Labor, Room N-4456, 200 Constitution Avenue, NW., Washington, DC 20210. (Paperwork Reduction Project 1205-0310). DO NOT SEND THE COMPLETED FORM TO THIS OFFICE.

Employer's Control Number ☐☐☐☐☐☐

Page - 3 of 4

Draft

SAMPLE PROPOSED LABOR CONDITION APPLICATION (CONTINUED)

Labor Condition Application for H-1B Nonimmigrants

U.S. Department of Labor
Employment and Training Administration
U.S. Employment Service

ETA Form 9035
OMB Approval:
Expiration Date:

Employers who, as of the date of this application, are H-1B dependent (as defined in Item 7 of the Instructions) or who have been found to have committed a willful violation or misrepresentation during the past five (5) years (and after October 20, 1998) must complete this section:

8. Additional Employer Labor Condition Statements:

All applicants are required to develop and maintain documentation supporting labor condition statements 8(a), (b), and (c). Employers are also required to make available for public examination a copy of the labor condition application and necessary supporting documentation within one (1) working day after the date on which the application is filed with DOL. The Employer must mark (X) in any of the appropriate box(es) below:

☐ Is H-1B dependent; *and/or*

☐ Has been found to have committed a willful violation or misrepresentation during the five (5) year period preceding the filing of this application,

and hereby agrees to observe the following labor condition statements unless the exemption requirements noted below are met:

(a) The employer will not displace any similarly employed U.S. worker within the period beginning 90 days before and ending 90 days after the date of filing a visa petition supported by this application.

(b) The employer will not place any H-1B nonimmigrant employed pursuant to this application with any other employer or at another employer's worksite *unless* the employer first makes a *bona fide* inquiry as to whether the other employer has displaced or intends to displace a similarly employed U.S. worker within the period beginning 90 days before and ending 90 days after the placement, and the employer has no contrary knowledge. NOTE: If the other employer displaces a U.S. worker during the period described, the displacement will constitute a failure to comply with the terms of the labor condition application and the employer applicant may be subject to civil money penalties and debarment.

(c) Prior to filing this application, or prior to filing any petition for an H-1B nonimmigrant pursuant to this application, the employer took or will take good faith steps meeting industry-wide standards to recruit U.S. workers for the job for which the nonimmigrant is sought, and offering compensation as least as great as offered to the H-1B nonimmigrant. The employer will (has) offer(ed) the job to any U.S. worker who (has) applies and is equally or better qualified for the job for which the H-1B nonimmigrant is sought. NOTE: This requirement does not apply to the employment of an H-1B nonimmigrant who is a "priority worker" (persons with extraordinary ability, or outstanding professors or researchers, or certain multinational executives or managers) within the meaning of Section 203(b)(1)(A), (B), or (C) of the Immigration and Nationality Act.

☐ NOTE: An employer who uses this application *only* to support visa petitions for H-1B nonimmigrants who are exempt because they receive wages at a rate equal to at least $60,000 per year, or have attained a Master's degree (or its equivalent) or a higher degree in a specialty related to the employment, is not required to comply with the requirements of this Item 8 and should mark (X) this box. Employers are cautioned that if this application is used to petition for *any* non-exempt employees, they will be required to comply with these additional labor condition statements with respect to *all* of its H-1B nonimmigrants whether or not this box is marked (X).

9. Declaration Of Employer

By signing this form, I, personally and on behalf of the employer, agree to comply with the Department of Labor regulations (see 20 CFR Part 655 Subparts H and I) governing this program and, in particular, to make this application, supporting documentation, and other records, files and documents available to officials of the Department of Labor, upon request, during any investigation under the Immigration and Nationality Act. If the employer is or becomes an H-1B dependent employer, or is found to have committed a willful violation or misrepresentation of these provisions, I personally and on behalf of the employer, further agree to comply with the attestation elements set forth in Item 8.

Name of Hiring or Other Designated Official

Title of Hiring or Other Designated Official

Signature — DO NOT let signature extend beyond the box.   M M / D D / Y Y Y Y

NOTE: Falsification of any statements on this form may subject the employer to civil or criminal prosecution (see 18 U.S.C. 1001), as well as to civil money penalties and debarment.

Complaints alleging misrepresentation of material facts in the labor condition application and/or failure to comply with the terms of the labor condition application may be filed with any office of the Wage and Hour Division of the United States Department of Labor.

FOR U.S. GOVERNMENT AGENCY USE ONLY:

By virtue of my signature below
I acknowledge that this application is hereby certified and will be valid from ________________ through ________________ .

Signature and Title of Authorized DOL Official _______ ETA Case No. _______ Date _______

The Department of Labor is not the guarantor of the accuracy, truthfulness or adequacy of a certified labor condition application.

NOTE: See OMB notice on page 3 of this form.

Employer's Control Number

Page - 4 of 4

Draft

THREE DIGIT OCCUPATIONAL CODES FOR USE WITH LABOR CONDITION APPLICATION

OCCUPATIONS IN ARCHITECTURE, ENGINEERING, AND SURVEYING

001 ARCHITECTURAL OCCUPATIONS
002 AERONAUTICAL ENGINEERING OCCUPATIONS
003 ELECTRICAL/ELECTONICS ENGINEERING OCCUPATIONS
005 CIVIL ENGINEERING OCCUPATIONS
006 CERAMIC ENGINEERING OCCUPATIONS
007 MECHANICAL ENGINEERING OCCUPATIONS
008 CHEMICAL ENGINEERING OCCUPATIONS
010 MINING AND PETROLEUM ENGINEERING OCCUPATIONS
011 METALLURGY AND METALLURGICAL ENGINEERING OCCUPATIONS
012 INDUSTRIAL ENGINEERING OCCUPATIONS
013 AGRICULTURAL ENGINEERING OCCUPATIONS
014 MARINE ENGINEERING OCCUPATIONS
015 NUCULEAR ENGINEERING OCCUPATIONS
017 DRAFTERS
018 SURVEYING/CARTOGRAPHIC OCCUPATIONS
019 OTHER OCCUPATIONS IN ARCHITECTURE, ENGINEERING, AND SURVEYING

OCCUPATIONS IN MATHEMATICS AND PHYSICAL SCIENCES

020 OCCUPATIONS IN MATHEMATICS
021 OCCUPATIONS IN ASTRONOMY
022 OCCUPATIONS IN CHEMISTRY
023 OCCUPATIONS IN PHYSICS
024 OCCUPATIONS IN GEOLOGY
025 OCCUPATIONS IN METEROLOGY
029 OTHER OCCUPATIONS IN MATHEMATICS AND PHYSICAL SCIENCES

COMPUTER-RELATED OCCUPATIONS

030 OCCUPATIONS IN SYSTEMS ANALYSIS AND PROGRAMMING
031 OCCUPATIONS IN DATA COMMUNICATIONS AND NETWORKS
032 OCCUPATIONS IN COMPUTER SYSTEM USER SUPPORT
033 OCCUPATIONS IN COMPUTER SYSTEM TECHNICAL SUPPORT
039 OTHER COMPUTER-RELATED OCCUPATIONS

OCCUPATIONS IN LIFE SCIENCES

040 OCCUPATIONS IN AGRICULTURAL SCIENCES
041 OCCUPATIONS IN BIOLOGICAL SCIENCES
045 OCCUPATIONS IN PSYCHOLOGY
049 OTHER OCCUPATIONS IN LIFE SCIENCES

OCCUPATIONS IN SOCIAL SCIENCES

050 OCCUPATIONS IN ECONOMICS
051 OCCUPATIONS IN POLITICAL SCIENCE
052 OCCUPATIONS IN HISTORY
054 OCCUPATIONS IN SOCIOLOGY
055 OCCUPATIONS IN ANTHROPOLOGY
059 OTHER OCCUPATIONS IN SOCIAL SCIENCES

OCCUPATIONS IN MEDICINE AND HEALTH

070 PHYSICIANS AND SURGEONS
071 OSTEOPATHS
072 DENTISTS
073 VETERINARIANS
074 PHARMACISTS
076 THERAPISTS
077 DIETICIANS
078 OCCUPATIONS IN MEDICAL AND DENTAL TECHNOLOGY
079 OTHER OCCUPATIONS IN MEDICINE AND HEALTH

OCCUPATIONS IN EDUCATION

090 OCCUPATIONS IN COLLEGE AN UNIVERSITY EDUCATION
091 OCCUPATIONS IN SECONDARY SCHOOL EDUCATION
092 OCCUPATIONS IN PRESCHOOL, PRIMARY SCHOOL, AND KINDERGARTEN EDUCATION
094 OCCUPATIONS IN EDUCATION OF PERSONS WITH DISABILITIES
096 HOME ECONOMICS AND FARM ADVISERS
097 OCCUPATIONS IN VOCATIONAL EDUCATION
099 OTHER OCCUPATIONS IN EDUCATION

OCCUPATIONS IN MESEUM, LIBRARY, AND ARCHIVAL SCIENCES

100 LIBRARIANS
101 ARCHIVISTS
102 MUSEUM CURATORS AND RELATED OCCUPATIONS
109 OTHER OCCUPATIONS IN MUSEUM, LIBRARY, AND ARCHIV SCIENCES

OCCUPATIONS IN LAW AND JURISPRUDENCE

110 LAWYERS
111 JUDGES
119 OTHER OCCUPATIONS IN LAW AND JURISPRUDENCE

OCCUPATIONS IN RELIGION AND THEOLOGY

120 CLERGY
129 OTHER OCCUPATIONS IN RELIGION AND THEOLOGY

OCCUPATIONS IN WRITING

131 WRITERS
132 EDITORS: PUBLICATION, BROADCASTS, AND SCRIPT
139 OTHER OCCUPATIONS IN WRITING

OCCUPATIONS IN ART

141 COMMERCIAL ARTISTS: DESIGNERS AND ILLUSTRATORS, G ARTS
142 ENVIRONMENTAL, PRODUCT, AND RELATED DESIGNERS
149 OTHER OCCUPATIONS IN ART

OCCUPATIONS IN ENTERTAINMENT AND RECREATION

152 0CCUPATIONS IN MUSIC
159 OTHER OCCUPATIONS IN ENTERTAINMENT AND RECREATI

OCCUPATIONS IN ADMINISTRATIVE SPECIALIZATIONS

160 ACCOUNTANTS, AUDITORS, AND RELATED OCCUPATIONS
161 BUDGET AND MANAGEMENT SYSTEMS ANALYSIS OCCUPA
162 PURCHASING MANAGEMENT OCCUPATIONS
163 SALES AND DISTRIBUTION MANAGEMENT OCCUPATIONS
164 ADVERTISING MANAGEMENT OCCUPATIONS
165 PUBLIC RELATIONS MANAGEMENT OCCUPATIONS
166 PERSONNEL ADMINSTRATION OCCUPATIONS
168 INSPECTORS AND INVESTIGATORS, MANAGERIAL AND PUB SERVICE
169 OTHER OCCUPATIONS IN ADMINSTRATIVE OCCUPATIONS

MANAGERS AND OFFICIALS

180 AGRICULTURE, FORESTRY AND FISHING INDUSTRY MANA OFFICIALS
181 MINING INDUSTRY MANAGERS AND OFFICIALS
182 CONSTRUCTION INDUSTRY MANAGERS AND OFFICIALS
183 MANUFACTURING INDUSTRY MANAGERS AND OFFICIALS
184 TRANSPORTATIONS, COMMUNICATION, AND UTILITIES IND MANAGERS AND OFFICIALS
185 WHOLESALE AND RETAIL TRADE MANAGERS AND OFFICIA
186 FINANCE, INSURANCE, AND REAL ESTATE MANAGERS AND OFFICIALS
187 SERVICE INDUSTRY MANAGERS AND OFFICIALS
188 PUBLIC ADMINISTRATION MANAGERS AND OFFICIALS
189 MISCELLANEOUS MANAGERS AND OFFICIALS

MISCELLANEOUS PROFESSIONAL, TECHNICAL, AND MANAGERIA OCCUPATIONS

195 OCCUPATIONS IN SOCIAL AND WELFARE WORK
199 MISCELLANEOUS PROFESSIONAL, TECHNICAL, AND MANA OCCUPATIONS

SALES PROMOTION OCCUPATIONS

297 FASHION MODELS

Return Travel Expenses

Since the 1990 Act, an employer who prematurely dismisses an H-1B alien is required to reimburse the employee for travel expenses back to the individual's last place of foreign residence. Employers do not have to pay for return transportation if the employee voluntarily terminates the employment.

No "Benching" Rule

Another important addition made to the H-1B program by the 1998 Act is the no "benching" rule. Employers are required to pay H-1B nonimmigrants the required wage for the full hours specified on the H-1B visa petition even if the beneficiary is in nonproductive status due to a decision by the employer, or based on the nonimmigrant's lack of a permit or license. Employers must pay the H-1B nonimmigrant the required wage beginning no later than thirty days after the date the nonimmigrant is admitted to the U.S. pursuant to the petition, or 60 days after the nonimmigrant becomes eligible to work for the employer. The benching provision does not apply if the reason for the nonproductive time is due to circumstances rendering the individual unable to work or voluntary absence. Violation of the no benching provision is considered to be a violation of the wage requirement and subject to the same penalties discussed earlier in this chapter.

Validity Period for H-1B Visas

The initial maximum validity period for an H-1B visa for specialty occupations and fashion models of distinguished merit and ability is three years. After the initial three years has expired, a three-year extension may be granted, for a maximum stay of six years. H-1B visaholders are authorized to enter the United States 10 days before the beginning of authorized stay, and may remain 10 days beyond the expiration of authorized stay. However, H-1B nonimmigrants may not be employed during the ten days before and after the dates of employment.

The H-1B petition may not be filed or approved earlier than six months before the start date of the applicant's employment. In some parts of the country it may be prudent to file an H-1B petition as soon as possible during the six-month window due to significant backlogs at certain Service Centers. Filing early may be beneficial because the additional requirement of filing a labor condition application may lengthen the petitioning process. In addition, since the H-1B visa category is subject to an overall numerical cap there may not be visas left for the time period in question if the petitioner does not file in a timely manner.

Spouse and Children of H Visaholder

The spouse and minor children of an H visaholder are eligible to enter the United States as H-4 visaholders. An H-4 nonimmigrant is not authorized to accept employment in the United States.

New Fee for Scholarship and Training

The 1998 Act imposed a new $500 fee (over and above the usual filing fee) on petitioning employers who file H-1B petitions on behalf of foreign workers. Employers must submit the new fee with petitions filed after December 1, 1998 and before October 1, 2001. The proceeds of the fee are to be used to fund scholarship and training programs, and to fund Department of Labor administration and enforcement activities under the H-1B program. The petitioning employer must submit the $500 fee at the time of filing of an initial petition for H-1B status, upon the first petition to extend the stay of an H-1B nonimmigrant, and upon a petition by a different employer for concurrent or new employment. The $500 fee is not required when filing for extensions of stay after the initial extension by the same employer or for amended petitions that do not request an extension of stay.

Employers are prohibited from requiring H-1B nonimmigrants to reimburse or otherwise compensate the employer for the cost of the fee. An employer who violates this provision is subject to a $1,000 fine per violation.

Institutions of higher education (e.g., colleges and universities) and nonprofit governmental research organizations are exempt from the $500 fee and should submit Form I-129W (Petition for Nonimmigrant Worker Filing Fee Exemption) at the time of filing the H-1B petition.

SAMPLE LETTER IN SUPPORT OF H-1B PETITION

U.S. Department of Justice
Immigration & Naturalization Service
St. Albans, Vermont

Re: International Printing (America), Inc. – Petitioner
Samuel Katanga – Beneficiary
I-129 Petition for Alien Worker

Dear Sir/Madam:

This letter is written in support of the petition of International Printing (America), Inc. to classify Mr. Samuel Katanga as an H-1B nonimmigrant performing in a specialty occupation as International Marketing Analyst in the Decorative Paper Division of our New York Office.

The Petitioner

International Printing (America), Inc. is a New York Corporation established in 1964 as a sales representative office of our parent company International Printing, Inc. of London.

International Printing, Inc. founded in 1900, is the world's largest comprehensive printing company, employing over 10,000 people worldwide and enjoying an annual sales volume in excess of $6.7 million.

Its activities comprise of publications printing, commercial printing, business forms, micro-precision products, decorative interiors, packaging and related graphics and design activities. The U.S. subsidiary now employs a total of approximately 200 individuals including five local managers, at sales offices located in Atlanta, New York, Pittsburgh, San Jose and Seattle.

The Position Offered

Mr. Katanga is being offered the position of International Marketing Analyst in the Decorative Paper Division. He will prepare market penetration reports, conduct market studies employing a cost price analysis and survey different geographic markets to determine the needs of various industrial areas in the United States. He will also be required to write marketing reports for submission and study by the home office in London. These reports will enable the home office to accurately assess the U.S. decorative paper market.

Additionally, Mr. Katanga will be responsible for studying current economic reports as well as forecasting international sales increase potential to be used for discussion between sales and executive personnel.

International Printing's success in the ever-expanding publications printing business can be attributed to its ability to move with the flow of the market in anticipating client's needs as well as its active pursuit of new possibilities for expanding the world of printing.

International Printing was a late-comer to the urethane coated decorative printed paper market (a paper used for Ready to Assemble furniture), but we have been able to quickly catch up by virtue of the high quality of our product and service as well as our strong sales power. Presently, we have a top share in the coated paper market.

In order to sustain this market share, we are compelled to seek an individual possessing at minimum a Bachelor's Degree in Economics from an accredited United States or foreign institution as well as substantial experience conducting marketing studies in this particular type of printed decorative paper.

The Beneficiary

Mr. Katanga is the ideal candidate for this position in light of his extensive experience with International Printing and his educational achievements.

Mr. Katanga earned a Bachelor of Arts Degree in Economics from Stanford University, where he concentrated on econometrics and theoretical economics. He undertook a program that is highly related to his position at International Printing and that included course work in Information Processing, Industrial Organization, General Economic History, Principles of Economics, Bookkeeping, Theory of Modern Capitalism, Econometrics, Agricultural Economics, Welfare Economics, Industrial Organization, Labor Market, Labor Economics, Commercial Law, Economic Policy, Application to Information Processing, Statistics and Theory of Economic Fluctuation.

Mr. Katanga's educational background is highly relevant to the proposed position where he will be required to analyze different markets to determine how he can increase existing business and develop further business. Further, since joining International Printing in 1987, Mr. Katanga has worked as a Marketing Analyst in the International Operations Sales Department. Mr. Katanga's focus was on North and South American clients, mainly dealing with Ready to Assemble manufacturers accounts. He conducted marketing and consumer studies with a directed approach toward Machinery Makers, Base Paper Mills and Particle Board Makers.

We now wish to utilize the temporary professional skills of Mr. Katanga as an International Marketing Analyst for a three-year period. Mr. Katanga's degree in Economics is a prerequisite for the position of International Marketing Analyst. He will be required to utilize knowledge of principles and theories in economics acquired through university studies in the field and through his work experience in order to prepare crucial marketing and management reports and studies. Commensurate with his specialty occupation status, he will be remunerated at $70,000 per annum.

Please be advised that International Printing (America), Inc. has agreed to be liable for the reasonable costs of return transportation of Mr. Katanga abroad if he is dismissed by our organization before the end of his authorized period of stay.

We respectfully request the expeditious approval of the enclosed petition so that we can benefit from Mr. Katanga's services. Thank you for your assistance in this matter.

Very truly yours,

Paul Angus Brooks
Director
International Paper Products
International Printing

SAMPLE FORM I-129 PETITION FOR NONIMMIGRANT WORKER

START HERE - Please Type or Print

Part 1. Information about the employer filing this petition.

If the employer is an individual, use the top name line. Organizations should use the second line.

Family Name	Given Name	Middle Initial

Company or Organization Name: International Printing (America) Inc.

Address - Attn:

Street Number and Name: 222 Park Avenue	Apt. #
City: New York	State or Province: New York
Country: USA	Zip/Postal Code: 10001

IRS Tax #: 13-1111111

Part 2. Information about this Petition.

(See instructions to determine the fee)

1. **Requested Nonimmigrant classification:** (write classification symbol at right) H-1B
2. **Basis for Classification** (check one)
   a. ☒ New employment
   b. ☐ Continuation of previously approved employment without change
   c. ☐ Change in previously approved employment
   d. ☐ New concurrent employment
3. **Prior Petition.** If you checked other than "New Employment" in item 2 (above) give the most recent prior petition numbers for the worker(s): ____________
4. **Requested Action:** (check one)
   a. ☒ Notify the office in Part 4 so the person(s) can obtain a visa or be admitted (NOTE: a petition is not required for an E-1, E-2, or R visa)
   b. ☐ Change the person(s) status and extend their stay since they are all now in the U.S. in another status (see instructions for limitations). This is available only where you check "New Employment" in item 2, above.
   c. ☐ Extend or amend the stay of the person(s) since they now hold this status.
5. **Total number of workers in petition:** 1

   (See instructions for where more than one worker can be included)

Part 3. Information about the person(s) you are filing for.

Complete the blocks below. Use the continuation sheet to name each person included in this petition.

If an entertainment group, give their group name.

Family Name: Katanga	Given Name: Samuel	Middle Initial
Date of Birth (Month/Day/Year): 05/15/1960	Country of Birth: Kenya	
Social Security #: N/A	A #: N/A	

If in the United States, complete the following:

Date of Arrival (Month/Day/Year)	I-94 #
Current Nonimmigrant Status	Expires (Month/Day/Year)

FOR INS USE ONLY

Returned	Receipt
Resubmitted	
Reloc Sent	
Reloc Rec'd	
Interviewed ☐ Petitioner ☐ Beneficiary	

Class: ______
# of Workers: ______
Priority Number: ______
Validity Dates: From ______ To ______

☐ **Classification Approved**
☐ Consulate/POE/PFI Notified
At: ______
☐ Extension Granted
☐ COS/Extension Granted

Partial Approval (explain)

Action Block

To be Completed by Attorney or Representative, if any

☐ Fill in box if G-28 is attached to represent the applicant

VOLAG#

ATTY State License #

Form I-129 (Rev. 12/11/91)N

Continued on back.

SAMPLE FORM I-129 (CONTINUED)

Part 4. Processing Information

a. If the person named in Part 3 is outside the U.S. or a requested extension of stay or change of status cannot be granted, give the U.S. consulate inspection facility you want to be notified if this petition is approved.

Type of Office (check one): ☒ Consulate ☐ Pre-flight inspection ☐ Port of Entry

Office Address (City): London — U.S. State or Foreign Country: United Kingdom

Person's Foreign Address: 2 Grand Street, London England

b. Does each person in this petition have a valid passport? ☐ Not required to have passport ☐ No - explain on separate paper ☒ Yes

c. Are you filing any other petitions with this one? ☒ No ☐ Yes - How many?

d. Are applications for replacement/Initial I-94's being filed with this petition? ☒ No ☐ Yes - How many?

e. Are applications by dependents being filed with this petition? ☐ No ☒ Yes - How many? 1

f. Is any person in this petition in exclusion or deportation proceedings? ☒ No ☐ Yes - explain on separate pape

g. Have you ever filed an immigrant petition for any person in this petition? ☒ No ☐ Yes - explain on separate pape

h. If you indicated you were filing a new petition in Part 2, within the past seven years has any person in this petition:

1) ever been given the classification you are now requesting? ☒ No ☐ Yes - explain on separate pape

2) ever been denied the classification you are now requesting? ☒ No ☐ Yes - explain on separate pape

i. If you are filing for an entertainment group, has any person in this petition not been with the group for at least 1 year? ☐ No ☐ Yes - explain on separate pape

Part 5. Basic Information about the proposed employment and employer.

Attach the supplement relating to the classification you are requesting.

Job Title: International Marketing Analyst — Nontechnical Description of Job: see attached letter in support

Address where the person(s) will work if different from the address in Part 1.

Is this a full-time position? ☐ No - Hours per week ☒ Yes — Wages per week or per year: $70,000 per yr

Other Compensation (Explain) — Value per week or per year — Dates of Intended employment From: 5/1/1999 To: 4/30/2002

Type of petitioner - check one ☐ U.S. citizen or permanent resident ☒ Organization ☐ Other - explain on separate paper

Type of business: Printing Company — Year established: 1964

Current number of employees: 200 — Gross Annual Income: 6.7 million — Net Annual Income:

Part 6. Signature.

Read the information on penalties in the instructions before completing this section.

I certify, under penalty of perjury under the laws of the United States of America, that this petition, and the evidence submitted with it, is all true and correct. If filing this on behalf of an organization, I certify that I am empowered to do so by that organization. If this petition is to extend a prior petition, I certify that the proposed employment is under the same terms and conditions as in the prior approved petition. I authorize the release of any information from my records, or from petitioning organization's records, which the Immigration and Naturalization Service needs to determine eligibility for the benefit being sought.

Signature and title	Print Name	Date

Please note: If you do not completely fill out this form and the required supplement, or fail to submit required documents listed in the instructions, then the person(s) filed for may not be found eligible for the requested benefit, and this petition may be denied.

Part 7. Signature of person preparing form if other than above.

I declare that I prepared this application at the request of the above person and it is based on all information of which I have knowledge.

Signature	Print Name	Date

Firm Name and Address

SAMPLE H CLASSIFICATION SUPPLEMENT TO FORM I-129

OMB No. 1115-0168
H Classification
Supplement to Form I-129

Name of person or organization filing petition: International Printing (America) Inc.

Name of person or total number of workers you are filing for: Samuel Katanga

List the alien's and any dependent family members' prior periods of stay in H classification in the U.S. for the last six years. Be sure to list only those periods in which the alien and/or family members were actually in the U.S. in an H classification. If more space is needed, attach an additional sheet.
N/A

Classification sought (check one):

- ☐ H-1A Registered Professional nurse
- ☒ H-1B1 Specialty occupation
- ☐ H-1B2 Exceptional services relating to a cooperative research and development project administered by the U.S. Department of Defense
- ☐ H-1B3 Artist, entertainer or fashion model of national or international acclaim
- ☐ H-1B4 Artist or entertainer in unique or traditional art form
- ☐ H-1B5 Athlete
- ☐ H-1BS Essential support personnel for H-1B entertainer or athlete
- ☐ H-2A Agricultural worker
- ☐ H-2B Nonagricultural worker
- ☐ H-3 Trainee
- ☐ H-3 Special education exchange visitor program

Section 1. Complete this section if filing for H-1A or H1B classification.

Describe the proposed duties
Prepare market penetration reports, conduct market surveys, and surveys of various geographic markets. See also attached letter in support

Alien's present occupation and summary of prior work experience
International Market Analyst, 1987-Present

Statement for H-1B specialty occupations only:
By filing this petition, I agree to the terms of the labor condition application for the duration of the alien's authorized period of stay for H1-B employment
Petitioner's Signature Date

Statement for H-1B specialty occupations and DOD projects:
As an authorized official of the employer, I certify that the employer will be liable for the reasonable costs of the return transportation of the alien abroad if the alien is dismissed from employment by the employer before the end of the period of the authorized stay.
Signature of authorized official of employer Date

Statement for H1-B DOD projects only:
I certify that the alien will be working on a cooperative research and development project under a reciprocal Government-to-Government agreement administered by the Department of Defense.
DOD project manager's signature Date

Section 2. Complete this section if filing for H-2A or H-2B classification.

Employment is: (check one)

- ☐ Seasonal
- ☐ Peakload
- ☐ Intermittent
- ☐ One-time occurrence

Temporary need is: (check one)

- ☐ Unpredictable
- ☐ Periodic
- ☐ Recurrent Annually

Explain your temporary need for alien's services (attach a separate paper if additional space is needed).

Continued on back.

SAMPLE H CLASSIFICATION SUPPLEMENT TO FORM I-129 (CONTINUED)

The petitioner and each employer consent to allow government access to the site where the labor is being performed for the purpose of determining compliance with H-2A requirements. The petitioner further agrees to notify the Service in the manner and within the time frame specified if an H-2A worker absconds or if the authorized employment ends more than five days before the relating certification document expires, and pay liquidated damages of ten dollars for each instance where it cannot demonstrate compliance with this notification requirement. The petitioner also agrees to pay liquidated damages of two hundred dollars for each instance where it cannot be demonstrated that the H-2A worker either departed the United States or obtained authorized status during the period of admission or within five days of early termination, whichever comes first.

The petitioner must execute Part A. If the petitioner is the employer's agent the employer must execute Part B. If there are joint employers, they must each execute Part C.

Part A. Petitioner:

By filing this petition, I agree to the conditions of H-2A employment, and agree to the notice requirements and limited liabilities defined in 8 CFR 214.2 (h) (3) (vi).

Petitioner's signature | Date

Part B. Employer who is not petitioner:

I certify that I have authorized the party filing this petition to act as my agent in this regard. I assume full responsibility for all representations made by this agent on my behalf, and agree to the conditions of H-2A eligibility.

Employer's signature | Date

Part C. Joint Employers:

I agree to the conditions of H-2A eligibility.

Joint employer's signature(s) | Date

Joint employer's signature(s) | Date

Joint employer's signature(s) | Date

Joint employer's signature(s) | Date

Joint employer's signature(s) | Date

Section 4. Complete this section if filing for H-3 classification.

If you answer "yes" to any of the following questions, attach a full explanation.

a. Is the training you intend to provide, or similar training available in the alien's country? ☐ No ☐ Yes

b. Will the training benefit the alien in pursuing a career abroad? ☐ No ☐ Yes

c. Does the training involve productive employment incidental to training? ☐ No ☐ Yes

d. Does the alien already have skills related to the training? ☐ No ☐ Yes

e. Is this training an effort to overcome a labor shortage? ☐ No ☐ Yes

f. Do you intend to employ the alien abroad at the end of the training? ☐ No ☐ Yes

If you do not intend to employ this person abroad at the end of this training, explain why you wish to incur the cost of providing this training, and your expected return from this training.

PRACTICAL CONSIDERATIONS FOR COMPLETING FORM I-129 AND H SUPPLEMENT

1. Part 2 - The employer must check only one box in each of the numbered sections because the computer is incapable of reading more than one.

- Box (a) should be checked if this is the first petition being filed for this worker with this employer, if there was a break in employment with the same employer or if the beneficiary is changing status.

- Box (b) should be checked if the employer is requesting an extension of stay for the beneficiary.

- Box (c) should be checked if there is a change in the previously approved employment with the same employer.

- Box (d) should be checked for additional employment to be performed at the same time as employment that was authorized in a prior petition.

- The prior petition number is found on the I-797 Approval Notice; a copy of this notice should also be included with the petition.

- Even if two actions are requested, only one box may be checked. If, for example, both consular notification and extension of stay are requested, box (c) should be checked and Form I-824 should be included to procure consular cable notification.

2. Part 5 - Nontechnical Description of Job - Write a short phrase followed by "See attached letter;" The accompanying letter should contain a complete description of the job.

3. If a question does not apply, do not leave it blank; write "N/A."

4. "H" Supplement - When petitioning for H-1B specialty Occupations, the petitioner must sign twice where marked in Section 1.

SAMPLE FORM I-824 APPLICATION FOR ACTION ON APPROVED APPLICATION OR PETITION

START HERE - Please Type or Print (Instructions on back)

FOR INS USE ONLY

Part 1. Information about the person that filed the original application or petition.

(Individuals should use the top name line; Organizations should use the second line)

Family Name	Given Name	Middle Initial
Company or Organization Name: International Printing (America) Inc.		
Address - Attn:		
Street Number and Name: 222 Park Avenue		Apt. #
City: New York	State or Province: New York	
Country: USA	ZIP/Postal Code: 10001	
Date of Birth (Month/Day/Year)	Country of Birth	
Social Security #: N/A	IRS Tax #: 13-1111111	A #

Part 2. Application Type (check one).

a. ☐ I am applying for a duplicate approval notice

b. ☒ I am requesting that a new U.S. Consulate or Port of Entry be notified of the previous approval of a petition. Please notify the U.S. Consulate or Port of Entry at: London, United Kingdom

c. ☐ I am requesting that a new U.S. Consulate be notified that my status has been adjusted to permanent resident. Please notify the U.S. Consulate at: ______

Part 3. Processing Information.

Type of Petition/Application (Form #): I-129 & H supplement	Filing Receipt #: EAC-111-111-1111
Date of Filing (Month/Day/Year)	Date Approved (Month/Day/Year): N/A

If Petition is filed for another person - give the following about the person you filed for:

Family Name: Katanga	Given Name: Samuel	Middle Initial
Date of birth (Month/Day/Year): 05/15/1960	Country of Birth: Kenya	
A#: N/A		

Part 4. Signature

Read the information on penalties in the instructions before completing this section.

I certify under penalty of perjury under the laws of the United States of America that this application, and the evidence submitted with it, is all true and correct. I authorize the release of any information from my records which the Immigration and Naturalization Service needs to determine eligibility for the benefit I am seeking.

Signature	Date
Print Your Name: Paul Angus Brooks, Director	

Returned	Receipt
Resubmitted	
Reloc Sent	
Reloc Rec'd	
☐ Applicant Interviewed	

☐ Duplicate Notice Sent
☐ American Consulate Notified at (Location):
☐ Application Denied

Action block

To Be Completed by Attorney or Representative, if any

☐ Fill in Box if G-28 is attached to represent the applicant.

VOLAG#

ATTY State License #

Form I-824 (Rev. 10/01/91)

For sale by the U.S. Government Printing Office
Superintendent of Documents, Mail Stop: SSOP, Washington, DC 20402-9328

SAMPLE FORM I-129W PETITION FOR NONIMMIGRANT WORKER FILING FEE EXEMPTION

On October 21, 1998, Congress enacted the "American Competitiveness and Workforce Improvement Act," (ACWIA) Public Law No. 105-277. Section 414(a) of ACWIA created an additional **$500** filing fee for all petitions to classify an alien as an H-1B nonimmigrant worker, filed on or after December 1, 1998.

A United States employer petitioning for new H-1B employment, concurrent employment, sequential employment, and the first extensi of stay, must file a completed Form I-129, accompanied by the **$110** filing fee **PLUS** an additional **$500** in a single remittanc (one check or money order) of **$610.** A United States employer is not required to submit the additional $500 fee if the employer is an "exempt organization" (institution of higher education or related or affiliated nonprofit entity, or nonprofit or Governmental researcl organization) as defined at 8 CFR 214.2(h) (19) (iii).

PART A

In order for the Immigration and Naturalization Service (Service) to determine if you must pay the additional $500 fee, please answer all of the following questions:

	YES	NO	
A.	☐	☐	Are you an institution of higher education as defined in Section 101 (a) of the Higher Education Act of 1965 and 8 CFR 214.2(h) (19) (iii)?
B.	☐	☐	Are you a nonprofit organization or entity related to or affiliated with an institution of higher education, as defined under 8 CFR 214.2(h) (19) (iii)?
C.	☐	☐	Are you a nonprofit research organization or a Governmental research organization, as defined under 8 CFR 214.2(h) (19) (iii)?
D.	☐	☐	Is this the second or subsequent request for an extension of stay that you have filed for this alien?

If you answered **YES** to any of the sections above, you are required to submit **ONLY** the fee for your H-1B Form I-129 petition, which is $110.

PART B

A United States employer claiming an exemption from the $500 filing fee, based on responses to part A, must submit evide as a nonprofit organization, as established by tax exempt status under sections 501(c) (3), (4) or (6) of the Internal Revenue Code of 1ʻ 26 U.S.C.A. 501 et esq.

I certify under penalty of perjury, under the laws of the United States of America, that this attachment and the evidence submitted with it, is all true and correct. If filing this on behalf of an organization, I certify that I am empowered to do so by that organization. I authorize the release of any information from my records or from the petitioning organization's records, that the Immigration and Naturalization Service needs to determine eligibility for the exemption being sought.

____________________	____________________	____________________
Signature and Title	*Print Name*	*Date*

Authority

Authority to collect this information is contained in Public Law 105-277 (The American Competitiveness and Workforce Improvement Act of 1998). Failure to provide all requested information may delay the final decision or result in denial of your request. INS, Department of State (DOS), and Department of Labor (DOL) will use the information to determine eligibility for the benefit requested, and may provide other agencies with the information.

Public Reporting Burden

Paperwork Reduction Act Notice. Under the Paperwork Reduction Act, a person is not required to respond to a collection of information unless i displays a currently valid OMB control number. We try to create forms and instructions that are accurate, can be easily understood, and which impose the least possible burden on you to provide us with information. Often this is difficult because some immigration laws are very complex. The estimated average time to complete and file this application is 15 minutes per application. If you have comments regarding the accuracy of this estimate, or suggestions for making this form simpler, you can write to the Immigration and Natualization Service, 425 I Street, N.W., Room 5307, Washington, D.C. 20536. **(DO NOT MAIL YOUR COMPLETED APPLICATION TO THIS ADDRESS).**

Extension of Temporary Stay

Form I-129 and the H Supplement are both used for the initial H petition and any subsequent extensions of stay. Additionally, a request for a petition extension may be filed only if the validity of the original petition has not expired. Therefore, it is important to keep in mind the validity dates of the alien's petition since supporting evidence for an extension will not normally be required unless requested by the Service Center. If the petitioner waits until the petition has expired, the petitioner will be required to submit a new petition along with all the required supporting documentation.

The request for an extension of temporary stay must be accompanied by a certified labor condition application certified for the time period in question, Form I-94 (Nonimmigrant Arrival/Departure Record), and a letter from the petitioner detailing the need for the extension. Family members of the primary H-1B visaholder who wish to extend their status are required to file Form I-539.

In some instances, an H-1B visaholder while in H-1B status in the United States may have begun the procedure to obtain "permanent residence." The procedure for obtaining permanent residence will be discussed in greater detail in the employment-based and family-based immigration chapters. In the case of employment-based immigration, the approval of an immigrant petition may be dependent upon approval of a "labor certification application" with the Department of Labor. The labor certification approval may not be the sole basis for denying an H-1B extension or change of status application. An H-1B nonimmigrant may legitimately come to the United States for a temporary period and depart voluntarily at the end of the period of authorized stay while at the same time lawfully seek to become a permanent resident of the United States.

The concept of dual intent is encountered in other nonimmigrant categories. H-1B nonimmigrants may possess a short-term intent to remain in the United States as provided for by their nonimmigrant classification, while at the same time possess a long-term intent to permanently immigrate to the United States.

However, this is not the case with regard to H-2A, H-2B and H-3 visaholders. If one of these visaholders has an approved permanent labor certification filed by their current H employer, the application for extension of stay may be denied for that reason alone. The reason for the distinction is that the H-2A, H-2B and H-3 categories of H visaholders are required to maintain a foreign residence abroad. Therefore, the permanent labor certification approval is clearly inconsistent with the intent to return abroad after temporary stay.

H-1B - Extensions of stay may be authorized for a total period of up to six years for a beneficiary of an H-1B petition in a specialty occupation. However, if at any time an H-1B employee's job duties materially change or the H-1B employee wishes to change employers a new or amended H-1B petition must be filed. Unless the beneficiary requests an extension of stay the dates of approval of the new or amended petition will be the same as the prior petition.

H-2A and H-2B - An extension of stay for the beneficiary of an H-2A or H-2B petition may be authorized for a period of up to one year except as otherwise provided for, and the individual's total period of stay as an H-2A or H-2B worker may not exceed three years.

H-3 - An H-3 extension of stay may be authorized for the length of the training program for a total period of stay as an H-3 trainee not to exceed two years, or for a total period of stay as a participant in a special education program not to exceed 18 months.

Once an H-1B nonimmigrant has been present in the United States under H visa classification for the maximum period of six years, he or she must spend at least one year outside of the United States before submitting a new petition for either an H or L classification. If a foreign nation who is subject to the one year waiting period must make brief trips to the United States for business or pleasure, the time spent in the U.S. will not count toward the minimum one-year period abroad.

SAMPLE FORM I-539 (TO BE USED FOR FAMILY MEMBERS' EXTENSION OF STAY)

START HERE - Please Type or Print

FOR INS USE ONLY

Part 1. Information about you.

Family Name Katanga	Given Name Elizabeth	Middle Initial

Address - In Care of:

Street # and Name 5700 Arlington Avenue	Apt. #
City Riverdale	State New York
Zip Code 10471	
Date of Birth (month/day/year) 10/06/1963	Country of Birth United Kingdom
Social Security # (if any) N/A	A# (if any) N/A
Date of Last Arrival Into the U.S. 4/28/1999	I-94# 55-5555555
Current Nonimmigrant Status H-4	Expires on (month/day/year) 4/30/02

Part 2. Application Type.

(See instructions for fee.)

1. **I am applying for:** (check one)
   a. ☒ an extension of stay in my current status
   b. ☐ a change of status. The new status I am requesting is: ____________
2. **Number of people included in this application:** (check one)
   a. ☐ I am the only applicant
   b. ☒ Members of my family are filing this application with me. The Total number of people included in this application is 2 (complete the supplement for each co-applicant)

Part 3. Processing Information.

1. I/We request that my/our current or requested status be extended until (month/day/year) 4/30/2005
2. Is this application based on an extension or change of status already granted to your spouse, child or parent?
   ☐ No ☒ Yes (receipt # EAC-111-111-0011)
3. Is this application being filed based on separate petition or application to give your spouse, child or parent an extension or change of status?
   ☐ No ☐ Yes, filed with this application ☐ Yes, filed previously and pending with INS
4. If you answered yes to question 3, give the petitioner or applicant name:
   Samuel Katanga
   If the application is pending with INS, also give the following information.
   Office filed at Filed on (date)

Part 4. Additional Information.

1. For applicant #1, provide passport information:

Country of issuance United Kingdom	Valid to: (month/day/year) 12/31/2005

2. Foreign Address:

Street # and Name 2 Grand Avenue	Apt#
City or Town London	State or Province
Country England	Zip or Postal Code 7UA 8HN

Form I-539 (Rev. 12-2-91)

Continued on back

FOR INS USE ONLY

Returned Date	Receipt
Resubmitted Date	
Reloc Sent Date	
Reloc Rec'd Date Date	
☐ Applicant Interviewed	

☐ Extension Granted to (date): ____________

☐ Change of Status/Extension Granted New Class: ______ To (date): ______

If denied:
☐ Still within period of stay
☐ V/D to: ____________
☐ S/D to: ____________
☐ Place under docket control

Remarks

Action Block

To be completed by Attorney or Representative, if any

☐ Fill in box if G-28 is attached to represent the applicant

VOLAG#

ATTY State License #

SAMPLE FORM I-539 (CONTINUED)

Answer the following questions. If you answer yes to any question, explain on separate paper.	Yes	No
Are you, or any other person included in this application, an applicant for an immigrant visa or adjustment of status to permanent residence?		X
Has an immigrant petition ever been filed for you, or for any other person included in this application?		X
Have you, or any other person included in this application ever been arrested or convicted of any criminal offense since last entering the U.S.?		X
Have you, or any other person included in this application done anything which violated the terms of the nonimmigrant status you now hold?		X
Are you, or any other person included in this application, now in exclusion or deportation proceedings?		X
Have you, or any other person included in this application been employed in the U.S. since last admitted or granted an extension or change of status?		X

you answered YES to question 3f, give the following information on a separate paper: Name of person, name of employer, address of employer, weekly ıcome, and whether specifically authorized by INS.

you answered No to question 3f, fully describe how you are supporting yourself on a separate paper. Include the source and the amount and basis for ny income. My husband fully supports me and our child pursuant to H-1B employment

Part 5. Signature Read the information on penalties in the instruction before completing this section. You must file this application while in the United States.

certify under penalty of perjury under the laws of the United States of America that this application, and the evidence submitted with it, is all true and correct. authorize the release of any information from my record which the Immigration and Naturalization Service needs to determine the eligibility for the benefit I am eeking.

Signature	Print your name	Date
	Elizabeth Katanga	

Please Note: If you do not completely fill out this form, or fail to submit required documents listed in the instructions, you cannot be found eligible or the requested document and this application will have to be denied.

Part 6. Signature of person preparing form if other than above. (Sign below)

declare that I prepared this application at the request of the above person and it is based on all information of which I have knowledge.

Signature	Print your name	Date

Firm Name and Address

(Please remember to enclose the mailing label with your application)

Form I-539 (Rev. 12-2-91)

SAMPLE FORM I-539 SUPPLEMENT

Attach to Form I-539 when more than one person is included in the petition or application. *(List each person separately. Do not include the person you named on the form).*

Family Name: Katanga	Given Name: Marisa	Middle Initial:	Date of Birth (month/day/year): 5/15/89
Country of Birth: United Kingdom	Social Security No.:		A#:
IF IN THE U.S. — Date of Arrival (month/day/year): 04/28/1999		I-94#: 55-5555554	
IF IN THE U.S. — Current Nonimmigrant Status: H-4		Expires on (month/day/year): 4/30/2002	
Country where passport issued: United Kingdom	Expiration Date (month/day/year): 12/31/2005		

Family Name:	Given Name:	Middle Initial:	Date of Birth (month/day/year):
Country of Birth:	Social Security No.:		A#:
IF IN THE U.S. — Date of Arrival (month/day/year):		I-94#:	
IF IN THE U.S. — Current Nonimmigrant Status:		Expires on (month/day/year):	
Country where passport issued:	Expiration Date (month/day/year):		

Family Name:	Given Name:	Middle Initial:	Date of Birth (month/day/year):
Country of Birth:	Social Security No.:		A#:
IF IN THE U.S. — Date of Arrival (month/day/year):		I-94#:	
IF IN THE U.S. — Current Nonimmigrant Status:		Expires on (month/day/year):	
Country where passport issued:	Expiration Date (month/day/year):		

Family Name:	Given Name:	Middle Initial:	Date of Birth (month/day/year):
Country of Birth:	Social Security No.:		A#:
IF IN THE U.S. — Date of Arrival (month/day/year):		I-94#:	
IF IN THE U.S. — Current Nonimmigrant Status:		Expires on (month/day/year):	
Country where passport issued:	Expiration Date (month/day/year):		

Family Name:	Given Name:	Middle Initial:	Date of Birth (month/day/year):
Country of Birth:	Social Security No.:		A#:
IF IN THE U.S. — Date of Arrival (month/day/year):		I-94#:	
IF IN THE U.S. — Current Nonimmigrant Status:		Expires on (month/day/year):	
Country where passport issued:	Expiration Date (month/day/year):		

PRACTICAL CONSIDERATIONS FOR COMPLETING FORM I-539 EXTENSION OF STAY FOR FAMILY MEMBERS

1. Part 2 - This form is only for accompanying family members. Therefore, do not include the principle beneficiary in the total number of family members included in the petition.

2. Part 3 - If the extension is based upon the authorization already granted to the principle beneficiary, place that person's file number (found on Form I-797) in the space provided in section

If the petition is being filed simultaneously with an extension of stay petition on behalf of the principle beneficiary, fill in the beneficiary's name in the box provided. In the case of a previously filed and pending application, provide the INS office with the filing date of the application.

3. Part 4, (#3f) - If the petitioner is supported by the principle beneficiary, write "supported by H-1B parent (or spouse)" and attach a copy of that person's I-797 approval notice.

G. <u>H-3 VISA FOR TRAINEES</u>

The H-3 visa category is designed for trainees who will undergo a training program in the United States for a period of no more than two years. The H-3 visa category may be a viable alternative for corporations who wish to bring employees to the U.S. but the proposed employee does not otherwise qualify for H-1B classification. Furthermore, the H-3 visa category does not require the employer to file a labor condition application, freeing the petitioner from prevailing wage constraints. In comparison with the H-1B visa, there is no limitation on the number of H-3 aliens who may enter the United States per year. Additionally, unlike the J exchange program, there is no requirement that the alien, subsequent to their stay in the United States, spend two years abroad prior to returning to the United States in another nonimmigrant or immigrant category.

Generally, an H-3 visaholder may not change status in the United States to another visa category once the H-3 program has ended. However, there may be instances when an H-3 visaholder may be able to change status. One possible situation is when a petitioner is willing and able to demonstrate that it had a need for the H-3 visaholder to fill a position as an H-1B professional in a specialty occupation. If the foreign national possesses a bachelor's degree in the field in question and otherwise meets the necessary prerequisites for the H-1B category, the INS may approve a change of status application.

The essential requirement with regard to H-3 nonimmigrants is that they must be coming to the United States to participate in a <u>bona fide</u> training program that involves "no productive employment." Therefore, the trainee's salary listed on the I-129 petition should reflect this factor, and should not be unusually high. Furthermore, the petitioner must show what benefit it will gain by providing this training for the foreign national, since by definition, this training will involve no productive employment. In the case of a multinational corporation that has branches in a number of geographic areas, the petitioner may show that the trainee will use the knowledge acquired in the U.S. when reassigned to employment in a foreign branch of the organization. The petitioner must also show how the proposed training will benefit the foreign national in their career, and whether the training is unavailable to the foreign national in their home country.

<u>Extensions of Stay</u>

The maximum length of stay accorded to an H-3 visaholder is two years. For example, if a petitioner initially requested one year for the period of training in question, the petitioner may be able to request an extension of stay for a period of another year. However, this request is likely to be viewed as an indication that the trainee is really involved in productive employment rather than in a <u>bona fide</u> training program. The petitioner is required to set forth the period of time required for the training program at the time of the initial filing of the application. If the petitioner sets a specific time period for the training it is unlikely the INS will approve an extension of stay unless the petitioner can demonstrate a need to extend the training program that was unanticipated at the time of initial filing.

<u>H-3 Alien Trainee Document Checklist</u>

Petitions on behalf of individuals participating in training programs must include the following documentation:

- Detailed training program for beneficiary broken down into chronological segments (weekly, monthly, etc.);

- Percentage of time the trainee will participate in academic and other training;

- Number of persons previously trained, currently being trained, and now employed in the same capacity as the beneficiary;

- Expected benefits to the beneficiary;

- Present duties of the beneficiary and chronicle of past employment and education with evidence demonstrating they are qualified to receive and in need of the proposed training;

- Manner in which the beneficiary came to the employer's attention and how the particular individual was selected for the proposed training;

- Demonstrate that the proposed training is unavailable in the beneficiary's home country;

- Letters from prospective employer(s) in the country in which the beneficiary intends to apply learned skills;

- Exact period of time required to complete the training and whether the beneficiary's anticipated stay in the United States will be in excess of that specified in the petition;

- Certified copy of the contractual agreement between petitioner and beneficiary;

- Evidence of the financial viability of petitioning organization, individual or firm;

- Description of the background and current activities of the petitioning organization including articles of incorporation and a current financial statement.

SAMPLE H-3 TRAINEE LETTER

U.S. Department of Justice
Immigration & Naturalization Service
St. Albans, Vermont

Re: **International Diamond, Inc. – Petitioner**
Simcha Aaron Levi – Beneficiary
I-129 - Petition for Alien Trainee

Dear Sir/Madam:

This letter is submitted in support of our petition for H-3 status on behalf of Mr. Simcha Aaron Levi for a temporary period of 18 months.

PETITIONER - INTERNATIONAL DIAMOND, INC.

International Diamond, Inc. (USA) is a duly registered New York Corporation established in 1970. International Diamond, Inc. (USA) is part of an international network of offices and affiliates throughout the world totaling six companies.

THE PARENT ORGANIZATION

International Diamond, Inc., our head office, is an international organization established in 1949 in Antwerp, Belgium. Our organization is engaged in the manufacture and marketing of instruments, tools and supplies for the diamond and jewelry trade.

Presently, International Diamond has six locations worldwide, Antwerp, Tel Aviv, London, Hong Kong, New York and Tokyo. International Diamond Inc. has earned the highest reputation for excellence and quality service worldwide, and continues to dominate the industry utilizing the most sophisticated tools and instruments. We attribute our success to our years of experience and quality service in attending to the needs of jewelers, and pride ourselves in being able to provide the advantage of superior output in all phases of jewelry manufacturing.

International Diamond employs sixty-eight people worldwide and enjoys gross annual sales in excess of $300 million.

U.S. SUCCESS OF INTERNATIONAL DIAMOND, INC. (USA)

The New York office, International Diamond, Inc. (USA), was established in 1970 in order to expand our market share and provide services in one of the major diamond capitals of the world. In order to compete nationally, the New York Office elected to concentrate on mail order sales rather than sales to walk-in customers in the diamond district.

International Diamond has been enormously successful in this regard. As a result of our efforts over the past decade, International Diamond now has approximately 20,000 active customers in the United States, including diamond dealers, retailers and jewelry manufacturers.

Indeed, International Diamond has acquired a reputation as the worldwide leader in the market, providing a product line that spans from the simplest to most sophisticated supplies. International Diamond has become synonymous with innovation among jewelers, diamond merchants and industry professionals around the world. We are one of the few companies to be trusted for the most advanced products, excellent values and courteous customer service.

Our success is largely attributed to the effectiveness of our award-winning mail order catalogue (a copy of which is enclosed) as well as the sophisticated nature of our computer systems and top of the line mail order software which processes all of our order entries, billing and inventory controls. This same software is used by many of the popular and successful mail-order firms in the United States.

THE TRAINING PROGRAM AND ITS PURPOSE

It is now our wish to build upon our success and experience in the United States by training Mr. Levi in the effective establishment of mail-order capabilities in Antwerp.

Previously, a mail-order operation had not seemed viable in Antwerp. However, it is expected that the successful use of the U.S. marketing strategies will enable us to move ahead in this regard, and we feel that this venture will be profitable.

International Diamond has an established program to provide its trainees with expertise in mail order distribution and instruction in the United States business procedures and regulation with regard to the sales and distribution of diamond and jewelry trade supplies.

The training program, the details of which are attached to this letter, incorporates two different approaches. This includes rotations through the various departments of our organization and a period of textbook training where the trainee is responsible for reviewing and assimilating extensive course materials.

While rotating through our various departments, the managerial trainee receives instruction from all the relevant departmental managers on all phases of a large mail order business. Mr. Levi will be instructed by all the personnel dealing with the exporting department, purchasing department, warehouse staff, display personnel and accounting department. Additionally, Mr. Levi will gain knowledge of the ABC software and hardware that we employ in our computer network. He will work with our in-house computer specialist as well as with our special consultant and attend intensive seminars to learn how to most effectively use this custom-designed software to its best advantage.

Additionally, Mr. Levi will participate in many national trade shows. International Diamond has found it critical to participate in these types of shows in order to maintain a high profile in a large country such as the United States. This experience will be indispensable to the trainee and will make him familiar with our customer demands.

The training that Mr. Levi will receive in the United States is not available in Belgium. Mail order, though commonplace in the United States, has not been very prominent in Belgium to date. Therefore, there is no place where Mr. Levi may learn the techniques and methodology to embark on this type of program.

We intend for Mr. Levi to utilize the knowledge he acquires concerning mail order techniques in the United States to implement a similar system when he returns to Belgium. He will then be able to assume a mid-level management position with our parent company.

We find the beneficiary is uniquely suited to benefit from this training and he will be fully qualified to fill this position in Belgium after completion of the training program. Mr. Levi is a graduate of the renowned University of Antwerp from which he holds a Bachelor's degree in International Marketing. Further the Belgian Tourist Office has engaged him in New York as their Assistant Public Relations Officer. As such, he possesses the type of experience that will enable him to benefit greatly from the program and will allow International Diamond to be competitive in the expanding world of mail order opportunities.

Accordingly, we respectfully request that Mr. Levi's H-3 status be approved for a temporary period of eighteen months.

Very truly yours,

Boris Sonorami
Executive Vice President
International Diamond, Inc. (USA)

INTERNATIONAL DIAMOND INC. UNITED STATES TRAINING PROGRAM

I. Introduction to U.S. Mail Order Methodology 3 Months

This stage of the training is designed to provide the trainee with an introductory view of the International Diamond Inc. U.S. method. The trainee will be introduced to the concepts employed in ABC mail order software and U.S. Sales Policy. The trainee will become familiar with the exclusive contracts utilized by the organization with regard to special clients and will become familiar with credit analysis in structuring fee arrangements for clients, U.S. shipping methods, insurance considerations etc.

Personnel from the following departments will instruct the trainee:

- Exporting
- Purchasing
- Warehouse Staff
- Display personnel
- Accounting Department

II. Attend Trade Shows and Meet U.S. Suppliers - 6 months

After undergoing the initial three-month introductory training, the trainee will attend National Trade Shows and meet with U.S. suppliers to understand and evaluate customer demands.

Trade Shows

1. Jewelers of America International (NY) Feb. 2 - 5, 1998
2. American Gem Trade Association (Tucson) Feb. 8 - 13, 1998
3. Southern Jewelry Travelers Assoc. (Atlanta) Mar. 1 - 3, 1998
4. Manufacturing Jewelers & Silversmiths (NY) July 20 - 24, 1998
5. Southern Jewelry Travelers Assoc. (Atlanta) Aug. 2 - 4, 1998
6. Fall Pacific Jewelry Show (San Diego) Aug. 8 - 10, 1998

III. Extensive Software Training - 3 months

During the third stage of the training, the trainee will attend Computer Seminars and learn how to maximize efficiency and customer service. The trainee will then be able to apply the software skills he acquires at the trade shows. In addition, the software training will enhance his ability to process customer queries, orders and complaints.

In this stage of the training the trainee will interact with various individuals with different areas of expertise. He will receive supervision and training from International Diamond Inc. and ABC computer specialists as well as ABC professional staff. The immersion in all facets of software application will provide the trainee with a sophisticated troubleshooting forum in which he will become fully prepared to confront any problems that he may have with the implementation of the program in Belgium.

IV. Advertising Strategies and Catalogue Production - 3 months

During this important stage of the training, the trainee will learn all of the marketing strategies that have been put to effective use for International Diamond Inc. These include phone and fax strategies, essentials of catalogue production, use of advertising, planning for trade show and promotional material, new production promotion and preferential discount treatment.

The trainee will participate in all aspects of the Quarterly Special Sale Mailings to better familiarize him with this marketing technique. He will also be involved in the production and distribution of our award-winning catalogue. He will meet with marketing consultants, designers and printers.

V. Advanced Client Management - 3 months

During the final stage of the training, the trainee will have sophisticated instruction in client management techniques that have worked successfully for International Diamond, Inc. in the United States. He will be taught how to assess a client's credit, when to award special fee and distribution arrangements for clients and how to coordinate advertising with suppliers in industry publications.

Textbooks that will be used are:

(1) Machinery and Tools for the Diamond Industry
(2) Gemological Instruments
(3) Diamond Cutting: A Complete Guide to Diamond Processing
(4) Diamond Grading ABC - Handbook of Diamond Grading.
(5) Consumer Guide to Colored Gemstones

The training received through textbook study will allow the trainee to familiarize himself with U.S. suppliers and products and apply this knowledge when learning more about the industry and its practices. He will then be able to effectively employ similar mail order techniques in Belgium.

Chapter Four
THE L VISA CATEGORY

A. INTRODUCTION

The L visa is a valuable tool for multinational corporations that have offices both in the United States and abroad. The L visa is designed to facilitate the temporary transfer of foreign nationals with management, executive and specialized knowledge skills to the United States to continue employment with an office of the same employer, its parent, subsidiary or affiliate. The L visa category provides for the transfer of employees between a number of different types of organizations including parent and subsidiary organizations, subsidiaries and parents, joint ventures and sibling organizations that share the same parent.

Foreign employees of multinational companies who possess management, executive and specialized knowledge skills are known as "intracompany transferees" and may qualify for the L-1 nonimmigrant visa classification subject to certain requirements that will be discussed in this chapter.

Who is classifiable as an intracompany transferee?

An "intracompany transferee" is a foreign national who, within three years preceding the time of his or her application for admission into the United States, has been employed abroad continuously for one year by a firm or corporation or other legal entity or parent, branch, affiliate, or subsidiary, who seeks to enter the United States temporarily in order to continue to render services to a branch of the same employer or a parent, affiliate or subsidiary in a capacity that is managerial, executive or involves specialized knowledge.

The benefits of the L-1 visa are substantial, and it is advisable for an employer to petition for an L-1 intracompany transferee visa when the necessary prerequisites for its issuance are present. Unlike the H-1B visa, there is no quota on the number of intracompany transferees who may work in the United States each year. Therefore, if an employee is eligible for both an H-1B and an L-1 visa, it is advisable for the employer to petition on the L-1 basis in order to avoid any possible delay or refusal based upon the exhaustion of the H-1B visa quota for the year in question. In addition, an employee who is eligible for a nonimmigrant L-1A visa based on his or her managerial or executive skills may also be eligible for priority worker status in the first employment based preference category for permanent residence. See Chapter Eight for a more detailed discussion of the employment-based immigrant categories.

Furthermore, unlike the H-1B visa, the L-1 visa does not require a labor condition application be filed with the Department of Labor. Eliminating the need for a labor condition application reduces the overall processing time for an L-1 visa in comparison to the possible backlogs associated with the H-1B visa category. In fact, regulations require that the INS adjudicate complete the individual and blanket L-1 petitions within 30 days. However, there is no mechanism in place to enforce this requirement. The processing time for a particular petition varies at each Service Center.

An L-1 visa may also be more beneficial than an H-1B visa because the maximum duration of stay is generally longer. L-1 visas are issued for an initial maximum period of three years, and are renewable in two year increments for a maximum of seven years total for employees who perform in a managerial or executive capacity, and up to five years for employees who perform in a capacity utilizing their specialized knowledge. Another added benefit of the L-1 visa is the ability of an individual who initially comes to the United States as a specialized knowledge employee to change positions and continue in a managerial or executive position for the maximum seven-year period.

The key factors in determining eligibility for L-1 visa classification are an assessment of whether the employer meets the standard set forth for a qualifying organization and whether the employee's role, both abroad and proposed role in the United States, is managerial, executive or one involving the use of specialized knowledge.

Prerequisites for L-1 Visa Classification

To qualify for L-1 visa classification, the following requirements must be satisfied:

1) There must be a qualifying relationship between the business entity in the United States and the foreign business entity that employs the intracompany transferee abroad (i.e. parent/subsidiary or affiliate).

2) The foreign employer must continue to do business both in the United States and in at least one other country, either directly or through one of the qualifying relationships during the entire time of the intracompany transferee's stay in the United States.

3) The intracompany transferee must have been employed abroad continuously by the foreign company for one year in the three years preceding the transfer.

4) The intracompany transferee's prior year of employment abroad must have been in a managerial, executive or specialized knowledge capacity. The proposed employment in the United States must also be in a managerial, executive or specialized knowledge capacity. However, there is no requirement that the position abroad and the position in the United States be identical. For example, an employee might be performing in an executive capacity abroad while the proposed position in the United States would be one involving specialized knowledge.

5) The petitioner and the employee must have the intent that the transfer from one of the operations abroad to the United States is temporary and the employee intends to return abroad at the end of authorized stay, unless the employee becomes a permanent resident during the authorized stay.

A qualifying organization for the purposes of petitioning for an L-1 intracompany transferee is defined by regulation as a United States or foreign firm or other legal entity which is a parent, branch, affiliate or subsidiary and is or will be doing business as an employer in the United States and in at least one other country directly, or through a parent, branch, affiliate or subsidiary for the duration of an employee's stay in the United States as an intracompany transferee.

A variety of different types of organizations may satisfy the qualifying relationship requirement. Generally, one of the corporate parties to the transfer must have effective control over the other organization, or both organizations may be effectively controlled by the same third company or individuals. If no legal relationship exists between the foreign company and the United States company, or a third organization, an L-1 petition will not be approved.

Doing business means the regular systematic and continuous provision of goods and/or services by a qualifying organization. Therefore, the mere presence of an agent or office in the United States and overseas **does not** constitute doing business for the purposes of the statute.

Since the L-1 category is specifically designed to benefit international business, there is no requirement that the petitioning organization be an American firm. Further, in order to qualify as a petitioning organization, the employer need not necessarily be engaged in foreign trade. A religious, charitable service or other non-profit organization may qualify as a firm, corporation or other legal entity, but these types of legal entities are prohibited from filing blanket petitions.

New Offices

One type of qualifying entity in the United States

covered under the L-1 category is the "new office." A foreign employer may send an employee to the United States not only to an existing office, but may also transfer an employee with the bona fide intent of setting up a new office in the United States to further the operations of the foreign company. The foreign entity from which the employee is being transferred must continue to do business for the duration of the intracompany transferee's stay in the United States. Alternatively, an American corporation with a foreign-based employee need not have an affiliate or subsidiary in that country. The employer need only show that the beneficiary will be reassigned to duties outside the United States when his temporary stay ends.

To petition for the intracompany transferee who is coming to set up a new office in the United States, the petitioner must show evidence that physical premises have been secured, either by a lease or purchase of property, as well as evidence that the petitioner has sufficient resources to remunerate the beneficiary. Additionally, establishment of a subsidiary or affiliate corporation or appropriate domestic registration of a branch office must have taken place. Blanket petitions are not issued to intracompany transferees coming to open up a new United States office. An individual petition must be filed, and the initial maximum authorization period is for a one year instead of the normal three year period. The initial period is subject to renewals in two-year increments. However, to remain eligible for an L-1 visa based on a new office the petitioner must show after one year that the U.S. entity still requires a managerial or executive employee to continue to operate the entity.

To obtain an L-1 extension for a new office the petitioner must show that the foreign and U.S. entities remain qualifying organizations, and that the U.S. entity has been doing business in the U.S. for the prior year, describe the intracompany transferee's duties over the past year and proposed duties for the next year, and submit a description of the U.S. entity's operation including staffing levels, number of employees, wages, financial records, and organizational structure.

An intracompany transferee who is coming to the United States to open a new branch, subsidiary or affiliate of the foreign employer, may be eligible for B-1 visa classification, provided the employee is not performing services for, or being paid a salary by a United States source. The individual may then become eligible for L-1 classification once the requisite creation of a new office has taken place.

Practical Consideration

In recent years, the INS has been increasing the documentation necessary to substantiate a new-office L-1, especially with regard to certain countries that are regarded as "high fraud" regions. These have included the People's Republic of China and the former Soviet Republics. In such instances, the INS requests voluminous documentation of the organization's structure and business activities of the foreign organization, detailed business plans, evidence of transfer of capital, and the business activities of the new U.S. entity. In fact, the INS' documentary requirements in such instances often lose sight of the fact that the new domestic business entity need not already be doing business at the time of L-1 petition submission.

The employee coming to the United States to open a new office may be classified as a manager or executive during the one year required to reach the "doing business" standard if the factors surrounding the establishment of the proposed organization are such that it can be expected that the organization will, within one year, support a managerial or executive position. The factors to be considered include amount of investment, intended personnel structure, product or service to be provided, physical premises, and viability of the foreign operation. It is expected that a manager or executive who is required to open a new business or office will be more actively involved in day-to-day operations during the initial phases of the business, but must also have authority, plans to hire staff and have wide latitude in making decisions about the goals and management of the organization.

Temporary Nature of Stay

The L-1 visa category allows companies to transfer intracompany personnel for a period not exceeding five or seven years, depending on the type of employee to be transferred. Managerial and executive employees are limited to a total seven-year stay and specialized knowledge employees are limited to a total five-year stay. The beneficiary must intend to return to the home country at the conclusion of the authorized stay.

Generally, intracompany transferee status involves a temporary transfer to the United States with the expectation that the employee will return to a position with the petitioner's operation abroad. The INS might have reason to believe that the petitioner and the employee intend permanent residence if there does not exist an appropriate position abroad to which the employee can be transferred back to and there also exists an approved labor certification application or a immigrant visa petition has been filed on behalf of the intracompany transferee.

However a petitioner may have more than one reason for a transfer with regard to a specific individual that is not inconsistent with the requirement that an L-1 intracompany transferee be coming to the United States for a temporary period of time. The doctrine of dual intent recognizes that a petitioner may legitimately have the intent to use the services of a foreign national for a temporary period, and in the future, intend to permanently employ the foreign national in the United States, if the petitioner is able to do so lawfully. The foreign national may also legitimately have the intent to come to the United States temporarily and depart voluntarily at the end of authorized stay unless, within that period, the foreign national has become a lawful permanent resident of the United States.

Generally, submitting a simple statement of the facts indicating the employee's proposed length of stay can satisfy proof of temporary stay. However, when the beneficiary is the principal owner/operator of the petitioning organization, a greater degree of proof evidencing the temporary nature of the employment may be required. Furthermore, there is no statutory requirement that the L-1 transferee have a permanent residence abroad that he or she has no intention of abandoning.

Factors which may be considered in determining the temporary nature of the stay may include the limited scope of the United States operation, the temporary services of the beneficiary are geared for a particular time period only and future plans of the beneficiary which will ultimately require his or her presence back in the foreign employer's office.

B. QUALIFYING ORGANIZATIONS

The exact nature of the international organization sponsoring the foreign national is critical to the determination of whether a qualifying relationship exists for immigration purposes. Therefore, it is important to understand the statutory definitions of the various organizations that may be considered "qualifying organizations" for the purposes of L-1 visa classification.

Parent Organization

A **parent** organization is a firm, corporation, or other legal entity that has subsidiaries. However, a subsidiary may own other subsidiaries and also be a parent, even though it has a parent. Subsidiaries are owned and controlled by the parent organization.

Branch Organization

A **branch** organization is an operating division or office of the same organization housed in a different location and is not established as a separate business entity.

Subsidiary

A **subsidiary** is a firm, corporation or other legal entity which a parent directly or indirectly owns more than half of the entity and has control, or a parent directly or indirectly owns 50% of a 50/50 joint venture and has equal control and veto power, or the parent directly or indirectly owns less than half of the entity, but has control because the stock of the subsidiary is widely distributed among the parent's shareholders.

Ownership

Ownership means the legal right of possession with full power and authority to control.

Control

Control means the right and authority to direct the management and operations of a business entity.

Ownership and control are important factors in establishing a qualifying relationship between business entities. Stock ownership and a substantial degree of managerial control often measure such a relationship. Control need not be demonstrated solely by majority ownership. There are situations where control may be demonstrated notwithstanding a lack of a majority. For example, the proxy votes of minor stockholders might give a larger stockholder a majority, or in the case of larger corporations, extremely diverse holdings of minor stockholders could give control to a larger stockholder. Control is generally presumed upon a showing of 51% stock ownership. Organizations where control is exercised with less than 51% stock ownership must present a larger amount of documentation.

Affiliate

The term affiliate may refer to any one of three following different kinds of associations:

1) One of two legal entities owned and controlled by the same parent or individual. Therefore, two subsidiaries of a parent company would qualify as affiliates of each other provided that the parent organization has actual control to move its employees from parent to subsidiary and also between affiliated subsidiaries. Each situation must be examined on the basis of the firm's corporate structure.

2) One of two legal entities owned and controlled by the same group of individuals, each individual owning and controlling approximately the same share or percentage of each entity.

3) A United States partnership organized to provide accounting services along with managerial and/or consulting services that markets its accounting services under an internationally recognized name under an agreement with a worldwide coordinating organization that is owned and controlled by the member accounting firms. (This is a special rule enacted by Congress for international accounting firms.)

Joint ventures may also qualify as petitioning organizations. For example an individual proprietorship with 50/50 ownership might qualify. Joint venture corporations include oil, chemical, electronic and atomic energy ventures.

An organization may not ultimately qualify as a petitioning organization if it is impossible to demonstrate the necessary measure of both ownership and control. This is usually the case where an agreement is merely contractual but involves no cross-ownership. This is precisely the same type of problem encountered with regard to licensing and franchising operations, since they are independent operations bound only by contract and not cross-ownership. In fact, the most common type of non-qualifying contractual relationships are licensing and franchising arrangements, which will normally not suffice to establish a qualifying relationship.

Employees

There are two categories of employees who may work in the United States under L-1 visa classification. These include individuals who will perform in a capacity that is executive or managerial in nature or one that requires the employee's use of specialized knowledge.

Employee performing in a Managerial Capacity

In order for an individual to be considered to be performing in a managerial capacity, he or she must:

- Manage the organization, or a department, subdivision, function or component of the organization;

- Supervise and control the work of other supervisory, professional or managerial employees, or manage an essential function within the organization or a department or subdivision of the organization;

- Have the authority to hire and fire or recommend those as well as other personnel actions (such as promotion and leave authorization) if another employee or employees are directly supervised. Or if no other employee is directly supervised, the employee functions at a senior level within the organizational hierarchy or with respect to the function managed; and

- Exercise discretion over the day-to-day operations of the activity or function for which the employee has authority. A first-line supervisor is not considered to be acting in a managerial capacity merely by virtue of the supervisor's supervisory duties unless the employees supervised are professional.

Employee performing in an Executive Capacity

An individual is considered to be performing in an executive capacity within an organization when he or she performs the following:

- Directs the management of the organization or a major component or function of the organization;

- Establishes the goals and policies of the organization, component or function;

- Exercises wide latitude in discretionary decision-making; and

- Receives only general supervision or direction from higher level executives, the board of directors, or stockholders of the organization.

Prior to the 1990 Act, the INS focussed heavily on the staffing levels of organizations when determining whether or not an individual could be considered a manager or executive for L-1 purposes. This prevented some individuals who were in fact performing in a managerial or executive capacity level from being able to obtain L-1 authorization if the company petitioning on their behalf did not have the appropriate staffing levels. Although staffing levels may still be considered in some organizations, an executive may manage a function within an organization without a staff of subordinates. This is currently considered an acceptable executive capacity as long as it can be clearly demonstrated that the executive is not directly performing the function.

Employee Performing in a Capacity Requiring Use of Specialized Knowledge

To qualify as an employee possessing "specialized knowledge," an individual must possess special knowledge of the petitioning organization's product, service, research, equipment, techniques, management, or other interests and its application to international markets, or an advanced level of knowledge or expertise in the organization's processes and procedures, that are not readily available in the United States labor market. An individual who possesses general industry knowledge or expertise necessary to produce a product or provide a service will not be considered to possess specialized knowledge for L-1 purposes. There is a general prohibition against classifying individuals in one of the above categories, when they are in reality merely skilled workers.

Characteristics of an employee with specialized knowledge include the following:

- The employee possesses knowledge that is valuable to the employer's competitiveness in the marketplace.

- The employee is uniquely qualified to contribute to the United States employer's knowledge of foreign operating conditions.

- The employee has been employed in a key position abroad and has been given significant assignments that have enhanced the employer's productivity, competitiveness, image or financial position.

- The employee possesses knowledge that can be gained only through extensive prior experience with that employer, and not through outside education or employment.

Exceptions to Bar on Reentry After the Five or Seven Year Period

After a five or seven year period of stay, the foreign national can not reenter the United States under H or L visa classification, unless the individual has resided and been physically present outside the United States for at least one year. This limitation does not apply to foreign nationals who do not reside continually in the United States and whose employment in the United States is seasonal, intermittent or an aggregate of six months or less per year.

C. TYPE OF EVIDENCE REQUIRED DEPENDING ON NATURE OF PETITIONING ORGANIZATION

Large Corporations

In the case of large, established organizations, the organization may submit a statement by the company's president, corporate attorney, corporate secretary, or other authorized official describing the ownership and control of each qualifying organization, accompanied by other evidence such as a copy of the organization's most recent annual report, Securities and Exchange Commission filings such as 10K statements, or other documentation which lists the parent and its subsidiaries.

Small Businesses

For small businesses and other marginal operations, in addition to a statement of an authorized official regarding ownership and control of each qualifying organization, other evidence of ownership and control should be submitted, such as records of stock ownership, profit and loss statements or other accountant's reports, tax returns or articles of incorporation, by-laws and minutes of board meetings.

New Offices

If the employee is coming to the United States to open a new office, proof of ownership and control, in addition to financial viability evidencing the petitioner's ability to remunerate the intracompany transferee is required. The petitioner's statement of ownership and control should be accompanied by appropriate evidence such as evidence of capitalization of the company or evidence of financial records of the foreign company, articles of incorporation, by-laws and minutes of board of directors meetings, corporate bank statements, profit and loss statements or other accountant reports or tax returns. Transfers from "suspect" regions may have to be over-documented.

Partnerships

To establish who owns and controls a partnership, a copy of the partnership agreement must be submitted. To establish what the partnership owns and controls, other evidence may be necessary.

Proprietorships

In cases where the business is not a separate legal entity from the owner, the petitioner's statement of ownership and control must be accompanied by evidence, such as a license to do business, record of registration as an employer with the Internal Revenue Service, business tax returns, or other evidence which identifies the owner of the business.

D. PROCEDURE FOR FILING L-1 PETITIONS

Form I-129

The prospective employer must submit a petition on behalf of the employee. The petitioner must submit in duplicate Form I-129 "Petition for a Nonimmigrant Worker" and the supplement "L Classification Supplement to Form I-129."

A filing fee set by the INS must also accompany the petition. The filing fee is subject to change and should be confirmed before the petition is submitted.

The petition must be submitted, along with the required supporting documentation, to the INS Service Center having jurisdiction over the place where the foreign national will be employed. See Appendix A for a list of the four Service Centers and their jurisdictions.

Supporting Documents for L-1 Petitions

- CPA certified financial statement or a copy of the Federal Income Tax Return of the United States entity.

- Statement of the foreign entity converted into United States dollars and translated into English. The statement is to be certified by a CPA, Chartered Accountant, or the equivalent.

- In the case of a newly established United States entity, evidence of a lease of purchase of facilities in the United States.

- Evidence establishing that the beneficiary has at least one year of experience in an executive, managerial or specialized knowledge position. This evidence should include a detailed description of the position abroad as well as in the United States.

- Personnel or payroll actions or notifications supporting the claimed employment relationship between the beneficiary and petitioner.

- Resume of the beneficiary, detailing education and work experience.

- Evidence linking the two companies as affiliates or evidence demonstrating the parent/subsidiary relationship.

- Articles of incorporation, partnership agreements, or other forms of business organization in the United States.

A United States company or foreign company doing business in the United States may petition for an employee who has worked in its parent or subsidiary or with the same company abroad in a managerial or executive capacity for at least one year and will be in such a position in the United States. A description of the foreign national's employment in the United States must be included in the submission to the Immigration and Naturalization Service.

The INS requires that the relationship between the two companies together with the dates and place of its establishment be documented to show its qualifying nature. The relationship between the foreign company and the United States operation may be established through official records, stock certificates or letters from the company's attorneys. Additionally, the United States company, whether parent, subsidiary, or affiliate must prove through financial statements or letters from its accountant, that it has sufficient annual income to support the employee's salary.

Corporate Documents from Overseas Company

- Evidence establishing that the beneficiary has at least one year of experience

- Address, description or nature of business, date of incorporation, number of employees.

- Certified copy of Certificate of Incorporation.

- Certified copy of latest financial statement or tax return.
- Certified copy of any current licenses (registrations) to operate business.
- Corporate brochures, annual report or other printed matter (e.g. newspaper and magazine articles).

<u>Corporate Documents from United States Corporation</u>

- Address, description or nature of business, date of incorporation, number of employees.
- Certified Copy of Certificate of Incorporation.
- Lease or deed evidencing office space in the United States.
- Certified copy of latest financial statement or tax return.
- Corporate brochures, annual report or other printed matter.

<u>Documents Establishing Corporate Relationship</u>

- Notarized statement by the Corporate Secretary, General Counsel, or independent accountant setting forth the manner of control.
- Minutes of the United States and foreign corporation confirming affiliate or subsidiary relationship.
- Copies of all issued stock certificates of the United States corporation. If all of the stock is not issued, a statement from the attorney for the corporation attesting to the proposed distribution of the remaining shares of the stock.

<u>Documents and Information Pertaining to Position Being Offered</u>

- Title of Position and detailed description of job responsibilities in overseas office. The position must be executive or managerial or one requiring specialized knowledge and the responsibilities must reflect the same.
- Evidence of alien's continued employment of at least one year, three years prior to transfer.
- Organizational charts of both United States and foreign corporation which indicate beneficiary's managerial, executive, or specialized knowledge position within the firm as well as the individuals (by title) that the beneficiary supervises and will supervise in the United States company.

SAMPLE FORM I-129 FOR A NONIMMIGRANT WORKER

U.S. Department of Justice
Immigration and Naturalization Service

OMB No. 1115-0168
Petition for a Nonimmigrant Worker

START HERE - Please Type or Print

Part 1. Information about the employer filing this petition.

If the employer is an individual, use the top name line. Organizations should use the second line.

Family Name	Given Name	Middle Initial
Company or Organization Name: Hong Kong Banking Group		

Address - Attn:

Street Number and Name: 1 Main Street		Apt. #
City: New York	State or Province: New York	
Country: USA		Zip/Postal Code: 11111

IRS Tax #: 13-4444444

Part 2. Information about this Petition.

(See instructions to determine the fee)

1. **Requested Nonimmigrant classification:** (write classification symbol at right) L-1B
2. **Basis for Classification** (check one)
   a. ☒ New employment
   b. ☐ Continuation of previously approved employment without change
   c. ☐ Change in previously approved employment
   d. ☐ New concurrent employment
3. **Prior Petition.** If you checked other than "New Employment" in item 2 (above) give the most recent prior petition numbers for the worker(s): ________
4. **Requested Action:** (check one)
   a. ☒ Notify the office in Part 4 so the person(s) can obtain a visa or be admitted (NOTE: a petition is not required for an E-1, E-2, or R visa)
   b. ☐ Change the person(s) status and extend their stay since they are all now in the U.S. in another status (see instructions for limitations). This is available only where you check "New Employment" in item 2, above.
   c. ☐ Extend or amend the stay of the person(s) since they now hold this status.
5. **Total number of workers in petition:** one (1)

   (See instructions for where more than one worker can be included)

Part 3. Information about the person(s) you are filing for.

Complete the blocks below. Use the continuation sheet to name each person included in this petition.

If an entertainment group, give their group name.

Family Name: Huang	Given Name: Shu-Hsin — Middle Initial:
Date of Birth (Month/Day/Year): 05/07/1963	Country of Birth: China (PRC)
Social Security #: N/A	A #: N/A

If in the United States, complete the following:

Date of Arrival (Month/Day/Year): N/A	I-94 #: N/A
Current Nonimmigrant Status: N/A	Expires (Month/Day/Year): N/A

FOR INS USE ONLY

Returned | Receipt
Resubmitted
Reloc Sent
Reloc Rec'd
Interviewed
☐ Petitioner
☐ Beneficiary

Class: ________
# of Workers: ________
Priority Number: ________
Validity Dates: From ________ To ________

☐ **Classification Approved**
☐ Consulate/POE/PFI Notified
At: ________
☐ Extension Granted
☐ COS/Extension Granted

Partial Approval (explain)

Action Block

To be Completed by Attorney or Representative, if any
☐ Fill in box if G-28 is attached to represent the applicant
VOLAG#
ATTY State License #

Form I-129 (Rev. 12/11/91)N

Continued on back.

SAMPLE FORM I-129 (CONTINUED)

Part 4. Processing Information

a. If the person named in Part 3 is outside the U.S. or a requested extension of stay or change of status cannot be granted, give the U.S. consulate or inspection facility you want to be notified if this petition is approved.

Type of Office (check one): ☒ Consulate ☐ Pre-flight inspection ☐ Port of Entry

Office Address (City): Hong Kong | U.S. State or Foreign Country:

Person's Foreign Address: 15 State Street Hong Kong

b. Does each person in this petition have a valid passport?
☐ Not required to have passport ☐ No - explain on separate paper ☒ Yes

c. Are you filing any other petitions with this one? ☒ No ☐ Yes - How many? ____

d. Are applications for replacement/Initial I-94's being filed with this petition? ☒ No ☐ Yes - How many? ____

e. Are applications by dependents being filed with this petition? ☒ No ☐ Yes - How many? ____

f. Is any person in this petition in exclusion or deportation proceedings? ☒ No ☐ Yes - explain on separate paper

g. Have you ever filed an immigrant petition for any person in this petition? ☒ No ☐ Yes - explain on separate paper

h. If you indicated you were filing a new petition in Part 2, within the past seven years has any person in this petition:
1) ever been given the classification you are now requesting? ☒ No ☐ Yes - explain on separate paper
2) ever been denied the classification you are now requesting? ☒ No ☐ Yes - explain on separate paper

i. If you are filing for an entertainment group, has any person in this petition not been with the group for at least 1 year?
☐ No ☐ Yes - explain on separate paper

Part 5. Basic Information about the proposed employment and employer.

Attach the supplement relating to the classification you are requesting.

Job Title: Manager, International Currency Transactions | Nontechnical Description of Job: Performing currency transactions (see attached letter)

Address where the person(s) will work if different from the address in Part 1.

Is this a full-time position? ☐ No - Hours per week ☒ Yes | Wages per week or per year: $100,000 per yr

Other Compensation (Explain): fringe benefits | Value per week or per year: 10% | Dates of Intended employment From: 10/1/99 To: 09/30/2002

Type of petitioner - check one ☐ U.S. citizen or permanent resident ☒ Organization ☐ Other - explain on separate paper

Type of business: Bank | Year established:

Current number of employees: 150 | Gross Annual Income: $15 billion + | Net Annual Income: $9 billion +

Part 6. Signature.

Read the information on penalties in the instructions before completing this section.

I certify, under penalty of perjury under the laws of the United States of America, that this petition, and the evidence submitted with it, is all true and correct. If filing this on behalf of an organization, I certify that I am empowered to do so by that organization. If this petition is to extend a prior petition, I certify that the proposed employment is under the same terms and conditions as in the prior approved petition. I authorize the release of any information from my records, or from petitioning organization's records, which the Immigration and Naturalization Service needs to determine eligibility for the benefit being sought.

Signature and title	Print Name	Date

Please note: If you do not completely fill out this form and the required supplement, or fail to submit required documents listed in the instructions, then the person(s) filed for may not be found eligible for the requested benefit, and this petition may be denied.

Part 7. Signature of person preparing form if other than above.

I declare that I prepared this application at the request of the above person and it is based on all information of which I have knowledge.

Signature	Print Name	Date

Firm Name and Address

SAMPLE L CLASSIFICATION SUPPLEMENT TO FORM I-129

OMB No. 1115-0168
L Classification
Supplement to Form I-129

Name of person or organization filing petition: Hong Kong Banking Group

Name of person you are filing for: Shu-Hsin Huang

This petition is (check one): ☒ An individual petition ☐ A blanket petition

Section 1. Complete this section if filing an individual petition

Classification (check one): ☐ L-1A manager or executive ☒ L-1B specialized knowledge

List the alien's, and any dependent family members' prior periods of stay in an L classification in the U.S. for the last seven years. Be sure to list only those periods in which the alien and/or family members were actually in the U.S. in an L classification.

NONE

Name and address of employer abroad Hong Kong Banking Group, 3 State Street, Hong Kong

Dates of alien's employment with this employer. Explain any interruptions in employment.

1987-Present

Description of alien's duties for the past three years.

1991 - Present: Treasury Division

Description of alien's proposed duties in the U.S.

International currency transactions (see attached letter)

Summarize the alien's education and work experience.

B.A., Harvard, Hong Kong banking Group 1987-Present

The U.S. company is, to the company abroad: (check one)

☐ Parent ☒ Branch ☐ Subsidiary ☐ Affiliate ☐ Joint Venture

Describe the stock ownership and managerial control of each company.

All stockholders are nationals of Hong Kong

Do the companies currently have the same qualifying relationship as they did during the one-year period of the alien's employment with the company abroad ☒ Yes ☐ No (attach explanation)

Is the alien coming to the U.S. to open a new office?

☐ Yes (explain in detail on separate paper) ☐ No

Section 2. Complete this section if filing a blanket petition.

List all U.S. and foreign parent, branches, subsidiaries and affiliates included in this petition.(Attach separate paper if additional space is needed)

Name and Address	Relationship

Explain in detail on separate paper.

PRACTICAL CONSIDERATIONS FOR COMPLETING FORM I-129 AND SUPPLEMENT

1. See Practical Considerations for Completing Form I-129 in the "H" Visa Chapter.

2. "L" Supplement - These questions should be answered in as much detail as possible. If there is not enough room in the spaces provided write "See attached letter" and provide a more complete explanation in the letter.

SAMPLE PETITIONER LETTER ON BEHALF OF AN EMPLOYEE UTILIZING SPECIALIZED KNOWLEDGE

Vermont Service Center
U.S. Department of Justice
Immigration & Naturalization Service
St. Albans, Vermont

Re: Shu-Hsin Huang

Dear Sir/Madam:

This letter is written in support of our L-1 petition on behalf of Mr. Shu-Hsin Huang as a Manager with Specialized Knowledge for the next three years. Mr. Huang has never been the beneficiary of an H or L visa.

The Hong Kong Banking Group

The Hong Kong Banking Group, headquartered in Hong Kong, is international in scope, and authorized to maintain a branch within the State of New York. Both our majority stockholders and the majority of our depositors are nationals of Hong Kong. We are one of the oldest banks in Hong Kong, with a global presence in over 156 locations worldwide and net annual revenues in excess of $9 billion dollars. We have enclosed a copy of our most recent financial statement and corporate brochure describing our operations. We presently have 150 employees in our New York Branch.

The Transferee

Mr. Huang began his career in finance after graduating from Harvard University in 1987. He joined the Hong Kong Banking Group in April of 1987, in the International Operations Administration Division, Foreign Trade and Remittance Group, in charge of export and remittance operations. His duties included the monitoring of currency exchange rates and payment as related to the Group's commercial banking operations. He was responsible for ensuring that our commercial banking operations were using the most favorable rates available and he monitored our payment schedules.

In January 1991, Mr. Huang was transferred to the Treasury Division, Administration Group. In this position he performed administrative duties relating to treasury operations. He monitored and controlled the balances due from banks and took the appropriate actions when necessary to maintain those balances. He performed settlement work for currency option, currency swap and interest rate swap transactions. He also performed profit and loss projections on currency option transactions. Through this position, Mr. Huang became an expert in several aspects of the Hong Kong Banking Group's unique financial techniques. His work on projecting profit and loss levels for our currency options business saved the Bank a great deal of money, and in turn, helped strengthen our market position.

In June 1991, Mr. Huang was transferred to the Options Group of the Treasury Division. He is currently in this position. Mr. Huang is in charge of the currency options dealing of USD/Sterling and Sterling/Yuan. He also performs specialized analysis using procedures and techniques specially developed for this purpose for the Hong Kong Banking Group. This type of analysis is necessary to perform foreign exchange position control and management. The techniques and programs developed allow Mr.

Huang to analyze the Bank's position in the world currency markets at any moment. This analysis is essential in the fast paced financial market, and allows our Group to successfully compete with other financial institutions. We believe that the continued use and application of the Group's specialized techniques is responsible for our maintaining a competitive edge.

Similar to his work in the Administration Group, Mr. Huang also performs profit and loss management and control. He applies other specialized techniques developed by the Bank to determine if the current profit/loss statement reflects our true market potential and assesses what measures are necessary to improve performance.

The Position

The Hong Kong Banking Group now wishes to transfer Mr. Huang to its New York Branch office as **Manager, International Currency Transactions**. This position will require Mr. Huang to use his specialized knowledge and experience in the area of international currency transactions including currency swaps, and options and dealings, as well as his first hand knowledge and experience of this bank and its procedures and techniques. International currency transactions are a highly complex process involving great sums of money on a daily, if not hourly basis.

Mr. Huang will be responsible for the transfer of monetary assets exclusively handled by branches of the Bank worldwide on behalf of our own funds and those of our customers. These international transfers involve several types of foreign currencies trading at different exchange rates at different times. Mr. Huang's experience in the methods, procedures and techniques developed specifically for Hong Kong Bank and our particular problems and concerns will be of vital importance in completing these complex transactions between Bank branches in different countries around the world. He will determine the most advantageous methods and form of the transfer. He will use his ability to recognize currency market trends and his ability to capitalize on these trends for the benefit of the bank and the client.

To best perform these services for our customers, we use a highly complex procedure internally designed by the Bank to obtain the best transfer rates in the most reliable and timely manner possible. Our strong position in the market is due to the application of the Bank's unique advanced financial engineering techniques. These techniques were specifically developed by the researchers of our bank to meet our strict performance requirements and standards. These methods are also pivotal in our efforts to use all resources available to the Bank to provide us with an edge over our competition. All large banking organizations have their own particular financial engineering techniques. Hong Kong Banking Group has developed their own specialized techniques. In fact, it is our belief that our techniques are the best in the field of international currency transactions as well as in the banking industry. This belief is supported by our financial successes and by our loyal worldwide corporate clientele who rely on our unique specialties.

Mr. Huang has become proficient in the application and use of our system and techniques over the course of his employment with the Hong Kong Banking Group. Mr. Huang has had the opportunity to work closely with all aspects of the system and has become an expert in adapting the system for each client's needs. His various assignments have all related, indirectly and directly, to the position for which he is presently needed for in the United States, Manager of International Currency Transactions.

We believe that his thorough knowledge and skill with our unique systems will help us to continue to maintain our competitive edge and expand our growth and profitability in these uncertain economic times.

Mr. Huang is eminently qualified for the position in question on the basis of his demonstrated specialized knowledge, extensive experience in international currency transfer transactions and familiarity with the procedures, policies and practices of the Hong Kong Banking Group. In accordance with his exceptional abilities, he will be compensated at a rate of $100,000 per year in U.S. dollars.

Thank you for your expeditious approval of the enclosed petition, so Mr. Huang may join us as soon as possible.

Very truly yours,

Baoheng Chiu
Senior Vice President
International Trading

SAMPLE PETITIONER LETTER ON BEHALF OF EMPLOYEE UTILIZING SPECIALIZED KNOWLEDGE

Vermont Service Center
U.S. Department of Justice
Immigration & Naturalization Service
St. Albans, Vermont

Re: St. Germaine & Associates, Ltd. – Petitioner
Elizabeth B. Monoco – Beneficiary
I-129 - L-1 petition for Alien Worker

Dear Sir or Madam:

This letter is written in support of our L-1 petition on behalf of Ms. Elizabeth B. Monoco whom we wish to transfer to the United States as an employee with specialized knowledge. Ms. Monoco will oversee the training of our underwriting staff and associates in our new in-house Computer System and she will manage the operation of the system in the United States. The project will last for three years.

THE PETITIONER

St. Germaine & Associates, Ltd. was incorporated in 1968 under the laws of the State of New York, as the 50% owned subsidiary of Richard Brown & Co. (London). Richard Brown & Co. employs the beneficiary, Elizabeth B. Monoco, in London. St. Germaine & Associates, Ltd. functions as an insurance broker and is the General Correspondent in the United States for mutual insurance associations managed by Richard Brown & Co. St. Germaine & Associates, Ltd. is responsible for all customers in the United States who are insured by mutual associations known as "clubs" that are managed by Richard Brown & Co. and it oversees all claims which arise in the United States. The petitioner, who operates offices in New York City and New Orleans, employs a total of thirty-eight people in the United States.

PARENT COMPANY

The parent company, Richard Brown & Co., provides management and agency services to a variety of mutual insurance associations, predominantly in the maritime industry. The company has been associated with the management of mutual insurance associations for over two hundred years and is the acknowledged world leader in maritime insurance coverage. It operates through a number of affiliate companies, each of which has responsibility for a particular mutual insurance association. A high level of specialized legal advice, claims handling/processing and general counseling is provided with respect to third-party liabilities to the organization's customers throughout the world. Richard Brown & Co. is an organization incorporated in the United Kingdom and its principal place of business is in London. Since a significant portion of claims arise in the United States, Richard Brown & Co. utilizes companies such as St. Germaine & Associates, Ltd. to provide services for its customers in the United States.

THE BENEFICIARY

Richard Brown & Co. has employed Elizabeth B. Monoco, a British citizen, in London, England since 1971. The company's principal activities center on providing insurance and reinsurance to customers engaged in transport operations. This past fiscal year Richard Brown & Co. employed 363 individuals and its gross assets were approximately $7,600,000 in U.S. currency.

Ms. Monoco currently holds the position of Chief Executive of the Underwriting Department with responsibility for worldwide training on the company's new Computer System. She works for a division of Robert Brown & Co., ABC Mutual Services in London. Ms. Monaco has never held H or L status in the United States.

The Computer System is a specialized computer system built for Robert Brown & Co. by in-house programmers at ABC Mutual Services and is designed to deal with all aspects of mutual insurance as applied to the transport and marine industries. The full details of how the system works are not in the public domain. However, it is capable of producing premium structure, based on specific criteria and questions and is programmed to hold all related information on customers so that at any time underwriters may access information. This enables them to assess risks, collate financial data and progress claims based on the data relating to the specific customer from both within the organization as well as data supplied by others via Electronic Data Interchange and other input methods.

The detailed use of the system can only be imparted by the trained staff of Richard Brown & Co. because no outside organization has been involved in the development of the system. No one outside of the company should be allowed access to data within the system. The system is designed for use by all related and associated offices throughout the world via regular connecting methods to the base in London.

Ms. Monoco is currently responsible for managing the training of underwriters in the London office in the new computer system. Her responsibilities also include coordinating the unification of documentation standards within all related or associated offices and the monitoring of service standards for the completion, correctness and dispatch of all documents.

THE PROPOSED POSITION

Ms. Monoco is being transferred to the United States to assume complete responsibility and management of the training of all underwriting associates on the new computer system and to manage the operation of the system. Upon transfer to the United States, she will become an employee of St. Germaine & Associates, Ltd. and will assume the position of Executive Assistant in Underwriting.

She will conduct training courses and will be responsible for continued staff ability evaluations and the review of performance after training. She will also manage the coordination and unification of documentation standards within all related or associated offices and provide computer connections and input to the computer based in London.

Her specialized knowledge of our in-house computer system and her experience managing its operations makes her the ideal candidate for this three-year project. Because it is a completely in-house system, it is impossible to bring in anyone from the outside to accomplish these tasks. In-house programmers purposely developed the system because the organization wished to keep its structure secret and its use confidential. Furthermore, Ms. Monoco is completely familiar with the system and has had extensive experience in managing the training of Richard Brown & Co. associates in its use.

Ms. Monoco will be compensated at the rate of $85,000 per year plus fringe benefits. Upon completion of the project, she will return to the United Kingdom and reassume her position with Richard Brown & Co.

Very truly yours,

Aloyshus D. St. Germaine
President
St. Germaine & Associates, Ltd.

SAMPLE PETITIONER LETTER ON BEHALF OF MANAGERIAL EMPLOYEE

Texas Service Center
United States Department of Justice
Immigration & Naturalization Service
Dallas, Texas

RE: Yoshi Tanaka

Dear Sir/Madam:

This letter is written in support of our petition for L-1 status on behalf of Mr. Yoshi Tanaka. Mr. Tanaka has never been in H-1 or L-1 status in the United States.

Brief Introduction to Ichi Electric Inc.

Ichi Electric Inc. is a subsidiary of Ichi Electric Inc. of Japan, a Japanese company engaged in the design and manufacture of telecommunications and information processing systems and electronic devices. Ichi Electric Inc. of Japan is a prestigious member of Japan's Fortunate 500. This growing international organization employees 20,000 individuals worldwide and has net sales in excess of $4.2 billion. Ichi Electric Inc. of America employees over 1,500 individuals and has gross income of $87 million. Both the parent company and the subsidiary will be fully operational during the temporary assignment period.

The transferee, Mr. Tanaka, will undertake a temporary assignment in the Tennessee offices of Ichi Electric Inc. of America. Ichi Electric Inc. of Japan currently employs the beneficiary in Japan.

The Transferee

Since graduating from Tokyo University in 1988 with an MBA in Finance and Economics, Mr. Tanaka has been continuously employed by the Ichi Organization. He first joined Ichi Electric Inc. of Japan in Osaka, Japan as an International Marketer. His outstanding performance led to several promotions. In April 1989 he assumed the position of Marketing Assistant at Ichi Electric World Headquarters in Kanagawa, Japan. In May 1990, he was promoted to Marketing Services Coordinator where he remained until December 1990.

Since January 1, 1991, Mr. Tanaka has held the position of Marketing Services manager in Kanagawa, Japan. As such, he is fully responsible for the activities of the Marketing Services Department of Ichi Electric International. This department is comprised of several staff members organized into three units-Market Intelligence, Competitor Information and Marketing Projects - all under Mr. Tanaka's control and supervision. Mr. Tanaka develops guidelines and procedures, supervises the implementation and evaluates the results of projects intended to supply strategic marketing information and marketing decision support to Ichi's fifty-seven marketing companies worldwide and to Ichi Group Management. In addition, he is project leader for the global information systems project within Ichi Electric. As such, he is responsible for the activities of ten staff members regarding the evaluation of the requirements for, design of and implementation of a global marketing information system, connecting Ichi operating units in fifty-seven countries. He reports directly to a member of the Ichi Electric Group Management.

The Position

Ichi Electric Inc. of Japan now wishes to transfer Mr. Tanaka to the United States in the managerial position of Area Business Manager. Utilizing his extensive experience as a manager in the international business activities of the Ichi Electric Organization, Mr. Tanaka will contribute significantly to our operations in the United States. He will be responsible for all of Ichi's business activities in the area covering Tennessee, Arkansas, Mississippi, Louisiana and Alabama. His managerial responsibilities will include:

Managing a regional staff of twenty sales and executive personnel in the Tennessee office.

Managing all of Ichi Electric's business activities in the region including marketing sales administration, finance and technical service;

Evaluating operating guidelines and procedures and formulating new business goals as needed.

Evaluating the unit's business performance and developing and implementing remedies as necessary to improve performance.

Directing and supervising the development and implementation of comprehensive business plans and strategies to expand Ichi Electric's business in this area.

Maintaining business contacts and relations with top executives of major Ichi Electric customers with headquarters in the relevant business areas;

Coordinating the unit's activities in national marketing projects with Ichi Electric staff and customers across the United States, including travelling to Ichi Electric Inc. offices throughout the United States.

Conducting all personnel evaluations including hiring personnel as necessary, firing and promotions.

It is the opinion of the board of Ichi Electric Inc., that based on Mr. Tanaka's success as Marketing Services Manager for Ichi Electric International, that he will be able to help guide Ichi Electric Inc. of America into continued dynamic growth, profitability and expansion in the world-wide marketplace.

Mr. Tanaka is eminently qualified for the position based on his demonstrated managerial abilities, extensive experience in the international communications industry, and intimate familiarity with the procedures, policies and practices of the Ichi Electric Organization. In accordance with his exceptional abilities, he will be remunerated at $90,000 per year.

Thank you for approving the enclosed petition as soon as possible so that Mr. Tanaka may join us as scheduled.

Very truly yours,

Kenichi Aragawa
President
Ichi Electric Inc. of America

SAMPLE LETTER IN SUPPORT OF EXECUTIVE EMPLOYEE

California Service Center
U.S. Department of Justice
Immigration & Naturalization Service
Laguna Niguel, California

Dear Sir/Madam:

This letter is written on behalf of Mr. Keniko Yamada in order to have him accorded L-1 visa classification as an executive employee of our organization.

The Petitioning Organization

Asahi Packaging, our parent, was established in Tokyo in 1950 and is one of the largest multi-purpose packaging organizations in Asia. With affiliated organizations on three continents, and in over forty countries in the world, Asahi is at the forefront of the international packaging market with annual revenues in excess of $50,000,000 U.S. dollars.

Asahi Packaging, USA Inc., a wholly owned subsidiary of Asahi Packaging, was established in Seattle, Washington in 1980 to capitalize on the heightened levels of commerce between the Pacific Northwest region of the United States and Asia. Presently, we seek to transfer Mr. Yamada to serve in an executive capacity as the Director of Finance.

The Beneficiary

Mr. Yamada began his long tenure with our organization after graduating from Tokyo University with a Masters Degree in Business Administration in 1982. From 1982 through 1987 he worked in a number of different capacities in our Finance and Administration department in our Tokyo Office, performing financial analysis. In 1987, Mr. Yamada's outstanding performance led to his promotion, to Vice President of Finance and Administration. He currently retains this position. He is responsible for directing the planning, implementation and formulation of all financial and administrative plans and policies. His executive responsibilities include:

Managing a staff of ten finance professionals working under his supervision;

Appraising financial position of Asahi Packaging Inc. and issuing periodic financial and operating reports;

Directing, consolidating and performing all cost and plant economy analyses together with other statistical and routine reports, including any desirable analysis of the monthly departmental reports;

Maintaining custody of all cash funds and securities of the corporation and being accountable for the custodianship of cash funds and financial assets;

Providing for arrangement and administration of lines of credit and working with depository accounts in banks and financial institutions; and

Directing studies of general economic, business and financial developments for minimizing cost and maximizing returns within established corporate guidelines.

The Position

Asahi Packaging Inc. now wishes to transfer Mr. Yamada to our Seattle office in an executive capacity, as Director of Finance. Utilizing his extensive experience as an executive in the international business activities of the Asahi Organization, Mr. Yamada will contribute significantly to our operations in the United States. He will have responsibility for the overall financial plans, policies and accounting practices for the corporation. In addition, Mr. Yamada will be responsible for:

Maintaining proper relationships with the government regulatory agencies and the U.S. financial community;

Directing procedures and systems necessary to maintain proper records as well as appropriate ac counting controls and services;

Directing a staff of Managers and Accountants having specific responsibility for developing and coordinating appropriate accounting and statistical data with and for all departments.

Directing and consolidating all cost and plant economy analyses together with other statistical and routine reports.

Appraising the financial position of Asahi in the United States and issuing periodic financial and operating reports to Asahi directors at the world headquarters in Kobe, Japan.

Supervising implementation and management of policies and procedures relating to credit and collections.

It is the opinion of the board of Asahi that based on Mr. Yamada's performance as Director of Finance and Vice President of Finance and Administration of Asahi Inc. Frankfurt, he will be able to guide Asahi Inc. into continued dynamic growth, profitability and expansion in the worldwide marketplace. Asahi Packaging has a long-standing corporate policy of rotating international executive personnel. This policy is based on the notion that the exposure of our executive personnel to the many facets of our organization benefits the employees, as well as the particular organization that utilizes their temporary services.

Mr. Yamada is eminently qualified for the position in question on the basis of his education, demonstrated executive abilities, extensive experience in the international food packaging industry and intimate familiarity with the procedures, policies and practices of the Asahi Organization. In accordance with his exceptional abilities, he will be remunerated at $125,000 per year.

Thank you for approving the enclosed petition as soon as possible, so that Mr. Yamada may join us as scheduled.

Very truly yours,

Akio Suzuki
Director-International Packaging

Denial of L-1 Petition

When an individual petition is denied, the petitioner has a right to appeal the decision to the Administrative Appeals Unit (AAU). In some cases the INS will request further documentation or deny the petition on the basis of evidence not included in the original petition. In those cases, the petitioner will be given thirty days to correct the defects in the petition, if possible, and submit an amended petition to the INS.

Issuance of Visa

Generally, the Consulate can not issue an L-1 visa until the Immigration & Naturalization Service approves the underlying L-1 petition.

Upon receipt of an approved petition, the consular officer makes a determination concerning the foreign national's qualification for admission. Once the consular officer is satisfied that the alien is admissible, a nonimmigrant visa is issued with the symbols L-1A or L-1B. The symbol L-1A is for managers and executives and L-1B is for employees with specialized knowledge. The accompanying spouse and children of an L-1 visaholder are issued L-2 visas.

If the consular officer is not satisfied of the admissibility of the foreign national, the officer may suspend action on the petition and submit a report to the INS suggesting that petition approval be withdrawn.

Employees being transferred pursuant to an approved blanket certification can apply directly to an American Consulate for issuance of an L-1 visa. Under NAFTA, Canadian nationals are not required to obtain prior approval by the INS and may directly petition for L-1 classification at ports of entry located on the United States/Canadian border and at certain locations in Canadian airports. However, individuals who apply directly at the border may find it cumbersome to carry all the required documentation and risk denial without an opportunity to present further evidence. It is more prudent to submit a petition to the INS before attempting to obtain a visa at the border or airport in case there are any defects in the petition.

Spouse and Children of L-1 visaholders

The spouse and minor children accompanying an L-1 intracompany transferee are eligible for classification as L-2 visaholders. L-2 visaholders may remain in the United States for the period granted to the primary visaholder and may engage in all activities except gainful employment in the United States. In order to be authorized to work in the United States, the L-2 visaholder must be the beneficiary of a separate approved nonimmigrant or immigrant petition filed on his or her behalf.

L-2 spouses or minor children are authorized to attend school on either a full or part-time basis without any further change of status. It may however, be advantageous for L-2 visaholders who are nearing the age of twenty-one to apply for a change of status to the F-1 student visa category. Obtaining an F-1 visa in this situation may be beneficial because an F-1 visa will enable the individual to remain in the United States for a longer period of time, since the L-2 is no longer valid once the individual reaches the age of 21. In addition, the F-1 visaholder can obtain work authorization and practical training while in school and during school vacations, as well as for a period of time subsequent to graduation or completion of studies.

Extension of L-1 Temporary Stay

To seek an extension of L-1 authorization, the visaholder must submit the following to the Immigration Service:

- Letter from the petitioner explaining the reasons for the extension.

- If family members will be applying for an extension as well, they will need to file an Application to Extend Time of Temporary Stay (Form I-539).

- Certified copy of the original petition Approval Notice (Form I-797).

- Original Form I-94 of principal applicant and family members, if any.

- Filing Fee.

The petitioner should prepare a statement of continued need in addition to the extension application. Extensions may be granted in increments of two years.

The factors that the INS will consider in determining whether to issue an L-1 extension to an intracompany transferee is in a managerial or executive role, include but are not limited to the following:

- Whether there has been an increase in the number of employees whom the transferee supervises;

- Whether there is a significant growth in cash flow; and/or

- The presence of significant customers and clientele.

Over recent years the demand for documents in support of a petition for the extension of an L-1 visa has increased dramatically. It is important to demonstrate that the petitioning entity remains, or has become a viable commercial enterprise with significant cash flow, large numbers of transactions and a sufficient staff to require the continued services of a manager or managers. Many believe the INS has gone too far in this requirement given the definition of a functional manager and express statutory admonition that staffing levels are not to control. However, with regard to smaller and privately held entities it can not be taken for granted that an L-1 petition previously approved for either a new company or existing company will automatically be extended after the initial period of authorization.

U.S. Department of Justice
Immigration and Naturalization Service

OMB #1115-0093
Application to Extend/Change Nonimmigrant Status

START HERE - Please Type or Print

FOR INS USE ONLY

Part 1. Information about you.

Family Name Orosco	Given Name Luis	Middle Initial

Address - In Care of:

Street # and Name 2 Abbott Drive	Apt. #
City Rye	State New York
Zip Code 11482	
Date of Birth (month/day/year) 02/26/1957	Country of Birth Argentina
Social Security # (if any) N/A	A# (if any) N/A
Date of Last Arrival Into the U.S. 05/15/1997	I-94# 123-56-7888
Current Nonimmigrant Status L-1	Expires on (month/day/year) 06/30/1998

Part 2. Application Type.

(See instructions for fee.)

1. I am applying for: (check one)
   a. ☒ an extension of stay in my current status
   b. ☐ a change of status. The new status I am requesting is: L-1
2. Number of people included in this application: (check one)
   a. ☐ I am the only applicant
   b. ☒ Members of my family are filing this application with me. The Total number of people included in this application is 3 (complete the supplement for each co-applicant)

Part 3. Processing Information.

1. I/We request that my/our current or requested status be extended until (month/day/year) 08/30/1999
2. Is this application based on an extension or change of status already granted to your spouse, child or parent?
   ☒ No ☐ Yes (receipt # ______________________)
3. Is this application being filed based on separate petition or application to give your spouse, child or parent an extension or change of status?
   ☒ No ☐ Yes, filed with this application ☐ Yes, filed previously and pending with INS
4. If you answered yes to question 3, give the petitioner or applicant name:

   If the application is pending with INS, also give the following information.

   Office filed at ______ Filed on ______ (date)

Part 4. Additional Information.

1. For applicant #1, provide passport information:

Country of issuance Argentina	Valid to: (month/day/year) 03/03/2002

2. Foreign Address:

Street # and Name 34 Calle Juarez	Apt#
City or Town Buenas Aires	State or Province
Country Argentina	Zip or Postal Code

120

Form I-539 (Rev. 12-2-91)

Continued on back

FOR INS USE ONLY

Returned	Receipt
Date	
Resubmitted	
Date	
Reloc Sent	
Date	
Reloc Rec'd	
Date	
Date	
☐ Applicant Interviewed	

☐ Extension Granted to (date): ______

☐ Change of Status/Extension Granted
New Class: ______ To (date): ______

If denied:
☐ Still within period of stay
☐ V/D to: ______
☐ S/D to: ______
☐ Place under docket control

Remarks

Action Block

To be completed by Attorney or Representative, if any

☐ Fill in box if G-28 is attached to represent the applicant

VOLAG#

ATTY State License #

Part 4. Additional Information. (continued)

3. Answer the following questions. If you answer yes to any question, explain on separate paper.	Yes	No
a. Are you, or any other person included in this application, an applicant for an immigrant visa or adjustment of status to permanent residence?		X
b. Has an immigrant petition ever been filed for you, or for any other person included in this application?		X
c. Have you, or any other person included in this application ever been arrested or convicted of any criminal offense since last entering the U.S.?		X
d. Have you, or any other person included in this application done anything which violated the terms of the nonimmigrant status you now hold?		X
e. Are you, or any other person included in this application, now in exclusion or deportation proceedings?		X
f. Have you, or any other person included in this application been employed in the U.S. since last admitted or granted an extension or change of status?	X	

If you answered YES to question 3f, give the following information on a separate paper: Name of person, name of employer, address of employer, weekly income, and whether specifically authorized by INS see attached letter in support

If you answered No to question 3f, fully describe how you are supporting yourself on a separate paper. Include the source and the amount and basis for any income.

Part 5. Signature

Read the information on penalties in the instruction before completing this section. You must file this application while in the United States.

I certify under penalty of perjury under the laws of the United States of America that this application, and the evidence submitted with it, is all true and correct. I authorize the release of any information from my record which the Immigration and Naturalization Service needs to determine the eligibility for the benefit I am seeking.

Signature	Print your name	Date
	Luis Orosco	

Please Note: If you do not completely fill out this form, or fail to submit required documents listed in the instructions, you cannot be found eligible for the requested document and this application will have to be denied.

Part 6. Signature of person preparing form if other than above. (Sign below)

I declare that I prepared this application at the request of the above person and it is based on all information of which I have knowledge.

Signature	Print your name	Date

Firm Name and Address

(Please remember to enclose the mailing label with your application)

Form I-539 (Rev. 12-2-91)

SAMPLE FORM I-539 SUPPLEMENT

Supplement-1

Attach to Form I-539 when more than one person is included in the petition or application. *(List each person separately. Do not include the person you named on the form).*

Family Name Orosco	Given Name Manuella	Middle Initial C.	Date of Birth (month/day/year) 05/01/1960
Country of Birth Spain	Social Security No. N/A		A# N/A
IF IN THE U.S.	Date of Arrival (month/day/year) 05/15/1997	I-94# 123-56-7889	
	Current Nonimmigrant Status L-2	Expires on (month/day/year) 06/30/1998	
Country where passport issued Argentina	Expiration Date (month/day/year) 01/15/2000		
Family Name Orosco	Given Name Susanna	Middle Initial C.	Date of Birth (month/day/year) 02/14/1989
Country of Birth Argentina	Social Security No. N/A		A# N/A
IF IN THE U.S.	Date of Arrival (month/day/year) 05/15/1997	I-94# 123-56-7890	
	Current Nonimmigrant Status L-2	Expires on (month/day/year) 06/30/1998	
Country where passport issued	Expiration Date (month/day/year)		
Family Name	Given Name	Middle Initial	Date of Birth (month/day/year)
Country of Birth	Social Security No.		A#
IF IN THE U.S.	Date of Arrival (month/day/year)	I-94#	
	Current Nonimmigrant Status	Expires on (month/day/year)	
Country where passport issued	Expiration Date (month/day/year)		
Family Name	Given Name	Middle Initial	Date of Birth (month/day/year)
Country of Birth	Social Security No.		A#
IF IN THE U.S.	Date of Arrival (month/day/year)	I-94#	
	Current Nonimmigrant Status	Expires on (month/day/year)	
Country where passport issued	Expiration Date (month/day/year)		
Family Name	Given Name	Middle Initial	Date of Birth (month/day/year)
Country of Birth	Social Security No.		A#
IF IN THE U.S.	Date of Arrival (month/day/year)	I-94#	
	Current Nonimmigrant Status	Expires on (month/day/year)	
Country where passport issued	Expiration Date (month/day/year)		

SAMPLE LETTER FOR EXTENSION OF L-1 VISA

Vermont Service Center
U.S. Department of Justice
Immigration & Naturalization Service
St. Albans, Vermont 05479-0001

Dear Sir/Madam:

This letter is written in support of our application for an extension of L-1 petition and status for Mr. Luis Orosco.

RCR Industries (USA) Inc. was established in the United States in 1988 to serve as the United States affiliate of RCR Textile Mills (Argentina) P.A. RCR Textile Mills (Argentina) was established in 1957 as a textile manufacturer and distributor. The Argentine company has extremely close relations with the Economics Development Board of Argentina and similar governmental trade organizations. It is the purpose of our organization to further expand and develop the Argentine textile industry on an international level. To this end, RCR Textile Mills (Argentina) includes a wholly owned subsidiary, Export Fabric Manufacturing Company, which is a leading manufacturer of textiles.

RCR Industries (USA) Inc. operates as the United States agent of both RCR Textile Mills (Argentina) and Export Fabric Manufacturing Company. The 100 shares of stock issued and outstanding of RCR Industries (USA) Inc. continue to be owned on an equal basis by Mr. Roberto Santiago and Mr. David Lev who are the same stockholders who own 100% of RCR Textile Mills (Argentina). They are directors of both corporations.

RCR Textile Mills (Argentina) presently has in excess of 2,000 employees. It earns approximately $6,700,000 in annual exports to the United States, making the management of our United States arm crucial to the success or our company.

Mr. Luis Orosco served as Managing Director of RCR Textile Mills (Argentina) from May 1979, until he was transferred to the United States in January 1991, to head up our United States operation. In this position, Mr. Orosco has served as the Chief Executive Officer of the United States corporation and has been responsible for the direction and implementation of the international marketing programs in our organization.

In particular, Mr. Orosco has been responsible for recruiting United States employees, developing organization and distribution systems, setting marketing goals for Argentine textile, handicrafts and agricultural products and marketing of American products in Argentina. This has been accomplished through our own offices in Argentina as well as associates in Venezuela, Mexico, Costa Rica, Guatemala and Chile.

Mr. Orosco was granted L-1 status from July 1, 1991 until June 30, 1994. In 1994, this was extended until June 30, 1994, and in 1996 it was extended until June 30, 1998 for a total of seven years. However, between July, 1991 and the present time, Mr. Orosco has been outside of the United States for a total of 14 months, making his period of presence in the United States less than seven years (See enclosed list of absences and copies of Form I-94).

We now request an additional fourteen-month extension of Mr. Orosco's L-1 status until August 30, 1999. Due to the continued expansion of our Argentine manufacturing facility, his role in managing and directing the global import and distribution network has become increasingly important. It is anticipated that RCR Industries (USA) Inc. will gross in excess of $5,500,000 during 1998 and Mr. Orosco's continued executive services are essential to assure appropriate management of our enterprise.

Mr. Orosco will be compensated at an annual rate of $100,000, paid to him both in the United States and Argentina and it is our intention to transfer him back to our company in Argentina upon completion of the additional period of L-1 status which we are now requesting.

We thank you for a favorable consideration of this application.

Very truly yours,

Roberto Santiago
President
RCR Industries (USA)

Revalidation of L visas by the Department of State

The following documentation is required in order to apply for a renewal of an L visa by the Department of State in Washington, D.C.

- The applicant's passport, valid for at least six months. The passport must contain a previous visa bearing the same classification as the one for which renewal is being sought. If the visa is still valid, it must not have a remaining validity of more than sixty days.

- The original Form I-94 issued to the applicant by the Immigration & Naturalization Service when the applicant last entered the United States (usually this form is stapled to the passport near the visa).

- A comprehensive letter from the applicant's employer identifying the applicant and describing in detail the nature and function of the applicant's position, the type of business, naming the dependents, if any.

- A properly executed visa application form (OF-156) for each person requesting visa revalidation.

- Evidence that the applicant's work assignment in the United States is temporary and that the applicant will depart from the United States at the end of that temporary work assignment.

- A valid petition approval notice (Form I-797) covering the period of the renewal.

- Passport sized photograph for each individual applying for renewal.

- A money order, certified check, or personal check payable to the Department of State for visa fees. Fees vary from country to country. The specific fee should be confirmed with the Department of State.

- A self-addressed stamped return envelope.

Send the applicable requested items to the following address:

U.S. Department of State
Diplomatic Liaison Visa Office
2401 E Street, N.W.
Washington, D.C. 20522-0113

E. BLANKET PETITIONS

The blanket petition program for the L visa category was introduced in 1983, appeared in the regulations in 1987, and was codified in the 1990 Immigration Act. The blanket petition program is designed to facilitate the transfer of foreign employees to the United States to certain eligible companies who on a regular basis utilize the L-1 visa. The program eliminates the need for companies to make frequent repetitive filings and reduces the INS' workload by decreasing the number of repetitive adjudications. Under the blanket visa program approved petitioners do not have to file individual petitions on behalf of each employee but instead are authorized to issue certificates of eligibility. The proposed transferee will then use the certificate of eligibility in addition to other documentation to obtain a L-1 visa at a consulate abroad or a change of status in the United States.

In order to qualify for the blanket petition program, an organization must prove the following:

- The organization and its branches, subsidiaries and affiliates are engaged in commercial trade or services.

- The organization has an office in the United States that has been doing business for one year or more.

- The organization has three or more domestic and foreign branches, subsidiaries, or affiliates.

- The organization has obtained approved petitions for at least 10 L-1 managers, executives or specialized knowledge professionals during the previous 12 months, and has United States subsidiaries or affiliates that enjoy a combined annual sales of at least $25 million dollars, or have a United States work force of at least 1,000 employees.

Employees who have specialized knowledge skills but are not professionals may not participate in the blanket petition program. A specialized knowledge professional is an individual who is engaged in an occupation that requires theoretical and practical application of a body of highly specialized knowledge, performing in such fields as architecture, physical and social sciences, business specialties, and the arts, and the minimum requirement for the occupation is a bachelor's degree.

The blanket petition is filed, adjudicated and maintained at the INS Service Center with geographical jurisdiction over the proposed place of employment. A blanket petition is approved for an initial three-year period and an extension may be granted indefinitely if the petitioner applies before the expiration of the initial blanket L-1 visa. If the petitioner fails to request an extension or an extension is denied the petitioner is then barred from reapplying for the blanket petition program for three years. The petitioner may continue to file individual petitions.

The L blanket petition procedure may be a difficult one to utilize because most organizations do not possess all of the required elements. Therefore, it may be generally advisable to use the individual procedure in place of the blanket petition. The L blanket petition is also not frequently used because it requires additional approval to be obtained at the Consular level. This adds a substantial and often subjective level of review to the process that is not always advisable.

When a qualifying company seeks to transfer an employee to the United States under blanket L authorization, the employee must present Form I-797 (Approval Notice of the company's Blanket Petition) and Form I-129S, Certificate of Eligibility for Intracompany Transferee under a Blanket Petition, at an American Consulate for visa issuance. The consular officer determines whether the employee qualifies as an intracompany transferee. If the employee is seeking to change status in the United States to an L-1 under a blanket petition, Form I-129 and the L supplement is used in place of Form I-129S and the package is submitted to the INS Service Center where the blanket petition was filed.

Applicants who are exempt from obtaining visas (i.e. Canadian citizens and landed immigrants) are required to submit the certificate of eligibility, copy of the blanket petition approval notice, and all supporting documentation to the INS office where the original petition was filed.

A foreign national who receives an approval from the INS on the basis of a blanket petition is required to go to the appropriate American Consulate in order to have the visa stamp placed in his or her passport. The foreign national is not normally required to obtain a secondary approval from the consular officer. The consular officer's role is merely to determine that there is no indication of fraud and that the visaholder intends to abide by the conditions of the petition, and the foreign national is not otherwise inadmissible to the United States. In addition, a determination must also be made that the applicant is in fact an executive, manager or specialized knowledge professional.

Extensions for transferees under blanket petitions are filed with the INS office that approved the original petition. In addition to the above, an extension of a blanket petition must be accompanied by Form I-129S.

SAMPLE FORM I-129S NONIMMIGRANT BASED ON BLANKET L PETITION

U.S. Department of Justice
Immigration and Naturalization Service

OMB #1115-0128
Nonimmigrant Petition based on Blanket L Petition

START HERE - Please Type or Print

Part 1. Information about employer.

Sponsoring company or Organization's Name: Alexander Pharmaceutical Group

Address - ATTN:

Street Number and Name 310 East 42nd Street		Room #
City or Town New York	State or Province New York	
Country USA	ZIP/Postal Code 10001	

Part 2. Information about employment.

This alien will be a:

a. ☐ manager/executive
b. ☒ specialized knowledge professional

Blanket petition approval number is: 1234567

Part 3. Information about employee.

Family Name Stockler	Given Name Irving	Middle Name
Foreign Address Street Number and Name 55 Berlin Plaza		Apt. #
City Berlin	State or Province	
Country Germany	ZIP/Postal Code	
Date of Birth (Month/Day/Year) 01/15/1954	Country of Birth Germany	

Part 4. Additional information about the employment.

Address: Route 4, Box 1

Street Number and Name		Room #
City or Town Leslie	State or Province Michigan	
Country USA	ZIP/Postal Code 35101	
Dates of intended employment (Month/Day/Year) From 02/05/1999	To 02/04/2001	
Weekly Wage $65,000 per yr.	Hours per Week 40	

Title and detailed description of duties to be performed.

Research Scientist: research on pharmaceutical products
(see attached letter)

FOR INS USE ONLY

Returned	Receipt
Resubmitted	
Reloc Sent	
Reloc Rec'd	
☐ Petitioner Interviewed ☐ Beneficiary Interviewed	

Approved as:
☐ manager/executive
☐ specialized knowledge professional

Validity dates
From:
To:

Denied (give reason)

Action Block

To Be Completed by Attorney or Representative, if any
☐ Fill in box if G-28 is attached to represent the petitioner

VOLAG#

ATTY State License #

Continued on back.

Part 4. (Continued).

Give the aliens dates of prior periods of stay in the U.S. in a worked authorized capacity and the type of visa.

November 1, 1993 - October 31, 1995

Give the alien's dates of employment and job duties for the immediate prior three years.

1980 - Present: Research Scientist for Alexander Pharmaceuticals

Summarize the alien's education and other work experience.

B.A., Mainz University 1975

Ph.D., Hamburg College of Science 1980

Part 5. Signature. Read the information on penalties in the instructions before completing this section.

I certify, under penalty of perjury under the laws of the United States of America, that this petition, and the evidence submitted with it, is all true and correct. I filing this on behalf of an organization, I certify that I am empowered to do so by that organization. If this petition is to extend a prior petition, I certify that th proposed employment is under the same terms and conditions as in the prior approved petition. I authorize the release of any information from my records, o from the petitioning organization's records, which the Immigration and Naturalization Service needs to determine eligibility for the benefit being sought.

Signature	Print Name	Date

Please Note: If you do not completely fill out this form, or fail to submit required documents listed in the instructions, then the person(s) filed for cannot be fou eligible for the requested benefit, and your petition may be denied.

Part 6. Signature of person preparing form if other than above.

I declare that I prepared this application at the request of the above person and it is based on all information of which I have knowledge.

Signature	Print Name	Date

Firm Name
and Address

*U.S. Government Printing Office: 1992 - 312-328/5

PRACTICAL CONSIDERATIONS FOR COMPLETING FORM I-129S

1. Part 1 - Fill in the United States company's name

2. Part 4 - Provide as detailed information as possible regarding each one of the questions. If there is not enough room, write, "See attached letter" and provide a more complete answer in the letter.

SAMPLE LETTER FOR BLANKET L PETITION

Nebraska Service Center
United States Department of Justice
Immigration & Naturalization Service
Lincoln, Nebraska

Dear Sir/Madam:

This letter is written in support of our petition for **Blanket L Classification** on behalf of all Alexander Pharmaceutical companies in the United States. The Alexander Pharmaceutical Group of Companies wishes to facilitate the transfer of key executive, management and specialized knowledge personnel among their companies worldwide. A "Blanket L" visa would allow Alexander Pharmaceutical in the United States to transfer key personnel as necessary to ensure the continued growth necessary for it success in the competitive pharmaceutical market.

Alexander Pharmaceutical's Background

Our roots go back to 1900 when the company was first founded in Mainz, Germany. The Alexander name, which is synonymous with high quality pharmaceuticals, can now be found on all seven continents. Worldwide gross annual sales for 1998 were $10 billion. There are over 100 members in our international family of companies, each with its own national profile.

Established in 1966 in the United States, Alexander's executive, managerial, professional and support staff number 2,715 while gross sales exceeded $30 million last year. We are particularly proud of our dynamic growth since our pharmaceuticals were only introduced to the U.S. in 1983. In breaking into the huge North American pharmaceutical market, Alexander utilized its impressive array of worldwide resources, including technical, financial and personnel skills. The skills and experience of Alexander's operations worldwide were necessary to meet the demands for quality, reliability and service demanded by the U.S. market and to meet the stringent standards of the regulations established by the U.S. Food and Drug Administration.

Alexander's Worldwide Activities

Since Alexander was established in the United States in 1966, it has grown to become a family of five companies - Alexander, Inc., Alexander Materials Inc., Alexander West Inc., Alexander Systems Inc. and Alexander Americas Inc. - with offices in fifteen states and the District of Columbia. We have 27 offices in the U.S. and over 50 offices in countries worldwide. These companies are all owned and controlled by the Alexander Group of Companies whose international headquarters is located in Mainz, Germany. A complete list of Alexander companies and locations in the United States and worldwide is attached.

Alexander's Eligibility for Blanket L Classification

Alexander's United States operation is engaged in the commercial activities of pharmaceutical manufacturing. We research, design, manufacture, package and market high quality pharmaceuticals.

Alexander has been doing business from offices in the United States since 1966. As their business success in the U.S. market has increased over the years, Alexander has increased its presence. At this time, Alexander in the U.S. is composed of five companies that employ 2,715 workers at locations in 15 states and the District of Columbia. Please see the attached list of all of Alexander's U.S. offices and their addresses.

The Alexander Group of companies has affiliates in over 50 countries around the world. As already noted, there are five Alexander companies in the United States alone. From our international headquarters, the activities of Alexander's affiliates in over 45 companies in North America, South America, Europe, Asia, Africa and Australia are coordinated to the mutual benefit of our international organization.

Alexander has obtained approval of 25 managers, executives or specialized knowledge professionals over the previous 12 months (please see attached copies of each Form I-797, Notice of Approval). In addition, Alexander's combined U.S. sales exceed $25 million and its work force of 2,715 employees exceeds the minimum required.

Alexander requires the freedom afforded by Blanket L classification in order to transfer key personnel between offices in different countries. This freedom is essential for Alexander to maintain its competitive edge in this highly competitive industry. Alexander is currently the leader in the pharmaceutical industry in terms of sales volume, research and development budgets. Since its inception in Germany and in the United States, Alexander has been an innovator in the pharmaceutical industry.

Alexander is under intense competition in both the world and U.S. markets. To maintain our competitive edge, we keep up continuous research and development efforts. Our scientists and researchers are constantly developing new technology and designing new and better pharmaceuticals. Currently, we are dramatically expanding our U.S. research and development capabilities by opening new laboratories at our Alexander Packaging Systems office in Leslie, Michigan. Alexander's scientists, who are the worlds leading experts, will be transferred there from our central laboratories at our international headquarters in Mainz, Germany.

We intend to remain the world leader in this industry and believe that this can be accomplished by employing the best executive and managerial personnel and the best research and development scientists. By assembling a pool of experienced and talent leaders, Alexander will be able to maintain its position of industry leadership and continue its history of innovations in the pharmaceutical industry.

We have attached to this petition documentation establishing our eligibility for Blanket L classification. This evidence includes a listing of all Alexander companies and locations in the U.S. and a listing of Alexander's companies around the world. In addition, we have included several issues of our in-house corporate magazine, "Alexander House Magazine." The nature of our commercial pharmaceutical activities, the size of our U.S. and worldwide workforce and the frequency with which we relocate key personnel illustrate our qualifications for Blanket L classification.

Thank you for approving the enclosed petition as soon as possible.

Very truly yours,

Wolfgang Alexander
President

Chapter Five

THE E VISA CATEGORY

A. INTRODUCTION

The E visa classification is an extremely useful visa category preferred by many executive and business people for the benefits it provides its holders. In response to the increase in trade and investment between foreign countries and the United States, many foreign corporations, investors and entrepreneurs favor the E visa category. The E visa is particularly beneficial because it can provide easy and continued access to the United States.

E nonimmigrant visa classification is available to prospective nonimmigrants provided they are nationals of a foreign state that has entered into a treaty of commerce and navigation with the United States, or has been specifically included in the Immigration and Nationality Act.

The Department of State and the Immigration and Naturalization Service share responsibility for the implementation of the E nonimmigrant visa category. Under the INA the Department of State has exclusive jurisdiction over E visa issuance and the INS has exclusive jurisdiction to adjudicate E applications for admission to the United States, change of status and extension of stay.

On August 30, 1991 and September 3, 1991, the Immigration and Naturalization Service and Department of State respectively, published separate rules governing E nonimmigrant visa classification. In an attempt to standardize both sets of rules and ensure consistent adjudication of E applications the Department of State and the INS undertook the process of revising their respective rules. After seven years of study, the Department of State and the INS simultaneously published final rules for E nonimmigrant classification on September 12, 1997. The final rules took effect on November 12, 1997.

Overall, the final rules have not significantly altered the policies and regulations of the E visa category that have been in place since 1991. The final rules are meant to be substantively the same even though at times the Department of State and the INS employ different language in their respective publications. Any reference to the final rules in this chapter refers to both the Department of State's rules contained in the Code of Federal Regulations, the Foreign Affairs Manual (FAM) and the INS' regulations.

One significant factor to be taken into consideration in E visa issuance is the individual requirements and preferences of each issuing consular post abroad. Every Consulate has developed its own procedures and methods for E visa issuance within the framework of the Department of State's published rules. Even within a particular consular district, each officer may require a different kind of documentation and utilize different standards to determine visa eligibility. As a practical consideration, applicants should be informed and prepared for the particular requirements at the Consulate adjudicating their application. Furthermore, because most E visaholders travel and require visas, the rules and procedures of the Department of State usually have a more significant impact on the E nonimmigrant.

In order to qualify for E classification the applicant must be entering the United States individually or as the qualified employee of a company as either an:

- **E-1 Treaty Trader**: Solely to carry on **substantial trade**, including trade in services or trade in technology, principally between the United States and the foreign state of which the applicant is a national; or

- **E-2 Treaty Investor**: Solely to develop and direct the operations of a bona fide enterprise in which the applicant has invested a **substantial amount of capital** or is actively in the process of investing.

The United States has treaty trader relationships with over 40 countries, and treaty investor relationships with over 60 countries. Both E-1 and E-2 visas are available to citizens of many countries including France, Germany, the Netherlands, Japan, Switzerland, the Philippines, the United Kingdom, Thailand and Austria. For a full list of participating countries see the end of this chapter and Appendix C.

Although the United States does not have a treaty agreement with the government of the People's Republic of China, a 1948 Treaty of Friendship, Commerce and Navigation with the Republic of China has not been rescinded and remains in force. Consequently, both types of E visas are available to Nationalist Chinese (Republic of China at Taiwan). Similarly, a treaty with Iran remains in effect although Iran does not currently enjoy diplomatic relations with the United States. In practice, however, under a 1985 executive order Iranian nationals are barred from receiving Treaty Trader (E-1) visas. Under very limited circumstances Iranian nationals are eligible for Treaty Investor (E-2) visas.

Prerequisites for E Classification

- There must be a treaty between the United States and the foreign country providing for such visas (or a specific statutory provision).

- The E applicant must be a national of the treaty country. If the applicant is an employee of a company, the stock of that company must be at least 50% owned by the nationals of the treaty country, either directly or indirectly, who are not permanent residents of the United States.

- Either substantial trade between the United States and the treaty country must be in place (E-1), or substantial investment in the United States must have been made, or be actively in the process of being made (E-2).

The Benefits of E Status

The benefits of E status are substantial. In both the treaty trader and treaty investor categories the E visa can provide some of the benefits that are available to individuals who have lawful permanent resident status in the United States. E visas are generally issued for a five-year period with five-year extensions available at American Consulates or with the Department of State in Washington, D.C. Upon each entry to the United States, E visaholders may be granted stay in E status for a two-year period with extensions available in increments of up to two years. Extensions are normally available without restriction.

Furthermore, if the visaholder travels outside of the United States at least once every two years, there may be no need to apply for status extensions since a new period of two-year authorization is granted upon each new entry that the visaholder makes to the United States. This process virtually enables the visaholder a limitless stay in the United States, provided that the E visaholder continues to meet the requirements necessary to maintain status.

CAVEAT

One important issue to note is that although the primary visaholder may not have the need to extend his status authorization, it is often the case that derivative E visaholders, (i.e. spouses and children) may need to extend their status. This situation occurs when the primary E visaholder travels outside of the United States on business trips, but does so without the family. The family members do not automatically receive the same two-year admission period that the primary holder receives upon re-entry. Therefore, it is important to timely file for extensions for family members who do not travel, to ensure that the visaholder's spouse and children under twenty-one do not inadvertently fall out of status.

Remaining in status is now especially crucial in the face of the penalties created by the Illegal Immigration Reform and Immigrant Responsibility Act of 1996. If the derivative E visaholders overstay E visa status they will be subject to section 222(g) of the INA. Section 222(g) penalizes those who overstay their nonimmigrant status, even by one day, by automatically invalidating their nonimmigrant visa. Except in circumstances of exceptional hardship, a new nonimmigrant visa can only be obtained in the country of nationality.

If the derivative E visaholders fail to realize that they are out of status and remain in the U.S. past the date stamped on the I-94, they will then become subject to the penalties for unlawful presence in the United States. If an alien is unlawfully present in the U.S. for more than 180 days but less than one year, upon departure from the U.S. the alien will be inadmissible for 3 years from the date of departure. If an alien is unlawfully present for one year or more, following departure from the U.S. the alien is inadmissible for 10 years from the date of departure. Note that the bar on re-admission is only triggered after the alien has departed the U.S. This is one of the many traps for the unwary, contained within the immigration laws. For a complete discussion of the penalties and bars for unlawful presence see Chapter Eleven.

Additional Benefits

E nonimmigrants are not required to maintain a foreign residence abroad, however, they must maintain an intention to depart the United States upon expiration or termination of E-1 or E-2 status. Applicants for E classification are permitted to maintain a dual intent by regulation and can not be denied initial admission, change of status, or extension of stay solely on the basis of an approved labor certification application or a filed or approved immigrant visa preference petition, or any other indicia of intent to establish lawful permanent residence.

The applicant's children under twenty-one years of age, as well as the applicant's spouse are entitled to E status regardless of their nationality. Therefore, dependents may be accorded E status even if their nationality is different than that of the primary E visaholder.

One of the major benefits of E status is that the initial two-year admission time period may generally be extended almost without limit. The holder of an E visa is entitled to make an application for admission (subject to any inadmissibility provisions) in order to gain entry to the United States. Therefore, assuming no special problems are present that would lead to a finding of inadmissibility, the E visaholder is normally assured of immediate entry and continued presence in the United States. In fact, the authors of this book have represented clients who have held E visa and status in excess of thirty years. While beyond the scope of this volume, there are usually substantial income tax benefits that motivate a client's decision to maintain long term E status rather than converting to permanent residence.

B. **TREATY TRADER STATUS: E-1 VISA**

In order to be classifiable as a nonimmigrant treaty trader, the corporate or individual applicant bears the burden of proving that the employee will be in the United States to conduct trade of a "substantial" nature between the United States and the home country.

TRADE: Items of trade include, but are not limited to goods, services, international banking, insurance, monies, transportation, communications, data processing, advertising, accounting, design and engineering, management consulting, tourism, technology and its transfer, and some news-gathering activities. Goods are tangible commodities or merchandise having intrinsic value and services are legitimate economic activities that provide other than tangible goods.

The substantiality of the trade required depends on the particular situation. There are no precise rules. Therefore, substantiality is largely a factual determination, determined on a case-by-case basis. It is clear however, that at least over 50% of the activity of the company must be between the United States and the home country. The trade must be international in scope and the trade must include some sort of exchange.

The important factor to be considered is the overall picture and view the transactions in relation to the overall situation, i.e. the market, the number of transactions, the percentage of United States sales, trade worldwide, continued course of trade and the dollar value of the trade. The final rules direct the Department of State and the INS to take into consideration the conditions in the foreign national's home country that may possibly impact the alien's ability to establish substantial trade with the United States.

The substantial trade requirement for treaty trader status classification is not necessarily geared toward ruling out smaller companies from consideration. In fact, proof of numerous transactions, although each may be small in value, may be sufficient to establish a continuing course of international trade. A significant number of smaller transactions will be generally deemed substantial, while one large transaction will generally not be considered sufficient for the purposes of establishing substantiality of trade. What is important is that a constant flow of trade be shown to exist. In fact, one or two large sales of great value during a one-year period may not qualify, while a flow of numerous transactions of lesser total value during the year may be sufficient.

It is also important to bear in mind that companies can be structured with the purpose of qualifying for E-1 Treaty Trader visas. For instance, a large Taiwanese manufacturing and export concern selling 30% of its output to the United States and 40% to other countries would not qualify for E-1 visa issuance. This would be true even if it established an unincorporated branch office in the United States. However, if a United States subsidiary, at least 50% owned by Taiwanese nationals is established, and that company imports at least 51% of its merchandise from Taiwan, Taiwanese employees of that company may qualify for issuance of E-1 visas. What governs is that the foreign trade must be substantial, and the majority of that trade must be between the U.S. and the treaty country

C. TREATY INVESTOR STATUS - E-2 VISA

To qualify for E-2 treaty investor status, the applicant must show that he or she is entering the United States solely to develop and direct the operations of an enterprise in which a substantial amount of capital has been invested or is actively in the process of being invested.

What Constitutes "Investing" or Being "In the Process of Investing"

To prove that the applicant has invested or is in the process of investing in the enterprise, the applicant must show that he or she has control of the funds to be invested. The mere presence of intent to invest or prospective investment arrangements entailing no present commitment will not suffice to prove the requisite investment. Therefore, mere possession of uncommitted funds in a bank account would not qualify. Indebtedness such as mortgage debt or commercial loans secured by the enterprise assets can not be counted toward the investment because the requisite element of risk does not exist.

However, a reasonable amount of cash held in a business bank account or similar fund used for routine business operations may be counted as investment funds. Similarly, loans secured by the applicant's own personal assets, such as a second mortgage on a home, or an unsecured loan guaranteed by applicant's personal signature, may be included since the applicant's funds are at risk in the event of business failure.

The applicant must be close to the start of actual business operations and not merely at the stage of signing contracts or looking for suitable locations or properties. Furthermore, the applicant must show that the investment is "substantial," the enterprise is a real and active commercial or entrepreneurial enterprise that produces some service or commodity for profit, and the enterprise is more than a marginal one established solely for earning a living.

The investment must be substantial in order to entitle the applicant to E-2 Treaty Investor Status.

There is **no set dollar amount** that automatically qualifies as substantial. Under the final rules the INS and the Department of State now define "a substantial amount of capital" as consisting of an amount that is:

- Substantial in relationship to the total cost of either purchasing an established entity or creating the type of enterprise under consideration;

- Sufficient to ensure the treaty investor's financial commitment to the successful operation of the enterprise under consideration; and

- Of a magnitude to support the likelihood that the treaty investor will successfully develop and direct the enterprise. Generally, the lower the cost of the enterprise, the higher proportionality the investment must be to be considered a substantial amount of capital.

This definition codifies the existing "proportionality test." The proportionality test weighed the amount invested against either the total value of the particular enterprise in question or the amount normally considered necessary to establish a viable enterprise of the nature contemplated.

In assessing the amount normally required to establish a particular enterprise, the consular officer must draw upon his or her personal knowledge of the United States business scene to determine whether the amount the applicant proposes to invest is reasonable to that type of business. If the consular officer is in doubt, he or she may seek additional evidence to help establish a reasonable amount. Additional evidence can include letters from Chambers of Commerce or statistics from trade associations.

The definition set out in the final rules is meant to be flexible and is not geared toward excluding small businesses. In fact, many E-2 visas involve relatively small investments. In the case of small to medium-sized businesses market, "substantial" generally means an investment of more than half the value of the enterprise, or an amount normally considered necessary to establish an enterprise.

In some instances, the dollar amount of an investment may be so great as to warrant issuance of E-2 visas even though the investment is not a large proportion of the total value of the enterprise. This can be the situation when a large foreign corporation, capable of multi-million dollar capital transactions, invests in an enterprise in the United States and seeks to dispatch managerial and essential employees to that enterprise.

The meaning of the term "investment" for treaty investor purposes is the placing of funds or other capital assets at risk in the commercial sense in the hope of generating a return on the funds risked. The treaty investor must be in possession of and have control over the capital invested or being invested. If the funds are not subject to partial or total loss, it is not an investment for treaty investor purposes. The applicant has the burden of establishing that the investment is irrevocably committed. However, the final rules explicitly allow the use of any legal mechanism available, including the use of escrowed funds, to protect the investor's funds pending admission in, or approval of, E classification and protecting the investor in case of denial.

The Applicant Must Show That the Enterprise is More Than Marginal

A marginal enterprise is an enterprise that does not have the present or future capacity to generate income over and above the amount needed to provide a minimal living for the treaty investor and his or her family.

The final rules state that an enterprise will not be considered marginal even if at the time of investment it does not have the capability of generating more than minimal income, if it can be shown that it's future income-generating capacity will be generally realizable within five years from the date the enterprise begins. The burden is on the applicant to demonstrate that the enterprise has the capability of becoming a viable entity within five years. This may be demonstrated by the presentation of a credible business plan.

D. COMPANY REQUIREMENTS FOR E-1 TREATY TRADER AND E-2 TREATY INVESTOR CLASSIFICATIONS

In order for a company to qualify for E-1/E-2 treaty trader or investor classification, the applicant must show that the company is 50% owned by a person or persons who are nationals of the treaty country.

In Parent/Subsidiary Relationships the nationality of the corporation that will directly employ the applicant is the key factor in determining whether a company may qualify for E classification. The place of incorporation of the company is not relevant. For example, if a company is French-owned (50% owned by French nationals), the fact that the company's place of incorporation is in the Grand Cayman Islands will have no bearing on the E application in determining whether the requisite element of nationality is met. However, company ownership will be traced back through holding companies, and the ultimate stockholders must be at least 50% nationals of the treaty country. Shares of a business owned by United States permanent residents (green card holders) cannot be considered in making determinations of majority ownership by nationals of the treaty country.

In many countries, the American Consulate keeps a separate folder on each company and keeps track on how many E visas are issued to that company. In general, there is a great concern about the number of individuals sent to the United States and the incidence of visa fraud. The consular officer may require that once a certain level of staffing is reached, new employees be sent only as replacements rather than as initial E-1/E-2 Treaty Trader or Treaty Investor Employees. It is also important that the United States company hire sufficient United States employees.

If the company in question is a publicly traded company where actual names and percentage of ownership are difficult to determine, the firm's nationality is presumed to be that of the country in which the firm's stock is principally listed and traded on the stock exchange.

E. HOW TO QUALIFY AS AN EMPLOYEE OF A TREATY TRADER OR TREATY INVESTOR COMPANY

Although many treaty traders and investors are self-employed individuals carrying on their own businesses, the vast majority of applicants tend to be employees of large companies who are being dispatched to United States. In order to qualify for an E visa, it must be demonstrated that:

- The employee is or will be engaged in duties of an executive or supervisory character, or

- The employee has special qualifications that make the services to be rendered essential to the efficient operation of the enterprise.

Although, the final rules eliminated the terms "manager" and "managerial" from the description of authorized employees of treaty traders and investors, employees who are titled managers or who perform managerial skills may still qualify for E-1 and E-2 classification.

When assessing the supervisory or executive nature of the position, the factors to be considered are:

- Whether the executive position is one that provides the employee with great authority to determine the policy of, and the direction for the enterprise;

- Whether a position of supervisory character provides the employee supervisory responsibility for a significant proportion of an enterprise's operations and does not generally involve the direct supervision of low-level employees, and;

- Whether the applicant possesses executive and

supervisory skills and experience; a salary and position title commensurate with executive or supervisory employment; recognition or indicia of the position as one of authority and responsibility in the overall organizational structure; responsibility for making discretionary decisions, setting policies, directing and managing business operations, supervising other professional and supervisory personnel; and that, if the position requires some routine work usually performed by a staff employee, such functions may only be incidental in nature.

The size and nature of the organization will determine the significance of the title concerned. For example, the title of "Executive Vice President" or "Department Supervisor" might be of use in assessing the supervisory nature of a position if the applicant is coming to a major operation having numerous employees. However, if the applicant is coming to a small two-person office, such a title in and of itself would be of little significance in determining whether the applicant's position is supervisory or executive in nature.

Furthermore, in order to qualify for E status, the applicant must show that the executive and supervisory duties are the employee's principal and primary function, and not an incidental or collateral function. It is also important to bear in mind that the staffing levels must be proportionate, i.e. the staff should not be composed of all E-1/E-2 managers without any local staff. In light of the increasing popularity of E status classification, qualifications for E status are strictly construed. It is generally easier for someone at a higher level in an organization to qualify for E status than it is for someone who is not highly placed within a corporation.

Applicants seeking visas as employees of treaty trader companies must normally apply for their visas at the appropriate Consulate having jurisdiction over their place of residence, regardless of where the treaty trader company visa was initially established. However, certain posts, including most of the U.S. consulates in Canada and Mexico will often entertain out-of-district cases for applicants present in the United States.

Employees With Essential Skills

In the event that the applicant seeking E visa classification for a treaty trader or investor employee will not perform duties of an executive or supervisory nature, they may nonetheless be accorded E visa classification if the applicant can show that they possesses special qualifications, and the services to be rendered are essential to the efficient operation of the enterprise.

In order to demonstrate that the employee possesses essential skills, the applicant must show that the employee possesses special qualifications that are needed by the E-1 or E-2 treaty trader or investor organization. Such knowledge must be demonstrated to be generally unavailable in the United States to support the assertion that United States workers are unavailable for the position. The company must also show how the E applicant will eventually train United States workers to perform this function. In addition, the visa application on behalf of an essential employee must specify the amount of time that the applicant's skills will be required.

In such instances, highly trained and specially qualified technicians may be employed by E-1 or E-2 firms to train or supervise personnel employed in manufacturing, maintenance and repair functions, even though these employees may perform some manual duties.

In the case of highly trained technicians there is the presumption that they will train United States workers in a reasonable period of time to replace the foreign technicians. If the treaty trader or investor company continually requests visas for foreign technicians, the consular officer will remind them of their obligation to train United States workers and will view the absence of a training program for United States workers as a negative factor in examining future visa applications for technicians.

It is important to note that the possession of language skills alone is not normally considered a special qualification to qualify as an essential employee of a treaty visa holder. An essential skill employee is not required to be currently working for the treaty employer but may have obtained the requisite skills with another employer.

E-2 Employees Considered Essential For Start-up Enterprises

In the instance of E-2 employees of treaty investors who will engage in starting up the treaty investor's enterprise in the United States, the essentiality of their services derives from their familiarity with the overseas operations of the treaty organization rather than from the nature of their skills. This factor is unique to E-2 employees and usually applies where an established foreign firm seeks to use some skilled foreign personnel in the early stages of a United States investment, usually for a period not to exceed one or two years.

Spouse and Children of Treaty Trader or Treaty Investor

Spouses and minor children are entitled to accompany or follow to join E visaholders and are accorded the same status as the primary E visaholder. The nationality of a spouse or child of an E treaty visaholder is not material to E classification. Family members are authorized to attend school without the need to make any change in their nonimmigrant status.

E derivative visaholders are not authorized to work. If E derivative visaholders do accept unauthorized employment in the United States they will not be subject to removal, unlike the family members of other types of nonimmigrant workers who work without authorization. Although not subject to removal, working without authorization will make the E derivative visaholder ineligible to adjust status to that of a lawful permanent resident.

Traveling with an E Visa

Each time the E visaholder departs the United States (other than to a contiguous country), the carrier is required to collect the visaholder's I-94 Form (Arrival/Departure Record) for submission to the INS. Upon a new entry to the United States, the E visaholder will present their visa to the Immigration Inspector and receive a new I-94. The new I-94 will generally reflect a new two-year period of E status authorization regardless of whether the former two-year period for which the visaholder was previously authorized had expired. As previously mentioned, this is one of the major benefits of E status, since travel abroad and return to the United States automatically triggers a new two-year period of admission without any other effort required on the part of the visaholder.

Travel to Canada and Mexico from the United States for less than a 30 day time period will generally **NOT** enable the applicant to receive a new two-year extension, unlike the situation where the visaholder is traveling abroad and then re-entering the United States. This occurs because upon departure to Canada or Mexico the applicant generally retains the original I-94 (Arrival and Departure Record). Furthermore, Immigration Inspectors at the Canadian and Mexican border are often reluctant to issue a new I-94 when there is any time remaining on the existing I-94.

F. HOW TO FILE AN APPLICATION FOR AN E VISA WITH THE AMERICAN CONSULATE: ORGANIZATIONS AND INDIVIDUALS

Documentation Required for Employee of Treaty Trader or Treaty Investor

The following represents the type of documentation often necessary for submission of an E visa application for an employee of a treaty trader or treaty investor. Again, the specific requirements will vary from Consulate to Consulate. In order for the application to be acceptable, the treaty trader or investor must be in E status as evidenced by the submission of the requisite company documentation.

1) Passport
2) Form OF-156E (E Nonimmigrant Visa Application)
3) Form OF-156 (Nonimmigrant Visa Application)
4) Photograph of the applicant
3) Employee Profile
4) Recommendation Letter (In support of Employee Profile)
5) For dependents - A copy of principal alien's visa or I-94 (Arrival Departure Record)

Each Consulate has their own requirements for supporting documentation and often produces their own intake forms. For example, the Consulates in Japan require that the applicant fill out a Form issued by the Consulate, which requires a "Company Profile," and is especially concerned with the structure and hierarchy of the company.

Required Supporting Documents

The following items represent the type of supporting documents which may be submitted in order to establish a company's qualification for either E-1 or E-2 visa classification.

Detailed company report on the nature of the business, current and projected investment and other business plans, current and planned employment of foreign and United States citizens, ties to United States corporations etc.

- Foreign Exchange License from a foreign bank, if any, and evidence of remittances.

- Evidence of establishment of United States company or branch office:
  - Certificate/Articles of Incorporation
  - Business License

- Evidence of Actual trade between the United States company or office and the foreign country. The submission of invoices, letters of credit, bills of lading and correspondence showing trading activity may be used as evidence.

- Evidence of investment in the United States. This may be shown by submitting proof of purchase of capital goods and inventory, lease or purchase of property contracts, construction contracts, blueprints, property valuations, photographs of building sites, and newspaper reports on new business ventures.

- Evidence of the applicant company's business volume in the United States. This can be established by submission of the company's balance sheet, orders for goods shipped or awaiting shipment and by providing copies of the company's tax returns.

- The foreign company's annual report.

- Organizational Charts for both the United States and foreign companies.

SAMPLE FORM OF-156E

*ESTIMATED BURDEN: 2 HOURS

NONIMMIGRANT TREATY TRADER/INVESTOR VISA APPLICATION
SUPPLEMENT TO FORM OF-156

(USE ADDITIONAL SHEETS OF PAPER, AS NECESSARY, TO COMPLETE RESPONSES)

PART I - BUSINESS PROFILE

1. NAME OF U.S. ENTERPRISE, BUSINESS, OR COMPANY

Black Enterprises, Inc.

2. TYPE OF BUSINESS ENTERPRISE:

☒ Corporation ☐ Branch/Liaison Office ☐ Partnership
☐ Privately owned ☐ Joint Venture ☐ Subsidiary ☐ Other ______

3. ADDRESS OF HEADQUARTERS, SUBSIDIARIES AND BRANCH OFFICES OF U.S. ENTERPRISE *(Specify type of office)*

Headquarters

1 Bleeker Lane
London, UA3 5HY
United Kingdom

4. DATE AND PLACE BUSINESS WAS ESTABLISHED OR INCORPORATED IN UNITED STATES *(Attach appropriate documentation; e.g., corporate paper, partnership agreement, etc.)*

State of Delaware
July 5, 1998

5. WHAT IS THE NATURE OF THE BUSINESS?

☐ General Trade ☐ Exports from U.S. ☐ Retail Sales ☐ Other *(describe)*
☐ Imports to U.S. ☐ Manufacturing ☒ Services/Technology

6. DESCRIBE FULLY THE SERVICES, PRODUCTION, OR OTHER ACTIVITY IN NO. 5 ABOVE.

Corporation owns and operates Victoria's Inn.
Full service hotel and luxurious accommodations located in New York City.

7. NAME AND ADDRESS OF FOREIGN PARENT BUSINESS *(If any)*

8. NATIONALITY OF FOREIGN ENTITY *(Corporation, Partnership, etc.)* OR FOREIGN INDIVIDUAL OWNER OF U.S. BUSINESS *(Attach documentation)*.

NAME	NATIONALITY	IF INDIVIDUAL INVESTOR IMMIGRATION STATUS/ COUNTRY OF RESIDENCE	PERCENT OF OWNERSHIP
Victoria Black	British	United Kingdom	75%
			Total - 100%

9. FINANCIAL STATEMENT FOR YEAR 1998 . ☐ CALENDAR YEAR ☒ FISCAL YEAR *(Attach most recent financial statement or auditor's report)*

	Before Taxes		After Taxes
Total Assets of U.S. Business	$ 2,203,224.00	☒ Current Cash	☐ Historical Cost
Total Liabilities:	$ 890,000.00		
Owner's Equity:*	$ 2,190,000.00		
Total Annual Operating Income:	$ 2,000,000.00		$ 950,000.00

* Owner's equity of a corporation refers to paid-in capital plus retained earnings; partners capital accounts in a partnership; and owner's capital account in a sole proprietorship.

PREVIOUS EDITIONS OBSOLETE

OPTIONAL FORM 156E (Rev. 5-94)
DEPT. OF STATE

SAMPLE FORM OF-156E (CONTINUED)

10. To measure the amount of international trade with the United States, please complete the following. (For trade in merchandise, exports and imports, refer to shipment and sale of goods across international boundaries. For trade in services and technology, exports and imports, refer to the sale of services by treaty-country nationals to nationals of the United States and other countries)

Gross International Trade of the U.S. Enterprise in ________ (year): ☐ Calendar Year ☐ Fiscal Year Ending ____________

	DOLLAR VALUE	NO. OF TRANSACTIONS (Optional)	PERCENT OF TOTAL TRADE
Imports from treaty country to U.S. business	$		
Exports from U.S. business to treaty country	$		
Imports from third countries to U.S. business	$		
Exports from United States to third countries	$		
Domestic trade (items bought and sold in U.S.)	$		
Domestic U.S. production/manufacturing	$		
Total:	$		100%

11. TYPE OF INVESTMENT *(Check one)*

☐ Creation of a new business ☐ Purchase of an existing business ☒ Continuation of an existing business

12. TOTAL INVESTMENT FROM ABROAD MADE IN THE UNITED STATES *(Attach documentation)*

FOR YEAR 1998 ☐ Calendar ☒ Fiscal

	ANNUAL INVESTMENT	TOTAL CUMULATIVE INVESTMENT
Cash:	$ 950,000.00	$ 2,450,000.00
Inventory:	$	$
Equipment:	$	$
Premises:	$	$
Other	$	$
TOTAL:	$ 950,000.00	$ 2,450,000.00

13. SOURCE OF INVESTMENT CAPITAL *(personal funds, corporate funds, loans, stocks, debentures, bonds, etc.)*; EVIDENCE OF POSSESSION AND CONTROL OF FUNDS IN THE UNITED STATES *(Attach full documentation; see instructions.)*

PART II - STAFF

14. TYPE OF PERSONNEL IN THE UNITED STATES *(attach staffing chart)*

Specify: ☐ Calendar Year ☐ Fiscal Year

	MANAGERIAL/ EXECUTIVE		SPECIALIZED ESSENTIAL		ALL OTHER EMPLOYEES	
	This Year	Next Year	This Year	Next Year	This Year	Next Year
Nationals of Treaty Country on E, H, and L Visas:						
U.S. Citizens and Legal Permanent Residents:						
Other (Third- Country Nationals):						
TOTAL:						

15. List all personnel of the U.S. business holding executive, managerial and/or specialist positions by subsidiary/branch office. If aliens, indicate nonimmigrant visa status or permanent resident (LPR) status.

NAME AND POSITION/TITLE/DIVISION	NATIONALITY	U.S. VISA TYPE	DATE	PLACE OF ISSUANCE

SAMPLE FORM OF-156E (CONTINUED)

PART III APPLICANT

16. NAME OF APPLICANT

(Family Name)	*(First Name)*	*(Middle Name)*
Black	Victoria	

17. TYPE OF APPLICANT

☒ Principal owner/investor/trader ☐ Supervisor ☐ Specialist
☐ Manager ☐ Executive ☐ Other________

18. PRESENT POSITION AND DUTIES *(Describe in detail)*
Hotel Manager
Oversee and direct management of Victoria's Inn.

19. NAME AND ADDRESS OF EMPLOYER
Black Enterprises, Inc. 1 Bleeker Lane, London, United Kingdom

20. YEARS WITH PRESENT EMPLOYER
25

21. HIGHEST LEVEL OF EDUCATION
School: Major/Subject: Degree: Year:
Suffolk University , Mathematics, Bachelor's Degree, 1973

22. OTHER RELEVANT EXPERIENCE AND EDUCATION *(Attach curriculum vitae - Optional)*

23. POSITION IN UNITED STATES Title: Hotel Manger
Description of duties (include names and titles of all immediate subordinates):

24. ANNUAL U.S. SALARY AND BENEFIT PACKAGE
$ 350,000 Salary
$ ______ Allowances/Benefits
$ 350,000 TOTAL

25. NAME OF PERSON IN UNITED STATES BEING REPLACED: ______

Type of Visa: ______
Date issued: ______
Place issued: ______

If NOT a replacement, is this:
a. An increase in staff? ☒ Yes ☐ No
b. Continuation of existing employment in the United States? ☐ Yes ☐ No

26. IF THE APPLICANT IS A SPECIALIST OR ESSENTIAL SKILLED WORKER, CAN A U.S. WORKER FILL THIS POSITION? *(NOTE: Questions 26-28 not applicable to executives/managers)*
☐ Yes ☐ No IF NO, WHY NOT?

27. WILL A U.S. WORKER BE TRAINED TO REPLACE THIS INDIVIDUAL?
☒ Yes ☐ No

28. DESCRIBE THE BUSINESS PRESENT OR PLANNED TRAINING PROGRAM FOR U.S. SPECIALISTS AND ESSENTIAL PERSONNEL

29. I do solemnly swear or affirm that all statements which appear in this application and attachments are true and complete to the best of my knowledge and belief.

______	______	/ /
Signature of Responsible Officer	*Printed Name and Position or Office*	*Date*

30. NAME AND ADDRESS OF PERSON WHO MAY BE CONTACTED ABOUT THIS APPLICATION

Telephone:

FAX:

SAMPLE FORM OF-156

PLEASE TYPE OR PRINT YOUR ANSWERS IN THE SPACE PROVIDED BELOW EACH ITEM.

1. SURNAMES OR FAMILY NAMES *(Exactly as in Passport)*
Black

2. FIRST NAME AND MIDDLE NAME *(Exactly as in Passport)*
Victoria

3. OTHER NAMES *(Maiden, Religious, Professional, Aliases)*
N/A

4. DATE OF BIRTH *(Day, Month, Year)*
17/8/55

8. PASSPORT NUMBER
1234123-00

5. PLACE OF BIRTH
City, Province: Leeds
Country: England

DATE PASSPORT ISSUED *(Day, Month, Year)*
5/7/98

6. NATIONALITY
British

7. SEX
☐ Male
☒ Female

DATE PASSPORT EXPIRES *(Day, Month, Year)*
5/7/04

9. HOME ADDRESS *(Include apartment no., street, city, province, and postal zone)*
18 St. James Place, London, United Kingdom

10. NAME AND STREET ADDRESS OF PRESENT EMPLOYER OR SCHOOL *(Postal box number unacceptable)*
Black Enterprises
1 Bleeker Lane, London, United Kingdom

11. HOME TELEPHONE NO.
044-234-2345

12. BUSINESS TELEPHONE NO.
044-123-1234

13. COLOR OF HAIR
Blonde

14. COLOR OF EYES
Green

15. COMPLEXION
Fair

16. HEIGHT
170cm.

17. MARKS OF IDENTIFICATION
N/A

18. MARITAL STATUS
☐ Married ☒ Single ☐ Widowed ☐ Divorced ☐ Separated
If married, give name and nationality of spouse.

19. NAMES AND RELATIONSHIPS OF PERSONS TRAVELING WITH YOU(NOTE: *A separate application must be made for a visa for each traveler, regardless of age.)*
N/A

20. HAVE YOU EVER APPLIED FOR A U.S. VISA BEFORE, WHETHER IMMIGRANT OR NONIMMIGRANT?
☐ No
☒ Yes Where? London, UK
When? 1992, 1997 Type of visa? B-1
☒ Visa was issued ☐ Visa was refused

21. HAS YOUR U.S. VISA EVER BEEN CANCELED?
☒ No
☐ Yes Where? ____________
When? ____________ By whom? ____________

22. Bearers of visitors visas may generally not work or study in the U.S.
DO YOU INTEND TO WORK IN THE U.S.? ☐ No ☒ Yes
If YES, explain.
Pursuant to E-2 status

23. DO YOU INTEND TO STUDY IN THE U.S.? ☒ No ☐ Yes
If YES, write name and address of school as it appears on form I-20.

DO NOT WRITE IN THIS SPACE

B-1/B-2 MAX B-1 MAX B-2 MAX

OTHER____________MAX
Visa Classification

MULT OR ____________
Number Applications

MONTHS____________
Validity

L.O. CHECKED ____________

ISSUED /REFUSED

ON____________ BY ____________

UNDER SEC.____________ INA

REFUSAL REVIEWED BY ____________

MRV# ____________

24. PRESENT OCCUPATION *(If retired, state past occupation)*
Hotel Manager

25. WHO WILL FURNISH FINANCIAL SUPPORT INCLUDING TICKETS?
myself

26. AT WHAT ADDRESS WILL YOU STAY IN THE U.S.A.? *(City and State)*
1 Fifth Avenue, New York, New York

27. WHAT IS THE PURPOSE OF YOUR TRIP?
E-2 Employment

28. WHEN DO YOU INTEND TO ARRIVE IN THE U.S.A.?
as soon as possible

29. HOW LONG DO YOU PLAN TO STAY IN THE U.S.A.?
3 years

30. HAVE YOU EVER BEEN IN THE U.S.A.?
☐ No
☒ Yes When? 12/92 -3/93
For how long? 5/97-10/97

NONIMMIGRANT VISA APPLICATION

COMPLETE ALL QUESTIONS ON REVERSE OF FORM

OPTIONAL FORM 156 (REV. 6/96) PAGE 1 50156-106
Department of State

SAMPLE FORM OF-156 (CONTINUED)

31. (a) HAVE YOU OR ANYONE ACTING FOR YOU EVER INDICATED TO A U.S. CONSULAR OR IMMIGRATION EMPLOYEE A DESIRE TO IMMIGRATE TO THE U.S.? (b)HAS ANYONE EVER FILED AN IMMIGRANT VISA PETITION ON YOUR BEHALF?(c) HAS LABOR CERTIFICATION FOR EMPLOYMENT IN THE U.S. EVER BEEN REQUESTED BY YOU OR ON YOUR BEHALF?

(a) ☒ No ☐ Yes (b) ☒ No ☐ Yes (c) ☒ No ☐ Yes

32. ARE ANY OF THE FOLLOWING IN THE U.S.? (X) NO ( ) YES (If YES, circle appropriate relationship and indicate that person's status in the U.S., i.e., studying, working, U.S. permanent resident, U.S. citizen, etc.)

HUSBAND/WIFE________ FIANCE/FIANCEE ________ BROTHER/SISTER ________

FATHER/MOTHER________ SON/DAUGHTER ________

33. PLEASE LIST THE COUNTRIES WHERE YOU HAVE LIVED FOR MORE THAN 6 MONTHS DURING THE PAST 5 YEARS BEGIN WITH YOUR PRESENT RESIDENCE.

Countries	Cities	Approximate Dates
England	London	1970-Present

34. IMPORTANT: ALL APPLICANTS MUST READ AND CHECK THE APPROPRIATE BOX FOR EACH ITEM.

A visa may not be issued to persons who are within specific categories defined by law as inadmissible to the United States (except when a waiver is obtained in advance). Are any of the following applicable to you?

- Have you ever been afflicted with a communicable disease of public health significance, a dangerous physical or mental disorder, or been a drug abuser or addict? ☐ Yes ☒ No
- Have you ever been arrested or convicted for any offense or crime, even though subject of a pardon, amnesty, or other such legal action? ☐ Yes ☒ No
- Have You ever been a controlled substance (drug) trafficker, or a prostitute or procurer? ☐ Yes ☒ No
- Have you ever sought to obtain or assist others to obtain a visa, entry into the U.S., or any U.S. Immigration benefit by fraud or willful misrepresentation? ☐ Yes ☒ No
- Were you deported from the U.S.A. within the last 5 years? ☐ Yes ☒ No
- Do you seek to enter the United States to engage in export control violations, subversive or terrorist activities, or any unlawful purpose? ☐ Yes ☒ No
- Have you ever ordered, incited, assisted, or otherwise participated in the persecution of any person because of race, religion, national origin, or political opinion under the control, direct or indirect, of the Nazi Government of Germany, or of the government of any area occupied by, or allied with, the Nazi Government of Germany; or have you ever participated in genocide? ☐ Yes ☒ No
- Have you ever voted in the U.S.A. in violation of law? ☐ Yes ☒ No
- Are you a former U.S. Citizen who renounced citizenship after 09/30/1996 to avoid taxation? ☐ Yes ☒ No
- Are you a member or representative of a terrorist organization? ☐ Yes ☒ No

A YES answer does not automatically signify ineligibility for a visa, but if you answered YES to any of the above, or if you have any question in this regard, personal appearance at this office is recommended. If appearance is not possible at this time, attach a statement of facts in your case to this application.

35. I certify that I have read and understood all the questions set forth in this application and the answers I have furnished on this form are true and correct to the best of my knowledge and belief. I understand that any false or misleading statement may result in the permanent refusal of a visa or denial of entry into the United States. I understand that possession of a visa does not entitle the bearer to enter the United States of America upon arrival at port of entry if he or she is found inadmissible.

DATE OF APPLICATION ________

APPLICANT'S SIGNATURE________

If this application has been prepared by a travel agency or another person on your behalf, the agent should indicate name and address of agency or person with appropriate signature of individual preparing form.

SIGNATURE OF PERSON PREPARING FORM
(if other than applicant) ________

DO NOT WRITE IN THIS SPACE

37 mm x 37 mm

PHOTO

Glue photo here

SAMPLE LETTER OF E-2 VISA APPLICATION TO AMERICAN CONSUL

American Consulate
London, England

RE: **E-2 Nonimmigrant Visa Application of Victoria Black**

Dear Sir/Madam:

I am writing this letter in support of my application for an E-2 Treaty Investor Visa. Kindly be advised as follows:

I am an English national, and the majority owner of Black Enterprises Inc., a United States corporation. I have made a substantial investment in Black Enterprises Inc., in the United States. Further, I have substantial capital for the investment and absolute control of the company by virtue of my majority ownership. Black Enterprises Inc. has recorded total assets of $2,203,244.00

Black Enterprises Inc. was incorporated in the State of Delaware on July 5, 1988. There are currently 100 shares issued and outstanding of which I own seventy-five percent. I enclose as proof of my ownership, copies of issued corporate stock certificates, attorney's letter summarizing ownership of Black Enterprises Inc. and Certificate of Incorporation and Filing Receipt of Black Enterprises Inc.

The corporation owns and operates Victoria's Inn located at 1 Fifth Avenue, New York, New York. Victoria's Inn is a hotel modeled after British Victorian style hotels. In 1997, the Inn underwent complete renovations and remodeling.

I have made a substantial investment in Black Enterprises Inc. and expect substantial future profits and continued expansion. To date, over $1.5 million has been invested. This sum represents the total amount necessary to establish a viable enterprise. I enclose an accounting statement and bank statements together with numerous invoices and canceled checks as evidence of this investment.

I have provided for all of the capital contributions and will continue to make additional capital contributions as required by the company. I have already transferred an additional $950,000 to Black Enterprises' U.S. bank account, for prospective additional capital expenditures. These funds are my own and are within my possession and control. There is no question that these funds have been placed at risk, and subject to potential or total loss, should the venture not be successful.

The investment is more than a marginal one solely for earning a living. My investments are listed in the personal financial statement that I attach herewith. I am not relying on the anticipated profits from this investment in the U.S. to support my other business ventures or myself.

A suitable location was carefully chosen for Victoria's Inn to ensure adequate space and client volume. There has been major redesigning and reconstruction of the entire building, indicating a bona fide commitment by myself to the success of this venture. All municipal regulations and requirements have been adhered to.

In addition to the basic requirements of the enterprise, I have undertaken considerable expense to enhance the appearance and quality of Victoria's Inn. The interior decorating was completed with numerous authentic materials imported from England. Genuine commitment to quality was necessary in order for the hotel to successfully compete in the affluent New York market. I am attaching photographs and blueprints to my submission.

Under my supervision and control, Victoria's Inn is expected to be a landmark on the New York horizon. I have worked in the hotel business in London for the past twenty years. My experience and expert skill are essential for the proper management and quality control of the enterprise. It is essential that I be present and actively participating in the running of this hotel.

I have committed time, money, and above all, my professional reputation to the positive outcome of this investment. I am in a position to develop and direct the enterprise as the owner of 75% of all outstanding stock.

I intend to depart from the United States when my investment ends, or when my status otherwise terminates. My ties and business holdings in England remain intact and I will be returning to England upon completion of this investment enterprise.

On the basis of the information now submitted, it is respectfully requested that my E-2 visa petition be approved. Thank you for your expeditious processing of this matter.

Very truly yours,

Victoria Black
President & General Manager
Black Enterprises Inc.

SAMPLE LETTER OF UNITED STATES COMPANY ON BEHALF OF APPLICANT

American Institute in Taiwan
Taipei, Taiwan

Re: E-1 Application of Li Electronic Inc. on behalf of Da-Yuen Lee

Dear Sir or Madam:

This letter is submitted in support of the above-captioned E-1 visa application for Mr. Da-Yuen Lee, to enable him to accept a temporary position in an executive capacity with Li Electronic Inc. Mr. Lee seeks an E-1 visa to be employed temporarily by Li Electronic Inc. on the basis of a management position and as an essential employee.

Li Electronic Inc. is a New York Corporation established in 1980 as a wholly owned subsidiary of Chang Corp. of Taiwan. Chang Corp, founded in 1950, is one of the world's largest comprehensive semiconductor producers and distributors with subsidiary affiliations in over 200 locations throughout the world. Li Electronic Inc. qualifies as a trading company under the provisions of the treaty of commerce and navigation between the United States and Taiwan. We are engaged in substantial trade between the United States and Taiwan representing eighty-five percent of our total international trade.

Mr. Lee is an integral member of Chang Corp., whose responsibilities include settling the consolidated accounts of the Chang Group, including our 200 subsidiaries. We have decided to replace Mr. Chiu Ho, the current Treasurer of Li Electronic Inc., with Mr. Lee, as he possesses the requisite executive experience as well as the advanced knowledge of our customized management systems.

His duties will include full responsibility for all-around functions, annual accounts, monthly accounts, budgeting, financing, billing, collection and tax arrangement.

Mr. Lee is eminently qualified for the position of Treasurer. In August 1982, Mr. Lee joined the Chang Group in Taiwan immediately following his graduation from the Wharton School of Business where he was awarded a Masters in Accounting.

Given the increased complexity of our accounting management system and our utilization of a network of over thirty personal computers, we are in need of an experienced individual who has extensive training and skill.

Li Electronic Inc. has no other employee who can effectively perform in this position and it is for this reason that we seek to employ the executive services of Mr. Lee for a temporary period of five years at a salary of $150,000 per year.

We trust that you will give Mr. Lee's application prompt consideration.

Very truly yours,

Wai Yin Leung
Vice President and General Manager

SAMPLE LETTER FROM FOREIGN COMPANY TO BE SUBMITTED TO UNITED STATES CONSULATE

US Embassy
Nonimmigrant Visa Unit
Tokyo, Japan

Re: **E-1 Application of Nippon Kaisha Inc. on Behalf of OGAWA, Masahiro**

Dear Sir or Madam:

This letter is submitted in support of the application for an E-1 visa by Mr. Masahiro Ogawa to assume temporary employment as Treasurer of Nippon Kaisha, our wholly owned subsidiary in the United States. Mr. Ogawa will succeed Mr. Takashi Suzuki who has been in this capacity since April 1990 in E-1 status.

The E-1 Organization

Nippon Kaisha Inc. is a New York corporation that was established in 1980 as our sales representative and wholly owned subsidiary of Yamada Corp. of Japan.

Yamada Corp, founded in 1950, is one of the world's largest comprehensive producers and distributors of semiconductors. The Yamada Group employs over 30,000 individuals worldwide, and has annual sales in excess of $15 billion. The U.S. subsidiary now employs a total of approximately 300 individuals, including local managers in sales offices located in New York, Boston, San Diego and San Francisco.

The transferee, Mr. Ogawa, will undertake a temporary assignment in the New York Office of Nippon Kaisha. He is currently employed by Nippon Kaisha's parent organization, Yamada Corp. of Japan.

The Executive Nature of the Position

The executive position that we are sponsoring Mr. Ogawa for is a key position in our organization. The Treasurer operates independently and is directly responsible for the preparation of all the critical financial documents required in a diversified enterprise such as our own. In his capacity as Treasurer, Mr. Ogawa will be required to manage five assistants as well as interact and advise managerial and executive staff concerning appropriate tax and financial strategies. Attached please find an organizational chart detailing the corporate structure of our New York Office. You will note that Mr. Ogawa will be replacing Mr. Suzuki, who has been employed in E-1 capacity since April 1990.

This position also requires specialized knowledge of Yamada's Japanese operations, products and systems. As a result of the remarkable change and expansion in the company's business, the Treasurer's responsibilities have increased and become more diversified in many respects.

To insure greater production and efficiency we have designed a special computer network that has been custom-made to meet the particular needs of our multinational conglomerate. Mr. Ogawa has been specially trained in the optimal use of this system. In addition, Mr. Ogawa possesses intimate knowledge of our clientele and the nature of their transactions.

The Treasurer is responsible for general accounting duties including annual accounts, monthly accounts, budgeting, financing, billing, collection and tax arrangements. Given the increased complexities of our accounting management, the Treasurer is required to have a great deal of skill and experience so that he may exercise proper judgement in areas reserved exclusively to his discretion.

Mr. Ogawa has acquired vast experience as a result of seventeen years with Yamada Corp. His familiarity with the internal and external accounting procedures of Yamada Corp is unsurpassed. It is this unique knowledge that is essential to satisfy the stringent requirements of the position.

Yamada Corp. is a leader in its field because of its commitment to excellence through its well-trained employees. Only a professional with distinctive and unique knowledge derived from years of experience in key positions within our organization will be suitable to fill the vacant position. The proposed transfer of Mr. Ogawa satisfies our goals in filling the open position with an executive-level employee that has specialized knowledge in our systems, products and clientele.

The Applicant

To successfully perform the duties of this position it is necessary for the applicant to possess a Bachelor's degree in commerce and significant experience with internal and external accounting procedure of Yamada Corp.

Mr. Ogawa is currently a key employee of our organization in Japan acting as the Senior Assistant Manager of the Accounts Settlements Section, (Accounting Division). In this capacity, he is responsible for settling the consolidated accounts of the Yamada Group, composed of 200 subsidiaries as a single economic entity.

Mr. Ogawa graduated from the renowned Sophia University in March 1981, where he received the U.S. equivalent of a Bachelor's degree in Commerce. Thereafter, he joined Yamada Corp., to work in the Accounting Department. After completing a full study of Yamada's accounting procedures, he was transferred to the accounting section for semiconductor parts where for three years he focussed on accounts receivable.

In 1983, he was then transferred to the accounting section for microprocessors. In July 1987, he was transferred to the Accounts Settlement Section of the Accounting Division. After one year he was promoted to Assistant Manager in charge of settling consolidated accounts of Yamada Group as a single economic entity. The consolidated financial statements were prepared on the basis of accounting principles generally accepted in the United States and have been audited by the accounting firm of Ackerman and Cohen LLP.

In June 1990, in recognition of his three years of experience in consolidated financial statement work, Mr. Ogawa was promoted to Senior Assistant Manager of the Accounts Settlement Section. He has held this position for the last eight years.

The applicant is knowledgeable of both Japanese and U.S. accounting standards and is very familiar with the aspect of financing jobs for overseas business. Additionally, he has broad-based training and experience with our clientele and transactions for our International Operations. Moreover, his fluency in both Japanese and English guarantees effective communication with local staff, accountants, banks and other individuals concerned with the United States as well as those key people located in the home office in Japan.

We now wish to employ Mr. Ogawa on a temporary basis at a salary of $200,000 per year, for a five-year period. We understand the temporary scope of this position and have informed Mr. Ogawa of this condition.

We respectfully request the favorable and expeditious review of our petition to classify Mr. Ogawa as an E-1.

Thank you for your kind attention to this matter.

Very truly yours,
Yamada Corp.

Akio Watanabe
Director/International Operations

SAMPLE LETTER TO HAVE SUBSIDIARY ORGANIZATION ACCORDED E-2 STATUS AND PETITION FOR E-2 EMPLOYEE VISA

American Consul
London, England

Attn: Treaty Visa Officer

Dear Sir/Madam:

This letter is respectfully submitted in support of our request to obtain E-2 employer status for our wholly owned subsidiary, I.T. Electronics (USA) Inc. I.T. Electronics Inc. is located in Portland, Oregon, and was recently incorporated under the laws of that state. Additionally, we request that Mr. Jung-Ho Kim be granted an E-2 visa, as he will serve as President and Chief Executive Officer at I.T. Electronics Inc.

THE PETITIONER

I.T. Electronics is a Korean company engaged in the design and manufacture of telecommunications and information processing systems and electronic devices. The Company employs over 10,000 individuals worldwide and has net sales in excess of $5 billion.

I.T. Electronics is strongly positioned for growth in such rapidly progressing areas as integrated services digital networks, artificial intelligence, submicron devices and advanced computer products. The Company supplies its products and expertise to customers around the world through an extensive sales and service network.

Over the past few years, we have been upgrading production capacity through an active capital investment program. The company's goal is to situate manufacturing operations as close to customers as possible, thus reducing lead-time and enhancing customer service.

Research and development is critical to I.T. Electronics' future growth. By increasing research and development expenditures, the company has been able to diversify product offerings and improve its response to customer needs. This program will continue over the next decade to fuel our growth in the industry.

The Company is currently experimenting with high-efficiency voice and image compression technologies to improve our Telecommunications Division. The primary goal of information processing research is to introduce practical, artificial intelligence into a broad variety of systems. Additionally, the Company is heavily involved in expanding and improving its position in the field of computer software.

The future will yield challenges and opportunities as production cycles shorten and new services and sophisticated products are introduced. As a leading producer of electronic systems and devices, I.T. Electronics is well placed to thrive in this new environment.

THE CORPORATE STRUCTURE

In order to maintain a position of leadership in the market and insure future growth, it is necessary to keep abreast of the changing needs and expectations of customers and be prepared to diversify or expand to meet any new challenges. It is with this purpose in mind that I.T. Electronics (USA) Inc. was formed in an effort to expand the possibilities of the company's trade with the United States. To date, I.T. Electronics has invested $6,000,000 into I.T. Electronics (USA) Inc., $4,500,000 of which was utilized to purchase all outstanding shares of San Jose Micro software business, thereby giving I.T. Electronics 100% ownership in operations. The remaining $1.5 million is allotted for use as working capital.

I.T. Electronics (USA) Inc. is a wholly owned subsidiary of I.T. Electronics, this is evidenced by the submission of stock certificates, I.T. Electronics (USA) Inc.'s Articles of Incorporation and by letters from the corporate attorneys' indicating ownership.

POSITION OFFERED

Mr. Kim will serve as President and Chief Executive Officer of the recently formed I.T. Electronics (USA) Inc. In this key executive position, Mr. Kim will be completely responsible for overseeing the expansion and improvement of our software technology with a view toward consolidating our position in the market. Only an executive with distinctive and unique knowledge of the software business derived from years of experience in key high-level executive roles within our organization will be suitable to fill this position. The proposed employment of Mr. Kim satisfies our goal in filling the position available with an executive-level employee having intimate knowledge of our software systems, products and corporate structure. Mr. Kim's presence in the United States will ensure I.T. Electronics maintains a competitive edge in the electronics market.

Attached please find an organizational chart detailing I.T. Electronics (USA) Inc.'s corporate structure. You will note that Mr. Kim will be responsible for several high level executives including the Company's Controller, the Vice President of Marketing and Sales, the Vice President of Engineering and the Director of Engineering. Additionally, he will be responsible for at least forty subordinate employees.

THE APPLICANT

In 1963, Mr. Kim graduated with the equivalent of a Bachelor's degree in Mathematics from the University of Seoul, South Korea. Immediately thereafter, he joined I.T. Electronics and has been employed by the Company in various capacities since that time.

From 1963 to 1969, Mr. Kim was assigned to the Logics Design Department where his primary duties involved creating and developing logics for electronic equipment such as computers and related software peripherals.

After the successful completion of his duties at our Logics Design Department, Mr. Kim joined the Automation Design Division in 1970. There he worked with other software specialists and was responsible for the design and development of software products for automatic electronic machinery. Mr. Kim's exceptional performance as a software specialist lead to his promotion in 1978. In his position as head of the Division, Mr. Kim supervised and managed all subordinates in the division. Additionally, he was responsible for overseeing the Mecatronics Section of the Division that transformed hardware electronic machinery controls to software controls.

As Chief of Corporate Planning since 1980, Mr. Kim has assumed responsibility for settling the Company's short, middle and long term goals with regard to engineering practices and future developments. During this time, he has spearheaded I.T. Electronics' development and construction of various highly complex CAD or Computer Aided Design Systems for introduction into worldwide electronics markets. Mr. Kim is responsible for expanding the Company's software product line, and has played a key role in the research and development of Application Specific Integrated Circuits.

TERMS OF EMPLOYMENT

I.T. Electronics (USA) Inc. wishes to employ Mr. Kim on a temporary basis as President and Chief Executive Officer for a period of five years. He will be compensated at a salary of $225,000 per year plus fringe benefits. We understand the temporary scope of this position and have informed Mr. Kim of this stipulation.

Thank you for your expeditious processing of this application.

Very truly yours,

Young-Min Park
General Manager
I.T. Electronics

G. APPLICATION FOR E VISA CLASSIFICATION IF THE APPLICANT IS ALREADY IN THE UNITED STATES

There are three courses of action available to foreign nationals seeking E visa classification if they are already present in the United States.

The best course of action when applying for an E visa when the applicant is already in the U.S. may be for the applicant to return to their home country and present the application directly to the American Consulate. Consular officers deal with treaty applications frequently and are best able to process them in an informed and intelligent fashion. Furthermore, application via the Consulate is the only means of obtaining a visa because processing of the application at INS Service Centers produces only status change, and not a visa.

If a trip back to the applicant's home country is not feasible, there are two other means of obtaining an E visa. An E visa may be obtained by going to the United States Consulate in another country and presenting the E application. For example, a Japanese national might seek to obtain an E visa in Toronto rather than returning to Japan to obtain the visa. In this situation it is important to note that American Consulates in different countries require different information. Furthermore, many consular posts are reluctant to process E applications for nationals from other countries due to the large volume of extra work that this will create. Consular officers often do everything possible to discourage such applications and frequently deny them for lack of sufficient information. This is particularly true of American consular posts in Canada which receive large numbers of applications from individuals coming from the United States for the exclusive purpose of applying for a visa.

In the event that it is not feasible for the applicant to return to the home country or a third country to obtain an E visa the applicant may file Form I-129 and E Supplement with the Immigration and Naturalization Service to change status. INS requires an E supplement that incorporates some of the same types of questions as the Department of State's Form OF-156E. Accompanying family members of the principal E applicant are required to file Form I-539 to change status to that of a derivative E nonimmigrant. Although INS processing may take longer, it does allow the applicant the benefit of not having to travel outside the United States. Acceptance of employment in the United States is not authorized until after the application is approved.

When making a change of nonimmigrant status from the United States, the appearance of intent is relevant. Therefore, if it appears that this course of action was premeditated, as evidenced by filing for E status soon after arrival in the United States, the change of nonimmigrant status may be denied. Frequently, treaty traders and investors will come to the United States initially under B-1 status seeking to evaluate the conditions of the marketplace. It is only after the individual has spent time in the U.S. that he or she will seek to change status. This is generally consistent with the initial intent to make entry as a business visitor and should not be viewed as contrary to proper procedure.

Another important consideration to keep in mind when evaluating an individual's choice of the place of processing, is the applicant's present and future need to travel. If the individual chooses to apply for E classification within the U.S. the individual will unable to travel outside of the U.S. after the application has been submitted. If the individual travels while the application is pending the application will be considered abandoned. Therefore, the best time to apply for status through the INS is when there are no travel plans in existence and the applicant does not foresee an immediate need to travel.

It is also of great significance that change of status to E-1 or E-2 granted by the INS loses all legal force as soon as the applicant leaves the United States (Except for trips to Canada or Mexico of less than 30 days). In order to reenter in E status, the applicant must apply for an E-1 or E-2 visa at the consulate in the normal manner. Furthermore, unlike pre-petition cases such as H-1B, H-2 H-3 or L-

1, the fact that the INS already approved change of status to E has no continuing legal effect whatsoever, and the applicant must prepare and present a full initial application to the Consulate. Change of status in the United States to E-1 or E-2 is generally not advisable, except for those not planning to travel out of the United States for a considerable time period.

Forms Necessary to Make an Application for Change of Non-immigrant Status

1) Form I-129 and E Supplement
2) Form I-539 - Application for change of nonimmigrant status for all accompanying family members
3) Supporting documentation from treaty organization
4) Form I-94 (Arrival Departure Record)
5) Filing Fee

E-1 and E-2 nonimmigrant applications filed in the United States may only be filed with two of the four INS Service Centers. If the applicant is under the jurisdiction of either the Vermont or Texas Service Center the application should be filed with the Texas Service Center. If the applicant is under the jurisdiction of either the Nebraska or California Service Center the application should be filed with the California Service Center. For example, if the applicant lives in New York the application for E classification should be filed with the Texas Service Center. For a complete list of the jurisdiction of each Service Center see Appendix A.

SAMPLE FORM I-129

OMB No. 1115-0168

Petition for a Nonimmigrant Worker

START HERE - Please Type or Print

Part 1. Information about the employer filing this petition.

If the employer is an individual, use the top name line. Organizations should use the second line.

Family Name	Given Name	Middle Initial

Company or Organization Name: E.G. Transport, Co.

Address - Attn: Eric Jorgenson, Managing Director

Street Number and Name: 9999 Northern Blvd.		Apt. #
City: Miami	State or Province: Florida	
Country: USA	Zip/Postal Code: 00010	

IRS Tax #: 11-1111110

Part 2. Information about this Petition.

(See instructions to determine the fee)

1. **Requested Nonimmigrant classification:** (write classification symbol at right) E-1
2. **Basis for Classification** (check one)
   - a. ☒ New employment
   - b. ☐ Continuation of previously approved employment without change
   - c. ☐ Change in previously approved employment
   - d. ☐ New concurrent employment
3. **Prior Petition.** If you checked other than "New Employment" in item 2 (above) give the most recent prior petition numbers for the worker(s): ______
4. **Requested Action:** (check one)
   - a. ☐ Notify the office in Part 4 so the person(s) can obtain a visa or be admitted (NOTE: a petition is not required for an E-1, E-2, or R visa)
   - b. ☒ Change the person(s) status and extend their stay since they are all now in the U.S. in another status (see instructions for limitations). This is available only where you check "New Employment" in item 2, above.
   - c. ☐ Extend or amend the stay of the person(s) since they now hold this status.
5. **Total number of workers in petition:** 1

   (See instructions for where more than one worker can be included)

Part 3. Information about the person(s) you are filing for.

Complete the blocks below. Use the continuation sheet to name each person included in this petition.

If an entertainment group, give their group name.

Family Name: Olson	Given Name: Hans	Middle Initial
Date of Birth (Month/Day/Year): 02/26/1959	Country of Birth: Norway	
Social Security #: N/A	A #: N/A	

If in the United States, complete the following:

Date of Arrival (Month/Day/Year): 1/15/97	I-94 #: 01 01111110
Current Nonimmigrant Status: H-3	Expires (Month/Day/Year): 1/31/98

FOR INS USE ONLY

Returned	Receipt
Resubmitted	
Reloc Sent	
Reloc Rec'd	
Interviewed ☐ Petitioner ☐ Beneficiary	

Class: ______
\# of Workers: ______
Priority Number: ______
Validity Dates: From ______ To ______

☐ **Classification Approved**
☐ Consulate/POE/PFI Notified
At: ______
☐ Extension Granted
☐ COS/Extension Granted

Partial Approval (explain)

Action Block

To be Completed by Attorney or Representative, if any

☐ Fill in box if G-28 is attached to represent the applicant

VOLAG#

ATTY State License #

Continued on back.

SAMPLE FORM I-129 (CONTINUED)

Part 4. Processing Information

a. If the person named in Part 3 is outside the U.S. or a requested extension of stay or change of status cannot be granted, give the U.S. consulate or inspection facility you want to be notified if this petition is approved.

Type of Office (check one): ☒ Consulate ☐ Pre-flight inspection ☐ Port of Entry

Office Address (City) Oslo

U.S. State or Foreign Country Norway

Person's Foreign Address 1 Oak Drive, Oslo Norway

b. Does each person in this petition have a valid passport?
☐ Not required to have passport ☐ No - explain on separate paper ☒ Yes

c. Are you filing any other petitions with this one? ☒ No ☐ Yes - How many?

d. Are applications for replacement/Initial I-94's being filed with this petition? ☒ No ☐ Yes - How many? ______

e. Are applications by dependents being filed with this petition? ☒ No ☐ Yes - How many? ______

f. Is any person in this petition in exclusion or deportation proceedings? ☒ No ☐ Yes - explain on separate paper

g. Have you ever filed an immigrant petition for any person in this petition? ☒ No ☐ Yes - explain on separate paper

h. If you indicated you were filing a new petition in Part 2, within the past seven years has any person in this petition:

1) ever been given the classification you are now requesting? ☒ No ☐ Yes - explain on separate paper

2) ever been denied the classification you are now requesting? ☒ No ☐ Yes - explain on separate paper

i. If you are filing for an entertainment group, has any person in this petition not been with the group for at least 1 year?
☐ No ☐ Yes - explain on separate paper

Part 5. Basic Information about the proposed employment and employer.

Attach the supplement relating to the classification you are requesting.

Job Title Sales/Marketing/Booking Manager

Nontechnical Description of Job see attached letter in support

Address where the person(s) will work if different from the address in Part 1.

Is this a full-time position? ☐ No - Hours per week ☒ Yes

Wages per week or per year $ 85,000 per yr

Other Compensation (Explain) fringe benefits

Value per week or per year 10%

Dates of Intended employment From: 2/1/99 To: 1/31/01

Type of petitioner - check one ☐ U.S. citizen or permanent resident ☒ Organization ☐ Other - explain on separate paper

Type of business International freight forwarding

Year established 1971

Current number of employees 350

Gross Annual Income $25.5 million

Net Annual Income

Part 6. Signature.

Read the information on penalties in the instructions before completing this section.

I certify, under penalty of perjury under the laws of the United States of America, that this petition, and the evidence submitted with it, is all true and correct. If filing this on behalf of an organization, I certify that I am empowered to do so by that organization. If this petition is to extend a prior petition, I certify that the proposed employment is under the same terms and conditions as in the prior approved petition. I authorize the release of any information from my records, or from petitioning organization's records, which the Immigration and Naturalization Service needs to determine eligibility for the benefit being sought.

Signature and title	Print Name	Date

Please note: If you do not completely fill out this form and the required supplement, or fail to submit required documents listed in the instructions, then the person(s) filed for may not be found eligible for the requested benefit, and this petition may be denied.

Part 7. Signature of person preparing form if other than above.

I declare that I prepared this application at the request of the above person and it is based on all information of which I have knowledge.

Signature	Print Name	Date

Firm Name and Address

SAMPLE E SUPPLEMENT TO FORM I-129

Name of person or organization filing petition: E.G. Transport, Co.

Name of person you are filing for: Hans Olson

Classification sought (check one): ☒ E-1 Treaty trader ☐ E-2 Treaty investor

Name of country signatory to treaty with U.S. Norway

Section 1. Information about the Employer outside the U.S. (if any)

Name: World Transport Co.

Address: 1 Main Street, Oslo, Norway

Alien's Position - Title, duties and number of years employed: see attached letter

Principal Product, merchandise or service: International freight forwarding

Total number of Employees: 3,000 + worldwide

Section 2. Additional information about the U.S. Employer.

The U.S. company is, to the company outside the U.S. (check one):
☐ Parent ☐ Branch ☒ Subsidiary ☐ Affiliate ☐ Joint Venture

Date and Place of Incorporation or establishment in the U.S.: Florida, February 1, 1971

Nationality of Ownership (Individual or Corporate)

Name	Nationality	Immigration Status	% Ownership
World Transport Co.	Norwegian	N/A	100%

Assets: 50,000,000

Net Worth: 350,000,000

Total Annual Income: approx. 25,500,000

Staff in the U.S.	Executive/Manager	Specialized Qualifications or Knowledge
Nationals of Treaty Country in E or L Status		
Total number of employees in the U.S.		

Total number of employees the alien would supervise; or describe the nature of specialized skills essential to the U.S. company.

Section 3. Complete if filing for an E-1 Treaty Trader

Total Annual Gross Trade/Business of the U.S. company: $ 25,500,000

For Year Ending: 1997

Percent of total gross trade which is between the U.S. and the country of which the treaty trader organization is a national.
65%

Section 4. Complete if filing for an E-2 Treaty Investor

Total Investment

Cash	Equipment	Other
$	$	$
Inventory	**Premises**	**Total**
$	$	$

Form I-129 Supplement E/L (12/11/91)N

SAMPLE LETTER OF E-1 TREATY TRADER EMPLOYEE APPLICATION THROUGH APPLICATION TO THE IMMIGRATION AND NATURALIZATION SERVICE

Texas Service Center
U.S. Department of Justice
Immigration & Naturalization Service

Re: Hans Olson

Dear Sir/Madam:

This letter is submitted in support of our petition to classify Mr. Hans Olson, a Norwegian national, as an E-1 treaty trader to assume a position within our United States organization.

THE TREATY ORGANIZATION

E.G. Transport Co., a Florida corporation, was founded in 1971. E.G. Transport Co. is a wholly owned subsidiary of the Norwegian company, World Transport Co. The stock of World Transport Co. is publicly owned and listed on the Norwegian Stock Exchange.

World Transport Co. is an international freight forwarder of products imported and exported between countries all over the world. In addition, World Transport Co. is authorized to perform various services connected with the transportation of goods within the United States.

The worldwide services that we provide our clients include storage, wharfage, warehousing and forwarding of property. World Transport Co. facilitates the shipment of a variety of goods from video games and roller coasters to volatile chemicals.

World Transport Co. is a leader in the freight forwarding industry because we have created a customized import/export operation and information system, which is tailored exclusively to the needs of the individual customer. This method of operation is not utilized by our competitors, and thus sets our services apart from the rest of the industry.

World Transport's information system provides our clients with daily information on the status of their freight. This technique allows the client to alter the course of the freight or to change the arrival date while the goods are still in transit.

Over 65% of the business transacted by World Transport Co. involves trade between the United States and Norway. During 1996 - 1997, annual revenues from transporting 3408 shipments of imported good into the United States from Norway was $12,138,500; annual revenue from transporting 267 shipments of exported goods from the U.S. to Norway totaled $1,211,500. The balance of 210 shipments that were transported worldwide provided $849,000 in revenue for our organization. Our total gross annual revenue for 1997 totaled more than $25.5 million, which represents the transportation of merchandise valued at billions of dollars.

THE APPLICANT

Mr. Hans Olson has been in employed in the freight forwarding industry for the past nineteen years. From 1979-1982, Norway Shipping International employed Mr. Olson as the Manager of the Consolidated Cargo Department. As manager he was responsible for improving existing cargo operating procedures, organizing and determining routing and transportation of cargo, negotiating with carriers to develop transportation options and expeditious service, calculating freight quotations and executing proper procedures by agents in order to assure the safe and efficient transport of goods for customers. In addition to his other duties, Mr. Olson exercised hire and fire authority over a mid-level tier of three to five managers and professional employees.

On the basis of Mr. Olson's reputation and demonstrated ability, World Transport Co. later recruited Mr. Olson. In 1997, Mr. Olson was granted H-3 status valid through January 31, 1998, to come to the United States in order to learn all facets of our U.S. operation. Mr. Olson's training in our U.S. company has been quite successful. He has participated in rotational assignments in all of our corporate departments and has been instructed in the operational aspects of our import and export procedures. His training has included attending regular departmental briefings and seminars, preparing freight quotations, advising customers and arranging cargo forwarding. He has also developed expertise in insurance matters, and marketing and advertising techniques.

The purpose of Mr. Olson's training was to prepare him for a position as Manager in our Sales/Marketing Department in Oslo, Norway. However, the circumstances within our company and the general industry conditions have altered our current needs. Given the recent changes in world trade, it is our desire to increase business through aggressive marketing and sales programs aimed at industrial bookings. Rather than send Mr. Olson to fill the position in Oslo, it would better serve our needs to employ Mr. Olson in the United States so that he may develop these new strategies. Now that Mr. Olson is familiar with the U.S. operation, his expert skill and knowledge of Norwegian and European industry will be a great asset to our growing business opportunities. We wish to employ Mr. Olson as the Sales/Marketing/Booking Manager to supervise and develop a vigorous marketing and customer service system in an effort to bolster sales.

Mr. Olson is the only logical choice for this important executive position by virtue of his educational credentials, managerial expertise and extensive training in the United States.

As Sales/Marketing/Booking Manager, Mr. Olson will be responsible for the following:

- Developing marketing and customer service programs by establishing research methodology and design formats for gathering data.

- Examining and analyzing statistical data to forecast market trends and formulate sales policy.

- Supervising the review of various industry records and journals to seek new exporters.

- Supervising the preparation of proposals and sales marketing presentations tailored to potential clients' needs.

- Contracting with new export accounts and supervising the maintenance of the new accounts.

- Directing a staff of four documentation and booking coordinators, and one special booking coordinator for hazardous substances.

- Reviewing and updating existing client accounts to assure efficient and cost effective service and thus insure continued business.

- Evaluating data on competitors in formulating price structure and sales/marketing effectiveness.

- Determining personnel requirements for the department including: hiring, firing, and promotion.

Mr. Olson will retain managerial control of a substantial department within our organization. Specifically, seven professional employees will report directly to him. Mr. Olson will be responsible for the ultimate success of our increased marketing and customer service programs.

We are confident that Mr. Olson's managerial abilities and technical expertise will prove to be a valuable asset to our U.S. organization. Commensurate with his exceptional abilities, we will compensate Mr. Olson at a rate of $85,000 per year plus fringe benefits. We expect that Mr. Olson's services will be needed through January 2001.

We are quite anxious for Mr. Olson to embark on this new campaign as Manager of our Sales/Marketing/Booking Department and we respectfully request that his status be changed from H-3 to E-1 at your earliest convenience.

Thank you for your attention to this matter.

Very truly yours,

World Transport Co.
Robert Nielson

Options available to the applicant in the event of a denial

A denial of a change of status application may not be appealed. There are however, two other options available to the applicant. First, a motion to reconsider may be presented, requesting that the INS reconsider the application based on the documentation already submitted. Second, a motion to reopen may be made with new evidence. These motions may be made within thirty days of the denial. Motions to reconsider are rarely granted. Motions to reopen are often granted if the new evidence is persuasive. If the motions are not successful the applicant will have to return their home country. Although it may appear more convenient to stay in the United States and apply for E status through the INS, in reality, the likelihood of success via the consular alternative may be greater especially considering the possible delays at INS Service Centers.

H. HOW TO APPLY FOR AN EXTENSION OF E STATUS THROUGH THE INS

Although E visas are generally authorized for a five-year period of time, E status from the INS is initially granted for a two-year period with incremental extensions of up to two years. Similarly, admission with an E visa is generally for a two-year period. Therefore, if the E visaholder has not made any trips abroad that would have triggered a new status period, he or she will be required to submit an application for extension of stay to the INS.

The following documentation is required for an extension application:

1) Form I-129 and E Supplement
2) Form I-539 for family members of the E applicant
3) Original Form I-94 (Arrival Departure Record)
4) Documentation from treaty organization supporting the continued need for employee.
5) Filing Fee

A denial of an extension application may not be appealed. It is an anomaly in the immigration laws that an E-2 visaholder will generally be granted a new two-year admission period upon re-entry by merely presenting his or her passport at an airport. The same applicant will need to prove his or her entire case with a multitude of documentation if the applicant does not travel and applies for an extension while in the United States.

SAMPLE FORM I-129

OMB No. 1115-0168

Petition for a Nonimmigrant Worker

START HERE - Please Type or Print

Part 1. Information about the employer filing this petition.

If the employer is an individual, use the top name line. Organizations should use the second line.

Family Name	Given Name	Middle Initial

Company or Organization Name: Yamada Corporation

Address - Attn: Akio Watanabe, Director of International Operations

Street Number and Name: 102-10 Tsudaka	Apt. #:
City: Tokyo	State or Province:
Country: Japan	Zip/Postal Code:

IRS Tax #: 34-565656

Part 2. Information about this Petition.

(See instructions to determine the fee)

1. **Requested Nonimmigrant classification:** (write classification symbol at right) E-1
2. **Basis for Classification** (check one)
   - a. ☐ New employment
   - b. ☒ Continuation of previously approved employment without change
   - c. ☐ Change in previously approved employment
   - d. ☐ New concurrent employment
3. **Prior Petition.** If you checked other than "New Employment" in item 2 (above) give the most recent prior petition numbers for the worker(s): N/A
4. **Requested Action:** (check one)
   - a. ☐ Notify the office in Part 4 so the person(s) can obtain a visa or be admitted (NOTE: a petition is not required for an E-1, E-2, or R visa)
   - b. ☐ Change the person(s) status and extend their stay since they are all now in the U.S. in another status (see instructions for limitations). This is available only where you check "New Employment" in item 2, above.
   - c. ☒ Extend or amend the stay of the person(s) since they now hold this status.
5. **Total number of workers in petition:** 1

   (See instructions for where more than one worker can be included)

Part 3. Information about the person(s) you are filing for.

Complete the blocks below. Use the continuation sheet to name each person included in this petition.

If an entertainment group, give their group name.

Family Name: Ogawa	Given Name: Masahiro	Middle Initial:
Date of Birth (Month/Day/Year): 07/12/1957	Country of Birth: Japan	
Social Security #: N/A	A #: N/A	

If in the United States, complete the following:

Date of Arrival (Month/Day/Year): 3/17/97	I-94 #: 56-88989
Current Nonimmigrant Status: E-1	Expires (Month/Day/Year): 3/16/99

FOR INS USE ONLY

Returned	Receipt
Resubmitted	
Reloc Sent	
Reloc Rec'd	
Interviewed ☐ Petitioner ☐ Beneficiary	

Class:
\# of Workers:
Priority Number:
Validity Dates: From
To

☐ **Classification Approved**
☐ Consulate/POE/PFI Notified
At:
☐ Extension Granted
☐ COS/Extension Granted

Partial Approval (explain)

Action Block

To be Completed by Attorney or Representative, if any

☐ Fill in box if G-28 is attached to represent the applicant

VOLAG#

ATTY State License #

Continued on back.

SAMPLE FORM I-129 (CONTINUED)

Part 4. Processing Information

a. If the person named in Part 3 is outside the U.S. or a requested extension of stay or change of status cannot be granted, give the U.S. consulate or inspection facility you want to be notified if this petition is approved.

Type of Office (check one): ☒ Consulate ☐ Pre-flight inspection ☐ Port of Entry

Office Address (City) Tokyo U.S. State or Foreign Country Japan

Person's Foreign Address 135 Okayama Tokyo Japan

b. Does each person in this petition have a valid passport?
☐ Not required to have passport ☐ No - explain on separate paper ☒ Yes

c. Are you filing any other petitions with this one? ☒ No ☐ Yes - How many? ______

d. Are applications for replacement/Initial I-94's being filed with this petition? ☒ No ☐ Yes - How many? ______

e. Are applications by dependents being filed with this petition? ☐ No ☒ Yes - How many? ______

f. Is any person in this petition in exclusion or deportation proceedings? ☒ No ☐ Yes - explain on separate paper

g. Have you ever filed an immigrant petition for any person in this petition? ☒ No ☐ Yes - explain on separate paper

h. If you indicated you were filing a new petition in Part 2, within the past seven years has any person in this petition:

1) ever been given the classification you are now requesting? ☐ No ☒ Yes - explain on separate paper

2) ever been denied the classification you are now requesting? ☒ No ☐ Yes - explain on separate paper

i. If you are filing for an entertainment group, has any person in this petition not been with the group for at least 1 year?
☐ No ☐ Yes - explain on separate paper

Part 5. Basic Information about the proposed employment and employer.

Attach the supplement relating to the classification you are requesting.

Job Title Treasurer

Nontechnical Description of Job see attached letter

Address where the person(s) will work if different from the address in Part 1. 1740 Broadway, New York, New York

Is this a full-time position? ☐ No - Hours per week ☒ Yes

Wages per week or per year 200,000 per yr.

Other Compensation (Explain) N/A

Value per week or per year

Dates of Intended employment From: 03/16/99 To: 03/15/01

Type of petitioner - check one ☐ U.S. citizen or permanent resident ☒ Organization ☐ Other - explain on separate paper

Type of business Producer & Distributor of Semiconductors

Year established 1950

Current number of employees 30,000+

Gross Annual Income 15 billion

Net Annual Income

Part 6. Signature.

Read the information on penalties in the instructions before completing this section.

I certify, under penalty of perjury under the laws of the United States of America, that this petition, and the evidence submitted with it, is all true and correct. If filing this on behalf of an organization, I certify that I am empowered to do so by that organization. If this petition is to extend a prior petition, I certify that the proposed employment is under the same terms and conditions as in the prior approved petition. I authorize the release of any information from my records, or from petitioning organization's records, which the Immigration and Naturalization Service needs to determine eligibility for the benefit being sought.

Signature and title	Print Name	Date

Please note: If you do not completely fill out this form and the required supplement, or fail to submit required documents listed in the instructions, then the person(s) filed for may not be found eligible for the requested benefit, and this petition may be denied.

Part 7. Signature of person preparing form if other than above.

I declare that I prepared this application at the request of the above person and it is based on all information of which I have knowledge.

Signature	Print Name	Date

Firm Name and Address

SAMPLE E SUPPLEMENT TO I-129

Name of person or organization filing petition:	Name of person you are filing for:
Yamada Corporation	Masahiro Ogawa
Classification sought (check one): ☒ E-1 Treaty trader ☐ E-2 Treaty investor	Name of country signatory to treaty with U.S.

Section 1. Information about the Employer outside the U.S. (if any)

Name	Address
Yamada Corporation	102 Tsudaka, Tokyo, Japan
Alien's Position - Title, duties and number of years employed Treasurer - see attached letter	Principal Product, merchandise or service Semiconductors
Total number of Employees 30,000+	

Section 2. Additional information about the U.S. Employer.

The U.S. company is, to the company outside the U.S. (check one):

☐ Parent ☐ Branch ☒ Subsidiary ☐ Affiliate ☐ Joint Venture

Date and Place of Incorporation or establishment in the U.S.

New York State, October 19, 1980

Nationality of Ownership (Individual or Corporate)

Name	Nationality	Immigration Status	% Ownership
Yamada Corporation	Japanese	N/A	100%

Assets	Net Worth	Total Annual Income

Staff in the U.S.	Executive/Manager	Specialized Qualifications or Knowledge
Nationals of Treaty Country in E or L Status		
Total number of employees in the U.S.	300	

Total number of employees the alien would supervise; or describe the nature of specialized skills essential to the U.S. company.

Section 3. Complete if filing for an E-1 Treaty Trader

Total Annual Gross Trade/Business of the U.S. company	For Year Ending
$	

Percent of total gross trade which is between the U.S. and the country of which the treaty trader organization is a national.

Section 4. Complete if filing for an E-2 Treaty Investor

Total Investment	Cash	Equipment	Other
	$	$	$
	Inventory	Premises	Total
	$	$	$

Form I-129 Supplement E/L (12/11/91)N

SAMPLE FORM I-539 APPLICATION TO EXTEND/CHANGE NONIMMIGRANT STATUS

START HERE - Please Type or Print

Part 1. Information about you.

Family Name: Ogawa	Given Name: Yukiko	Middle Initial
Address - In Care of:		
Street # and Name		Apt. #
City	State	
Zip Code		
Date of Birth (month/day/year) 08/10/1965	Country of Birth Japan	
Social Security # (if any) N/A	A# (if any) N/A	
Date of Last Arrival into the U.S. 3/17/97	I-94# 56-88990	
Current Nonimmigrant Status E-1	Expires on (month/day/year) 3/16/99	

Part 2. Application Type.

(See instructions for fee.)

1. I am applying for: (check one)
   - a. ☒ an extension of stay in my current status
   - b. ☐ a change of status. The new status I am requesting is: ____________
2. Number of people included in this application: (check one)
   - a. ☒ I am the only applicant
   - b. ☐ Members of my family are filing this application with me. The Total number of people included in this application is ____________ (complete the supplement for each co-applicant)

Part 3. Processing Information.

1. I/We request that my/our current or requested status be extended until (month/day/year) 03/15/01
2. Is this application based on an extension or change of status already granted to your spouse, child or parent?
   ☐ No ☐ Yes (receipt # ____________________)
3. Is this application being filed based on separate petition or application to give your spouse, child or parent an extension or change of status?
   ☐ No ☒ Yes, filed with this application ☐ Yes, filed previously and pending with INS
4. If you answered yes to question 3, give the petitioner or applicant name: ____________________

   If the application is pending with INS, also give the following information.

   Office filed at ____________ Filed on ____________ (date)

Part 4. Additional Information.

1. For applicant #1, provide passport information:

Country of issuance: Japan	Valid to: (month/day/year) 04/07/2002

2. Foreign Address:

Street # and Name 135 Okayama	Apt#
City or Town Tokyo	State or Province
Country Japan	Zip or Postal Code

Form I-539 (Rev. 12-2-91)

Continued on back

FOR INS USE ONLY

Returned	Receipt
Date	
Resubmitted	
Date	
Reloc Sent	
Date	
Reloc Rec'd	
Date	
☐ Applicant Interviewed	

☐ Extension Granted to (date): ____________

☐ Change of Status/Extension Granted New Class: ______ To (date): ______

If denied:
☐ Still within period of stay
☐ V/D to: ________
☐ S/D to: ________
☐ Place under docket control

Remarks

Action Block

To be completed by Attorney or Representative, if any

☐ Fill in box if G-28 is attached to represent the applicant

VOLAG#

ATTY State License #

3. Answer the following questions. If you answer yes to any question, explain on separate paper.	Yes	No
a. Are you, or any other person included in this application, an applicant for an immigrant visa or adjustment of status to permanent residence?		X
b. Has an immigrant petition ever been filed for you, or for any other person included in this application?		X
c. Have you, or any other person included in this application ever been arrested or convicted of any criminal offense since last entering the U.S.?		X
d. Have you, or any other person included in this application done anything which violated the terms of the nonimmigrant status you now hold?		X
e. Are you, or any other person included in this application, now in exclusion or deportation proceedings?		X
f. Have you, or any other person included in this application been employed in the U.S. since last admitted or granted an extension or change of status?		X

If you answered YES to question 3f, give the following information on a separate paper: Name of person, name of employer, address of employer, weekly income, and whether specifically authorized by INS.

If you answered No to question 3f, fully describe how you are supporting yourself on a separate paper. Include the source and the amount and basis for any income. My husband fully supports me.

Part 5. Signature

Read the information on penalties in the instruction before completing this section. You must file this application while in the United States.

I certify under penalty of perjury under the laws of the United States of America that this application, and the evidence submitted with it, is all true and correct. I authorize the release of any information from my record which the Immigration and Naturalization Service needs to determine the eligibility for the benefit I am seeking.

Signature	Print your name	Date
	Yukiko Ogawa	

Please Note: If you do not completely fill out this form, or fail to submit required documents listed in the instructions, you cannot be found eligible for the requested document and this application will have to be denied.

Part 6. Signature of person preparing form if other than above. (Sign below)

I declare that I prepared this application at the request of the above person and it is based on all information of which I have knowledge.

Signature	Print your name	Date

Firm Name and Address

(Please remember to enclose the mailing label with your application)

SAMPLE COVER LETTER IN SUPPORT OF EXTENSION OF STAY

Vermont Service Center
U.S. Department of Justice
Immigration and Naturalization Service
St. Albans, Vermont

Re: E-1 Extension of Stay on behalf of Masahiro Ogawa

Dear Sir/Madam:

This letter is written on behalf of Mr. Masahiro Ogawa's application for extension of stay in line with his duties as Treasurer of Nippon Kaisha Inc., the qualifying treaty organization. Mr. Ogawa was initially granted E-1 authorization on July 31, 1996 through August 1, 1998 and it is presently requested that this be extended to July 31, 2000.

Nippon Kaisha Inc. is a New York corporation that was established in 1980 as the sales representative arm and wholly owned subsidiary of Yamada Corp. of Japan. Nippon Kaisha Inc. continues to engage in 100% of its trade activities with Japan, with the most recent trade figures reflecting sales of over $540 million, and as such continue to qualify as an E-1 treaty trader organization.

Mr. Ogawa is a valued employee of both Nippon Kaisha and Yamada Corp. having been in our employ since 1981 in a variety of managerial and executive positions. Presently, Mr. Ogawa has been performing the duties of Treasurer, which involves the complex intricacies of settling the consolidated accounts of the Yamada Group as a whole, which includes over 200 subsidiaries worldwide.

We continue to require the temporary services of Mr. Ogawa to perform this important role in our organization and continue to offer him compensation of $200,000 per year.

Since Mr. Ogawa's present status is due to expire on August 1, 1998, it is respectfully requested that he be granted an additional two-year period of extension to expire on July 31, 2000.

Your expeditious approval of this status extension is greatly appreciated.

Very truly yours,

Kunihiko Takahashi
General Manager
Nippon Kaisha Inc.

I. <u>VISA RENEWAL</u>

Visa renewal, also known as visa "revalidation," is necessary when the visa's period of validation is due to expire. The process may be accomplished through any one of three ways:

The first option to revalidate a visa is by going to the consulate in person where the initial visa was granted. When obtaining the visa revalidation by this option, the applicant should go to the consulate accompanied with proof that all the relevant information with regard to the treaty organization remains the same. The applicant must provide recent documentation that demonstrates that the treaty organization continues to remain active.

<u>Treaty Trader Organizations</u>: the documentation must reflect current trade figures and serve to update the consular officer of recent trade activity.

<u>Treaty Investor Organizations</u>: the documentation should include recent purchase and ledger statements and accountant's statements to show the continuing substantial investment.

The second option to revalidate a visa is through the Visa Office in Washington, D.C. The following documentation is required:

1) Form OF-156E
2) Passport of visaholder
3) Form I-94 (Arrival/Departure Record) showing valid status
4) Filing Fee
5) State Department Fee
6) Letter of Support and accompanying documentation
7) Self-addressed, stamped or pre-paid envelope

The address for the visa office is:

VISA OFFICE - ACCREDITATION AND ISSUANCE BRANCH

U.S. STATE DEPARTMENT ANNEX NO. 1
401 E STREET, NW
WASHINGTON, D.C. 20522-0113

The final option, available only at some Consulates (e.g. Japan) is to mail a revalidation request to the original Consulate that issued the visa. For this option, the same documentation is required as that through the Visa Office in Washington. However, at present time, most consular posts do not permit issuance of visas by mail from "stateside" applicants.

Treaty Trader Countries (E-1 Visas & Status)

1) Argentina
2) Australia
3) Austria
4) Belgium
5) Bolivia
6) Brunei
7) Canada
8) China (Taiwan only)
9) Colombia
10) Costa Rica
11) Denmark
12) Estonia
13) Ethiopia
14) Finland
15) France
16) Germany
17) Greece
18) Honduras
19) Iran
20) Ireland
21) Israel
22) Italy
23) Japan
24) Korea
25) Liberia
26) Luxembourg
27) Mexico
28) Netherlands
29) Norway
30) Oman
31) Pakistan
32) Paraguay
33) Philippines
34) Spain
35) Suriname
36) Sweden
37) Switzerland
38) Thailand
39) Togo
40) Turkey
41) United Kingdom
42) Yugoslavia

Treaty Investor Countries (E-2) Bilateral Investment Treaty

1) Argentina
2) Armenia
3) Australia
4) Austria
5) Bangladesh
6) Belgium
7) Bulgaria
8) Cameroon
9) Canada
10) China (Taiwan)
11) Columbia
12) Congo
13) Costa Rica
14) Czech Republic
15) Ecuador
16) Egypt
17) Estonia
18) Ethiopia
19) Finland
20) France
21) Georgia
22) Germany
23) Grenada
24) Honduras
25) Iran
26) Ireland
27) Italy
28) Jamaica
29) Japan
30) Kazakhstan
31) Korea
32) Kyrgyzstan
33) Latvia
34) Liberia
35) Luxembourg
36) Mexico
37) Moldova
38) Mongolia
39) Morocco
40) Netherlands
41) Norway
42) Oman
43) Pakistan
44) Panama
45) Paraguay
46) Philippines
47) Poland
48) Romania
49) Senegal
50) Slovak Republic
51) Spain
52) Sri Lanka
53) Suriname
54) Sweden
55) Switzerland
56) Thailand
57) Togo
58) Trinidad & Tobago
59) Tunisia
60) Turkey
61) Ukraine
62) United Kingdom
63) Yugoslavia
64) Zaire

Chapter Six

O AND P NONIMMIGRANT VISAS

A. INTRODUCTION

The O and P nonimmigrant visa categories were created by the Immigration Act of 1990 for aliens of extraordinary ability in the sciences, arts, business, education and athletics, aliens of extraordinary achievement in motion pictures and television and artists, athletes and entertainers. The O an P categories were designed to cover the aliens who were previously included under the old H-1B visa category as aliens of distinction and exceptional ability. Since the 1990 Act, the H-1B visa category has been limited to professional "Specialty Occupations" enumerated in the statute that require at least a Bachelor's degree or its equivalent for entry into the occupation. The O and P categories should be used for individuals who possess extraordinary ability or have achieved significant recognition and acclaim within their field, but do not necessarily possess a college degree. Unfortunately, the O and P categories are much more narrow and select than the former H-1B category for "distinguished" individuals.

Both the O and P visa categories have a number of different sub-categories, which will be discussed in this chapter. However, one of the more important distinctions between the O and P visa categories is that the O visa is designed for individuals, while the P category, particularly the P-1B, P-2 and P-3 categories are designed for members of a group, either entertainment, athletic or "culturally unique."

The specific characteristics of each sub-category will be addressed in detail in this chapter. The following is a list of each of the sub-categories of O and P classification.

O-1 **Aliens of Extraordinary Ability in Sciences, Arts, Business, Education or Athletics and Aliens of Extraordinary Achievement in Motion Pictures and Television**

O-2 **Accompanying Support Personnel**

O-3 **Spouses and Minor Children Of O-1 and O-2 Visaholders**

P-1A **Individual Athletes and Teams**

P-1B **Entertainment Groups**

P-2 **Entertainer or Entertainment Group Reciprocal Exchange Program**

P-3 **Performer or Group in a Culturally Unique Program**

P-4 **Spouses or Minor Children of P-1, P-2, P-3 Aliens**

B. O NONIMMIGRANT VISA

The "O" visa category is available to foreign nationals who have extraordinary ability in the sciences, arts, education, business or athletics, or have a demonstrated record of extraordinary achievement in the motion picture or television industry. In addition, the foreign national must be coming temporarily to the United States to continue work in the area of extraordinary ability or achievement.

There are three different standards of proof to be met to demonstrate eligibility for an O-1 visa:

Extraordinary Ability

The highest standard, **"extraordinary ability"** applies to foreign nationals in the sciences, education, business and athletics. Extraordinary ability means a level of expertise indicating that the person is one of the small percentage who have arisen to the very top of the field of endeavor.

Distinction

Foreign nationals in the arts are required to be of **"distinction."** Distinction means a high level of achievement in the field of arts evidenced by a degree of skill and recognition substantially above that ordinarily encountered to the extent that a person described as prominent is renowned, leading or well known in the field of arts.

Extraordinary Achievement

Aliens in the motion picture and television industry must have earned "extraordinary achievement" in their field. Extraordinary achievement, as commonly defined in the industry, means a very high level of accomplishment in the motion picture or television industry evidenced by a degree of skill and recognition significantly above that ordinarily encountered to the extent that the person is recognized as outstanding, notable, or leading in the motion picture or television field.

Other Important Definitions for the Purposes of O Classifications

Event means an activity such as, but not limited to, a scientific project, conference, convention, lecture series, tour, exhibit, business project, academic year, or an engagement. Such activity can include short inactive interludes, promotional appearances and stopovers that are incidental and/or related to the event. A group of related activities will also be considered an event. In the case of an O-1 athlete, the event can be the foreign national's contract.

Arts include any field of creative activity or endeavor such as, but not limited to, fine arts, visual arts, and performing arts.

Foreign nationals engaged in the arts include not only the principal creators and performers but other essential persons such as, but not limited to, directors, set designers, lighting designers, sound designers, choreographers, choreologists, conductors, orchestrators, coaches, arrangers, musical supervisors, costume designers, makeup artists, fight masters, stage technicians, and animal trainers.

Peer Group means a group or organization that is comprised of practitioners in the foreign national's occupation. If there is a collective bargaining representative of an employer's employees in the occupational classification for which the foreign national is being sought, such a representative may be considered the appropriate peer group for purposes of consultation.

Extraordinary ability in the sciences, arts, education, business, or athletics, or extraordinary achievement in the case of an alien in the motion picture or television industry, must be established for each foreign national. A petition filed on behalf of a foreign national for O classification must be accompanied by evidence that the work the foreign national is coming to the United States to perform requires extraordinary ability, and the foreign national meets the criteria for classification as an alien of extraordinary ability, extraordinary achievement, or distinction.

Evidence Required for an O-1 Alien of Extraordinary Ability in the Sciences, Education, Athletics or Business

To demonstrate eligibility for this category, a foreign national must demonstrate sustained national or international acclaim and recognition for achievements in the field of expertise by providing evidence of receipt of a major, internationally-recognized award, such as the Nobel Prize; or at least three of the following categories of documentation:

1) Documentation of the foreign national's receipt of nationally or internationally recognized prizes or awards for excellence in the field of endeavor;

2) Documentation of the foreign national's membership in associations in the field for which classification is sought, which require outstanding achievements of their members, as judged by rec-

ognized national or international experts in their disciplines or fields;

3) Published material in professional or major trade publications or major media about the foreign national, relating to the foreign national's work in the field for which classification is sought, which shall include the title, date, and author of such published material, and any necessary translation;

4) Evidence of the foreign national's participation on a panel, or individually, as a judge of the work of others in the same or in an allied field of specialization to that for which classification is sought;

5) Evidence of the foreign national's original scientific, scholarly, or business-related contributions of major significance in the field;

6) Evidence of the foreign national's authorship of scholarly articles in the field, in professional journals, or other major media;

7) Evidence that the foreign national has been employed in a critical or essential capacity for organizations and establishments that have a distinguished reputation;

8) Evidence that the foreign national has commanded and now commands a high salary or other remuneration for services, evidenced by contracts or other reliable evidence; or

If the above standards do not readily apply to the beneficiary's occupation, the petitioner may submit comparable evidence in order to establish the beneficiary's eligibility.

Evidence Required for an O-1 Alien of Extraordinary Ability in the Arts

To qualify as an alien of extraordinary ability in the field of arts, the foreign national must be recognized as being prominent in his or her field of endeavor as demonstrated by evidence that the foreign national has been nominated for, or has been the recipient of, significant national or international awards or prizes in the particular field such as an Academy Award, an Emmy, a Grammy, or a Director's Guild Award or at least three of the following forms of documentation:

1) Evidence that the foreign national has performed and will perform services as a lead or starring participant in productions or events which have a distinguished reputation as evidenced by critical reviews, advertisements, publicity releases, publications contracts or endorsements;

2) Evidence that the foreign national has achieved national or international recognition for achievements evidenced by critical reviews or other published materials by or about the individual in major newspapers, trade journals, magazines, or other publications;

3) Evidence that the foreign national has performed in a lead, starring, or critical role for organizations and establishments that have a distinguished reputation evidenced by articles in newspapers, trade journals, publications, or testimonials;

4) Evidence that the foreign national has a record of major commercial or critically acclaimed successes as evidenced by such indicators as title, rating, standing in the field, box office receipts, motion picture or television ratings, and other occupational achievements reported in trade journals, major newspapers, or other publications;

5) Evidence that the foreign national has received significant recognition for achievements from organizations, critics, government agencies, or other recognized experts in the field in which the foreign national is engaged. Such testimonials must be in a form which clearly indicates the author's authority, expertise, and knowledge of the foreign national's achievements; or

6) Evidence that the foreign national has commanded or now commands a high salary or other substantial remuneration for services in relation to

others in the field, as evidenced by contracts or other reliable evidence; or

If the above standards do not readily apply to the beneficiary's occupation, the petitioner may submit comparable evidence in order to establish the beneficiary's eligibility.

Evidence Required for an O-1 Alien of Extraordinary Achievement in the Motion Picture or Television Industry

To qualify as an alien of extraordinary achievement in the motion picture or television industry, the foreign national must show that he or she has attained a very high level of accomplishment evidenced by a degree of skill and recognition significantly above that ordinarily encountered and are recognized as outstanding, notable or leading. Extraordinary achievement may be demonstrated by evidence that the foreign national has been nominated for, or has been the recipient of, significant national or international awards or prizes in the particular field such as an Academy Award, an Emmy, a Grammy, or a Director's Guild Award or at least three of the following forms of documentation:

1) Evidence that the foreign national has performed and will perform services as a lead or starring participant in productions or events which have a distinguished reputation as evidenced by critical reviews, advertisements, publicity releases, publications contracts or endorsements;

2) Evidence that the foreign national has achieved national or international recognition for achievements evidenced by critical reviews or other published materials by or about the individual in major newspapers, trade journals, magazines, or other publications;

3) Evidence that the foreign national has performed in a lead, starring, or critical role for organizations and establishments that have a distinguished reputation evidenced by articles in newspapers, trade journals, publications, or testimonials;

4) Evidence that the foreign national has a record of major commercial or critically acclaimed successes as evidenced by such indicators as title, rating, standing in the field, box office receipts, motion picture or television ratings, and other occupational achievements reported in trade journals, major newspapers, or other publications;

5) Evidence that the foreign national has received significant recognition for achievements from organizations, critics, government agencies, or other recognized experts in the field in which the foreign national is engaged. Such testimonials must be in a form which clearly indicates the author's authority, expertise, and knowledge of the foreign national's achievements; or

6) Evidence that the foreign national has commanded or now commands a high salary or other substantial remuneration for services in relation to others in the field, as evidenced by contracts or other reliable evidence.

Consultation

Written evidence of consultation with an appropriate individual, peer group, labor organization, or management organization in the area of the foreign national's ability or achievement, regarding the nature of the work to be done and the alien's qualifications is **mandatory** before a petition for an O-1 classification can be adjudicated. Under the 1991 Amendments to the 1990 Act, individuals as well as peer groups may provide consultations for O-1 petitions.

Consultation requirements for an O-1 alien of extraordinary ability

A petition for O-1 classification for extraordinary ability requires the submission of a written consultation from a peer group in the area of the foreign national's ability. The peer group must be an appropriate association or entity with expertise in that area and may be a labor organization. The advisory opinion provided by the peer group must describe the foreign national's ability and achievements in the field of endeavor, describe the nature of the duties to be performed, and state whether the position requires the services of an alien of extraordinary ability. A consulting organization may also submit a letter of no objection in lieu of an advisory opinion, if it has no objection to the approval of the petition. An authorized official of the organization must sign the written opinion.

Although a petitioner is free to choose the type of consulting organization, the INS will delay the petition process if it determines that the appropriate labor organization has not been consulted. In that situation, the INS will send the petition and supporting documentation to the national office of the union the INS designates as the appropriate entity within five days of the INS' receipt of the petition. If there is a collective bargaining representative for the occupational classification for which the alien is being sought the INS will contact that entity. The organization will have fifteen days after the receipt of the petition to submit a written advisory opinion, comment or no objection letter. Once the fifteen-day period has expired, the INS has fourteen days to adjudicate the petition. The INS will render a decision utilizing the evidence on record, if the labor organization or union has not responded to the request for an advisory opinion within the fifteen-day period.

Consultations are advisory in nature and are not binding on the INS. Written evidence of consultation must be included in the record in every approved O petition.

In the case of an alien of extraordinary achievement who will be working on a motion picture or television production, consultation must be made with the appropriate union representing the foreign national's occupational peers as well as a management organization in the area of the foreign national's ability. The advisory opinion from the labor and management organizations must describe the foreign national's achievements in the motion picture or television field and state whether the position requires the services of an alien of extraordinary achievement.

Exceptions to the Consultation Requirement

There are three instances in which an advisory opinion need not always be submitted with an O petition:

The burden of submitting a consultation is lifted from the petitioner when the petitioner requests expeditious handling of the O petition. A petitioner may only request expeditious handling of a petition in the fields of art, entertainment, and athletics. If the INS determines that a petition merits expeditious handling, the INS will telephonically contact the appropriate labor and/or management organization and request an advisory opinion if the petitioner does not submit one. The labor and/or management organization then has 24 hours to respond telephonically to the INS' request. The INS will adjudicate the petition after receipt of the telephonic response from the labor and/or management organization. The labor and/or management group must furnish the INS a written advisory opinion within five days of the initiating request. If the organization fails to respond, the INS will render a decision on the petition without the advisory opinion.

However, the INS will not liberally grant expedites, and if the expedite request is not granted, the petition may ultimately be denied or at least returned to allow the petitioner time to secure the requisite peer group letter.

Another exception to the consultation requirement is when there is no appropriate consulting entity in existence. The petitioner has the burden of establishing that an appropriate peer group, including a labor organization, does not exist. The INS will then render a decision based on the evidence on record. To establish that an appropriate peer group does not exist the petitioner should include affidavits or statements from practitioners in the foreign national's field or from a related labor organization attesting that an appropriate peer group does not exist. The petitioner should also include a statement detailing the attempt to locate an appropriate group.

Finally, the consultation requirement will be waived for an alien of extraordinary ability in the field of arts in those instances where the foreign national seeks readmission to the U.S. to perform similar services within two years of the date of a previous consultation. The INS will, within five days of granting the waiver, forward a copy of the petition and supporting documentation to the national office of an appropriate labor organization. The petitioner should include a copy of the previous consultation when requesting this type of waiver.

C. O-2 ALIENS ACCOMPANYING O-1 ALIENS OF EXTRAORDINARY ACHIEVEMENT

O-2 classification applies to an accompanying alien who is coming temporarily to the United States solely to assist in the artistic or athletic performance of the primary O-1 visaholder or to assist an O-1 visaholder on a specific motion picture or television production. O-2 status is not available to aliens who accompany O-1 aliens in the fields of science, education or business. To qualify for O-2 classification the applicant must:

- Be an **integral** part of the actual performance or events and possess **critical skills** and **experience** with the O-1 visaholder that are **not of a general nature** and cannot be performed by others; or

- In the case of a motion picture or television production, have skills and experience with the O-1 visaholder which are **not of a general nature** and which are **critical**, either based on a **pre-existing and longstanding** working relationship or, if in connection with a specific production only, because significant production (including pre - and post-production) will take place both inside and outside the United States and the continuing participation of the alien is **essential** to the successful completion of the production.

In order to meet the requirements of this category, the evidence must establish the current essentiality, critical skills, and experience of the foreign national with the O-1 visaholder and that the foreign national has substantial experience performing the critical skills and essential support services for the O-1 alien. In the case of a specific motion picture or television production, the evidence must establish that significant production has taken place outside the United States and will take place inside the United States and that the continuing participation of the foreign national is essential to the successful completion of the production.

An employer can petition for an individual to be an O-2 employee to either provide direct support to the O-1 visaholder or provide continuity to the performance, engagement or production that includes the O-1 visaholder. In addition, the use of O-2 nonimmigrant category is not limited to performances before a live audience. O-2 employees may include but are not limited to managers, trainers, accompanists, lighting engineers, and backline stage crewmembers. Other types of employees may be petitioned for as O-2 employees as long as they are essential to the performance of the O-1 visaholder.

Although an O-2 nonimmigrant must obtain his or her own classification, it does not entitle him or her to work separate and apart from the primary O-1 visaholder to whom he or she provides support. In addition, O-2 visaholders are not authorized to change employer unless it is in conjunction with a change of employer by the primary O-1 visaholder, since the O-2 nonimmigrant is expected to have critical skills relating to the O-1's performance or a preexisting, longstanding, working relationship with the O-1 visaholder.

Multiple Beneficiaries

O-2 nonimmigrants must be petitioned for on a separate petition from the primary O-1 visaholder, however, more than one O-2 accompanying alien may be included on the petition. Multiple beneficiaries may be included on the petition if they are assisting the same O-1 visaholder for the same events or performances, during the same period of time and in the same location. If the beneficiaries will be applying for visas at more than one consulate, the petitioner should submit a separate petition for each consulate. If the beneficiaries who are exempt from visa requirements will be applying for admission at more than one port of entry, the petitioner should submit a separate petition for each port of entry.

Consultation Requirements for an O-2 Accompanying Alien

Consultation with a labor organization with expertise in the skill area involved is required for an O-2 nonimmigrant accompanying an O-1 alien of extraordinary ability. For instance, a musicians union may be the appropriate labor organization to contact on behalf of a pianist accompanying a famous singer. In the case of a foreign national who seeks entry to work on a motion picture or television production, consultation with a labor organization and a management organization in the area of the foreign national's ability is required. The opinion provided by the labor and/or management organization must describe the foreign national's essentiality to, and working relationship with the O-1 artist or athlete and state whether there are available United States workers who can perform the support services.

If the foreign national will accompany an O-1 visaholder involved in a motion picture or television production, the advisory opinion must address the foreign national's skills and experience with the O-1 visaholder and whether the foreign national has had a preexisting longstanding working relationship with the O-1 visaholder, or whether significant production will take place in the United States and abroad and if the continuing participation of the foreign national is essential to the successful completion of the production. A single advisory opinion may be submitted in conjunction with multiple accompanying foreign nationals.

O-1 and O-2 Visaholders: Foreign Residence Requirement and Dual Intent

O-1 visaholders are not required to maintain a foreign residence abroad that they have no intention of abandoning and may harbor dual intent. Dual intent allows O-1 visaholders to come legitimately to the U.S. for a temporary period, while at the same time lawfully seek to become permanent residents of the United States. The approval of a permanent labor certification or the filing of an immigrant preference petition is statutorily not a basis for denying an O-1 petition, an extension request, or a change of status application. O-2 visaholders, however, must maintain a foreign residence abroad that they have no intention of abandoning and may not harbor a dual intent to remain permanently in the United States.

Individuals who meet the criteria for O-1 nonimmigrant classification based on extraordinary ability in the sciences, arts, education, business or athletics may also be eligible for employment-based permanent residence in the United States. In fact, the evidentiary requirements for permanent residence based on extraordinary ability in some ways are less burdensome than the requirements for O-1 nonimmigrant classification. For example, the petition for permanent residence does not require a peer group consultation or a job offer from an employer. From a practical standpoint, an individual with extraordinary ability in the sciences, arts, education, business or athletics should evaluate the options for nonimmigrant or immigrant classification carefully and decide which option best suits their needs. See Chapter Eight for a complete discussion of the employment based immigration categories.

Return Transportation Requirement

Employers of O nonimmigrants are required to pay the return trip costs of O employees whose employment is terminated before the end of the O nonimmigrant's authorized stay.

D. **O-3 CLASSIFICATION**

O-3 classification is available to the spouse and children of O-1 or O-2 visaholders accompanying, or following to join the O primary visaholder. O-3 visaholders are not authorized to accept employment unless they qualify for work authorization on an independent basis in another nonimmigrant or immigrant visa category.

PROCEDURE FOR FILING O PETITIONS

Who may petition for an O employee?

To be eligible to petition for an O-1 and O-2 nonimmigrant, the petitioner must be a United States employer, a U.S. agent, or a U.S. agent on behalf of a foreign employer. A foreign national can not self-petition for O status. Foreign employers are no longer permitted to petition for O nonimmigrants, however, foreign employers may retain the services of an U.S. agent. An U.S. agent may be required in three circumstances:

- When the O beneficiary is traditionally self-employed a U.S. agent may perform the function of an employer. A contract must be signed between the agent and foreign national, specifying the salary and terms and conditions of employment.

- When the O beneficiary will be employed by numerous employers the U.S. agent may act as a representative of both the employers and the foreign national. A contract must also be signed between the parties specifying the salary and terms and conditions of employment.

- United States agents are necessary when a foreign employer employs the O beneficiary. In this instance, the agent acts as a business representative of the foreign employer. The foreign employer must submit a letter with the petition stating that the U.S. agent is authorized to file the petition and will accept service of process in any proceeding under the employer sanctions provisions of the immigration statute. A contract between the parties must also be submitted specifying the salary and terms and conditions of employment.

General Documentary Requirements for O Classification

The evidence submitted with an O petition should include the following:

- The evidence specified for each particular classification (i.e. extraordinary ability, distinction or extraordinary achievement);

- Copies of any written contracts between the petitioner and the beneficiary, or if there is no written contract, a summary of the terms of the oral agreement under which the beneficiary will be employed;

- In a letter of support, an explanation of the nature of events or activities, the beginning and ending dates for the events or activities, and a copy of any itinerary for the events or activities; and

- A written advisory opinion(s) from the appropriate consulting entity or entities.

The evidence submitted with the O petition may take the form of the following:

Affidavits, contracts, awards, and similar documentation that reflect the nature of the foreign national's achievement and are executed by the person in charge of the institution, firm, establishment, or organization where the work was performed.

Affidavits written by present or former employers or recognized experts certifying to the recognition and extraordinary ability and specifically describe the foreign national's recognition and ability or achievement in factual terms and set forth the expertise of the affiant and the manner in which the affiant acquired such information.

Legible photocopies of documents referenced in the letter of support (e.g. certificates of achievement, publications, and promotional materials).

Additional filing requirements

In addition to the documentary requirements listed above, Form I-129 Petition for Nonimmigrant Worker with O/P supplement must be completed, signed, and submitted to the INS by the petitioner.

The petition, all supporting documentation and filing fee should be filed with the INS Service Center that has jurisdiction in the area where the foreign national will work. If the foreign national will work in more than one location the petition and supporting documentation should be filed with the INS Service Center that has jurisdiction over the area in which the petitioner is located. For a list of the four INS Service Centers and jurisdictions see Appendix A. Family members accompanying or following to join the O-1 and O-2 beneficiaries may be included on Form I-129 and O/P supplement and do not require a separate petition.

Generally, the petition will be approved for a period of time determined by the INS to be necessary to accomplish the event or activity. The initial petition may not be approved for a period of time to exceed three years. Extensions of stay may be granted in increments of up to one year. Unlike H and L status, there is no time limit an alien may remain in authorized O status.

Denial

If the INS denies the petition on the basis of information that is unknown to the petitioner, the INS must give notice of the intent to deny and the basis of the denial. The petitioner is given thirty days to inspect and rebut the evidence and resubmit an amended petition addressing the reasons for denial. If the INS Service Center ultimately denies the petition, the petitioner may appeal the decision to the Administrative Appeals Unit (AAU).

VISA ISSUANCE

Once an O petition has been approved and petition approval has been transmitted on Form I-797 the beneficiary can arrange to obtain the nonimmigrant visa abroad. Although the INS has sole authority to determine whether the requirements for O status have been met, an approved petition does not guarantee visa issuance. The beneficiary still has the burden of proving visa eligibility and admissibility to the United States Consular Officer. Consular officers are directed to consider the approved petition as prima facie evidence that the beneficiary has met the requirements for O classification. Consular officers may ask for additional evidence of visa eligibility and are allowed to refer a petition for reconsideration to the INS in instances of obvious error or in light of evidence related to the petition that was unavailable to the INS at the time of petition approval.

E. EXTENSIONS AND AMENDED PETITIONS

O visaholders may request extensions of stay by the INS in increments of up to one year to continue or complete the same activity or event indicated on the initial petition. The extension application filed with the INS includes both a request to extend the petition and a request to extend the visaholder's duration of stay. Extensions may be granted without concern of an overall time limit, however, it is important to note that extensions will only be granted to continue the same event or activity that the O visaholder was admitted to participate in the original petition.

A petition for an extension of stay is filed on Form I-129 and O/P supplement and should include a letter in support detailing the reasons for the extension, including current salary and conditions of employment. In addition, a copy of the initial approval notice or notices, Form I-797, should accompany the extension request and a copy of the current I-94 of each person included in the petition. Family members accompanying the O visaholder should petition for an extension on Form I-539 and file it concurrently with the primary O visaholder's petition. The entire package should be submitted to the INS Service Center with jurisdiction over the beneficiary's place of employment.

The O visaholder must be physically present in the United States at the time of filing of the extension. If the beneficiary needs to travel while the extension request is pending, the petitioner may request that notification of approval be cabled to the consulate abroad where the beneficiary will apply for a new visa. A denial of an extension request may not be appealed.

A petitioner is required to submit an amended petition when there are any material changes in the terms and conditions of employment or the O visaholder's eligibility presented in the original petition has changed. An amended petition does not have to be filed in the case of a petitioner of an artist or entertainer who merely wishes to add additional performances or engagements during the validity period of the initial petition. The new performance or events must require the services of an alien of O-1 caliber.

SAMPLE FORM I-129 PETITION FOR NONIMMIGRANT WORKER

START HERE - Please Type or Print

Part 1. Information about the employer filing this petition.

If the employer is an individual, use the top name line. Organizations should use the second line.

Family Name	Given Name	Middle Initial

Company or Organization Name: World Press Corporation

Address - Attn:

Street Number and Name: 245 Madison Avenue	Apt. #:
City: New York	State or Province: New York
Country: USA	Zip/Postal Code: 100010

IRS Tax #: 13-8888888

Part 2. Information about this Petition.

(See instructions to determine the fee)

1. **Requested Nonimmigrant classification:**
   (write classification symbol at right) O-1
2. **Basis for Classification** (check one)
   - a. ☒ New employment
   - b. ☐ Continuation of previously approved employment without change
   - c. ☐ Change in previously approved employment
   - d. ☐ New concurrent employment
3. **Prior Petition.** If you checked other than "New Employment" in item 2 (above) give the most recent prior petition numbers for the worker(s):
4. **Requested Action:** (check one)
   - a. ☒ Notify the office in Part 4 so the person(s) can obtain a visa or be admitted (NOTE: a petition is not required for an E-1, E-2, or R visa)
   - b. ☐ Change the person(s) status and extend their stay since they are all now in the U.S. in another status (see instructions for limitations). This is available only where you check "New Employment" in item 2, above.
   - c. ☐ Extend or amend the stay of the person(s) since they now hold this status.
5. **Total number of workers in petition:** one (1)
   (See instructions for where more than one worker can be included)

Part 3. Information about the person(s) you are filing for.

Complete the blocks below. Use the continuation sheet to name each person included in this petition.

If an entertainment group, give their group name.

Family Name: Dillion	Given Name: Kim	Middle Initial:
Date of Birth (Month/Day/Year): 06/04/1959	Country of Birth: United Kingdom	
Social Security #: N/A	A #:	

If in the United States, complete the following:

Date of Arrival (Month/Day/Year): N/A	I-94 #: N/A
Current Nonimmigrant Status: N/A	Expires (Month/Day/Year): N/A

FOR INS USE ONLY

Returned	Receipt
Resubmitted	
Reloc Sent	
Reloc Rec'd	
Interviewed ☐ Petitioner ☐ Beneficiary	

Class:
\# of Workers:
Priority Number:
Validity Dates: From
To

☐ **Classification Approved**
☐ Consulate/POE/PFI Notified
At:
☐ Extension Granted
☐ COS/Extension Granted

Partial Approval (explain)

Action Block

To be Completed by Attorney or Representative, if any

☐ Fill in box if G-28 is attached to represent the applicant

VOLAG#

ATTY State License #

Continued on back.

SAMPLE FORM I-129 PETITION FOR NONIMMIGRANT WORKER (CONTINUED)

Part 4. Processing Information

a. If the person named in Part 3 is outside the U.S. or a requested extension of stay or change of status cannot be granted, give the U.S. consulate or inspection facility you want to be notified if this petition is approved.

Type of Office (check one): ☒ Consulate ☐ Pre-flight inspection ☐ Port of Entry

Office Address (City): Hong Kong | U.S. State or Foreign Country:

Person's Foreign Address: 45 State Street Hong Kong

b. Does each person in this petition have a valid passport?
☐ Not required to have passport ☐ No - explain on separate paper ☒ Yes

c. Are you filing any other petitions with this one? ☒ No ☐ Yes - How many? ____

d. Are applications for replacement/Initial I-94's being filed with this petition? ☒ No ☐ Yes - How many? ____

e. Are applications by dependents being filed with this petition? ☒ No ☐ Yes - How many? ____

f. Is any person in this petition in exclusion or deportation proceedings? ☒ No ☐ Yes - explain on separate paper

g. Have you ever filed an immigrant petition for any person in this petition? ☒ No ☐ Yes - explain on separate paper

h. If you indicated you were filing a new petition in Part 2, within the past seven years has any person in this petition:

1) ever been given the classification you are now requesting? ☒ No ☐ Yes - explain on separate paper

2) ever been denied the classification you are now requesting? ☒ No ☐ Yes - explain on separate paper

i. If you are filing for an entertainment group, has any person in this petition not been with the group for at least 1 year?
☐ No ☐ Yes - explain on separate paper

Part 5. Basic Information about the proposed employment and employer.

Attach the supplement relating to the classification you are requesting.

Job Title: Editor-in-Chief | Nontechnical Description of Job: see attached letter in support

Address where the person(s) will work if different from the address in Part 1. 1740 Broadway, New York, New York 10019

Is this a full-time position? ☐ No - Hours per week ☐ Yes | Wages per week or per year

Other Compensation (Explain) | Value per week or per year | Dates of Intended employment From: To:

Type of petitioner - check one ☐ U.S. citizen or permanent resident ☒ Organization ☐ Other - explain on separate paper

Type of business: Communications | Year established: 1933

Current number of employees: 20,000 | Gross Annual Income: $1,000,000,000.00 | Net Annual Income: $750,000,000.00

Part 6. Signature.

Read the information on penalties in the instructions before completing this section.

I certify, under penalty of perjury under the laws of the United States of America, that this petition, and the evidence submitted with it, is all true and correct. If filing this on behalf of an organization, I certify that I am empowered to do so by that organization. If this petition is to extend a prior petition, I certify that the proposed employment is under the same terms and conditions as in the prior approved petition. I authorize the release of any information from my records, or from petitioning organization's records, which the Immigration and Naturalization Service needs to determine eligibility for the benefit being sought.

Signature and title	Print Name	Date
	Francis Cho, Vice-President	

Please note: If you do not completely fill out this form and the required supplement, or fail to submit required documents listed in the instructions, then the person(s) filed for may not be found eligible for the requested benefit, and this petition may be denied.

Part 7. Signature of person preparing form if other than above.

I declare that I prepared this application at the request of the above person and it is based on all information of which I have knowledge.

Signature	Print Name	Date

Firm Name and Address

SAMPLE SUPPLEMENT TO FORM I-129 FOR "O" NONIMMIGRANT WORKERS

Name of person or organization filing petition: World Press Corporation

Name of person or group or total number of workers you are filing for: DILLION, Kim

Classification sought (check one):

- [X] O-1 Alien of extraordinary ability in sciences, art, education, or business
- [ ] P-2 Artist or entertainer for reciprocal exchange program
- [ ] P-2S Essential Support Personnel for P-2

Explain the nature of the event

Describe the duties to be performed

Editor-in-Chief of Spectra Magazine

(see attached letter in support)

If filing for O-2 or P support alien, dates of alien's prior experience with the O-1 or P alien.

Have you obtained the required written consultation(s)? [X] Yes - attached [ ] No - Copy of request attached

If not, give the following information about the organization(s) to which you have sent a duplicate of this petition.

O-1 Extraordinary ability

Name of recognized peer group: International Communication Group

Phone #: 212-555-5555

Address: 100 Broadway, New York, New York 10000

Date sent:

O-1 Extraordinary achievement in motion pictures or television

Name of labor organization

Phone #

Address

Date sent

Name of management organization

Phone #

Address

Date sent

O-2 or P alien

Name of labor organization

Phone #

Address

Date sent

Form I-129 Supplement O/P/Q/R (12/11/91) N

SAMPLE LETTER OF SUPPORT ON BEHALF OF O-1 ALIEN OF EXTRAORDINARY ABILITY

Vermont Service Center
Immigration & Naturalization Service
St. Albans, Vermont

RE: World Press Corporation - Petitioner
Kim Dillion - Beneficiary
Petition for Classification as an O-1 Alien of Extraordinary Ability in Business

Dear Sir/Madam:

Pursuant to Section 101 (a)(15)(O)(i) of the Immigration and Nationality Act, we submit the above for processing to accord Mr. Kim Dillion status as a business executive of extraordinary ability for a temporary period of three years to serve as the Editor-In-Chief of Spectra Magazine. Mr. Dillion is part of the small percentage who has arisen to the very top of his field of endeavor.

The Petitioner

The World Press Corporation is one of the nation's leading diversified communications companies with extensive interests in newspapers, magazines, books, business publications, television and radio broadcasting, cable television programming services, newspaper features distribution and television production and distribution.

Spectra Magazine, founded in 1958, is one of the leading monthly magazines in the world. It is estimated that over one million people read it each month.

The Beneficiary

Mr. Dillion is an internationally known and acclaimed news editor regarded by many as one of the leading news editors in the world today. Most recently, he served as Editor-in-Chief of **Viewpoint** in Hong Kong and as Director of World Publications. As Editor-in-Chief of **Viewpoint**, Mr. Dillion's activities, statements and contributions to the publishing field were regularly reported in newspapers and magazines throughout the world. Furthermore, Mr. Dillion was credited with boosting and augmenting the circulation, advertising revenue, and international stature of **Viewpoint** in the world of print journalism. Mr. Dillion is also a member of the Executive Committee and Chairman of the Press Committee of the Hong Kong Foreign Policy Council, one of the most prestigious press organizations in the world.

The Proposed Position, Temporary Business Project and Basis for O-1 Eligibility

The World Press Corporation seeks to completely rejuvenate, rehabilitate and refocus **Spectra Magazine** over a three-year period. It aims to increase its share of the United States news magazine circulation and advertising markets and to recoup revenue, which was lost during the 1980's. A period of three years is needed for Mr. Dillion to accomplish these project objectives.

Mr. Dillion was selected for the position of Editor-in-Chief of **Spectra Magazine** after a one-year international search for the most appropriate individual to accomplish the Corporation's objectives. By definition, the Editor-in-Chief must understand the importance of ideas and trends throughout the world and then be able to inject these ideas into the structure and fabric of the magazine. Only a person of Mr. Dillion's extraordinary caliber can bring to **Spectra Magazine** the combination of celebrity and business acumen necessary to achieve these goals.

Mr. Dillion clearly qualifies as an O-1 alien of extraordinary ability in business as evidenced by the extensive material in professional publications and major media outlets that have been published about him. His business-related contributions of major significance to the field have been extensively documented in the media. Please see enclosed articles.

Further, as Editor-in-Chief of **Viewpoint**, Mr. Dillion was employed in a critical or essential capacity for an establishment that has a distinguished reputation worldwide.

Additionally, Mr. Dillion is a member of the Executive Committee and Chairman of the Press Committee of the Pacific Rim Foreign Policy Council (See enclosed exhibit). Formed in 1981, the Pacific Rim Foreign Policy Council is the most prestigious regional organization in the field. It is responsible for coordinating Pacific Rim Foreign Policy events, particularly the "Foreign Policy Forum, a highly esteemed event attended by professionals from all around the world.

Finally, as reflected by Mr. Dillion's contracts with the World Press Corporation and **Spectra Magazine**, he will be compensated at a salary of $700,000 per year plus fringe benefits and stock incentives. Previously, as Editor-In-Chief of **Viewpoint**, Mr. Dillion earned $500,000 per year plus fringe benefits. This reflects his statutory eligibility as an alien who has commanded and now commands a high salary or other remuneration for services.

As required by statute, we are submitting an advisory opinion by The International Communications Group, which is a leading organization in the world of print journalism. The International Communications Group, founded in 1950, is one of the most powerful and diversified association of professionals in the field of journalism today. Highly respected in the United States and abroad, its membership includes the most successful people in this field.

The enclosed letter by The International Communications Group demonstrates that Mr. Dillion is indeed an individual of extraordinary ability and accomplishment.

On the basis of the above, we submit that Mr. Dillion and the proposed position with **Spectra Magazine** are clearly within the O-1 petition standards, and therefore, we respectfully request that this petition by approved.

Thank your for your attention to this matter.

Very truly yours,

Francis Cho
Vice-President
Media Department
The World Press Corporation

F. P-1 NONIMMIGRANT VISA

P-1 classification applies to an alien who is coming temporarily to the United States to:

1) To perform at a specific athletic competition as an athlete, individually or as part of a group or team, at an internationally recognized level of performance.

2) To perform with, or as an integral and essential part of the performance of, an entertainment group that has been recognized internationally as being outstanding in the discipline for a sustained and substantial period of time, and who has a sustained a substantial relationship with the group (for at least one year) and provides functions integral to the performance of the group. There are certain exceptions to the one-year requirement that will be discussed in greater detail later in this chapter.

Foreign Residence Requirement and Dual Intent

P visaholders, unlike O-1 visaholders are required to maintain a foreign residence abroad that they have no intention of abandoning. However, P visaholders, excluding essential support personnel, may legitimately come to the United States for a temporary period as a P nonimmigrant and depart voluntarily at the end of authorized stay and at the same time lawfully seek to become a permanent resident of the United States. The approval of a permanent labor certification or the filing of a preference petition for an individual should not be considered as a basis for denying a P petition, a request for extension of stay or an application for change of status. P support personnel may not apply for permanent residence while in P nonimmigrant status.

P-1A Classification as an Athlete in an Individual Capacity or as part of a Team

P-1A classification may be granted to a foreign national who is coming temporarily to perform at a specific athletic competition as an athlete, individually or as a part of a group or team, at an internationally recognized level of performance.

P-1B Classification as a Member of an Entertainment Group

A P-1B classification may be granted to individuals who perform with or are an integral part of the performance of an entertainment group that has been recognized as being outstanding for a sustained and substantial period of time. Individual entertainers may not be granted P-1B status to perform separate and apart from the group. An entertainment group must have been established for a minimum of one year or more, and seventy-five percent of the members of the group must have been performing entertainment services for the group during the prior year.

Standards for an Internationally Recognized Athlete or Athletic Team

A petition for an athlete or athletic team must be accompanied by evidence that the team as a unit has achieved international recognition in the sport. Each member of the team is accorded P-1A classification based on the international reputation of the team. A petition for an athlete who will compete individually or as a member of a United States team must be accompanied by evidence that the athlete has achieved international recognition in the sport based on his or her reputation.

Internationally Recognized means having a high level of achievement in a field evidenced by a degree of skill and recognition substantially above that ordinarily encountered, to the extent that such achievement is renowned, leading or well-known in more than one country.

Arts includes fields of creative activity or endeavor such as, but not limited to, fine arts, visual arts, and performing arts.

Competition, event, or performance means an activity such as an athletic competition, athletic season, tournament, tour, exhibit, project, entertainment event, or engagement.

Contract means the written agreement between the petitioner and the beneficiary that explains the terms and conditions of employment. The contract must describe the services to be performed, and specify the wages, hours of work, working conditions, and any fringe benefits.

Group means two or more persons established as one entity or unit to provide a service.

Member of a Group means a person who is actually performing the entertaining services.

Sponsor means an established organization in the United States which will not directly employ a P-1, P-2, or P-3 alien, but will assume responsibility for the accuracy of the terms and conditions specified in the petition.

Team means two or more persons organized to perform together as a competitive unit in a competitive event.

Documentary Evidence Required P-1A Petition for an Individual Athlete or Athletic Team:

A petition for a P-1A athlete or athletic team must include:

- A tendered contract with a major United States sports league or team, or a tendered contract in an individual sport commensurate with international recognition in that sport, if such contracts are normally executed in the sport, and

- Documentation of at least two of the following:

- Evidence of having participated to a significant extent in a prior season with a major United States sports league.

- Evidence of having participated in international competition with a national team;

- Evidence of having participated to a significant extent in a prior season for a United States college or university of intercollegiate competition.

- A written statement from an official of a major United States sports league or an official of the governing body of the sport which details how the foreign national or team is internationally recognized;

- A written statement from a member of the sports media or a recognized expert in the sport which details how the foreign national or team is internationally recognized;

- Evidence that the individual or team is ranked if the sport has international rankings; or

- Evidence that the foreign national or team has received a significant honor or award in the sport.

Documentary evidence required for P-1B Members of Internationally Recognized Entertainment Groups:

A petition for P-1B classification for the members of an entertainment group must be accompanied by:

- Evidence that the group has been established and performing regularly for a period of at least one-year;

- A statement from the petitioner listing each member of the group and the exact dates for which each member has been employed on a regular basis by the group; and

- Evidence that the group has been internationally recognized in the discipline for a sustained and substantial period of time. This may be demonstrated by the submission of evidence of the group's nomination or receipt of significant international awards or prizes for outstanding achievement in its field or by three of the following different types of documentation:

- Evidence that the group has performed and will perform as a starring or leading entertainment group in productions or events which have a distinguished reputation as evidenced by critical reviews, advertisements, publicity releases, publications, contracts or endorsements;

- Evidence that the group has achieved international recognition and acclaim for outstanding achievement in its field as evidenced by reviews in major newspapers, trade journals, magazines, or other published material;

- Evidence that the group has performed and will perform services as a leading or starring group for organizations and establishments that have a distinguished reputation evidenced by articles in newspapers, trade journals, publications or testimonials;

- Evidence that the group has a record of major commercial or critically acclaimed successes, as evidenced by such indicators as ratings, standing in the field, box office receipts, record, cassette or video sales, and other achievements in the field as reported in trade journals, major newspapers or other publications;

- Evidence that the group has achieved significant recognition for achievements from organizations, critics, government agencies, or other recognized experts in the field. Such testimonials must be in a form that clearly indicates the author's authority, expertise and knowledge of the group's achievements; or

- Evidence that the group has commanded or now commands a high salary or other substantial remuneration for services comparable to others similarly situated in the field as evidenced by contracts or other reliable evidence.

Alien Circus Personnel

The one-year group membership and international recognition requirement are not applicable to alien circus personnel who perform as part of a circus or circus group, or who constitute an integral and essential part of the performance of such circus or circus group. The one-year requirement is waived provided that the foreign national is coming to join a circus that has been recognized nationally as outstanding for a sustained and substantial period of time.

Other Types of Waiver of International Recognition Requirement and One-Year Member of Group Requirement

In addition to alien circus personnel, the one-year group membership requirement may be waived in cases where an individual is replacing an essential member of an P-1B entertainment group due to illness or unanticipated and exigent circumstances or in the case of an individual who augments the group by performing a critical role.

The international recognition requirement may be waived in the case of an entertainment group that is recognized nationally (not internationally), and is outstanding in its discipline for a sustained and substantial period of time. INS regulations suggest that an entertainment group may find it difficult to demonstrate recognition in more than one country when the group has had limited access to international news media or because of the limitations of geography. For example, a popular music group from an island in the South Pacific may find it difficult to show international recognition but instead the group can show enormous popularity for over twenty-years in most of the islands located in the South Pacific.

Consultation Requirements for P-1 Athletes and Entertainment Groups

Consultation with a labor organization that has expertise in the area of the foreign national's sport or entertainment field is required in a P-1 petition. The advisory opinion provided by the labor organization must evaluate and/or describe the individual or the group's ability and achievements in the field of endeavor, comment on whether the individual or group is internationally recognized for achievements, and state whether the services the individual or group is coming to perform are appropriate for an internationally recognized athlete or entertainment group. In lieu of an advisory opinion, the labor organization may also submit a no objection letter.

Consultation Requirements for P-1 Circus Personnel

The consultation by the labor organization required for a P-1 petition on behalf of circus personnel should comment on whether the circus that will employ the individual has national recognition as well as any other aspect of the individual's qualifications that the labor organization deems appropriate. A letter of no objection may also be submitted in lieu of an advisory opinion.

G. P-2 NONIMMIGRANT VISA: RECIPROCAL EXCHANGE GROUPS AND PERFORMERS

P-2 classification may be accorded to individuals who are coming temporarily to the United States to perform as artists or entertainers, individually or as part of a group, who will be performing under a reciprocal exchange program which is between an organization or organizations in the United States and that provides for the temporary exchange of artists and entertainers, or groups of artists and entertainers. The P-2 visaholder does not have to attain a certain level of recognition or expertise, but must be part of a genuine reciprocal program. However, the artists and entertainers from each participating country should be of similar quality and expertise. There is no requirement that the exchange consist of the same number of individuals. A foreign national country may send to the United States one person while the United States may send abroad an entire group.

Consultation Requirement for P-2 Alien in a Reciprocal Exchange Program

In P-2 petitions where an artist or entertainer is coming to the United States under a reciprocal exchange program, consultation with the appropriate labor organization is required to verify the existence of a viable exchange program. The advisory opinion from the labor organization must comment on the bona fides of the reciprocal exchange program and specify whether the exchange meets the statutory requirements.

Written evidence of consultation with an appropriate labor organization regarding the nature of the work to be done and the foreign national's qualifications are mandatory before a petition for P-2 classification can be approved.

Evidence Required For a P-2 Petition

A petition for P-2 classification must be accompanied by the following:

- A copy of the formal reciprocal exchange agreement between the U.S. organization or organizations which sponsor the foreign nationals and an organization or organizations in a foreign country which will receive the U.S. artists or entertainers;

- A statement from the sponsoring organization describing the reciprocal exchange of U.S. artists or entertainers as it relates to the specific petition for which P-2 classification is sought;

- Evidence that an appropriate labor organization in the United States was involved in negotiating, or has concurred with, the reciprocal exchange of U.S. and foreign artists and entertainers; and

- Evidence that the foreign nationals for whom P-2 classification is being sought and the U.S. artist or entertainers subject to the reciprocal agreement are artists and entertainers with comparable skills, and that the terms and conditions of employment are similar.

H. P-3 NONIMMIGRANT VISA

P-3 classification may be given to artists or entertainers, individually or as a group, coming to the U.S. for the purpose of developing, interpreting, representing, coaching or teaching a unique or traditional ethnic, folk, cultural, musical, theatrical, or artistic performance or presentation. The artist or entertainer must be coming to the United States to participate in a cultural event or events that will further the understanding or development of his or her art form. The program may be of a commercial or noncommercial nature.

"**Culturally unique**" means a style of artistic expression, methodology, or medium which is unique to a particular country, nation, society, class, ethnicity, religion, tribe or other group of persons.

Documentary Requirements for a Petition Involving a Culturally Unique Program

A petition for P-3 classification must be accompanied by:

- Affidavits, testimonials, or letters from recognized experts attesting to the authenticity and excellence of the individual's or group's skills in performing, presenting, coaching, or teaching the unique or traditional art form, explaining the level of recognition accorded the individual or group in the native country or another country, and giving the credentials of the expert, including the basis of his or her knowledge of the individual's or group's skills and recognition; and

- Documentation that the performance of the individual or group is culturally unique, as evidenced by reviews in newspapers, journals, or other published materials; and

- Evidence that all of the performances or presentations will be culturally unique events.

Consultation Requirements for P-3 in a Culturally Unique Program

Consultation with an appropriate labor organization is required for P-3 petitions involving foreign nationals in culturally unique programs. The advisory opinion should evaluate the cultural uniqueness of the foreign national's skills, state whether the events are cultural in nature and state whether the event or activity is appropriate for P-3 classification. A no objection letter may be substituted for an advisory opinion.

Essential Support Aliens

An essential support alien may be granted the same classification as the primary P visaholder based on a support relationship.

Essential Support Alien means a highly skilled, essential person, determined by the INS to be an integral part of the performance of a P-1, P-2 or P-3 visaholder because he or she performs support services which cannot be readily performed by a United States worker and which are essential to the successful performance of services by the P visaholder. Such foreign nationals must have appropriate qualifications to perform the services, critical knowledge of the specific services to be performed, and experience providing such support to the P-1, P-2 or P-3 visaholder. Qualified support personnel may include, but are not limited to, trainers or managers for athletes, lighting engineers, riggers, backline stage crew and other technical support for stage and film productions.

Consultation Requirements for Essential Support Aliens

Written consultation on petitions for P-1, P-2 or P-3 essential support aliens must be made with a labor organization with expertise in the skill area involved. The advisory opinion provided by the labor organization must evaluate the foreign national's essentiality to and working relationship with the artist or entertainer, and state whether

United States workers are available who can perform the support services.

Exceptions to the Consultation Requirement

There are two instances in which an advisory opinion need not always be submitted with a P petition:

The burden of submitting a consultation is lifted from the petitioner when the petitioner requests expeditious handling of the P petition. If the INS determines that a petition merits expeditious handling, the INS will telephonically contact the appropriate labor and/or management organization and request an advisory opinion. The labor and/or management organization then has 24 hours to respond the Service's request. If the organization fails to respond, the INS will render a decision on the petition without the advisory opinion.

If there is no appropriate consulting entity in existence the consultation requirement will be waived. The petitioner has the burden of establishing that an appropriate peer group, including a labor organization, does not exist. The INS will render a decision based on the evidence on record. To establish that an appropriate peer group does not exist, the petitioner should include affidavits or statements from practitioners in the foreign national's field or from a related labor organization attesting that an appropriate peer group does not exist. The petitioner should also include a statement detailing the attempt to locate an appropriate group.

Spouses and Dependents

The spouse and unmarried minor children of P-1, P-2 or P-3 visaholders are entitled to **P-4** nonimmigrant classification, subject to the same period of admission and limitations as the principal alien beneficiary, if they are accompanying or following to join the alien beneficiary in the United States. Neither the spouse nor the children of a P primary visaholder may accept employment unless he or she has been granted employment authorization under a separate immigrant or nonimmigrant visa category.

Duration of Stay

For all P nonimmigrants, the maximum initial period of admission that will be granted by the INS will be the time period necessary to complete the event, activity, or performance, not to exceed one year, with the exception of individual athletes who may be admitted for up to a period of five years.

An extension of stay for a P-1 individual athlete and support personnel may be authorized for a period of five years, for a total period of authorization not to exceed ten years. Extensions of stay for all other P-1, P-2, and P-3 visaholders may be granted for periods of up to one year, to continue or complete the same event or activity for which they were originally admitted.

Return Transportation Requirement

The employer and petitioner whose offer of employment formed the basis of an approved O or P nonimmigrant petition are jointly and severally liable for the reasonable cost of return transportation for O and P nonimmigrants whose employment terminates for reasons other than voluntary resignation.

I. FILING REQUIREMENTS

The filing requirements for P petitions are substantially the same as for O petitions. Form I-129 with O/P supplement and all accompanying documentation should be filed with the INS Service Center having jurisdiction over the beneficiary's place of employment or performance. In the case of multiple employment or performance sites the petition, supporting documentation including a complete itinerary should be filed with the INS Service Center having jurisdiction in the area where the petitioner is located. The petitioner on behalf of a P nonimmigrant must be a U.S. employer, a U.S. sponsoring organization, a U.S. agent, or a foreign employer through a U.S. agent. For more detailed information concerning U.S. agents filing on behalf of foreign employers see the filing requirements for O petitions discussed earlier in this chapter. O and P petitions may not be filed more than six months in advance of the actual need of the beneficiary's services. There is no limit to the number of O and P nonimmigrants who may be admitted to the United States each year.

J. **"30 Day Rule" for Professional Athletes**

INS regulations include a special provision for professional athletes who are traded between U.S. sports teams. The "30 day rule" for O and P professional athletes was codified in final rules that took effect in April 1997. The 30-day rule allows an O or P athlete who is traded to a new team to play for the new team prior to the filing of a new petition as long as the new petition is filed within 30 days. During the thirty-day period the traded athlete is deemed to be in valid O or P status and may continue to play for the new team while the petition is being adjudicated, as long as the new petition was submitted during the initial thirty days. If the petition is denied, employment authorization will automatically cease.

SAMPLE LETTER ON BEHALF OF P-3 GROUP PERFORMING IN A CULTURALLY UNIQUE EXCHANGE GROUP

Re: P-3 Application of The Japanese Ancient Dance Troupe

Dear Sir/Madam:

The enclosed petition is submitted on behalf of the Japanese Ancient Dance Troupe, as a P-3 Culturally Unique Group, for a period of one year.

The Petitioner

The Japanese Ancient Dance Troupe is a world-renowned dance troupe composed of 50 individuals, that tours internationally delighting audiences with its unique presentation of these ancient cultural rituals dating back to the Meji Regime in Japan. The Japanese Ancient Dance Troupe is recognized by governmental agencies, entertainment and production organizations and is acclaimed in newspapers and national magazines.

In view of the enclosed documentation, it is evident that the Japanese Ancient Dance Troupe is indeed culturally unique, and we respectfully note that an appropriate labor organization does not exist for the representation of such performers. Therefore, we request that the Service render a decision on the evidence of the record as directed by statute.

The Group

We presently wish to have 14 members of the group classified as P-3 aliens so that the beneficiary group may travel to the United States where they are scheduled to perform in several major cities, both in the United States and Canada.

A complete list of all the performers is included on Form I-129 and its Supplement Form and we note that all of the aliens included in the petition have been employed by and associated with our troupe for over one year.

The Proposed Itinerary

We presently wish to have the beneficiary group accorded P-3 Classification so that they may participate in our upcoming scheduled tour of North America. Below we list a copy of our proposed itinerary:

May 9, 1999	Montreal, Canada
May 10, 1999	Washington, D.C.
May 16, 1999	Chicago, Illinois
May 17, 1999	Winnipeg, Canada
May 23, 1999	New York City
May 30, 1999	Edmonton, Canada

June 15, 1999	Calgary, Canada
July 4, 1999	San Francisco, California
August 1, 1999	Los Angeles, California
September 4, 1999	Houston, Texas
September 17, 1999	Dallas, Texas
October 20, 1999	Toronto, Canada
November 1, 1999	Santa Fe, New Mexico
November 30, 1999	Tucson, Arizona
December 20, 1999	Vancouver, British Columbia, Canada
February 14, 2000	Boston, Massachusetts
March 15, 2000	Charleston, South Carolina
April 1, 2000	Key West, Florida
May 1, 2000	New Orleans, Louisiana

Should any of the individuals in the beneficiary group's employment terminate for reasons other than voluntary resignation, we hereby accept responsibility to provide for his or her return transportation back to Japan.

U.S. citizens and residents of Japanese origin eagerly await the opening of this dance extravaganza, and we urge your expedited adjudication of this petition in order for the scheduled performances be held to the satisfaction and gratification of the this sector of the American population.

Please also find enclosed translated copies of Japanese newspaper articles describing and reviewing various performances of the Japanese Dance Group.

We respectfully request that the Japanese Ancient Dance Group be accorded P-3 classification on the basis of the enclosed documentation and that approval be cabled to the American Consulate in Tokyo.

Very truly yours,

Ken Yamaguchi
Artistic Director
The Japanese Ancient Dance Troupe

OMB No. 1115-0168

SAMPLE FORM I-129 FOR P-1B NONIMMIGRANT

Petition for a Nonimmigrant Worker

START HERE - Please Type or Print

Part 1. Information about the employer filing this petition.

If the employer is an individual, use the top name line. Organizations should use the second line.

Family Name | Given Name | Middle Initial

Company or Organization Name: French Gymnastic Team

Address - Attn:

Street Number and Name: 16 West Broadway | Apt. #

City: New York | State or Province: New York

Country: USA | Zip/Postal Code: 10100

IRS Tax #: 13-9999999

Part 2. Information about this Petition.

(See instructions to determine the fee)

1. **Requested Nonimmigrant classification:** (write classification symbol at right) P-1B
2. **Basis for Classification** (check one)
   - a. ☒ New employment
   - b. ☐ Continuation of previously approved employment without change
   - c. ☐ Change in previously approved employment
   - d. ☐ New concurrent employment
3. **Prior Petition.** If you checked other than "New Employment" in item 2 (above) give the most recent prior petition numbers for the worker(s):
4. **Requested Action:** (check one)
   - a. ☒ Notify the office in Part 4 so the person(s) can obtain a visa or be admitted (NOTE: a petition is not required for an E-1, E-2, or R visa)
   - b. ☐ Change the person(s) status and extend their stay since they are all now in the U.S. in another status (see instructions for limitations). This is available only where you check "New Employment" in item 2, above.
   - c. ☐ Extend or amend the stay of the person(s) since they now hold this status.
5. **Total number of workers in petition:** one (1)

   (See instructions for where more than one worker can be included)

Part 3. Information about the person(s) you are filing for.

Complete the blocks below. Use the continuation sheet to name each person included in this petition.

If an entertainment group, give their group name.

Family Name: Bouley | Given Name: Cisley | Middle Initial

Date of Birth (Month/Day/Year): 04/04/1984 | Country of Birth: France

Social Security #: N/A | A #: N/A

If in the United States, complete the following:

Date of Arrival (Month/Day/Year) | I-94 #

Current Nonimmigrant Status | Expires (Month/Day/Year)

FOR INS USE ONLY

Returned | Receipt

Resubmitted

Reloc Sent

Reloc Rec'd

Interviewed
- ☐ Petitioner
- ☐ Beneficiary

Class:
# of Workers:
Priority Number:
Validity Dates: From
To

☐ **Classification Approved**
- ☐ Consulate/POE/PFI Notified

At:
- ☐ Extension Granted
- ☐ COS/Extension Granted

Partial Approval (explain)

Action Block

To be Completed by Attorney or Representative, if any

☐ Fill in box if G-28 is attached to represent the applicant

VOLAG#

ATTY State License #

Continued on back.

SAMPLE FORM I-129 FOR P-1B NONIMMIGRANT (CONTINUED)

Part 4. Processing Information

a. If the person named in Part 3 is outside the U.S. or a requested extension of stay or change of status cannot be granted, give the U.S. consulate or inspection facility you want to be notified if this petition is approved.

Type of Office (check one): ☒ Consulate ☐ Pre-flight inspection ☐ Port of Entry

Office Address (City) Paris, France | U.S. State or Foreign Country

Person's Foreign Address 78 Rue Artistes, Paris, France

b. Does each person in this petition have a valid passport?
☐ Not required to have passport ☐ No - explain on separate paper ☒ Yes

c. Are you filing any other petitions with this one? ☒ No ☐ Yes - How many? ____

d. Are applications for replacement/Initial I-94's being filed with this petition? ☒ No ☐ Yes - How many? ____

e. Are applications by dependents being filed with this petition? ☒ No ☐ Yes - How many? ____

f. Is any person in this petition in exclusion or deportation proceedings? ☒ No ☐ Yes - explain on separate paper

g. Have you ever filed an immigrant petition for any person in this petition? ☒ No ☐ Yes - explain on separate paper

h. If you indicated you were filing a new petition in Part 2, within the past seven years has any person in this petition:

1) ever been given the classification you are now requesting? ☒ No ☐ Yes - explain on separate paper

2) ever been denied the classification you are now requesting? ☒ No ☐ Yes - explain on separate paper

i. If you are filing for an entertainment group, has any person in this petition not been with the group for at least 1 year?
☐ No ☐ Yes - explain on separate paper

Part 5. Basic Information about the proposed employment and employer.

Attach the supplement relating to the classification you are requesting.

Job Title: Gymnast

Nontechnical Description of Job: Participate in gymnastic events. See attached letter in support.

Address where the person(s) will work if different from the address in Part 1.

Is this a full-time position? ☐ No - Hours per week ☒ Yes

Wages per week or per year: $35,000 per yr.

Other Compensation (Explain): Awards & Prizes

Value per week or per year:

Dates of Intended employment From: 01/01/99 To: 01/01/2000

Type of petitioner - check one ☐ U.S. citizen or permanent resident ☒ Organization ☐ Other - explain on separate paper

Type of business: Athletic Team

Year established: 1956

Current number of employees: 85

Gross Annual Income: $30,000,000.00

Net Annual Income: $18,000,000.00

Part 6. Signature.

Read the information on penalties in the instructions before completing this section.

I certify, under penalty of perjury under the laws of the United States of America, that this petition, and the evidence submitted with it, is all true and correct. If filing this on behalf of an organization, I certify that I am empowered to do so by that organization. If this petition is to extend a prior petition, I certify that the proposed employment is under the same terms and conditions as in the prior approved petition. I authorize the release of any information from my records, or from petitioning organization's records, which the Immigration and Naturalization Service needs to determine eligibility for the benefit being sought.

Signature and title	Print Name	Date

Please note: If you do not completely fill out this form and the required supplement, or fail to submit required documents listed in the instructions, then the person(s) filed for may not be found eligible for the requested benefit, and this petition may be denied.

Part 7. Signature of person preparing form if other than above.

I declare that I prepared this application at the request of the above person and it is based on all information of which I have knowledge.

Signature	Print Name	Date

Firm Name and Address

OMB No. 1115-0168
O and P Classification
Supplement to Form I-129

O AND P SUPPLEMENT TO FORM I-129

Name of person or organization filing petition: French Gymnastic Team

Name of person or group or total number of workers you are filing for: Cisley Bouley

Classification sought (check one):

- ☐ O-1 Alien of extraordinary ability in sciences, art, education, or business
- ☐ P-2 Artist or entertainer for reciprocal exchange program
- ☐ P-2S Essential Support Personnel for P-2

P-1B as a member of an entertainment group or athletic team.

Explain the nature of the event

Participate in pre-Olympic Trials including the Pan American Games and Inter-Global preliminaries that will determine pre-Olympic trial qualifications.

Describe the duties to be performed

Train and prepare to be able to compete in various national athletic events on a team sponsored by the French Government's Ministry of Health and Welfare

If filing for O-2 or P support alien, dates of alien's prior experience with the O-1 or P alien.

Have you obtained the required written consultation(s)? ☒ Yes - attached ☐ No - Copy of request attached

If not, give the following information about the organization(s) to which you have sent a duplicate of this petition.

O-1 Extraordinary ability

Name of recognized peer group | Phone #

Address | Date sent

O-1 Extraordinary achievement in motion pictures or television

Name of labor organization | Phone #

Address | Date sent

Name of management organization | Phone #

Address | Date sent

O-2 or P alien

Name of labor organization: United States Gymnastics Federation | Phone #: 212-555-5555

Address: 190 Fifth Avenue, New York, New York 19010 | Date sent

Form I-129 Supplement O/P/Q/R (12/11/91) N

Chapter Seven
A,C,D,F,G,I,J,K,M,Q AND R VISAS

A. INTRODUCTION

This chapter is devoted to the nonimmigrant categories not previously discussed in earlier chapters.

Miscellaneous Nonimmigrant Visas

A-1 Ambassador, Public Minister, Career Diplomatic or Consular Officer and members of their immediate family.

A-2 Other Foreign Government Official or employee, and members of their immediate family.

A-3 Attendant, servant, or personal employee of A-1 and A-2 visaholder, and members of their immediate family.

C-1 Alien in Continuous Transit

C-2 Alien Qualified to pass in transit to and from UN Headquarters District and Foreign Country

C-3 Foreign Government Official, members of immediate family, attendant, servant and personal employee in transit

D-1/D-2 Crewmember

F-1 Full-time Academic Students attending approved schools

F-2 Spouse and minor children of student.

G-1 Principal resident representative of recognized foreign member government to international organization, staff and members of immediate family.

G-2 Other representatives of recognized foreign member government to international organization and members of immediate family.

G-3 Representative of non-recognized or non-member foreign government to international organization and members of immediate family.

G-4 International organization officer or employee, and members of immediate family.

G-5 Attendant, servant or personal employee of G-1, G-2, G-3 and G-4 visaholders and members of immediate family.

I Representative of foreign media spouse and children.

J-1 Exchange Visitors in approved programs

J-2 Spouse and children of J-1 exchange visitor

K-1 Fiance(e)s of U.S. citizens immigrating to the United States.

K-2 Minor children of K-1 fiance(e) of United States citizen.

M Students in approved Vocational Study Programs

Q International Cultural Exchange Program Participants

R-1 Religious Workers

R-2 Spouse or child of R-1 visaholder

B. THE A VISA FOR FOREIGN DIPLOMATS

The A visa is issued to foreign diplomats and

dignitaries who seek to enter the United States temporarily in connection with official business on behalf of a foreign government. A-1 classification is reserved for Ambassadors, Public Ministers, Counselors, Secretaries, Attaches, Consul Generals, Consuls, Vice Consuls, other career diplomats and consular officers and their immediate family. A-2 classification is reserved for other accredited officials of permanent diplomatic missions or consular posts established in the United States by a foreign government and for employees performing official duties on behalf of foreign governments who are not otherwise eligible for A-1 classification and their immediate family. A-3 classification is reserved for the attendants, servants, and personal employees of those individuals accorded A-1 or A-2 classification.

A foreign national is classifiable as A-1 or A-2, if the principal visaholder:

- Has been accredited by a foreign government legitimately recognized by the United States;

- Intends to engage solely in official activities for that foreign government while in the United States; and

- Has been accepted by the President, the Secretary of State, or a consular officer acting on behalf of the Secretary of State.

Foreign diplomatic personnel, whether they are A or G visaholders are entitled to bring with them members of their immediate family. A member of the immediate family of a principal alien is also classifiable as A-1 or A-2 nonimmigrant.

The Immediate Family, for the purposes of the A visa category, is defined as the spouse and unmarried sons and daughters, whether by blood or adoption, who are not members of some other household and who will reside regularly in the household of the principal alien.

"Immediate Family" also includes any other close relative of the principal alien or spouse who are:

- Recognized as dependents by the sending government, as demonstrated by eligibility for rights and benefits, such as the issuance of a diplomatic or official passport and travel and other allowances which would be granted to the spouse and children of the principal alien, and

- Any other person individually authorized by the Department of State.

A-1 and A-2 visaholders are admitted to the United States without a time limit and are not required to apply for an extension of stay as long as the A-1 or A-2 visaholder continues to be recognized by the Secretary of State as entitled to that status. A-3 attendants, servants, and personal employees of A-1 and A-2 visaholders are admitted to the United States for an initial period of up to three years and are eligible for extensions of temporary stay in increments of up to two years. Certain dependents of A-1 and A-2 visaholders are eligible for work authorization if they meet specific statutory requirements and receive the approval of the Secretary of State. A-3 dependents are not eligible for work authorization.

C. THE C VISA FOR ALIENS IN TRANSIT

The "C" visa is designed for aliens intending to proceed in immediate and continuous transit through the United States. Generally, four types of individuals are accorded C status. These are: general transits passing through the United States while traveling to a foreign destination, transits without visas (TWOV), individuals in transit to and from the United Nations Headquarter District, and foreign government officials and their immediate families, attendants, servants, and personal employees in immediate and continuous transit through the United States.

A transit alien may be admitted to the United States for a period not to exceed twenty-nine days.

Generally, transit aliens may not apply for a change of status to any other nonimmigrant category, except for officials of foreign governments or employees of international organizations. Transit aliens will not be granted an extension of stay and are not permitted to accept employment while in the United States.

D. THE D-1/D-2 VISA FOR ALIEN CREW MEMBERS

The D nonimmigrant visa category is reserved for alien crew members who are serving in good faith on board a vessel or aircraft, in any capacity required for the normal operation and service of that vessel or aircraft. In addition, to be eligible for classification as a D nonimmigrant, the alien crew member must intend to land temporarily and solely in pursuit of his or her calling as a crew member and must depart from the United States with the vessel or aircraft on which he or she arrived or on some other vessel or aircraft.

A foreign national in D nonimmigrant status may be employed only in a crew member capacity on the vessel or aircraft of arrival, or on a vessel or aircraft of the same transportation company, and may not be employed in connection with domestic flights or movements of a vessel or aircraft.

To qualify for D status, crew members must intend to depart from the United States with the vessel on which they arrived or some other vessel within twenty-nine days of admission to the United States.

In addition, alien crewmembers are prohibited from performing longshore work in the United States. The INS defines longshore work as any activity relating to the loading or unloading of cargo, the operation of cargo-related equipment, and the handling of mooring lines on the dock when the vessel is made fast or let go in the United States or on the coast water of the United States. Regulations provide four exceptions to the general prohibition against longshore work.

Alien crew members will be permitted to perform longshore work for safety or environmental reasons, if it is the prevailing practice to permit such work (through collective bargaining agreements or attestations made to the DOL). In addition, alien crew members are permitted to do longshore work in Alaska, and crew members will be permitted to perform longshore work in other parts of the U.S. if the alien's vessel is registered in a country that allows crew members of U.S. registered ships to engage in longshore work.

D visaholders may not receive an extension of stay or change status while in D nonimmigrant classification.

E. THE F-1 STUDENT VISA

To qualify for an F-1 student visa a foreign national must maintain a foreign residence abroad that he or she has no intention of abandoning and be coming to the U.S. temporarily for the sole purpose of pursuing a full course of study as a bona fide student. However, to be eligible for an F-1 visa the foreign national must first follow the correct procedure for enrollment in a school or program that has been granted the authority by the INS to issue a Certificate of Eligibility, Form I-20 A-B/I-20 ID. Form I-20 enables the foreign national to apply for an F-1 visa at the American Consulate in his or her home country or in a third country (if possible). Eligible schools include colleges, universities, seminaries, conservatories, academic high schools, elementary schools, other academic institutions and language training programs.

In order to be accredited by the INS as an institution authorized to issue Form I-20 A-B/I-20 ID, the educational institution must first complete a rigorous and complex procedure. The educational institution must submit a petition to the INS along with detailed documentation concerning the institution's State or City certification, the institution's finances, the size and nature of the institution's physical plant, the institution's attendance and scholastic grading policies, and the institution's general curriculum along with the salaries of its teachers. Upon INS approval, the institution must designate a school official that will administer the records of all nonimmigrant students. The Designated School Official (DSO) is required to keep detailed records of each nonimmigrant student as well as fulfill the INS reporting requirements. Each school term, the INS requires a list of all the F-1 students including a description of each student's course of study and status. The Illegal Immigration Reform and Immigrant Responsibility Act of 1996 (IIRAIRA) imposed additional record keeping responsibilities on schools and designated exchange visitor programs who issue F, J, and M visas.

The Designated School Official also handles the issuance of the Form I-20 A-B/I-20 ID to nonimmigrant students. A properly issued Form I-20 A-B/I-20 ID enables a foreign student to apply for an F-1 visa. It indicates on its face the proposed course of study, duration of study and expected completion date. The form also indicates the anticipated cost of tuition and living expenses. Form I-20 must be presented by the student to the Consulate in connection with his or her application for a student visa. The consular officer endorses the Form I-20 A-B and sends it to the school. The endorsed I-20 ID is returned to the student who must keep it with them at all times.

Duration of Status

F-1 students are admitted to the United States for the period of authorized stay required to complete the course of study indicated on the Form I-20. The foreign student's period of authorized stay is described as duration of status (D/S). Duration of status is defined as the time during which an F-1 student is pursuing a full course of study at an approved educational institution, or engaging in practical training following completion of studies, plus sixty days to prepare for departure from the United States. The student is considered to be maintaining status if he or she is making normal progress towards completion of a course of study. The DSO must indicate the period of time normally required for completion of the specified course of study on the face of the Form I-20. A foreign student is required to apply for an extension of stay if he or she fails to complete the educational objective within the normal time allotted for the particular course of study.

Full Course of Study

The applicant must enroll in a full course of study. In general, a student who is enrolled in the usual number of courses needed to complete a specific degree within the usual time satisfies this requirement. Specifically, INS regulations define a full course of study as one of the following:

- Postgraduate study or postdoctoral study at a college or university, or undergraduate or postgraduate study at a conservatory or religious seminary, certified by the DSO as a full course of study;

- Undergraduate study at a college or university, certified by a school official to consist of at least **12 semester or quarter hours** of instruction per academic term if that educational institution utilizes the standard semester, trimester, or quarter hour systems. In addition, to be considered a full course of study all undergraduate students who are enrolled for a minimum of 12 semester or quarter hours are charged full-time tuition or are considered full-time for other administrative purposes, or its equivalent, except if the student needs a lesser course load to complete the course of study during the current term.

- Study in a post-secondary language, liberal arts, fine arts, or other non-vocational program at a school which confers upon its graduates recognized associate or other degrees or has established that its credits have been and are accepted unconditionally by at least three institutions of higher learning which are either: 1) A school (or school system) owned and operated as a public educational institution by the United States or a State or political subdivision thereof; or 2) a school accredited by a nationally recognized accrediting body, and which has been certified by a DSO to consist of at least 12 clock hours of instruction a week, or its equivalent as determined by the district director in the school approval process;

- Study in any other language, liberal arts, fine arts, or other non-vocational training program, certified by a DSO to consist of at least 18 clock hours of attendance a week if the dominant part of the course of study consists of classroom instruction, or to consist of at least 22 clock hours a week if the dominant part of the course of study consists of laboratory work;

- Study in a primary school or academic high school curriculum certified by a DSO to consist of class attendance for not less than the minimum number of hours a week prescribed by the school for normal progress towards graduation.

Proof of Nonimmigrant Intent

In order to be eligible for classification as an F-1 student, a foreign national must establish that he or she has a residence in a foreign country which he or she has no intention of abandoning and the student intends to depart the United States upon completion of the anticipated course of study. An applicant may usually establish that they have an intention to return abroad by presenting evidence that he or she has compelling economic, social or family ties in the homeland which would cause the student to leave the United States after completion of studies.

Proof of Sufficient Funds

An applicant for an F-1 student visa must also demonstrate that sufficient funds exist to cover the student's expenses while in the United States. The student must submit evidence that he or she is not likely to become a public charge or to resort to unauthorized employment in order to maintain financial solvency during the course of the student's studies in the United States.

An F-1 student whose stay in the United States may last several years is not required to establish availability of "cash in advance" to cover the entire period of intended studies. The applicant may be required to submit specific documentary evidence that shows the student has funds immediately available to cover all expenses for the first year of study, and that, barring any unforeseen change in circumstances, adequate funds will be available each continuing year from the same source or other financially reliable sources. Sources include financial aid, scholarships, work-study programs, family resources or a United States "sponsor."

Proficiency in the English Language

The applicant must satisfy the school of his or her proficiency in English. This is usually accomplished through the passing of an English exam. If the student is not proficient in English, he or she must attend courses in a language in which he or she is proficient or enroll in a course of study involving both academic study and English instruction.

SAMPLE FORM I-20 A-B

Certificate of Eligibility for Nonimmigrant (F-1) Student Status - For Academic and Language Students

OMB No. 1115-0051

This page must be completed and signed in the U.S. by a designated school official.

1. Family Name (surname): Kang
   First (given) name (do not enter middle name): Hae Sook
   Country of birth: South Korea — Date of birth (mo./day/year): 3/25/72
   Country of citizenship: South Korea — Admission number (Complete if known):

2. School (school district) name: Cornell University
   School official to be notified of student's arrival in U.S. (Name and Title): Mary Jones, Director of Foreign Student Admissions
   School address (include zip code): Ithaca, New York
   School code (including 3-digit suffix, if any) and approval date: NYS 214F 1111.000 approved on 1965

For Immigration Official Use

Visa issuing post — Date Visa issued

Reinstated, extension granted to:

3. This certificate is issued to the student named above for: (Check and fill out as appropriate)
   - a. ☐ Initial attendance at this school
   - b. ☒ Continued attendance at this school
   - c. ☐ School transfer. Transferred from ______
   - d. ☐ Use by dependents for entering the United States.
   - e. ☐ Other ______

4. Level of education the student is pursuing or will pursue in the United States: (check only one)
   - a. ☐ Primary
   - b. ☐ Secondary
   - c. ☐ Associate
   - d. ☒ Bachelor's
   - e. ☐ Master's
   - f. ☐ Doctorate
   - g. ☐ Language training
   - h. ☐ Other

5. The student named above has been accepted for a full course of study at this school, majoring in Mathematics
   The student is expected to report to the school no later than (date) N/A and complete studies not later than (date) 08/31/01
   The normal length of study is four years

6. ☒ English proficiency is required:
   - ☐ The student has the required English proficiency
   - ☐ The student is not yet proficient, English instructions will be given at the school.
   - ☐ English proficiency is not required because ______

7. This school estimates the student's average costs for an academic term of 8 (up to 12) months to be:
   - a. Tuition and fees $ 30,000.00
   - b. Living expenses $ 10,000.00
   - c. Expenses of dependents $ ______
   - d. Other(specify): $ ______

   Total $ 40,000.00

8. This school has information showing the following as the students means of support, estimated for an academic term of 8 months (Use the same number of months given in item 7).
   - a. Student's personal funds $ ______
   - b. Funds from this school $ ______ (specify type) ______
   - c. Funds from another source $ 40,000.00 (specify type and source) Parents
   - d. On-campus employment (if any) $ ______

   Total $ 40,000.00

9. Remarks: ______

10. School Certification: I certify under penalty of perjury that all information provided above in items 1 through 8 was completed before I signed this form and is true and correct; I executed this form in the United States after review and evaluation in the United States by me or other officials of the school of the student's application, transcripts or other records of courses taken and proof of financial responsibility, which were received at the school prior to the execution of this form; the school has determined that the above named student's qualifications meet all standards for admission to the school; the student will be required to pursue a full course of study as defined by 8 CFR 214.2(f)(6); I am a designated official of the above named school and I am authorized to issue this form.

Signature of designated school official — Name of school official (print or type) — Title — Date issued — Place issued (city and state)

11. Student Certification: I have read and agreed to comply with the terms and conditions of my admission and those of any extension of stay as specified on page 2. I certify that all information provided on this form refers specifically to me and is true and correct to the best of my knowledge. I certify that I seek to enter or remain in the United States temporarily, and solely for the purpose of pursuing a full course of study at the school named on page 1 of this form. I also authorize the named school to release any information from my records which is needed by the INS pursuant to 8 CFR 214.3(g) to determine my nonimmigrant status.

Elizabeth GIBSON

Signature of student — Name of student — Date

Signature of parent or guardian if student is under 18 — Name of parent/guardian (Print or type) — Address(city) — (State or province) — (Country) — (Date)

Form I20 A-B/I20ID(Rev 04-27-88)N

For official use only
Microfilm Index Number

IF YOU NEED MORE INFORMATION CONCERNING YOUR F-1 NONIMMIGRANT STUDENT STATUS AND THE RELATING IMMIGRATION PROCEDURES, PLEASE CONTACT EITHER YOUR FOREIGN STUDENT ADVISOR ON CAMPUS OR A NEARBY IMMIGRATION AND NATURALIZATION SERVICE OFFICE.

THIS PAGE, WHEN PROPERLY ENDORSED, MAY BE USED FOR ENTRY OF THE SPOUSE AND CHILDREN OF AN F-1 STUDENT FOLLOWING TO JOIN THE STUDENT IN THE UNITED STATES OR FOR REENTRY OF THE STUDENT TO ATTEND THE SAME SCHOOL AFTER A TEMPORARY ABSENCE FROM THE UNITED STATES.

For reentry of the student and/or the F-2 dependents (EACH CERTIFICATION SIGNATURE IS VALID FOR ONLY ONE YEAR.)

Signature of Designated School Official | Name of School Official(print or type) | Title | Date

Signature of Designated School Official | Name of School Official(print or type) | Title | Date

Signature of Designated School Official | Name of School Official(print or type) | Title | Date

Signature of Designated School Official | Name of School Official(print or type) | Title | Date

Signature of Designated School Official | Name of School Official(print or type) | Title | Date

Signature of Designated School Official | Name of School Official(print or type) | Title | Date

Dependent spouse and children of the F-1 student who are seeking entry/reentry to the U.S.

Name family (caps) first	Date of birth	Country of birth	Relationship to the F-1 student

Student Employment Authorization and other Records

For sale by the Superintendent of Documents. U.S. Government Printing Office. Washington, D.C. 20402

PRACTICE POINTERS FOR COMPLETING FORM I-20 A-B

- The information on this form will be fed into an automated data system by the INS when the student enters the United States and the INS will refer to this document throughout the student's stay in F status.

- Page 1 is to be filled out and signed by the Designated Student Official of the school. The student must also sign this page.

- Page 3 (not provided) is the student's carbon copy of Page 1. The INS, at the port of entry, will return it after the student's admission number is noted.

- Page 4 is the reverse side of the student's copy. It can be used by the student to reenter the United States after a temporary trip overseas (no longer than five months) or by family members who are joining the student in the United States. If any of the information on Page 1 changes, the school must issue a new Form I-20 A-B.

EMPLOYMENT POSSIBILITIES FOR AN F-1 STUDENT

Authorized employment is available to an alien in F-1 student status under three prescribed and limited situations:

- On-Campus Employment
- Limited Off-Campus Employment
- Employment for Practical Training Purposes relating to the foreign national's area of study.

On-Campus Employment

The Immigration & Naturalization Service does not need to approve on-campus employment. On-campus employment may either be performed on the school's premises (including on-location commercial firms that provide services for students on campus such as the school bookstore or cafeteria), or at an off-campus location which is educationally affiliated with the school.

Employment with an on-site commercial firm, such as a construction company building a school building, which does not provide direct student services, is not deemed on-campus employment. In the case of off-campus locations, the educational affiliation must be associated with the school's established curriculum or related to contractually funded research projects at the post-graduate level. In any event, the employment must be an integral part of the student's educational program. Employment authorized as on-campus employment may not exceed twenty hours a week while school is in session. An F-1 student may work full-time while school is not in session and during the annual vacation.

Off-Campus Work Authorization

An F-1 student may be granted off-campus employment authorization based on severe economic hardship caused by unforeseen circumstances beyond the student's control. Such circumstances include:

- loss of financial aid or on-campus employment without fault on the part of the student;
- substantial fluctuations in the value of currency or exchange rates;
- inordinate increases in tuition and/or living costs;
- unexpected changes in the financial condition of the student's source of support, such as bankruptcy of sponsor or loss of scholarship fund; and
- medical bills or other substantial and unexpected expenses.

An F-1 student may be authorized for off-campus employment due to severe economic hardship if the student has been in F-1 student status for one full academic year and is in good academic standing. Off-campus employment will be granted for twenty hours per week while school is in session and the student may work full time during holidays or school vacation. Employment authorization will be automatically terminated if the student fails to maintain F-1 status.

To apply for off-campus employment the foreign student must first submit Form I-538 to the Designated School Official for certification. The DSO must certify that on-campus employment opportunities are unavailable or insufficient, the student has been in F-1 status for one full academic year, the student is in good standing and is carrying a full course of study, that acceptance of off-campus employment will not interfere with the student's carrying a full course of study and that the requisite severe economic hardship exists. Once the DSO has certified the Form I-538, the student must then submit to the INS the Form I-20 ID, and Form I-765 (application for work authorization) along with the requisite fee, photographs and any supporting affidavits or documents demonstrating the circumstances of the student's severe economic hardship. The application for work authorization should be filed with the INS Service Center having jurisdiction over the student's place of residence.

If employment authorization is granted, the student will be issued an Employment Authorization Document. The employment authorization document is a small plastic card that contains the student's photograph and information about the work authorization. The student may not begin working until the authorization is issued. Work authorization is granted in increments of one year.

In emergent circumstances and in response to world economic crises the INS may temporarily lift employment restrictions for designated F-1 nonimmigrant students. In 1998, the INS in response to a request made by the Secretary of State, temporarily lifted certain employment restrictions for F-1 students whose financial support came from Indonesia, Malaysia, the Philippines, South Korea and Thailand. In the wake of the Asian economic crisis of 1998, the INS initiated a special relief program that allowed eligible students to work more than twenty hours per week, either on or off-campus, while school was in session. In addition, qualified students were eligible for work authorization under this program even if they had not completed one full academic year of study before applying.

SAMPLE FORM I-538

OMB Approval No. 1115-0060
Certification by Designated School Official

SECTION A. This section must be completed by student as appropriate (Please print or type):

1. Name: *(Family in CAPS)*	*(First)*	*(Middle)*	2. Date of birth:
GIBSON	Elizabeth		03/17/1976

3. Student admission number:	4. Date first granted F-1 or M-1 status: 07/31/1996
5. Level of education being sought: Bachelor's Degree	6. Student's major field of study: Chemistry

7. Describe the proposed employment for practical training:
Laboratory work in advanced chemistry

Beginning date: 01/15/99 Ending date: 08/31/99 Number of hours per week: 20

8. List all periods of previously authorized employment for practical training:

A. Curricular or work study:	B. Post completion of studies:
1/15/98 - 8/31/98	

Signature of student: ______________________ Date: ____________

SECTION B. This Section must be completed by the designated school official of the school the student is attending or was last authorized to attend:

9. I hereby certify that:

The student named above:
- ☒ is taking a full course of study at this school and the expected date of completion is: 12/31/99
- ☐ is taking less than a full course of study at this school because ____________
- ☐ Completed the course of study at this school on (date): ________
- ☐ Did not complete the course of study. Terminated attendance on (date) ________

Check one:

☒ A. The employment is for practical training in the student's field of study. The student has been in the educational program for at least 9 months and is eligible for the requested practical training in accordance with INS regulations at 8CFR 214.2(f) (10).

☐ B. The Endorsement for off-campus employment is based on the wage-and-labor attestation filed by the employer in accordance with the requirements set forth by the Secretary of Labor. The student has been in F-1 status for at least one year and is in good academic standing. Copy of the employer's attestation is attached.

☐ C. The employment is for an internship with a recognized international organization and is within the scope of the organization's sponsorship. The student has been in F-1 status for at least 9 months and is in good academic standing

10. Name and title of DSO	Signature	Date / /
11. Name of school	School file number	Telephone no.

For Official Use Only
Microfilm Index Number:

Form I-538 (Rev. 07/08/91)N (See instructions on reverse)

Instructions

A Student seeking authorization for off-campus employment (F-1 only) or practical training (F-1 and M-1) must submit as supporting documentation to Form I-765, Application for Employment Authorization, a certification by the designated school official (DSO) of the school they were last authorized to attend. Certification by the DSO is required of all students (F-1 and M-1) seeking authorization for employment off campus or practical training, including required or optional curricular practical training. The DSO must certify on Form I-538 that the proposed employment is directly related to the student's field of study. A copy of the DSO's certification must be mailed to the STCS data processing center,P.O.Box 140, Highway 25 South, London, Ky. 40741

All students requesting school certification must complete questions 1 through 6. Students requesting recommendation for practical training must complete questions 7 and 8. Answers to questions 7 through 9 may be continued on this page if needed.

M-1 students seeking extensions of stay must submit a completed Form I-539, Application to Extend time of Temporary Stay, supported by a current Form I-20M-N as appropriate.

Reporting Burden

Public reporting burden for this collection of information is estimated to average 4 minutes per response, including the time for reviewing instructions, searching existing data sources, gathering and maintaining the data needed, and completing and reviewing the collection of information. Send comments regarding this burden estimate or any other aspect of this collection of information, including suggestions for reducing this burden, to: U. S. Department of Justice, Immigration and Naturalization Service (Room 5304), Washington, D.C. 20536; and to the Office Management and Budget, Paperwork Reduction Project, OMB No. 1115-0060 Washington, D.C. 20503.

Comments: ______________________________

SAMPLE FORM I-765 APPLICATION FOR EMPLOYMENT AUTHORIZATION

Action Stamp

Fee Stamp

☐ Application Approved. Employment Authorized / Extended (Circle one) ______________ (Date).
until ______________ (Date).

Subject to the following conditions: ______________

☐ Application Denied.

☐ Failed to establish eligibility under 8 CFR 274a.12(a) or (c)

☐ Failed to establish economic necessity as required in 8 CFR 274a.12(c) (14), (18) and 8 CFR 214.2(f)

I am applying for: ☒ Permission to accept employment

☐ Replacement (of lost employment authorization document).

☐ Renewal of my permission to accept employment (attach previous employment authorization document).

1. Name (Family Name in CAPS) (First) (Middle)
GIBSON Elizabeth

2. Other Names Used (Include Maiden Name)

3. Address in the United States (Number and Street) (Apt. Number)
University of Maryland, 9135 La Plata Hall

(Town or City) (State/Country) (ZIP Code)
College Park Maryland 20748

4. Country of Citizenship/Nationality
Ireland

5. Place of Birth (Town or City) (State/Province) (Country)
Limerick Ireland

6. Date of Birth (Month/Day/Year)
03/17/1976

7. Sex
☐ Male ☒ Female

8. Marital Status ☐ Married ☒ Single ☐ Widowed ☐ Divorced

9. Social Security Number (Include all Numbers you have ever used)
N/A

10. Alien Registration Number (A-Number) or I-94 Number (if any)
A11 111 112

11. Have you ever before applied for employment authorization from INS?
☒ Yes (If yes, complete below) ☐ No

Which INS office? Date(s)
Baltimore, Maryalnd 1/15/98

Results (Granted or Denied - attach all documentation)
Granted

12. Date of Last Entry into the U.S. (Month/Day/Year)
02/14/97

13. Place of Last Entry into the U.S.
Washington, D.C.

14. Manner of Last Entry (Visitor, Student, etc.)
Student

15. Current Immigration Status (Visitor, Student, etc.)
F-1

16. Go to Part 2 of the instructions, Eligibility Categories. In the space below, place the letter and number of the category you selected from the instructions (For example, (a)(8), (c)(17)(iii), etc.).
Eligibility under 8 CFR 274a.12

(c) (3) (i)

Certification

Your Certification: I certify, under penalty of perjury under the laws of the United States of America, that the foregoing is true and correct. Furthermore, I authorize the release of any information which the Immigration and Naturalization Service needs to determine eligibility for the benefit I am seeking. I have read the instructions in Part 2 and have identified the appropriate eligibility category in Block #16.

Signature Telephone Number Date

Signature of Person Preparing Form if Other Than Above: I declare that this document was prepared by me at the request of the applicant and is based on all information of which I have any knowledge.

Print Name Address Signature Date

Initial Receipt	Resubmitted	Relocated		Completed		
		Rec'd	Sent	Approved	Denied	Returned

SAMPLE FORM I-765 (CONTINUED)

GROUP A

The current immigration laws and regulations permit certain classes of aliens to work in the United States. If you are an alien described below, you do not need to request employment authorization be granted to you, but you do need to request a document to show that you are able to work in the United States. For aliens in classes (a) (3) through (a) (11), NO FEE will be required for the original card or for extension cards. A FEE will be required if a replacement employment authorization document is needed. A FEE IS REQUIRED for aliens in item (a) (12) who are over the age of 14 years and under the age of 65 years.

Place an X in the box next to the number which applies to you.

☐ (a) (3) - I have been admitted to the United States as a refugee.

☐ (a) (4) - I have been paroled to the United States as a refugee.

☐ (a) (5) - My application for asylum has been granted.

☐ (a) (6) - I am the fiance(e) of a United States citizen and I have K-1 nonimmigrant status; OR I am the dependent of a fiance(e) of a United States citizen and I have K-2 nonimmigrant status.

☐ (a) (7) - I have N-8 or N-9 nonimmigrant status in the United States.

☐ (a) (8) - I am a citizen of the Federated States of Micronesia or of the Marshall Islands.

☐ (a) (10) - I have been granted withholding of deportation.

☐ (a) (11) - I have been granted extended voluntary departure by the Attorney General.

☐ (a) (12) - I am an alien who has been registered for Temporary Protected Status (TPS) and I want an employment authorization document. FEE REQUIRED.

GROUP C

The immigration law and regulations allow certain aliens to apply for employment authorization. If you are an alien described in one of the classes below, you may request employment authorization from the INS and, if granted, you will receive an employment authorization document. The instruction FEE REQUIRED printed below refers to your initial document, replacement, and extension.

Place an X in the box next to the number which applies to you.

☐ (c) (1) - I am the dependent of a foreign government official (A-1 or A-2). I have attached certification from the Department of State recommending employment. NO FEE.

☐ (c) (2) - I am the dependent of an employee of the Coordination Council of North American Affairs and I have E-1 nonimmigrant status. I have attached certification of my status from the American Institute of Taiwan. FEE REQUIRED.

☒ (c) (3) (i) - I am a foreign student (F-1). I have attached certification from the designated school official recommending employment for economic necessity. I have also attached my INS Form I-20 ID copy. FEE REQUIRED.

☐ (c) (3) (ii) - I am a foreign student (F-1). I have attached certification from the designated school official recommending employment for practical training. I have also attached my INS Form I-20 ID copy. FEE REQUIRED.

☐ (c) (3) (iii) - I am a foreign student (F-1). I have attached certification from the designated school official and I have been offered employment under the sponsorship of an international organization within the meaning of the International Organization Immunities Act. I have certification from this sponsor and I have also attached my INS Form I-20 ID copy. FEE REQUIRED.

☐ (c) (4) - I am the dependent of an officer or employee of an international organization (G-1 or G-4). I have attached certification from the Department of State recommending employment. NO FEE.

☐ (c) (5) - I am the dependent of an exchange visitor and I have J-2 nonimmigrant status. FEE REQUIRED.

☐ (c) (6) - I am a vocational foreign student (M-1). I have attached certification from the designated school official recommending employment for practical training. I have also attached my INS Form I-20 ID Copy. FEE REQUIRED.

☐ (c) (7) - I am the dependent of an individual classified as NATO-1 through NATO-7. FEE REQUIRED.

☐ (c) (8) - I have filed a non-frivolous application for asylum in the United States and the application is pending. FEE REQUIRED FOR REPLACEMENT ONLY.

☐ (c) (9) - I have filed an application for adjustment of status to lawful permanent resident status and the application is pending. FEE REQUIRED.

☐ (c) (10) - I have filed an application for suspension of deportation and the application is pending. FEE REQUIRED.

☐ (c) (11) - I have been paroled into the United States for emergent reasons or for reasons in the public interest. FEE REQUIRED.

☐ (c) (12) - I am a deportable alien and I have been granted voluntary departure either prior to or after my hearing before the immigration judge. FEE REQUIRED.

☐ (c) (14) - I have been granted deferred action by INS as an act of administrative convenience to the government. I understand that I must show economic necessity and I will refer to the instructions concerning "Basic Criteria to Establish Economic Necessity." FEE REQUIRED.

☐ (c) (16) - I entered the United States prior to January 1, 1972 and have been here since January 1, 1972. I have applied for registry as a lawful permanent resident alien and my application is pending. FEE REQUIRED.

☐ (c) (17) (i) - I am a (B-1) visitor for business. I am and have been (before coming to the United States) the domestic or personal servant for my employer who is temporarily in the United States. FEE REQUIRED.

☐ (c) (17) (ii) - I am a visitor for business (B-1) and am the employee of a foreign airline. I have B-1 nonimmigrant classification because I am unable to obtain visa classification as a treaty trader. (E-1). FEE REQUIRED.

☐ (c) (18) - I am a deportable alien who has been under an order of supervision (OS). I understand that I must show economic necessity and I will refer to the instructions concerning "Basic Criteria to Establish Economic Necessity." FEE REQUIRED.

☐ (c)(19) - I am an alien who is prima facie eligible for temporary Protected Status (TPS) and (1) INS has not given me a reasonable chance to register during the first 30 days of the registration period [FEE REQUIRED], or (2) INS has not made a final decision as to my eligibility for TPS. FEE REQUIRED.

Renewal Procedure for Work Authorization

Employment authorization based upon severe economic hardship is valid for one year. Employment authorization is renewable in one-year increments until the expected date of the student's completion of the course of study. The student must maintain good academic standing and remain in student status. To renew the employment authorization, the student must file the following with the INS:

- Copy of Form I-94
- Form I-765;
- Form I-20 ID;
- Copy of previous EAD card;
- photographs; and
- Filing Fee.

Practical Training

Practical training is available to F-1 students who have been lawfully enrolled on a full-time basis in an INS approved college, university, conservatory, or seminary for at least nine consecutive months. Students in English language training programs are ineligible for practical training. An eligible F-1 student may request employment authorization for practical training in a position which is directly related to his or her major area of study. There are two types of practical training available: curricular practical training or optional practical training.

Curricular Practical Training Programs

Curricular practical training programs are programs, which generally take place during the course of an F-1 student's academic year as a supplement to the course of study. Curricular practical training must be an integral part of an established curriculum. It may be an alternate work/study program, internship, cooperative education, or any other type of required internship or practicum that is offered by sponsoring employers through cooperative agreements with the school.

An F-1 student must be authorized by the Designated School Official to participate in a curricular practical training program. The DSO will endorse the student's I-20 ID by writing "full-time (or part-time) curricular practical training authorized for (employer) at (location) from (date) to (date)." The DSO will also certify and forward a completed Form I-538 to the INS. INS approval is not required.

Students who have received one year or more of full-time curricular practical training are ineligible for optional practical training. To be eligible for curricular practical training, the student must have been in F-1 status for at least nine months. Exceptions to this requirement are provided for students enrolled in graduate studies that require immediate participation in curricular practical training.

Optional Practical Training Programs

Optional Practical Training is the term used by the INS to refer to temporary employment for practical training directly related to the student's major area of study. It may take place pre-graduation or post-graduation and is available in addition to curricular training. However, a student is only eligible for a total period of optional practical training of twelve months.

Optional practical training may be authorized:

- during the student's annual vacation or when school is not in session;

- while school is in session, provided that the training does not exceed twenty hours a week;

- after completion of all course requirements for the degree (excluding thesis or equivalent), if the student is in a bachelor's, master's, or doctoral degree program; or

- after completion of the course of study. All training must be completed within the fourteen-month period following the completion of study.

NOTE: An F-1 student can get his or her "foot in the door" with a particular employer by utilizing practical training work authorization. At the end of the training program, it is often possible to apply for an H-1B nonimmigrant visa with the same employer.

Procedure for Applying for Practical Training

The student should request a recommendation to accept practical training from the Designated Student Official within a 120-day period prior to commencement of employment and up to sixty days after completion of the course of study.

The student must request the recommendation by submitting Form I-538 and his or her Form I-20 ID. The DSO will certify the Form I-538 and forward it to the INS. The Form I-20 ID is endorsed by writing that practical training is recommended "full-time (or part-time) from (date) to (date)."

During the 120-day period that the Designated Official is authorized to recommend practical training, the student must apply for an Employment Authorization Document from the INS. The application must include:

- Copy of Form I-94;
- Form I-765;
- Form I-20 ID with the Designated School Official's recommendation; and
- Copy of previous EAD card;
- photographs; and
- Filing Fee.

The application for work authorization for optional practical training is filed at the INS Service Center having jurisdiction over the student's place of residence.

Extensions of Stay for F-1 Students

An F-1 student is not required to seek extensions of stay unless he or she fails to maintain status or fails to make normal progress towards completing the educational objective. When determining the program completion date on Form I-20 A-B, the Designated School Official should make a reasonable estimate based on the time an average foreign student would need to complete a similar program in the same discipline. No more than one year may be added on to the estimate made by the DSO.

An F-1 student who is unable to meet the program completion date on the Form I-20 may be granted an extension by the school if the student continually maintained F-1 status and the delay was caused by compelling academic or medical reasons. The DSO must forward Form I-538 to the INS within 30 days of any approved program extensions.

Transfers by F-1 Students

An F-1 student who has maintained status may transfer to another INS approved school by following specific notification procedures. An F-1 student who was not pursuing a full-course of study at the school he or she was last authorized to attend is ineligible for school transfer and must apply for reinstatement. While the request for reinstatement is pending, the student may be enrolled in school, subject to approval or denial of the request for reinstatement. In the case of a denial, the student must leave school and depart the United States upon notification by the INS.

To transfer to a new school, an F-1 student must first notify the school he or she is attending of the intent to transfer. Then he or she must obtain a Form I-20 A-B from the school to which he or she intends to transfer. The transfer will be conducted only if the student completes the student certification portion of Form I-20 A-B and returns the form to the DSO of the new school within fifteen days of beginning attendance at the new school. Upon receipt of the student's Form I-20 A-B, the Designated School Official must note the transfer completion date on the student's Form I-20 ID in the space provided by writing "transfer completed on (date)."

Annual Vacation

An F-1 student is considered to be in status during the annual (or summer) vacation if the student is otherwise eligible and intends to register for the next term. A student attending a school on a quarter or trimester calendar who takes only one vacation a year during any one of the quarters or trimesters instead of during the summer is considered to be in status during the vacation if the student has completed the equivalent of one academic year prior to taking the vacation.

F-2 Visa: Spouse and Children of F-1 Students

The spouse and minor children following to join an F-1 student are eligible for F-2 visas and admission to the United States if the F-1 student is, or will be within sixty days, enrolled in a full course of study or, if the student is engaged in approved practical training following completion of studies. The eligible spouse and minor children of an F-1 student may be admitted to the United States in F-2 status if they present the F-1 student's current I-20 ID properly endorsed by the designated school official at the school where the F-1 student will be enrolled.

F-2 visaholders are not authorized to engage in employment unless they qualify for work authorization under a separate visa category.

Important Changes made to the F nonimmigrant visa category by Illegal Immigration Reform and Immigrant Responsibility Act of 1996

The Illegal Immigration Reform and Immigrant Responsibility Act of 1996 (IIRAIRA) made significant changes to the F nonimmigrant visa category and added new penalties for certain violations of F nonimmigrant status. The following is a summary of the most important changes made by the 1996 Act.

Under no circumstances may a foreign student be accorded F-1 nonimmigrant classification to pursue a course of study at a public elementary school or in a publicly funded adult education program. F-1 students are also prohibited from attending public secondary schools. However, an F-1 student may attend a public secondary school under two limited exceptions. Under these exceptions an F-1 student may attend a public secondary school for a period of time not to exceed 12 months, however, the student must reimburse the local educational agency that administers the secondary school for the full, unsubsidized per capita cost of providing education at that school.

The 1996 Act also created a new penalty for "student visa abusers." If a foreign student obtains F-1 status in order to pursue a course of study at a private elementary or secondary school or in a language training program that is not publicly funded and then abandons or terminates study at the private school to attend a public elementary or secondary school or a publicly funded adult education language program, the student will be deemed to be a "student visa abuser." The student will be considered to have violated his or her status and the underlying F nonimmigrant visa will be voided. In addition, the student will be inadmissible to the United States for a period of five years from the date of the violation. This provision of the 1996 Act was meant to punish those children, popularly referred to as "parachute kids," who jump from private school to public school upon admission to the United States in F-1 status. A foreign student will not be subject to this ground of inadmissibility if he or she transfers to a public secondary school from a private secondary school, attends the public school for 12 months, and reimburses the local school for the per capita cost of education at that school.

The 1996 Act also created harsh new penalties for aliens who overstay the date of lawful admission indicated on the Form I-94 (Arrival/Departure record). Section 222(g) of the Immigration and Nationality Act renders void any nonimmigrant visa of a foreign national who remains in the U.S. beyond the period of authorized stay and prohibits the individual from being readmitted to the U.S. as a nonimmigrant, unless a new visa is issued by the consulate in the individual's home country.

However, F-1 students are not admitted for a date certain on the Form I-94. Instead F-1 visaholders are admitted for a period of time referred to as duration of status (D/S). Individuals admitted to the United States in D/S are not considered to have overstayed their visa until the INS or an Immigration Judge finds the individual has committed a status violation. This anomaly protects an F-1 student who inadvertently falls out of status from becoming subject to the penalties for visa overstays and unlawful presence. See Chapter Eleven for a full discussion of the penalties for visa overstays and unlawful presence.

Practice Pointers:

Dependents of E-1/E-2, H-4, J-2, and L-2 visaholders are permitted to attend schools in the United States without having to obtain separate F-1 classification. However, it may be advisable for those types of visaholders to change to F-1 classification in order to gain certain benefits of F-1 status. Namely, F-1 visaholders are eligible to apply for work authorization while E-1/E-2 dependents, H-4, J-2 and L-2 visaholders are statutorily prohibited from accepting employment in the United States. In addition, E-1/E-2 dependents, H-4, J-2 and L-2 visaholders are only entitled to those classifications if they are under the age of twenty-one and remain unmarried. To guard against inadvertently falling out of status by "aging out" or by marrying, it may be advisable for those individuals to obtain independent F-1 classification.

F. THE G VISA

The G visa is available for foreign nationals seeking entry for purposes connected with international organizations. The United Nations, and its related organizations, are the most important sources of G visas in the United States. Other well known organizations that utilize G visas to facilitate the entry of personnel in the United States include the European Bank for Reconstruction and Development, the World Health Organization, the World Trade Organization and the World Tourism Organization.

The G Visa is divided into the following subcategories:

G-1 Personnel of any rank, including clerical and custodial employees, assigned by a foreign member government legitimately recognized by the United States to represent that government and be resident at the headquarters of a designated international organization and members of their immediate family.

G-2 Personnel of any rank, including clerical and custodial employees, detailed by a foreign member government legitimately recognized by the United States as members of a temporary delegation of that government to a designated international organization, and members of their immediate family.

G-3 Personnel of any rank, including clerical and custodial employees, detailed by a foreign member government not legitimately recognized by the United States, or a nonmember government, before a designated international organization, and members of their immediate family.

G-4 Personnel of any rank on the payroll of a designated international organization, or appointed to the staff of a designated international organization, and proceeding to the United States to take up such appointment, and members of their immediate family; and

G-5 Attendants, servants and personal employees of persons in the G-1 through G-4 categories, and members of their immediate family.

G-1, G-2, G-3, and G-4 visaholders are admitted to the United States for the full term of their assignment in their official capacity, and as long as they are recognized by the Secretary of State. G-5 visaholders are limited to an initial three-year period of stay and may obtain extensions of stay for up to two-years.

Dependents of G-1, G-3, and G-4 visaholders may apply for work authorization. For the purposes of the G nonimmigrant category a dependent is defined as:

- spouses;
- unmarried children under the age of twenty-one;
- unmarried sons or daughters under the age of twenty-five who are in full-time attendance as students at post-secondary educational institutions;
- unmarried sons or daughters under the age of twenty-five who are in full-time attendance as students at post-secondary educational institutions if a formal bilateral employment agreement permits their employment; and
- unmarried sons or daughters who are physically or mentally disabled.

G. THE I VISA FOR FOREIGN PRESS REPRESENTATIVES

The I nonimmigrant visa category is available to bona fide representatives of foreign press, radio, film or other information media who seek to enter the United States solely to engage in those vocations. The I nonimmigrant category is only available to representatives of information media whose home office is located in a foreign country. I nonimmigrants, and their spouses and children are admitted to the United States based upon reciprocity agreements between the United States and the foreign country where the information medium has its home office. For the purposes of the I nonimmigrant category, reciprocity exists between the United States and all foreign countries.

The INS will admit an individual with a valid I visa to the United States for the duration of his or her employment. The initial admission and any subsequent extensions will be granted in one-year increments. I nonimmigrants do not have to maintain a residence abroad, may change nonimmigrant classification and status, and are permitted to adjust status to that of a lawful permanent resident. However, an I nonimmigrant must first receive permission from the INS before changing the information medium or his or her employer.

The spouse and children of I nonimmigrants are not authorized to work while in the United States. However, if the I nonimmigrant's spouse or children does accept unauthorized employment, the employment will not be viewed as a violation of I nonimmigrant status but may disqualify the spouse and children in future attempts to change or adjust status in the United States.

H. THE J-1 VISA FOR EXCHANGE VISITORS

The J-1 visa is designed for "exchange visitors" coming to the United States to participate in accredited programs. In 1948, Congress created the J-1 exchange visitor nonimmigrant visa program to promote and strengthen international relationships through the mutual exchange of persons between the U.S. and other countries. The J-1 program is administered by the United States Information Agency (USIA). However, on October 1, 1999 it is anticipated that the Department of State will absorb the functions of the USIA. Currently, the Department of State and the Immigration and Naturalization Service are responsible for determining the admissibility and fixing the conditions of stay for J-1 exchange visitors.

Individuals may be admitted to the United States in J-1 status if they have an unabandoned foreign residence and are coming temporarily to the U.S. to participate in an accredited J-1 exchange visitor program. Participation in an accredited J-1 exchange visitor program is open to individuals who are engaged in the following activities in the United States:

- Students;
- Professors and Research Scholars;
- Short-term Scholars;

- Trainees;
- Specialists;
- Foreign medical graduates;
- International and Government Visitors;
- Teachers;
- Camp Counselors; and
- Au Pairs.

Upon completion of the exchange program, in certain instances a J-1 visaholder will be subject to a two-year foreign residence requirement.

An accredited program may be run by any reputable United States federal, state, or local government agency, or a recognized international agency or organization of which the United States is a member and which has offices in the United States, or a reputable organization which is a citizen of the United States. Corporations or organizations that are not citizens of the United States may not be designated as sponsors. The procedure for J-1 Program authorization is similar to that for F-1 school accreditation.

An individual is classifiable as a J-1 exchange visitor if the consular officer is satisfied that the individual:

- Has been accepted to participate, and intends to participate in an exchange visitor program as evidenced by presentation of a properly executed Form IAP-66, Certificate of Eligibility for Exchange Visitor (J-1) Status.

- Has sufficient funds to cover expenses or has made other arrangements to provide for expenses.

- Has sufficient knowledge of the English language to undertake the program for which he or she has been selected, or, except for a foreign national coming to participate in a graduate medical education or training program, the sponsoring organization is aware of the language deficiency, and has nevertheless indicated its willingness to accept the foreign national.

- Will abide by the two-year foreign residence requirement (if applicable).

Two Year Foreign Residence Requirement

The J visa category is designed to promote the exchange of foreign visitors and to enable foreign nationals to obtain practical training or experience that is unavailable in their home country. The primary objective of the J-1 Exchange-Visitor Program is to provide a variety of educational and cultural exchanges between the United States and foreign countries in order to increase mutual understanding, promote international cooperation, strengthen ties between nations, and assist in the development of relations between nations.

In order to achieve this goal, the United States, in many cases places a foreign residence requirement on exchange visitors. When an exchange visitor is subject to the foreign residence requirement, the individual is required to return to his or her country of nationality or last residence for at least two years after completion of their specific J-1 program. This requirement was developed to help ensure that the exchange visitor utilizes the newly acquired skills derived from participation in the exchange program in his or her home country, and to guard against the "brain drain", wherein the U.S. was believed to be taking the best scholars from underdeveloped countries.

Specifically, a J-1 exchange visitor is subject to the two-year foreign residence requirement when:

- The individual's participation in one or more exchange programs was wholly or partially financed, directly or indirectly, by the U.S. government or by the government of the individual's country of last residence; or

- The individual is a national of a country which the Director of the USIA has designated, through publication by public notice in the Federal Register (the Skills List), as clearly requiring the services of persons engaged in the field of specialized knowledge or skill in which the individual will engage during the exchange visitor program; or

- The individual acquires exchange visitor status in order to receive graduate medical education training in the United States.

The policy underlying the development and use of the Skills List is to help ensure that the individual's home country or country of last residence will benefit from individual's acquisition of skills that are lacking in that country.

When subject to the foreign residence requirement the individual must return to his or her country of origin for a period of two years before that individual is permitted to return to the United States as a permanent resident or under a different nonimmigrant category.

The main disadvantage in utilizing the J-1 program often centers on the J-1 visaholder being subject to the two-year foreign residence requirement and thus not being able to obtain a "green card" or change to any other nonimmigrant status, upon the completion of the J-1 program. Further, spending two years in a third country can not satisfy the foreign residence requirement. The spouse and children of the J-1 principal visaholder are also subject to the same foreign residence requirement, notwithstanding the fact that they may be eligible in their own right for another nonimmigrant classification such as H or L. Even if a J-1 visaholder marries a United States citizen upon completion of the program, he or she is still obligated to fulfill the foreign residence requirement, and is not eligible to change status in the United States.

Prior to the Immigration Act of 1990, many doctors participating in residency programs in the United States were working in the United States under J-1 authorization. Foreign medical graduates who were admitted in J-1 status are still subject to the foreign residence requirement because such requirement was initially a condition of the individual's participation in the exchange program. However, under current law, many doctors participating in residency programs are now able to obtain H-1B classification. Foreign doctors who are admitted under H-1B classification may later change status to either another nonimmigrant or immigrant category without having to fulfill the foreign residence requirement.

Waiver of Foreign Residence Requirement

A waiver of the foreign residence requirement is available in five instances. First, a waiver is available if the J-1 visaholder can obtain a "No Objection Letter" from his or her country of origin, indicating that they do not object to the fact that the individual will not return to his or her country of origin to fulfill the foreign residence requirement. "No objection" waivers are not available to graduates of foreign medical schools who are participating in graduate medical education and training.

Second, a waiver may be obtained if the J-1 visaholder's departure from the United States would impose exceptional hardship upon the J-1 visaholder's spouse or child (if such spouse or child is a citizen or resident of the United States).

Third, a waiver may be obtained if the individual can substantiate a claim that he or she will be persecuted on account of race, religion, or political opinion, if the individual returns to the country of nationality or last residence. The burden of proof that must be met in this type of claim is higher than the burden of proof required to be met in a standard political asylum application.

Fourth, the Attorney General may waive the two-year foreign residence requirement in response to a recommendation made by an interested United States government agency.

Finally, a foreign medical graduate, upon a request made by a State's Public Health Department, or its equivalent may also obtain a waiver. The underlying public policy of this waiver is to help relieve shortages of health care professionals in designated geographic locations as determined by the Secretary of Health and Human Services. Each state may only receive 20 waivers of this type per year. In addition, the J-1 visaholder must meet stringent criteria to obtain this type of waiver. If the waiver is granted, the foreign medical graduate will be allowed to apply for a change of nonimmigrant status from J-1 to H-1B. A list of the areas in each State that are designated as shortage areas are published in the Federal Register.

Practice Pointer

While "no objection" waivers are often freely granted, hardship waivers are quite difficult to obtain and the hardship shown must usually be quite severe. Furthermore, even where hardship is found, the waiver may be denied for "program and policy" reasons. Similarly, where government funding or grants are involved in the program (such as a Fulbright Scholarship or funding from the National Endowment for the Arts) the views of the funding agency will generally be considered, and usually followed in granting or denying a "no objection", hardship, or interested government agency waiver.

J-2 Classification

The spouse and minor children of J-1 visaholders are entitled to classification as J-2 nonimmigrants. Unlike other derivative visa categories (e.g. H-4, L-2), J-2 visaholders may obtain work authorization. However, work authorization will only be granted if the income earned by the J-2 visaholder is used to support the family's customary recreational, cultural and travel activities. Employment will not be authorized if the income is needed to support the J-1 principal visaholder. J-2 employment may be authorized for the duration of the J-1 principal visaholder's authorized stay or a period of four years, whichever is shorter. A J-2 visaholder may only apply for renewal of work authorization if he or she has filed a timely application for extension of stay that has been approved.

Duration of Stay

A J-1 visaholder's duration of stay in the United States is determined by the general limitations for the specific J-1 category and the time the individual will need to complete a particular exchange program. In addition to the duration of stay an exchange visitor is granted in a specific category, the INS also grants J-1 visaholders an additional grace period of thirty days to depart the United States after program completion. The following is a brief summary of the authorized duration of stay for each J-1 category:

- College and university students in a degree program may be admitted to the U.S. for the duration of the course of study, plus eighteen months of academic training. Post-doctoral students are eligible for thirty-six months of academic training.

- College and university students in a non-degree program may be admitted for a total of twenty-four months, plus eighteen months of academic training.

- Professors and research scholars may be admitted to the U.S. for a period of up to three years.

- Short-term scholars may be admitted to the U.S. for a period of up to four months.

- Trainees may be admitted to the U.S. for a period of up to eighteen months. Exchange visitors participating in flight training programs may be admitted to the U.S. for up to twenty-four months.

- Specialists may be admitted to the United States for a period of up to one year.

- Foreign medical graduates may be admitted to the U.S. for the length of the individual program, up to a maximum of seven years. There are a few limited exceptions that may increase the authorized period of stay beyond the maximum of seven years.

- International visitors may be admitted to the U.S. for a period of up to one year.

- Government visitors may be admitted to the U.S. for a period of up to eighteen months.

- Teachers may be admitted to the U.S. for a period of up to three years.

- Secondary school students may be admitted to the U.S. for a period of up to one year.

- Camp Counselors may be admitted to the U.S. for a period of up to four months.

- Au pairs may be admitted to the U.S. for a period of up to one year.

I. THE K VISA FOR ALIEN FIANCE(E)S

The Immigration and Nationality Act provides K nonimmigrant classification for individuals who are the fiancées of U.S. citizens who seek to enter the United States solely to conclude a valid marriage within 90 days after entry. The minor children accompanying or following to join the foreign national are also accorded nonimmigrant classification. Of course, calling the K category a "nonimmigrant" category is really a misnomer, in that K visaholders are, by definition, really immigrants.

To be classified as a fiancé or fiancée, an alien must be the beneficiary of an approved visa petition filed on Form I-129F. The petition with supporting documentation must be filed by the petitioner with the INS Service Center having jurisdiction over the petitioner's place of residence in the United States. An approved I-129F petition is valid for a period of four months. The approval of any K nonimmigrant petition is automatically terminated when the petitioner dies or files a written withdrawal of the petition before the beneficiary arrives in the United States. Once approved, the I-129F petition will be forwarded to the American Consulate designated on the petition.

A consular officer will review the application for a K nonimmigrant visa as though it was a petition for an immigrant visa. The beneficiary must submit to the consular office a sworn statement of ability and intent to conclude a valid marriage within 90 days of admission to the U.S., a completed nonimmigrant visa application (OF-156), medical examination, birth certificate, any divorce decrees, police certificates, an affidavit of support and a passport. The consular officer must determine whether the beneficiary is eligible for admission to the United States as a permanent resident, i.e. not inadmissible even though technically a K visa is a nonimmigrant visa. If the consular officer determines that the beneficiary is inadmissible, the beneficiary may be eligible for a waiver of the particular ground of inadmissibility. The beneficiary is eligible for any waivers that would be available if the beneficiary was already married to the petitioner. The INS has the sole discretion to issue a waiver of a ground of inadmissibility.

Requirement that Petitioner and Beneficiary Have Met

The petitioner must establish to the satisfaction of the INS that the petitioner and beneficiary have met in person within the two years immediately preceding the filing of the petition. However, the INS in limited circumstances may waive this requirement. One exception and possible ground for a waiver is if a meeting of the beneficiary and the petitioner prior to marriage would violate strict and long-established customs of the beneficiary's foreign culture or social practice.

As previously mentioned, the K visa is essentially an immigrant visa rather than a nonimmigrant visa, since the intent of the individual is permanent and the consular officer clears the fiance(e) as an immigrant. The alien fiance(e) must marry the United States citizen petitioner within 90 days after the alien's arrival in the United States. An individual who enters the United States as a K visaholder must marry within the prescribed time period and then file an application to be classified as an Immediate Relative of the United States citizen spouse. Failure to do so will result in the individual's being considered out of legal status.

K visaholders have unrestricted work authorization incident to K nonimmigrant status. However, K visaholders must first apply to the INS for work authorization (Form I-765) prior to beginning to work in the United States.

OMB # 1115-0054

SAMPLE FORM I-129F, ALIEN FIANCE(E)

Petition for Alien Fiance(e)

DO NOT WRITE IN THIS BLOCK

Case ID#	Action Stamp	Fee Stamp
A#		
G-28 or Volag#		
The petition is approved for status under Section 101(a)(15)(k). It is valid for four months from date of action.		AMCON: ______ ☐ Personal Interview ☐ Previously Forwarded ☐ Document Check ☐ Field Investigations
Remarks:		

A. Information about you

1. Name (Family name in CAPS) (First) (Middle)
TYLER Anne K.

2. Address (Number and Street) (Apartment Number)
1014 East 41 St.

(Town or City) (State/Country) (ZIP/Postal Code)
New York New York 10017

3. Place of Birth (Town or City) (State/Country)
Bondville, Vermont

4. Date of Birth (Mo/Day/Yr) 01/18/65
5. Sex ☐ Male ☒ Female
6. Marital Status ☐ Married ☒ Single ☐ Widowed ☐ Divorced

7. Other Names Used (including maiden name)
N/A

8. Social Security Number 010-01-0101
9. Alien Registration Number (if any) N/A

10. Names of Prior Husbands/Wives 11. Dates(s) Marriage(s) Ended
N/A

12. If you are a U.S. citizen, complete the following:
My citizenship was acquired through (check one)
☒ Birth in the U.S.
☐ Naturalization
Give number of certificate, date and place it was issued
☐ Parents
Have you obtained a certificate of citizenship in your own name?
☐ Yes ☒ No
If "Yes", give number of certificate, date and place it was issued

13. Have you ever filed for this or any other alien fiance(e) or husband/wife before? ☐ Yes ☐ No
If you checked "yes", give name of alien, place and date of filing, and result

B. Information about your alien fiance(e)

1. Name (Family name in CAPS) (First) (Middle)
KING Franklin

2. Address (Number and Street) (Apartment Number)
56 Outback Road

(Town or City) (State/Country) (ZIP/Postal Code)
Sydney Australia

3. Place of Birth (Town or City) (State/Country)
Sydney Australia

4. Date of Birth (Mo/Day/Yr) 07/04/1963
5. Sex ☒ Male ☐ Female
6. Marital Status ☐ Married ☒ Single ☐ Widowed ☐ Divorced

7. Other Names Used (including maiden name)
N/A

8. Social Security Number N/A
9. Alien Registration Number (if any) N/A

10. Names of Prior Husbands/Wives 11. Dates(s) Marriage(s) Ended

12. Has your fiance(e) ever been in the U.S.?
☒ Yes ☐ No

13. If your fiance(e) is currently in the U.S. complete the following:
He or she last arrived as a (visitor, student, exchange alien, crewman, stowaway, temporary worker, without inspection etc.)

Arrival/Departure Record (I-94) Number Date arrived (Mo/Day/Yr)

Date authorized stay expired, or will expire as shown on form I-94 or I-95

INITIAL RECEIPT	RESUBMITTED	RELOCATED		COMPLETED		
		Rec'd	Sent	Approved	Denied	Returned

SAMPLE FORM I-129F (CONTINUED)

14. List all children of your alien fiance(e) (if any)

(Name)

N/A

15. Address in the United States where your fiance(e) intends to live

(Number and Street)

1014 East 41St.

16. Your fiance(e)'s address abroad

(Number and Street) (Town or City)

56 Outback Road

17. If your fiance(e)'s native alphabet is other than Roman letters, write his or her name and address abroad in the native alphabet

(Name) (Number and Street)

18. Your fiance(e) is related to you. ☐ Yes ☐ No

If you are related, state the nature and degree of the relationship, e.g. third cousin

19. Your fiance(e) has met and seen you. ☒ Yes ☐ No

Describe the circumstances under which you met. If you have not personally met each other, explain ... detail any reasons you may have for requesting that the requirement ...

We met and dated while I was ...

20. Your fiance(e) will apply for a visa abroad at the American Consulate in Sydney (City) ____ (Country)

(Designation of the consulate outside the country of your fiance(e)'s last residence does not guarantee acceptance for processing by that consulate. Acceptance is at the discretion of the designated consulate.)

C. Other Information

If you are serving overseas in the armed forces of the United States, please answer the following:

I presently reside or am stationed overseas and my current mailing address is Australia

I plan to return to the United States on or about ____

Penalties: You may, by law, be imprisoned for not more than five years, or fined $250,000, or both, for entering into a marriage contract for the purpose of evading any provision of the immigration laws and you may be fined up to $10,000 or imprisoned up to five years or both, for knowingly and willfully falsifying or concealing a material fact or using any false document in submitting this petition.

Your Certification

I am legally able to and intend to marry my alien fiance(e) within 90 days of his or her arrival in the United States. I certify under penalty of perjury under the laws of the United States of America, that the foregoing is true and correct. Furthermore, I authorize the release of any information from my records which the Immigration and Naturalization Service needs to determine eligibility for the benefit that I am seeking.

Signature ____ Date ____ Phone Number ____

Signature of Person Preparing Form if Other than Above

Print Name ____ (Address) ____ (Signature) ____ (Date) ____

G-28 ID Number ____

Volag Number ____

For sale by the Superintendent of Documents, Government Printing office
Washington, DC 20402

*U.S.GPO:1991-282-...

J. THE M VISA FOR VOCATIONAL NONACADEMIC STUDENTS

The M Visa is available to foreign students who wish to pursue a full-time course of study at an approved vocational or other recognized nonacademic institution. Foreign students are not permitted to attend language-training programs under M classification. However, M students are permitted to attend English language training classes in order to better understand the student's vocational or technical courses. Foreign students who are granted M nonimmigrant classification are designated as M-1 visaholders and any accompanying spouse or children are designated as M-2 visaholders.

To be eligible for M classification a foreign student must maintain a residence abroad that he or she has no intention of abandoning and must seek to enter the U.S. solely to pursue a full course of study at an approved vocational or other recognized nonacademic institution. The full-time course of study must lead to the attainment of a specific educational or vocational objective. Unlike F-1 students, M-1 students are not permitted to change the educational objective indicated on Form I-20M-N while in school. For example, a foreign student who has been given M classification to attend school to become an auto mechanic will not be permitted to transfer schools to become a computer programmer, unless the student obtains new M classification.

A full-time course of study for the purposes of M classification includes the following:

- Study at a community college or junior college, certified by a school official to consist of at least 12 semester or quarter hours of instruction per academic term in those institutions that use a standard, semester, trimester, or quarter-hour systems.

- Study at a post-secondary vocational or business school, other than in a language training program, which confers upon its graduates recognized associate or other degrees or has established that its credits have been or are accepted unconditionally by at least three institutions of higher learning which are either: 1) a school or school system owned and operated by the U.S. or a State or political subdivision thereof or; 2) a school accredited by a nationally recognized accrediting body, and that has been certified by a designated school official to consist of at least 12 hours of instruction a week or its equivalent as determined by the INS.

- Study in a vocational or other nonacademic curriculum, other than a language training program certified by a DSO to consist of at least 18 clock hours of attendance a week if the dominant part of the course of study consists of classroom instruction, or at least 22 clock hours a week if the dominant part of the course of study consists of shop or laboratory work; or

- Study in a vocational or other nonacademic high school curriculum, certified by a designated school official to consist of class attendance for not less than the minimum number of hours prescribed by the school for normal progress towards graduation.

Duration of Stay

An M-1 student may be admitted to the United States for the period of time necessary to complete the course of study indicated on the Certificate of Eligibility (Form I-20M-N) issued by the designated vocational or non-academic institution, or for one year, whichever period of time is less. In addition, an M-1 student has 30 days to depart the United States after the completion of the full course of study.

Employment Authorization

M-1 students are not authorized to work while completing their course of study but are eligible for post-study practical training. Practical training is only permitted after the student has completed the course of study. The application for work authorization (Form I-765) must be submitted prior to the expiration of the student's authorized period of stay in M-1 status and not more than 60 days before or 30 days after the completion of the course of study.

The application for work authorization for an M-1 student must be accompanied by a letter written by the student's designated school official that states the proposed employment is related to the student's course of study and that upon the DSO's information and belief there is no comparable employment available in the student's home country.

An M-1 student will be granted practical training authorization for one month for every four months of full-time study he or she has completed in M-1 status, not to exceed six months in the aggregate. For example, if an M-1 student's course of study were 16 months, the student would be eligible for four months of practical training. A student will not be granted employment authorization if he or she cannot complete the requested practical training in six months.

The INS' decision on applications for extension of status, permission to transfer schools and practical training can not be appealed.

Change of status

The INS will deny an application for change of status to M-1 student status if the INS determines that the applicant intends to pursue the course of study solely in order to qualify for a subsequent change to H temporary worker classification. In addition, an application for a change of status from M-1 to H-1B temporary worker will be denied if the education or training which the student received in M-1 status enables the student to meet the qualifications for H nonimmigrant classification. Finally, an M-1 student is not permitted to change status to that of an F-1 student.

Visa Issuance

The procedure for M visa issuance is virtually the same as that for F-1 visa issuance.

K. THE Q VISA FOR CULTURAL EXCHANGE ALIENS

Although many aspects of the Q nonimmigrant visa category are similar to the J-1 nonimmigrant visa category, Congress in the Immigration Act of 1990, established a separate nonimmigrant category for cultural exchange visitors. In the Q nonimmigrant category, a qualified employer may petition the INS for approval to bring in an individual in Q classification to engage in pre-arranged employment or training that helps facilitate the sharing of the individual's foreign culture with the American public. The international cultural program is designed to enhance the American public's knowledge and appreciation of different world cultures.

The Q visa is valid for the duration of the program or 15 months, whichever is shorter. The INS gives an additional 30 days to Q visaholders to depart from the United States after completion of the cultural exchange program.

In order to be eligible for Q classification, the petitioner must show both that the program for which it is sponsoring the individual is valid, and that the individual's employment or training in the United States is not independent of the cultural component of the international cultural exchange program.

An international cultural exchange program must meet all of the following requirements:

Accessibility to the public:

The international cultural exchange program must take place in a school, museum, business or other establishment where the American public, or a segment of the public sharing a common cultural interest, is exposed to aspects of a foreign culture as part of a structured program. Activities that take place in a private home or an isolated business setting to which the American public, or a segment of the public sharing a common cultural interest does not have direct access, do not qualify.

Cultural Component:

The international cultural exchange program must have a cultural component that is an essential and integral part of the Q nonimmigrant visaholder's employment or training. The cultural component must be designed, on the whole, to exhibit or explain the attitude, customs, history, heritage, philosophy, or traditions of the cultural visitor's country of nationality. A cultural component may include structured instructional activities, such as seminars, courses, lecture series, or language camps.

Work Component:

The cultural visitor's employment or training in the United States may not be independent of the cultural component of the international cultural exchange program. The work component must serve as the vehicle to achieve the objectives of the cultural component. The sharing of the culture of the Q nonimmigrant visaholder's country of nationality must result from his or her employment or training with the qualified employer in the United States.

Requirements for Cultural Visitors

In order for an individual to be eligible for cultural exchange visitor status, he or she must be at least 18 years old at the time the petition is filed. The alien must also be qualified to perform the service or labor or receive the type of training stated in the petition and must have the ability to communicate effectively about the cultural attributes of his or her country of nationality to the American public. Finally, the proposed cultural visitor must have resided and been physically present outside of the United States for the immediate prior year, if he or she was previously admitted as a Q nonimmigrant.

Application process for Q nonimmigrant cultural visitors

The petitioner must file the Form I-129 and Q supplement, applicable fee, and supporting documentation with the INS Service Center having jurisdiction over the area where the cultural visitor will perform services, labor or receive training. The petition may also be filed with the INS Service Center having jurisdiction over employer's headquarters.

Supporting Documentation Required for Submission of "Q" Petition

Documentation by the Employer

To establish eligibility as a qualified employer, the petitioner must submit appropriate supporting documentation evidencing that:

- the employer maintains an established cultural exchange program and has designated a qualified employee as a representative who will be responsible for administering the international cultural exchange program and serve as liaison to the INS;

- the employer does business in the United States (including providing lectures, seminars and other types of cultural programs) and has employees;

- the employer will offer the alien wages and working conditions comparable to those accorded local domestic workers similarly employed; and

- the employer has the financial ability to remunerate the cultural exchange visitor.

The employer must also provide the date of birth, country of nationality, level of education, position title, and a brief job description for each participant included in the petition.

Petitions for Multiple Participants

The petitioner may include more than one participant on the petition. The petitioner must include the name, date of birth, nationality, and other identifying information required on the petition for each participant.

Spouse and Children of Q Nonimmigrants

Unlike other nonimmigrant visa categories that allow for derivative nonimmigrant visa status to be conferred upon the accompanying minor children and spouse of the principal alien, the Q visa does not provide for derivative status for these family members.

Q-2 NONIMMIGRANT VISAS FOR NATIONALS OF NORTHERN IRELAND AND OTHER DESIGNATED COUNTIES OF IRELAND

In October 1998, Congress passed the Irish Peace Process Cultural Training Act which provided for the creation of "Q-2" visas for nationals from specific areas of Ireland. The Q-2 program was created to allow young people from disadvantaged areas of designated counties suffering from sectarian violence and high structural unemployment to temporarily enter the United States for the purpose of developing job skills and conflict resolution abilities in a diverse and peaceful environment.

Individuals, 35 years old or younger who have a residence in the six counties of Northern Ireland and the counties of Louth, Monaghan, Cavan, Leitrim, Sligo, and Donegal within the Republic of Ireland are eligible to participate in approved cultural and training programs in the United States for a period not to exceed thirty-six months. Up to 4,000 Q-2 visas are available each year. The Q-2 program is set to expire on October 1, 2005. The spouses and minor children of Q-2 visaholders are permitted to accompany or follow to join the primary Q-2 visaholder.

SAMPLE FORM I-129 FOR A "Q" NONIMMIGRANT

OMB No. 1115-0168
Petition for a Nonimmigrant Worker

START HERE - Please Type or Print

Part 1. Information about the employer filing this petition.

If the employer is an individual, use the top name line. Organizations should use the second line.

Family Name	Given Name	Middle Initial

Company or Organization Name: El Restuarante del Sol

Address - Attn:

Street Number and Name: 3 Aster Avenue	Apt. #:
City: New York	State or Province: New York
Country: USA	Zip/Postal Code: 10010

IRS Tax #: 13-9999999

Part 2. Information about this Petition.

(See instructions to determine the fee)

1. **Requested Nonimmigrant classification:**
   (write classification symbol at right) Q-1
2. **Basis for Classification** (check one)
   a. ☒ New employment
   b. ☐ Continuation of previously approved employment without change
   c. ☐ Change in previously approved employment
   d. ☐ New concurrent employment
3. **Prior Petition.** If you checked other than "New Employment" in item 2 (above) give the most recent prior petition numbers for the worker(s):
4. **Requested Action:** (check one)
   a. ☒ Notify the office in Part 4 so the person(s) can obtain a visa or be admitted (NOTE: a petition is not required for an E-1, E-2, or R visa)
   b. ☐ Change the person(s) status and extend their stay since they are all now in the U.S. in another status (see instructions for limitations). This is available only where you check "New Employment" in item 2, above.
   c. ☐ Extend or amend the stay of the person(s) since they now hold this status.
5. **Total number of workers in petition:** one (1)
   (See instructions for where more than one worker can be included)

Part 3. Information about the person(s) you are filing for.

Complete the blocks below. Use the continuation sheet to name each person included in this petition.

If an entertainment group, give their group name.

Family Name: Reyes	Given Name: Mauricio	Middle Initial:
Date of Birth (Month/Day/Year): 02/25/1960	Country of Birth: Spain	
Social Security #: N/A	A #: N/A	

If in the United States, complete the following:

Date of Arrival (Month/Day/Year)	I-94 #
Current Nonimmigrant Status	Expires (Month/Day/Year)

FOR INS USE ONLY

Returned	Receipt
Resubmitted	
Reloc Sent	
Reloc Rec'd	
Interviewed ☐ Petitioner ☐ Beneficiary	

Class:
\# of Workers:
Priority Number:
Validity Dates: From
To

☐ **Classification Approved**
☐ Consulate/POE/PFI Notified
At:
☐ Extension Granted
☐ COS/Extension Granted

Partial Approval (explain)

Action Block

To be Completed by Attorney or Representative, if any

☐ Fill in box if G-28 is attached to represent the applicant

VOLAG#

ATTY State License #

Continued on back.

SAMPLE FORM I-129 FOR A "Q" NONIMMIGRANT (CONTINUED)

Part 4. Processing Information

a. If the person named in Part 3 is outside the U.S. or a requested extension of stay or change of status cannot be granted, give the U.S. consulate or inspection facility you want to be notified if this petition is approved.

Type of Office (check one): ☒ Consulate ☐ Pre-flight inspection ☐ Port of Entry

Office Address (City) Madrid, Spain U.S. State or Foreign Country

Person's Foreign Address 1 Calle Primero Madrid, Spain

b. Does each person in this petition have a valid passport?
☐ Not required to have passport ☐ No - explain on separate paper ☒ Yes

c. Are you filing any other petitions with this one? ☒ No ☐ Yes - How many?

d. Are applications for replacement/Initial I-94's being filed with this petition? ☒ No ☐ Yes - How many?

e. Are applications by dependents being filed with this petition? ☒ No ☐ Yes - How many?

f. Is any person in this petition in exclusion or deportation proceedings? ☒ No ☐ Yes - explain on separate paper

g. Have you ever filed an immigrant petition for any person in this petition? ☒ No ☐ Yes - explain on separate paper

h. If you indicated you were filing a new petition in Part 2, within the past seven years has any person in this petition:

1) ever been given the classification you are now requesting? ☒ No ☐ Yes - explain on separate paper

2) ever been denied the classification you are now requesting? ☒ No ☐ Yes - explain on separate paper

i. If you are filing for an entertainment group, has any person in this petition not been with the group for at least 1 year?
☐ No ☐ Yes - explain on separate paper

Part 5. Basic Information about the proposed employment and employer.

Attach the supplement relating to the classification you are requesting.

Job Title: Maitre' D

Nontechnical Description of Job: Manage and Direct Spanish Restaurant. See attached letter in support

Address where the person(s) will work if different from the address in Part 1.

Is this a full-time position? ☐ No - Hours per week ☒ Yes

Wages per week or per year

Other Compensation (Explain): Tips

Value per week or per year: $65,000 per yr.

Dates of Intended employment From: 6/1/1999 To: 7/31/2000

Type of petitioner - check one ☐ U.S. citizen or permanent resident ☒ Organization ☐ Other - explain on separate paper

Type of business: Spanish Restaurant

Year established: 1919

Current number of employees	Gross Annual Income	Net Annual Income
45	$3,000,000.00	$950,000.00

Part 6. Signature.

Read the information on penalties in the instructions before completing this section.

I certify, under penalty of perjury under the laws of the United States of America, that this petition, and the evidence submitted with it, is all true and correct. If filing this on behalf of an organization, I certify that I am empowered to do so by that organization. If this petition is to extend a prior petition, I certify that the proposed employment is under the same terms and conditions as in the prior approved petition. I authorize the release of any information from my records, or from petitioning organization's records, which the Immigration and Naturalization Service needs to determine eligibility for the benefit being sought.

Signature and title	Print Name	Date

Please note: If you do not completely fill out this form and the required supplement, or fail to submit required documents listed in the instructions, then the person(s) filed for may not be found eligible for the requested benefit, and this petition may be denied.

Part 7. Signature of person preparing form if other than above.

I declare that I prepared this application at the request of the above person and it is based on all information of which I have knowledge.

Signature	Print Name	Date

Firm Name and Address

Q CLASSIFICATION SUPPLEMENT TO FORM I-129

OMB No. 1115-0168
Q & R Classifications
Supplement to Form I-129

Name of person or organization filing petition: El Restuarante del Sol

Name of person you are filing for: Mauricio Reyes

Section 1. Complete this section if you are filing for a Q international exchange alien.

I hereby that the participant(s) in this international exchange program:

- is at least 18 years of age,
- has the ability to communicate effectively about the cultural attributes of his or her country of nationality to the American public, and
- has not previously been in the United States as a Q nonimmigrant unless he/she has resided and has been physically present outside the U.S. for the immediate prior year

I also certify that the same wages and working conditions are accorded the participants as are provided to similarly employed U.S. workers.

Petitioner's signature   Date

Section 2. Complete this section if you are filing for an R religious worker.

List the alien's and any dependent family members, prior periods of stay in R classification in the U.S. for the last six years. Be sure to list only those periods in which the alien and/or family members were actually in the U.S. in an R classification.

Describe the alien's proposed duties in the U.S.

Describe the alien's qualifications for the vocation or occupation

Describe the relationship between the U.S. religious organization and the organization abroad of which the alien was a member.

SAMPLE "Q" LETTER

Vermont Service Center
Immigration & Naturalization Service
St. Albans, Vermont

Re: "Q" nonimmigrant Visa Petition by El Restaurante del Sol on behalf of Mauricio Reyes

Dear Sir or Madam:

This letter is submitted in support of the petition by El Restaurante del Sol on behalf of Mr. Mauricio Reyes in the capacity of Maitre'D. Mr. Reyes has never entered the United States.

El Restaurante del Sol is one of the oldest and most prestigious Spanish restaurants in New York City. It prides itself in preserving the unique cuisine of the various regions of Spain. The restaurant is a member of El Groupo Restaurantes Espanoles (EGRE), an organization composed of restaurants, educational institutions, importers, food writers an chefs from throughout the United States who have come together to promote and preserve the origins and status of Spanish gastronomy. It is EGRE's belief that Spanish cuisine deserves the same renown as French haute cuisine. EGRE'S goal is to elevate the image of Spanish regional cuisine.

In furtherance of its goal, EGRE has concentrated on clarifying, codifying and elevating the perception (by the press, the public and the hospitality industry itself) of the entire spectrum of Spanish wine and food. The theme and driving force of EGRE has been and always will be education. EGRE has accomplished many goals.

- It has set up a Spanish cuisine curriculum at the prestigious Culinary Institute of America.

- EGRE was one of the sponsors of the new Spanish Culinary Institute for Foreigners (SCIF) in Barcelona, Spain and was responsible for the creation of an advance scholarship for students from North America. Recently over 30 students from the United States and Canada completed a six-month course that was entirely underwritten by the Spanish government.

- EGRE created a computerized databank that will become the definitive information source for every known aspect of Spanish cuisine and wine. This information bank will be available to students, press, restaurateurs and educational institutions who require quick and reliable information on any aspect of Spanish cuisine.

- Since its inception, EGRE has sponsored annual gastronomic trips to various regions of Spain. Food and wine writers accompany EGRE members for a one-week program of intensive study of the customs, history and cuisine of a particular region of Spain. This program is done in coordination with officials of the Spanish government.

EGRE's newest program involves bringing Spanish chefs and Maitre'Ds to restaurants in the United States for limited time periods to enable the restaurants to enhance their creative knowledge of Spain and its heritage through its cuisine.

In conjunction with this program, El Restaurante del Sol wishes to temporarily "import" from Spain Mr. Reyes who is one of the most knowledgeable culinarians of regional cuisine. Mr. Reyes has worked in traditional Spanish restaurants his entire life. He grew up working in his father's famed restaurant in Sevilla and graduated from the Spanish Instituto de Servicio in 1977. Since that time he has worked as Maitre'D of several famous restaurants in Madrid, Cordoba and Leon.

In light of Mr. Reyes background, education, and significant work history we believe he is eminently qualified to participate in an exchange cultural program.

Thank you for your attention to this matter and we hope that this petition will be adjudicated promptly.

Very truly yours,

Alicia Sephardi
Owner
El Restaurante del Sol

L. THE R VISA FOR RELIGIOUS WORKERS

In the Immigration Act of 1990, Congress introduced the R nonimmigrant visa category. The R nonimmigrant visa category is very similar to the fourth employment-based preference immigrant visa category for ministers and religious workers. In addition to the obvious differences between immigrant and nonimmigrant classifications there are a number of significant distinctions between the R-1 and the fourth employment-based immigrant category. The fourth employment-based visa category is discussed in greater detail in Chapter Eight.

The R-1 Nonimmigrant Visa Category in comparison to the Fourth Employment-Based Immigrant Visa Category (EB-4)

There are four significant differences between the R-1 nonimmigrant and EB-4 immigrant categories that go beyond the threshold differences between any nonimmigrant and immigrant visa category.

The first significant difference between the two categories centers on the threshold eligibility requirements. To be eligible for an immigrant visa as a religious worker, an individual must not only have been a member of the particular religious denomination for the two years immediately proceeding the application, but the beneficiary must also demonstrate that he or she has work experience in the particular category (minister, professional, other worker) for at least two years prior to the filing of the immigrant visa petition. In the R-1 category, the beneficiary is only required to have been a member of the religious denomination for the immediately preceeding two years prior to the filing of the nonimmigrant visa petition. An individual who wishes to come to the United States permanently, but does not have the requisite two years of work experience may come to the U.S. in R-1 nonimmigrant status and subsequently apply for an immigrant visa once he or she obtains two years of work experience.

The second major difference is that there are no numerical limits on the number of R nonimmigrants who may come to the United States per fiscal year. Congress has placed an overall cap of 10,000 on the number of individuals who may be admitted to the U.S. in the EB-4 category per fiscal year. There is also a sub-cap of 5,000 put on the number of professional religious workers or other religious workers who may use immigrant visas per fiscal year. The existence of the cap and sub-cap has from time to time caused the immigrant religious worker category to become backlogged. When there is a backlog an individual will have to wait until the individual's priority date becomes current before he or she can become a lawful permanent resident of the United States. To avoid any possible backlog it may be advisable for an individual to first enter the U.S. in R-1 nonimmigrant status and then apply for an immigrant visa. Once in R nonimmigrant status, the individual will have at least three years and possibly up to five years to wait in the United States for his or her priority date to become current. He or she may then apply for adjustment of status or visa process abroad.

Another significant difference between R nonimmigrant classification and EB-4 immigrant classification is that applicants for an R nonimmigrant visa do not have to get pre-approval from the INS before submitting an application to the American Consulate. The applicant may directly apply for an R nonimmigrant visa at the consulate unless he or she is visa exempt, in which case he or she would apply with an immigration officer at a U.S. port of entry. However, extension of stay and change of status petitions must first be filed with the INS.

Finally, the most important difference between the two categories is that the EB-4 religious worker category (except for ministers) is set to expire on September 30, 2000, unless Congress passes legislation to extend the program. There is no expiration date for the equivalent categories in the R nonimmigrant visa category.

Requirements for R Nonimmigrant Visa Classification

An alien who, for at least the two years preceding the time of application for admission, has been a member of a religious denomination having a bona fide non-profit religious organization in the United States, may be admitted temporarily to the United States in R-1 status to carry on the activities of a religious worker.

- The individual must be coming to the United States for one of the following purposes:

- Solely to carry on the vocation of a minister of the religious denomination.

- To work for the religious organization at the request of the organization in a professional capacity.

- To work for the organization or a bona fide organization which is affiliated with the religious denomination, at the request of the organization in a religious vocation or occupation.

Definitions

Bona fide nonprofit religious organization in the United States means an organization exempt from taxation as provided by the Internal Revenue Code as it relates to religious organizations, or one that has never sought such exemption but establishes that it would be eligible if it had applied for tax-exempt status.

A **Minister** is an individual duly authorized by a recognized religious denomination to conduct religious worship and to perform other duties usually performed by authorized members of the clergy of that religion. In all cases, there must be a reasonable connection between the activities performed and the religious calling of the minister. The term does not include a lay preacher not authorized to perform such duties.

Professional Capacity means an activity in a religious vocation or occupation for which the minimum of a United States bachelor's degree or a foreign equivalent degree is required.

Religious Denomination means a religious group or community of believers having some form of ecclesiastical government, a creed or statement of faith, some form of worship, a formal or informal code of doctrine and discipline, religious services and ceremonies, established places of religious worship, and religious congregations, or comparable indicia of a bona fide religious denomination. For the purposes of this definition, an interdenominational religious organization that is exempt from taxation pursuant to the Internal Revenue Code will be treated as a religious denomination.

Religious Occupation means an activity that relates to a traditional religious function. Examples of persons in religious occupations include, but are not limited to, liturgical workers, religious instructors, religious counselors, cantors, catechists, workers in religious hospitals or religious health care facilities, missionaries, religious translators, or religious broadcasters. This group does not include janitors, maintenance workers, clerks, fundraisers, or persons involved solely in the solicitation of donations.

Religious Vocation means a calling to religious life evidenced by the demonstration of commitment practiced in the religious denomination, such as the taking of vows. Examples of persons with a religious vocation include, but are not limited to, nuns, monks and religious brothers and sisters.

Initial Evidence required for an R Nonimmigrant Visa

An individual who seeks classification as an R nonimmigrant religious worker must present to the consular officer, or, if visa exempt, to an immigration officer at a U.S. port of entry, documentation that establishes that the individual will be providing services to a bona fide nonprofit religious organization in the United States or to an affiliated religious organization and that the individual meets the criteria to perform such services. The beneficiary needs only to have been a member of the organization in the preceding two years and not a worker.

Evidence that the Organization qualifies as a Non-Profit Organization

In order to qualify as a petitioning organization for the purposes of R nonimmigrant classification, the petitioner must show that the organization qualifies as a non-profit organization. The documentation may consist of either:

- Documentation showing that it is exempt from taxation in accordance with the Internal Revenue Code, as it relates to religious organizations (in appropriate cases, evidence of the organization's assets and methods of operation and the organization's papers of incorporation under applicable state law may be requested); or

- Such documentation as is required by the Internal Revenue Service to establish eligibility for exemption under the Internal Revenue Code as it relates to religious organizations.

The petition to employ an R nonimmigrant must be accompanied by a letter from an authorized official of the specific organizational unit of the religious organization which will be employing the foreign national or engaging the foreign national's services in the United States. The letter must establish the following items:

- If the foreign national is a minister, he or she is authorized to conduct religious worship for that denomination and to perform other duties usually performed by authorized members of the clergy of that denomination, including a detailed description of those duties;

- If, immediately prior to the application for the nonimmigrant visa or application for admission to the United States, the foreign national has the required two years of membership in the religious denomination.

It is significant to note that there is no requirement that the alien actually have been employed by the petitioning organization for two years immediately prior to the petition, but rather that he or she only have been a member of the denomination.

Additionally as appropriate, the petitioner must show:

- If the foreign national is a minister, he or she is authorized to conduct religious worship for that denomination and to perform other duties usually performed by authorized members of the clergy of that denomination, including a detailed description of those duties.

- If the foreign national is a religious professional, he or she has at least a United States bachelor's degree or its foreign equivalent and that such a degree is required for entry into the religious profession; or

- If the foreign national is to work in another religious vocation or occupation, he or she is qualified in the religious vocation or occupation. Evidence of such qualification may include, but need not be limited to, evidence establishing that the foreign national is a monk, nun, or religious brother or that the type of work to be done relates to a traditional religious function.

Further, the letter must also provide details of the arrangements made, if any, for remuneration for services to be rendered by the beneficiary, including the amount and source of any salary, a description of any other types of remuneration to be received including housing, food, clothing, and any other benefits to which a monetary value may be affixed, and a statement whether such remuneration will be in exchange for services rendered.

Finally, the petitioner may submit any appropriate additional evidence that the examining officer may request relating to the religious organization, the beneficiary, or the affiliated organization.

Additional documentation may include, but need not be limited to, diplomas, degrees, financial statements, or certificates of ordination. No prior petition, labor certification, or prior approval is required.

Initial Admission

The initial admission of a religious worker, spouse and unmarried children less than 21 years of age may not exceed three years.

Extension of Stay

An extension of stay may be filed by a religious organization on the worker's behalf to extend the duration of stay. The petition must be filed at the INS Service Center having jurisdiction over the place of employment. The worker's total period of stay may not exceed five years. A letter must accompany the petition from an authorized official of the organizational unit confirming the worker's continuing eligibility for classification as an R-1 nonimmigrant.

Change of Employers

A different or additional organizational unit of the religious denomination seeking to employ or engage the services of a religious worker admitted under the R category is required to file Form I-129 and the appropriate fee to the INS Service Center having jurisdiction over the place of new employment. The petition must be accompanied by evidence establishing that the alien will continue to qualify as a religious worker under this section.

Any unauthorized change of employment to a new religious organizational unit will constitute a failure to maintain authorized immigration status.

Limitation on Re-entry as an R nonimmigrant

A foreign national who has spent five years in the United States as an R religious worker may not be readmitted to the United States under R visa classification, unless the foreign national has resided and been physically present outside the United States for the immediate prior year, except for brief visits for business or pleasure. Such visits do not end the period that the foreign national is considered to have resided and been physically present outside the United States. However, time spent in the U.S. does not count toward fulfillment of the foreign residence requirement.

R-2 Status for Spouse and Children of R-1 Nonimmigrant

The religious worker's spouse and unmarried children under twenty-one years of age are entitled to the same nonimmigrant classification and length of stay as the religious worker, if the religious worker will be employed and residing primarily in the United States, and if the spouse and unmarried minor children are accompanying or following to join the religious worker in the United States. Neither the spouse nor any child may accept employment while in the United States in R-2 nonimmigrant status.

SAMPLE FORM I-129 FOR AN "R" NONIMMIGRANT PETITION

START HERE - Please Type or Print

Part 1. Information about the employer filing this petition.

If the employer is an individual, use the top name line. Organizations should use the second line.

Family Name	Given Name	Middle Initial

Company or Organization Name: Temple Beth-El

Address - Attn: Rabbi Joshua Cohen

Street Number and Name: 23-26 Queens Boulevard | Apt. #:

City: Queens | State or Province: New York

Country: USA | Zip/Postal Code: 14456

IRS Tax #: 22-1111111

Part 2. Information about this Petition.

(See instructions to determine the fee)

1. **Requested Nonimmigrant classification:** (write classification symbol at right) R-1
2. **Basis for Classification** (check one)
   a. ☒ New employment
   b. ☐ Continuation of previously approved employment without change
   c. ☐ Change in previously approved employment
   d. ☐ New concurrent employment
3. **Prior Petition.** If you checked other than "New Employment" in item 2 (above) give the most recent prior petition numbers for the worker(s): ______
4. **Requested Action:** (check one)
   a. ☐ Notify the office in Part 4 so the person(s) can obtain a visa or be admitted (NOTE: a petition is not required for an E-1, E-2, or R visa)
   b. ☒ Change the person(s) status and extend their stay since they are all now in the U.S. in another status (see instructions for limitations). This is available only where you check "New Employment" in item 2, above.
   c. ☐ Extend or amend the stay of the person(s) since they now hold this status.
5. **Total number of workers in petition:** one (1)

   (See instructions for where more than one worker can be included)

Part 3. Information about the person(s) you are filing for.

Complete the blocks below. Use the continuation sheet to name each person included in this petition.

If an entertainment group, give their group name.

Family Name	Weiss	Given Name	Ethan
Middle Initial			
Date of Birth (Month/Day/Year)	02/26/1959	Country of Birth	Israel
Social Security #	N/A	A #	N/A

If in the United States, complete the following:

Date of Arrival (Month/Day/Year)	08/18/98	I-94 #	66666666661
Current Nonimmigrant Status	B-1	Expires (Month/Day/Year)	12/18/98

FOR INS USE ONLY

Returned	Receipt
Resubmitted	
Reloc Sent	
Reloc Rec'd	
Interviewed ☐ Petitioner ☐ Beneficiary	

Class: ______
\# of Workers: ______
Priority Number: ______
Validity Dates: From ______ To ______

☐ **Classification Approved**
☐ Consulate/POE/PFI Notified
At: ______
☐ Extension Granted
☐ COS/Extension Granted

Partial Approval (explain)

Action Block

To be Completed by Attorney or Representative, if any

☐ Fill in box if G-28 is attached to represent the applicant

VOLAG#

ATTY State License #

Continued on back.

SAMPLE FORM I-129 FOR AN "R" PETITION (CONTINUED)

Part 4. Processing Information

a. If the person named in Part 3 is outside the U.S. or a requested extension of stay or change of status cannot be granted, give the U.S. consulate or inspection facility you want to be notified if this petition is approved.

Type of Office (check one): ☒ Consulate ☐ Pre-flight inspection ☐ Port of Entry

Office Address (City): Jerusalem, Israel — U.S. State or Foreign Country

Person's Foreign Address: Ben Gurion St. Jerusalem, Israel

b. Does each person in this petition have a valid passport?
☐ Not required to have passport ☐ No - explain on separate paper ☒ Yes

c. Are you filing any other petitions with this one? ☒ No ☐ Yes - How many? ______

d. Are applications for replacement/Initial I-94's being filed with this petition? ☒ No ☐ Yes - How many? ______

e. Are applications by dependents being filed with this petition? ☒ No ☐ Yes - How many? ______

f. Is any person in this petition in exclusion or deportation proceedings? ☒ No ☐ Yes - explain on separate paper

g. Have you ever filed an immigrant petition for any person in this petition? ☒ No ☐ Yes - explain on separate paper

h. If you indicated you were filing a new petition in Part 2, within the past seven years has any person in this petition:

1) ever been given the classification you are now requesting? ☒ No ☐ Yes - explain on separate paper

2) ever been denied the classification you are now requesting? ☒ No ☐ Yes - explain on separate paper

i. If you are filing for an entertainment group, has any person in this petition not been with the group for at least 1 year?
☐ No ☐ Yes - explain on separate paper

Part 5. Basic Information about the proposed employment and employer.

Attach the supplement relating to the classification you are requesting.

Job Title: Assistant Rabbi	Nontechnical Description of Job: Lead weekday services and Bible instruction. See attached letter in support	
Address where the person(s) will work if different from the address in Part 1.		
Is this a full-time position? ☐ No - Hours per week	☒ Yes	Wages per week or per year: $35,000 per yr.
Other Compensation (Explain): Housing	Value per week or per year: $400	Dates of Intended employment From: 12/1/1998 To: 11/30/2001
Type of petitioner - check one: ☐ U.S. citizen or permanent resident	☒ Organization	☐ Other - explain on separate paper
Type of business: Synagogue		Year established: 1946
Current number of employees: 26	Gross Annual Income: $500,000	Net Annual Income: $270,000

Part 6. Signature.

Read the information on penalties in the instructions before completing this section.

I certify, under penalty of perjury under the laws of the United States of America, that this petition, and the evidence submitted with it, is all true and correct. If filing this on behalf of an organization, I certify that I am empowered to do so by that organization. If this petition is to extend a prior petition, I certify that the proposed employment is under the same terms and conditions as in the prior approved petition. I authorize the release of any information from my records, or from petitioning organization's records, which the Immigration and Naturalization Service needs to determine eligibility for the benefit being sought.

Signature and title	Print Name	Date

Please note: If you do not completely fill out this form and the required supplement, or fail to submit required documents listed in the instructions, then the person(s) filed for may not be found eligible for the requested benefit, and this petition may be denied.

Part 7. Signature of person preparing form if other than above.

I declare that I prepared this application at the request of the above person and it is based on all information of which I have knowledge.

Signature	Print Name	Date

Firm Name and Address

R CLASSIFICATION SUPPLEMENT TO FORM I-129

U.S. Department of Justice
Immigration and Naturalization Service

OMB No. 1115-0168
Q & R Classifications
Supplement to Form I-129

Name of person or organization filing petition: Temple Beth-El

Name of person you are filing for: Ethan Weiss

Section 1. Complete this section if you are filing for a Q international exchange alien.

I hereby that the participant(s) in this international exchange program:

- is at least 18 years of age,
- has the ability to communicate effectively about the cultural attributes of his or her country of nationality to the American public, and
- has not previously been in the United States as a Q nonimmigrant unless he/she has resided and has been physically present outside the U.S. for the immediate prior year

I also certify that the same wages and working conditions are accorded the participants as are provided to similarly employed U.S. workers.

Petitioner's signature   Date

Section 2. Complete this section if you are filing for an R religious worker.

List the alien's and any dependent family members, prior periods of stay in R classification in the U.S. for the last six years. Be sure to list only those periods in which the alien and/or family members were actually in the U.S. in an R classification.

None

Describe the alien's proposed duties in the U.S.

See attached letter in support for a detailed description of duties.

Describe the alien's qualifications for the vocation or occupation

1979-1998 Assistant Rabbi, Temple Bar-Shabbat, Jerusalem, Isreal

Describe the relationship between the U.S. religious organization and the organization abroad of which the alien was a member.

None

Chapter Eight
EMPLOYMENT-BASED IMMIGRATION

A. INTRODUCTION

As discussed in Chapter One, a foreign national may obtain an immigrant visa or adjust status to that of a permanent resident in the United States through an employment-based petition, family-based petition, or through the winning of a diversity visa (lottery). The focus of this chapter is on employment-based immigration. The Immigration Act of 1990 substantially changed the structure of the employment-based visa system and broadened the areas of employment eligible for participation. Overall, there are 140,000 visas available to employment-based immigrants in the United States each year. They are divided into the following categories and sub-categories:

First Employment-Based Category

Priority Workers - allotted 40,000 visas per year plus any left over from the Fourth and Fifth Employment Categories.

This category includes:

- Persons with Extraordinary Ability
- Outstanding Professors and Researchers
- Multinational executives and managers of international companies

Second Employment-Based Category

- Members of the Professions Holding Advanced Degrees
- Persons of Exceptional Ability in the Sciences, Arts, or Business

40,000 visas granted per year plus any unused visas from the first employment category. Individuals in this category are subject to the Labor Certification requirement, unless the INS approves a national interest waiver.

Third Employment-Based Category

- Skilled workers
- Professionals
- Other Workers – (limited to 10,000 visas per annum)

Overall 40,000 visas for this category are available per year plus any unused visas from employment category one and two. Individuals in this category are subject to the Labor Certification requirement.

Fourth Employment-Based Category

Special Immigrants - 10,000 visas allocated (No leftover visas from other immigrant categories).

This category includes ministers of religion and other religious workers, certain employees under the Panama Canal Act, certain persons declared dependent by a U.S. juvenile court or placed in state custody, certain employees or retired employees of the U.S. government who have served abroad, certain foreign medical graduates, certain officers and employees of international organizations, and certain immigrants who have served in the U.S. armed forces.

Fifth Employment-Based Category

Employment Creation Investors - Limited to 10,000 visas annually, no overlap from other categories.

B. General Overview: Petitioning Process in the Employment–Based Immigration Categories

If the employment category is one that requires the filing of a labor certification, the labor certification must be approved before an I-140 immigrant visa petition may be filed with the INS Service Centers having jurisdiction over the petitioner. If the employment-based category does not require a labor certification, as is always the case in the first employment category, and sometimes in other categories, Form I-140, Immigrant Petition for Alien Worker, may be filed directly with the INS Service Center having jurisdiction over the beneficiary's intended place of employment.

The effect of obtaining an immigrant visa or adjusting status is acquiring "permanent resident status" in the United States. Permanent Resident Status is evidenced by a Resident Alien Card, commonly known as a "Green Card." A lawful permanent resident may remain in the United States for an indefinite period of time, and is entitled to rights of entry, travel and employment as provided by law. However, a permanent resident is required to maintain his or her primary place of abode in the United States, except for "temporary" absences.

LABOR CERTIFICATION PROCESS

When required, "labor certification" is a complex process, requiring thorough research and preparation in order to satisfy Department of Labor (DOL) and INS requirements for ultimate approval of employment-based immigrant petitions. Labor certifications are generally required in the second and third employment based preference categories.

When labor certification is a prerequisite for INS approval, the prospective employer must show that the employment of the foreign national will not have the effect of displacing a United States citizen or permanent resident worker. The DOL must verify that there are no United States workers ready, willing, able and qualified for the position the employer wants to fill with a foreign national. In addition, the DOL must certify that the foreign national will be compensated at a rate in keeping with the prevailing wage for such employment in the United States to ensure that there will be no adverse effect upon the wages and working conditions of U.S. workers in similar positions.

The "Application for Alien Employment Certification" (Forms ETA-750 Parts A & B) set out the minimum requirements for the position to be filled as well as how the alien meets those requirements. The application is initially filed with the State Department of Labor office in the state of intended employment. The State DOL office will review the application and then forward it the DOL Regional Office with jurisdiction over the geographic area for further review. The DOL Regional office has the authority to approve the application.

The labor certification process will be discussed in greater detail in Chapter Nine. However, for the purposes of this chapter it is important to highlight some important issues and concepts. One important issue is the ability of the beneficiary to document prior relevant job experience. The beneficiary should secure letters from former employers prior to the filing of the labor certification to assure that the applicant will later be able to establish that he or she can meet the specific requirements of the approved labor certification. A job experience letter should be obtained from every prior employer detailing the job performed, the skills required or utilized in the position and the salary earned by the beneficiary.

Petitioner Requirements

In the employment-based categories, where a job offer is a prerequisite for eligibility, the petitioner is required to demonstrate that it has the ability to pay the wage offered to the beneficiary. The petitioner must show ability to pay the offered wage at the time the priority date of the petition is established and up until the time the beneficiary obtains lawful permanent residence. The priority date is established at the time of filing of a labor certification or the filing of an I-140 petition. The ability to pay the wage may be demonstrated either in the form of copies of annual reports, federal tax returns, or audited financial statements. If the United States employer employs 100 or more workers, the INS may accept a statement from a financial officer of the organization that establishes the prospective employer's ability to pay the offered wage. In other cases, additional evidence, such as profit/loss statements, bank account records, or personnel records may be submitted by the petitioner or requested by the Service. Normally, with small to medium sized organizations, the INS insists on reviewing copies of Federal income tax returns.

It is important to recognize that the evidence relating to the employer's ability to pay the offered wage is only applicable to immigrant petitions which require a job offer for the petitioning process. In the case of Persons with Extraordinary Ability, no job offer is required for the petition process, and the individual may petition on his or her own behalf. In this instance, the individual is required to demonstrate that he or she will continue to work in the area of extraordinary ability in the United States. This may be achieved by submitting letters from prospective employers, evidence of prearranged commitments such as contracts, or a statement from the beneficiary detailing plans on how the foreign national intends to continue his or her work in the United States.

Timing

The timing of the filing of a labor certification or immigrant petition may be an issue for the petitioner to consider. It is important to make sure the petitioner's financial situation is viable before filing any type of employment petition. A new business may have an evidentiary problem regarding expectations of future success. It is necessary to show that the petitioner's expectations of future financial profit are reasonable. If the new business has substansial start-up assets and gross revenues it should not be difficult to prove economic viability. The INS will scrutinize net income figures when the petitioner submits tax records with the petition. Other evidence which may indicate the employer's ability to pay the offered wage include W-2 and 1099 forms, personnel records, bank account records and profit and loss statements. If the business is experiencing a downward cycle, the presence of liquid assets/cash reserves, as demonstrated by bank account statements, may be sufficient to prove the employer's ability to pay the offered wage.

The economic viability of the petitioning organization at the time of application is a key prerequisite in the employment-based immigration process. If there are apparent losses to a company, this may affect the approval of the immigrant visa petition, unless there are justifiable reasons for the losses falling into a number of exceptions which we will detail below:

Exceptions

Subsidiary Organizations - If the subsidiary organization petitioning on behalf of a foreign national does not appear to be profitable at the time of application, the organization may still petition for the foreign national as long as the company can show that the parent organization will support the subsidiary organization until it becomes profitable. Often it is the case that a subsidiary organization is structured in such a way as to deliberately fail to earn a profit for tax reasons. Therefore, in this type of scenario, it is important to view the profitability of the whole worldwide operation of a company rather than view the subsidiary in isolation when assessing its ability to pay the offered wage.

In addition, the petitioner's ability to pay the foreign national's wage may not be questioned when a large amount of funds is set aside to cover employee payroll. In this case, even if an organization is not yet profitable, the ability to pay the wage will not be a relevant issue.

Finally, another common situation for new companies is where large and/or accelerated depreciation deductions were taken for a given year, which has, as its effect, the decrease of profit, but increase in cash flow. This should not reflect negatively upon the petitioner's ability to pay the wage since the cash flow is ultimately what will determine the petitioner's ability to pay the foreign national, rather than the amount of "profit" reflected for tax purposes. Similarly, in a closely held corporation, where management elects to take profits in the form of officer's salaries, the petitioner's ability to pay the foreign national's offered wage should not be an issue. In such cases, however, a special presentation should be made with the petition.

There are numerous similar situations that may explain a poor or negative "bottom line," and it is important to note that petitions are decided on a case-by-case basis.

Priority Dates

Priority dates are a critical element related to the employment-based immigration process. Priority dates become crucial because certain visa categories are often oversubscribed. Visa categories may become oversubscribed when the number of approved immigrant visa petitions in a year exceeds the visa numbers allocated to that particular category. If backlogs do exist a potential immigrant must wait until a visa number is available from the State Department for nationals from his or her country of birth before the individual is granted permanent residence. Visas are allocated on the basis of priority dates, much the same way as a bakery serves customers based on a sequential number card, with the earlier numbers called first.

Generally, a priority date is established on the date an I-140 immigrant visa petition is duly filed with the Immigration and Naturalization Service. In the case of employment categories that require a labor certification, the priority is the date the State DOL office accepts the labor certification application for filing.

In certain instances, a foreign national may be eligible in more than one employment-based category. It may be in the foreign national's best interest to petition in more than one category if he or she is unsure of which category is most likely to be approved. For example, in the case of an artist who may be qualified as a person with extraordinary ability (first employment-based category), the artist may also decide to petition simultaneously under the second employment-based category, with a national interest waiver. The artist may even start a labor certification, which could then be discontinued if either the extraordinary ability, or national interest waiver applications are approved.

There may be a consideration for employers with regard to the timing of the filing of the labor certification application and the I-140 petition. The effect of these two actions may serve to alert INS to possible unauthorized employment and potential employer penalties. In instances where the employee is working in the United States without authorization, the foreign national may be required to leave the United States until the immigrant visa is available.

C. FIRST EMPLOYMENT-BASED CATEGORY:

"PRIORITY WORKERS"

Persons with Extraordinary Ability, Outstanding Professors and Researchers, and Multinational Executives and Managers represent the three subcategories that comprise the first employment-based preference category (EB-1). The EB-1 category is allotted 40,000 visas per year from the total 140,000 visas available for employment based immigration under the INA. In addition, the EB-1 category will be allotted any left over visas from the fourth and fifth employment preference categories. The EB-1 category is extremely desirable because an approved labor certification from the Department of Labor is not required. The petitioning process is simplified when the need to obtain an approved labor certification is eliminated. Generally, the practical effect is that a petition under the EB-1 category will be adjudicated much faster than a petition under the employment-based categories that require labor certification (months instead of years).

EB-1-1: **Persons with Extraordinary Ability**

EB-1-2: **Outstanding Professors and Researchers**

EB-1-3: **Managerial or Executive Transferees**

EB-1-1: Persons with Extraordinary Ability

To obtain permanent residence based on extraordinary ability in the sciences, arts, education, business, or athletics, individuals must demonstrate that they are one of the small percentage who have risen to the very top of the field of endeavor. The definition of extraordinary ability and the evidentiary requirements for an EB-1-1 petition are almost identical to the requirements in the O nonimmigrant visa category. However, in comparison to the O nonimmigrant category, an EB-1-1 beneficiary may self-petition. A job offer, an approved labor certification, and peer group consultation are also not required.

A petition for a person of extraordinary ability must be accompanied by evidence that the foreign national has sustained national or international acclaim and that his or her achievements have been recognized in the field of expertise. Such evidence may include evidence of a one-time achievement like a major internationally recognized award such as a Nobel Prize, or at least **three** of the following:

- Documentation of the foreign national's receipt of lesser nationally or internationally recognized prizes or awards for excellence in the field of endeavor;

- Documentation of the foreign national's membership in associations in the field for which classification is sought, which require outstanding achievements of their members, as judged by recognized national or international experts in their disciplines or fields;

- Published material about the foreign national in professional or major trade publications or other major media, relating to the foreign national's work in the field for which classification is sought. Such evidence must include the title, date, and author of the material, and any necessary translation;

- Evidence of the foreign national's participation, either individually or on a panel, as a judge of the work of others in the same or an allied field of specification for which classification is sought;

- Evidence of the foreign national's original scientific, scholarly, artistic, athletic, or business-related contributions of major significance in the field;

- Evidence of the foreign national's authorship of scholarly articles in the field, in professional or major trade publications or other major media;

- Evidence of the display of the foreign national's work in the field at artistic exhibitions or showcases;

- Evidence that the foreign national has performed in a leading or critical role for organizations or establishments that have a distinguished reputation;

- Evidence that the foreign national has commanded a high salary or other significantly high remuneration for services, in relation to others in the field;

- Evidence of commercial successes in the performing arts, as shown by box office receipts or record, cassette, compact disc, or video sales.

If the above standards do not readily apply to the beneficiary's occupation, the petitioner may submit other "comparable evidence" to establish the beneficiary's eligibility.

Although there is no job offer requirement in the EB-1-1 category, the petition must be accompanied by clear evidence that the foreign national is coming to the United States to continue to work in the area of expertise. Such evidence may include letters from prospective employers, evidence of prearranged commitments such as contracts, or a statement from the beneficiary detailing plans on how he or she intends to continue his or her work in the United States.

The Immigration and Nationality Act also requires that the foreign national's admission "substantially benefit prospectively the United States." There are no separate evidentiary requirements to show that the foreign national's admission will substantially benefit prospectively the United States. Generally, the evidence used to show that the beneficiary will continue to work in their field of expertise is sufficient to meet the prospective benefit requirement.

SAMPLE LETTER FOR PERSON OF EXTRAORDINARY ABILITY IN THE ARTS

U.S. Department of Justice
Immigration & Naturalization Service
Nebraska Service Center
Lincoln, Nebraska

Re: **Schmidt, Boris**
Person with Extraordinary Ability in the Arts

Dear Sir/Madam:

This letter is submitted on behalf of Mr. Boris Schmidt as an EB-1-1 Priority Worker, Person with Extraordinary Ability in the Arts. To support classification as an E-1-1 Priority Worker, we submit the following index and supporting documentation demonstrating that Mr. Schmidt is one of the small percentage of individuals who are at the very top of their field, and therefore is qualified to be classified as a Priority Worker. Please find attached an index of Exhibits A-G submitted on Mr. Schmidt's behalf.

EXHIBITS

A. **Appraisers Association of America - Membership**

B. **Book Publisher**

C. **Letters of Attestation**

D. **Articles about Beneficiary**

E. **Articles by Beneficiary**

F. **Letters from Museums**

G. **Who's Who in Interior Design - Biography**

To demonstrate Mr. Schmidt's qualification in his field of expertise, we have enclosed documentation that meets the requirements from at least three of the ten categories enumerated in the statute for classification as an EB-1-1. His qualification as a person with extraordinary ability in the arts is evidenced by the many articles that have been written about him, articles he has written, letters from museums, letters from publishers, his membership in the Appraisers Association of America, and the recent publication of his book Post-Modernism, the definitive book on this specialized area of art. Please find following a detailed description of the evidence submitted:

ii) **Documentation of the foreign national's membership in associations in the field, which requires outstanding achievements of their members, as judged by recognized national or international experts in their disciplines of fields.**

Mr. Schmidt is a member of the Appraisers Association of America. The Appraisers Association of America is an elite national group of 1,000 members, founded in 1955, and having leaders in various fields relating to appraisals of different arts and antiquities. Membership in AAA is limited to individuals who possess outstanding achievements in their field, as judged by recognized international experts in their discipline or fields. In order to be accepted for membership, an applicant must submit an application along with a sponsor's written recommendation and numerous personal and professional references. After reviewing the applicant's qualifications and assessing the results of such written or oral examinations as are necessary, the Committee submits its report and recommendation to the Board of Directors. Election to Membership is subject to a 2/3 vote by the Membership Committee, which must subsequently be approved by a 2/3 vote of the Board of Directors.

In order to become a member, one must be sponsored by a current member and then be voted on by the Membership Committee. The Membership Committee is composed of experts in all the fields represented in the Association, as well as by the Board of Directors.

The Association is composed of individual professional appraisers who have been admitted to membership after meeting the critical standards set by the Association and proving their qualifications to the satisfaction of both the membership committee and the Board of Directors.

Exhibit A details the exact procedure for membership to the Appraisers Association of America as well as their by-laws and Membership Directory.

iii) **Published material about the foreign national in professional or major trade publications or other major media, relating to the alien's work in the field for which classification is sought**.

The name "Boris Schmidt" frequently appears in professional trade magazines and publications relating to his work in the field of post-modernism. As an international authority in this field he is often called upon to explain the artistic significance of particular works, and to lecture on different schools within this artistic realm. Attached as Exhibit B are representative articles published about the beneficiary.

iv) **Evidence of the foreign national's original scientific, scholarly, artistic, athletic, or business-related contributions of major significance in the field.**

Further evidence of the beneficiary's qualifications as a person with extraordinary ability in the arts is demonstrated by the publication of his most recent book on post-modernism, entitled Post-Modernism: A Critical Reexamination. Critically hailed as the definitive book on post-modernism, the book was enthusiastically received by the international press. In addition to the current German language version, this book is to be translated into Russian, English, Japanese and Italian. Please find critical reviews of the book and a copy of the text attached in **Exhibit C**.

v) **Evidence of the foreign national's authorship of scholarly articles in the field, in professional or major trade publications or other major media**.

Additionally, the beneficiary has also authored a number of articles on the subject of post-modernism. These articles appear in various professional and trade publications and are attached as **Exhibit E**.

vi) **Evidence that the foreign national has performed in a leading or critical role for organizations or establishments that have a distinguished reputation**.

Mr. Schmidt is frequently quoted by leading art magazines, and is sought after by museums, insurance companies and others who must rely on his expert advice and scholarship. Mr. Schmidt plays a critical role for these organizations by offering his advice and expertise. His role as Coordinator and Lecturer in the prestigious Post-Modernism Lecture Series at the Museum of Modern Art in New York further demonstrates his critical role and distinguished reputation in this field.

In light of Mr. Schmidt's record of achievement and the evidence attached to this petition, we respectfully request Mr. Schmidt's classification as an EB-1-1 Person with Extraordinary Ability be approved. Thank you for your immediate attention to this matter.

Very truly yours,

Hilda Mendelsohn
Senior Curator
German Society

SAMPLE EB-1-1 LETTER FOR PERSON WITH EXTRAORDINARY ABILITY

United States Department of Justice
Immigration & Naturalization Service
Vermont Service Center
St. Albans, Vermont

Re: **I-140 Petition - EB-1 Classification**
Person with Extraordinary Ability
Marcus Olivieri

Dear Sir/Madam:

This letter is written in support of Mr. Marcus Olivieri's I-140 petition as a Priority Worker. Mr. Olivieri is an Artist of Extraordinary Ability, who is currently employed by our gallery in H-1B status.

Mr. Olivieri's brilliant career and exceptional talent have been established in art shows, exhibits, galleries and auctions in both Europe and Latin America. His work has been shown in, or as a part of, collections at the finest galleries and museums in the world.

Mr. Olivieri was born in Grenada, and graduated in 1978 from the Faculty of Painting and Graphic Arts, Grenada Teachers Training College. In the ensuing twenty-year period, Mr. Olivieri has continuously exhibited his work in major international art shows. Please find attached the following evidence that demonstrates Mr. Olivieri's is an Artist of Extraordinary Ability.

Evidence of the display of the foreign national's work in the field at artistic exhibitions or showcases:

His one-man shows over the past six years include:

1992	Museo Moderno	Barcelona, Spain
1991	Soho Art Gallery	New York, USA
1991	Galleria Mexico	Guadalajara, Mexico
1990	Museo Moderno Buenos Aires	Buenos Aires, Argentina
1989	Galleria Della Fontana	Rome, Italy
1988	Salle Moderne	Paris, France

Group Exhibitions over the last sixteen years include:

1991	Pacific Fine Arts Center	Seattle, USA

1990	Goethe Institute Collection	Berlin, Germany
1989	Three Young Spanish Artists	London, England
	Museum of Modern Art	Zagreb, Yugoslavia
	Auction Sale	Cannes, France
1987	"Works by Young Artists"	Stockholm, Sweden
1986	Galleria Suisse	Basel, Switzerland
1982	"Works by Art Students"	St. Petersburg, Russia

Published material about the foreign national in professional or major trade publications or other major media, relating to the foreign national's work in the field for which classification is sought:

Mr. Olivieri's works have been reviewed by art critics in leading newspapers and by his peers in exhibition catalogues.

Catalogues

1991 Marcus Olivieri, one-man show catalogue, Rome, Italy

1990 Goethe Institute Collection, Berlin, Germany - "New Generations in Transition" exhibit.

1986 Galleria Suisse's catalogue of young Japanese artists from the Basel, Switzerland collection.

Publications

1997 Goya, Madrid, Spain

1996 Village Voice, New York, New York

1995 Goya, Madrid, Spain

1994 Apollo, London, England

1992 Artistos, Spain

1991 The New York Times Magazine, New York, New York.

1991 Art in America, New York, New York.

1990 Gallery Guide, New York, New York.

1989 Der Spiegel, Germany

1989 Moscow Artist, Moscow, Russia.

1988 Burlington, London, England

Additionally, Mr. Olivieri recently appeared on the New York television program "Today Show" in January 1999.

Evidence that the alien has commanded a high salary or other significantly high remuneration for services, in relation to others in the field:

Mr. Olivieri is currently paid $10,000 per month in addition to monies he receives upon the sale of his own highly acclaimed and sought after work. Mr. Olivieri's paintings range in price from $50,000 to $500,000 and his last five shows were completely sold out.

As one of the worlds's leading contemporary Spanish painters, Mr. Olivieri is uniquely suited to advise us on the selection of contemporary art for investment, exhibits and sale in the United States.

He will apply his well-demonstrated extraordinary ability in advising on purchases of art for our collection, concentrating on art produced by artists classified as contemporary living artists. He will arrange art shows throughout the United States, assist in the acquisition of and sale of limited mint collections, direct limited editions and print collections and provide his own works for sale, exhibit and promotion in our gallery.

Mr. Olivieri's extraordinary ability in the arts is demonstrated by his worldwide exhibits, numerous review of his works, his ability to command a high fee per painting and general worldwide acclaim. We respectfully submit this letter on his behalf.

Very truly yours,

Heather Smith
Curator
Picasso Gallery

EB-1-2 Outstanding Professors and Researchers

The second category of the first employment preference classification is comprised of professors and researchers who are "outstanding" in a specific "academic field."

The term "academic field" refers to a body of specialized knowledge offered for study at an accredited United States university or institution of higher education.

Evidence that the professor or researcher is recognized internationally as outstanding in the academic field should include at least two of the following types of documentation:

- Documentation of the foreign national's receipt of major prizes or awards for outstanding achievement in the academic field;

- Documentation of the foreign national's membership in associations in the academic field which require outstanding achievements of their members;

- Published material in professional publications written by others about the foreign national's work in the academic field. Such material should include the title, date and author of the material and any necessary translation;

- Evidence of the foreign national's participation, either individually or on a panel, as the judge of the work of others in the same or an allied academic field;

- Evidence of the foreign national's original scientific or scholarly research contributions to the academic field; or

- Evidence of the foreign national's authorship of scholarly books or articles in scholarly journals with international circulation, in the academic field.

The petition for an outstanding professor or researcher must also include evidence that the foreign national has at least three years of experience in teaching and/or research in the academic field. Experience in teaching or research while working on an advanced degree will only be acceptable if the foreign national has acquired the degree, and if the teaching duties were such that he or she had full responsibility for the class taught or if the research conducted toward the degree has been recognized within the academic field as outstanding. Evidence of teaching and/or research experience should be in the form of letters from current or former employers and should include the name, address, and title of the writer, and a specific description of the duties performed by the foreign national.

Additionally, the EB-1-2 category requires an offer of employment from a prospective United States employer. The "offer of employment" should be in the form of a letter from any of the following:

- A United States university or institution of higher learning offering the foreign national a tenured or tenure-track teaching position in the foreign national's academic field;

- A United States university or institution of higher learning offering the foreign national a permanent research position in the foreign national's academic field; or

- A department, division, or institute of a private employer offering the foreign national a permanent research position in the foreign national's academic field. The department, division, or institute must demonstrate that it employs at least three persons full-time in research positions, and that it has achieved documented accomplishments in an academic field.

In reference to a research position, **permanent** means either tenured, tenure-track, or for a term of indefinite or unlimited duration, and in which the employee will ordinarily have an exception of continued employment unless there is good cause for termination.

SAMPLE EMPLOYER LETTER FOR OUTSTANDING RESEARCHER

U.S. Department of Justice
Immigration & Naturalization Service
California Service Center
Laguna Niguel, California

Re: **Dr. Po-Hian Chin**

Dear Sir/Madam:

I am writing this letter in support of Dr. Po-Hian Chin's petition for an EB-1-2 immigrant visa as an outstanding researcher. He has worked as a research physicist in a permanent full-time position for Hawkes Technical Services since July 1997, at a salary of $175,000 per annum.

Hawkes Technical Services (HTS) was founded in 1956 and was incorporated under the laws of the State of Arizona. HTS is currently located in Phoenix, Arizona. HTS was established to provide technical services to government and industry. The company is renown for its comprehensive in-house capability to provide a wide variety of engineering, engineering support and prototype development services related to research and developmental programs. Fifteen full-time researchers, both physicists and engineers, as well as several part-time researchers are presently employed by HTS.

For the past two years, Dr. Chin has been performing important theoretical and experimental research in physics for HTS. He is presently involved in significant research concerning the possibilities of a better understanding of theoretical phenomenon. The theoretical work he performs involves calculating the atomic properties of solid state materials including the development of an atomic code that can solve the atomic orbital of all atoms. This work is vital for the development of ultra-high-speed electronic and photonic devices in the manometer spatial and femtosecond temporal scales.

A permanent position with our organization will remain immediately available to Dr. Chin pending the approval of his petition for an immigrant visa as an outstanding researcher. We trust that his petition will be approved so that he may continue this important and innovative work in the United States.

Very truly yours,

Andrew Spearman, Ph.D.
President

EB-1-3 Multinational Corporate Executives or Managers

The third sub-category of the first employment-based preference category is available to individuals who are multinational executives or managers. The definition of executives and managers in this category is the same as that of the executives and mangers in the L-1 nonimmigrant visa category. See Chapter Four for a complete discussion of the L nonimmigrant visa category. Employees with specialized knowledge are eligible for L-1B classification but are not eligible for permanent residence in the EB-1-3 category. In addition, executives and managers may not qualify for permanent residence based upon employment with a new office until that office has been in operation for at least one year.

The EB-1-3 category requires no labor certification from the Department of Labor, however the prospective employer in the United States must furnish a **job offer** in the form of a statement which indicates that the foreign national is to be employed in the United States in a managerial or executive capacity. Further, the letter must clearly describe the duties to be performed by the foreign national.

The inclusion of multinational executives and managers in the priority worker category, eliminating the need for labor certification, is a particular benefit to multinational businesses. Under prior law, multinational executives and managers were accorded a lower preference category subject to greater backlogs. Prior to the Immigration Act of 1990, high level managers and executives who did not have degrees, were ineligible for permanent residence based upon the offer of employment. In the interest of promoting multinational businesses in the United States, the 1990 Act specifically included multinational executives and managers in the first employment-based immigrant preference category.

In order for an employer to qualify as a petitioner, the business entity must be a "Multinational Entity." Multinational means that the qualifying entity, or its affiliate, or subsidiary conducts business in **two or more countries**, one of which is the United States.

Definition of Terms

Subsidiary means a firm, corporation, or other legal entity of which a parent owns, directly or indirectly, more than half of the entity and controls the entity, or owns, directly or indirectly 50 percent of a 50/50 joint venture and has equal control and veto power over the entity, or owns directly or indirectly, less than half of the entity, but in fact controls the entity.

Doing business means the regular, systematic, and continuous provision of goods and/or services by a firm, corporation, or other entity and does not include the mere presence of an agent or office.

Executive Capacity means an assignment within an organization in which the employee primarily:

- Directs the management of the organization or a major component or function of the organization;
- Establishes the goals and policies of the organization, component or function;
- Exercises wide latitude in discretionary decision making; and
- Receives only general supervision or direction from higher level executives, the board of directors, or stockholders of the organization.

Managerial Capacity means an assignment within an organization in which the employee primarily:

- Manages the organization, or a department, subdivision, function or component of the organization;
- Supervises and controls the work of other supervisory, professional, or managerial employees, or manages an essential function within the organization, or a department or subdivision of the orga-

nization;

- If another employee or other employees are directly supervised, has the authority to hire and fire or recommend those as well as other personnel actions (such as promotion and leave authorization) or, if no other employee is directly supervised, functions at a senior level within the organizational hierarchy or with respect to the function managed; and

- Exercises discretion over the day-to-day operations of the activity or function for which the employee has authority.

A statement must accompany a petition for a multinational executive or manager from an authorized official of the petitioning United States employer, which demonstrates that:

- If the foreign national is outside the United States, in the three years immediately preceding the filing of the petition the foreign national has been employed outside the United States for at least one year in a managerial or executive capacity by a firm or corporation, or other legal entity, or by an affiliate or subsidiary of such a firm or corporation or other legal entity; or

- If the foreign national is already in the United States working for the same employer or a subsidiary or affiliate of the firm or corporation, or other legal entity by which the foreign national was employed overseas, in the three years preceding entry as a nonimmigrant, the foreign national was employed by the entity abroad for at least one year in a managerial or executive capacity.

- The prospective employer in the United States is the same employer or a subsidiary or affiliate of the firm or corporation or other legal entity who employed the foreign national overseas; and

- The prospective United States employer has been doing business for at least one year, and is currently active both in the United States and at least one country abroad.

When assessing whether an employee is performing in a managerial or executive capacity, it is important to keep in mind that a first-line supervisor, by regulation, is not considered to be acting in a managerial capacity merely by virtue of his or her supervisory duties unless the employees supervised are professional.

If staffing levels are used as a factor in determining whether an individual is acting in a managerial or executive capacity, the reasonable needs of the organization, component, or function, in light of the overall purpose and stage of development of the organization, component, or function, are taken into account. An individual is not to be considered to be acting in a managerial or executive capacity merely on the basis of the number of employees that the individual supervises or has supervised or directs or has directed.

SAMPLE LETTER FOR MANAGERIAL OR EXECUTIVE TRANSFEREE

U.S. Department of Justice
Immigration & Naturalization Service
Vermont Service Center
St. Albans, Vermont

Re: **Sidney Yi Lam**

Dear Sir/Madam:

This letter is written in support of our petition for classification under the first employment preference as a multinational manager on behalf of Mr. Sidney Yi Lam who is presently employed in professional managerial capacity by Hong Kong Pharmaceuticals (HKP). Mr. Lam is currently in L-1A status.

THE PETITIONER

Established in 1903, HKP employs over 11,000 individuals. In 1997, HKP had gross revenues exceeding $2.25 billion and a net income of over $433 million. HKP is a global organization and an established leader in the pharmaceutical market.

During the last decade HKP has expanded its operations and dedicated its resources to becoming a research-driven enterprise. HKP has continuously increased research and development spending year by year. The most ambitious capital project in HKP's history is a $35 million Product Development Center in Fort Lee, New Jersey. This state-of-the-art facility will play a crucial part in ensuring our success in the 21st century and beyond.

CORPORATE INTERRELATIONSHIP

Hong Kong Pharmaceuticals of America Inc. is a wholly owned subsidiary of Hong Kong Pharmaceuticals Corporation of Hong Kong. The corporate interrelationship is one of subsidiary and parent. All of the directors of Hong Kong Pharmaceuticals USA Inc. are also members of Hong Kong Pharmaceuticals Corporation of Hong Kong. These directors set the corporate policy for the U.S. subsidiary and direct the ultimate assignments of all employees in the organization.

Established in 1984, Hong Kong Pharmaceuticals USA Inc. (HKP USA) manufactures and distributes pharmaceutical products. With over 200 employees, its gross annual income averages $35,000,000 million in U.S. dollars.

THE BENEFICIARY

The Hong Kong Pharmaceuticals Corporation has continuously employed Mr. Lam since June 1981, when he joined Hong Kong Pharmaceuticals in Hong Kong, as a Senior Accountant. In this capacity, he was responsible for designing and installing a financial accounting system, consolidating accounting records, as well as purchasing in three companies. He was also responsible for implementing corporate-related, procedures to ensure that strict internal accounting controls were applied. Mr. Lam also designed a capital project accounting system and automated financial and cost accounting system.

His outstanding performances and demonstrated abilities led Mr. Lam to be promoted to Manager of Finance in April 1988. This is a top management position within the HKP hierarchy that includes responsibility for total financial control of Hong Kong Pharmaceuticals USA Inc. The Manager of Finance reports directly to the Managing Director of HKP. The areas of responsibility included Treasury, Budgeting, Financial and Cost Accounting, Risk Management, Legal, Taxation and managing a staff of ten, including a Financial Accountant, a Management Accountant, six Accountants and two support personnel.

His specific duties included: Management and coordination of Internal and External Audits, including full statutory audits of the Hong Kong registered legal entities; implementation of corporate procedure and provision of financial control on Capital Projects; evaluation of Capital Expenditure proposals; generation of company minutes and all statutory returns; ensuring that all legal requirements were complied with; administering Profit Sharing Scheme; and ensuring that payment was tax effective and in compliance with Japanese tax legislation.

In addition, Mr. Lam's duties included preparation of Annual Operating Plan and management of departmental budgets, forecasting the latest estimate generation taxation strategy, regular review of current and potential exposures and opportunities for tax reduction in Hong Kong, making appropriate recommendations to Corporate Taxation and implementation of policy.

THE POSITION

In January 1997, after an international search, Mr. Lam was selected to assume the executive managerial position of **Director of Finance, Pharmaceutical Manufacturing**. Mr. Lam was chosen from the ranks of our professional executives to assume, in L-1 status, this top position at the American subsidiary location in Fort Lee, New Jersey. Mr. Lam was selected for the position because of his intimate familiarity with the policies, practices and procedures of HKP and his exceptional track record with our organization. This appointment reflects the high esteem in which the worldwide HKP group of companies holds Mr. Lam.

This is an extremely challenging high level executive position with overall direction of Cost Accounting, Inventory Control, Cost Analysis, Manufacturing Budget and Management reporting for all HKP labs pharmaceutical-manufacturing operations. In addition, Mr. Lam also participates in the planning and evaluation of the financial impact of present and proposed manufacturing activities and provides financial support to the Senior Vice President of Pharmaceutical Manufacturing.

As Director of Finance of the New Jersey subsidiary, Mr. Lam reports directly to the Vice President of Finance of the Hong Kong Pharmaceuticals Corporation. A professional staff of fifteen reports to Mr. Lam. His specific duties include:

- Directing, scheduling and coordinating the development of all Manufacturing operating plans; generating formal presentation material required at high-level management meetings and analysis of significant variances, working with the executive level Manufacturing and Finance Management, Directors and Managers in Manufacturing and staff support.

- Providing effective Cost Analysis and performance measurement of actual monthly results versus Plan and latest Estimate; identifying significant trends or potential problems and recommending alternatives for corrective action;

- Directing the development of all unit standard costs for products manufactured by HKP Labs Manufacturing;

- Evaluating existing Cost and Inventory Systems as to the adequacy of internal control, value of generated data, and time lines; developing and implementing enhancements; and

- Establishing and maintaining financial communication network that will ensure that all Cost/ Inventory data is being transmitted/coordinated with the appropriate functional areas; heavy interface with Manufacturing, Marketing, Quality Control, International Finance, Corporate Audits and outside auditors.

Mr. Lam's thorough familiarity with the policies, practices and procedures of the Hong Kong Pharmaceuticals Corporation, as well as his solid academic background and high-level experience in Advanced Corporate Accounting all relate directly to the position in question at which he is remunerated $234,000 per annum.

The Hong Kong Pharmaceuticals Corporation now requires his exceptional abilities and dynamic professional and managerial leadership in the United States on a long-term basis so that he may continue contributing to our corporate growth.

We respectfully request your expeditious approval of the enclosed immigrant petition. Thank you for your assistance in this matter.

Very truly yours,

Baoheng Chin
Senior Vice President - International Accounting

D. **EB-2: SECOND EMPLOYMENT-BASED IMMIGRANT CATEGORY**

The second employment-based category is available to the following two categories of individuals:

- Persons who are members of the professions holding advanced degrees or their equivalent; or

- Persons of exceptional ability in the sciences, arts or business who, because of their exceptional ability, will substantially benefit prospectively the national economy, cultural or educational interests, or welfare of the United States.

Similar to the first employment category, the EB-2 category has 40,000 visas available per year, plus any left over from the first category.

Definitions:

An **advanced degree** for the purposes of this category refers to any United States academic or professional degree or a foreign equivalent degree above that of baccalaureate. A U.S. baccalaureate degree or a foreign equivalent degree followed by at least five years of progressive experience in the specialty will be considered the equivalent of a master's degree. If a doctoral degree is customarily required by the specialty the foreign national must have a United States doctorate or a foreign equivalent degree.

The definition of **profession** includes, but is not limited to, architects, engineers, lawyers, physicians, surgeons, teachers in elementary or secondary schools, colleges, academics, or seminaries, as well as any occupation for which a United States baccalaureate degree or its foreign equivalent is the minimum requirement for entry into the occupation.

Exceptional Ability in the Sciences, Arts, or Business means a level of expertise significantly above that ordinarily encountered in the sciences, arts, or business.

Who may petition?

Any United States employer may file a petition on Form I-140 on behalf of an individual for classification as a member of the professions holding an advanced degree or a person of exceptional ability in the sciences, arts, or business. If a foreign national is claiming exceptional ability in the sciences, arts, or business and is seeking an exemption from the requirement of a job offer in the United States (through a **national interest waiver** discussed below), then the foreign national, or anyone on the foreign national's behalf, may be the petitioner.

Petition Requirements

To show that the individual is a **professional holding an advanced degree**, the petition must be accompanied by:

- An official academic record showing that the foreign national has a United States advanced degree or a foreign equivalent degree; or

- An official academic record showing that the foreign national has a United States baccalaureate degree or a foreign equivalent degree, and evidence in the form of letters from current or former employers showing that the foreign national has at least five years of progressive post-baccalaureate experience in the specialty.

If the beneficiary has obtained a foreign degree an education evaluation of the foreign degree must be submitted along with the petition. An education evaluation is required to show that the foreign degree is equivalent to a U.S. degree and the foreign national has met the requisite educational requirements for the position.

To show that the individual is a **person of exceptional ability in the sciences, arts, or business**, the petition must be accompanied by at least three of the following:

- An official academic record showing that the foreign national has a degree, diploma, certificate, or similar award from a college, university, school, or other institution of learning relating to the area of exceptional ability;

- Evidence in the form of letter(s) from the current or former employer(s) showing that the foreign national has at least ten years of full-time experience in the occupation for which he or she is being sought;

- A license to practice the profession or certification for a particular profession or occupation;

- Evidence that the foreign national has commanded a salary, or other remuneration for services, which demonstrates exceptional ability;

- Evidence of membership in professional associations; or

- Evidence of recognition for achievements and significant contributions to the industry or field by peers, governmental entities, or professional or business organizations.

If the above standards do not readily apply to the beneficiary's occupation, the petitioner may submit "comparable evidence" to establish the beneficiary's eligibility.

The main use of the exceptional ability component in the EB-2 category is to avoid the advanced degree requirement.

Prior to 1995, the INS did not permit professional athletes to be considered for classification as "exceptional ability" aliens in the second employment-based category. Professional athletes may now be considered for the second preference category as persons of exceptional ability in the arts.

NATIONAL INTEREST WAIVERS

Both the job offer and the labor certification requirement may be waived for professionals with advanced degrees and persons with exceptional ability if the exemption is shown to be "in the national interest." The term "in the national interest" has never been explicitly defined and each application is decided on a case-by-case basis. However, in 1992, the Administrative Appeals Unit of the Immigration and Naturalization Service enunciated seven factors to be considered regarding the foreign national's admission:

- Whether the foreign national's admission will improve the United States economy;

- Whether the foreign national's admission will improve the wages and working conditions of United States workers;

- Whether the foreign national's admission will improve educational and training programs for United States children and under qualified workers;

- Whether the foreign national's admission will improve health care;

- Whether the foreign national's admission will provide more affordable housing for young, aged or poor United States residents;

- Whether the foreign national's admission will improve the United States environment and the productive use of natural resources; or

- Whether the foreign national's admission is requested by an interested United States government agency.

A petitioner in a standard EB-2 petition for exceptional ability does not have to provide any additional evidence to show the foreign national's admission will have a prospective national benefit. However, in the case of a foreign national who is submitting a national interest waiver, both the AAU and INS have stated that the foreign national must provide a benefit to the country **beyond** the general prospective national benefit required in the standard petition.

The key factors that are considered in regard to a national interest waiver application are the level of documentation, the level of support from important local government or business in the region where the foreign national will be employed, and the beneficiary's expertise and special skills.

The application for a national interest waiver in the second employment based visa category must include Form ETA-750 Part B of the Labor Certification Application in duplicate and supporting documentation. In addition, the petitioner must include evidence to support the claim that the admission of the foreign national is in the national interest. This evidence may take the form of letters, affidavits, articles, and other types of supporting documentation that addresses the foreign national's qualifications and background. The documentation submitted should demonstrate that the foreign national possesses unique knowledge, abilities, or experience and that the foreign national will utilize their unique knowledge, abilities, or experience to benefit the United States or a particular geographic area of the United States.

The principal advantage of the national interest waiver is the avoidance of the labor certification requirement, otherwise required in the EB-2 category. The labor certification process is discussed in greater detail in Chapter Nine. The labor certification process can be a frustrating, cumbersome, and difficult process often taking more than two years to complete. Generally, the avoidance of the labor certification process is quite advisable whenever possible.

E. EB-3: THIRD EMPLOYMENT-BASED IMMIGRANT CATEGORY

The third employment-based category is designed for the following three groups of individuals:

- **Skilled Workers**
- **Professionals**
- **Other Workers ("E-W")**

A **Skilled Worker** is a foreign national who is capable, at the time of petitioning for classification, of performing skilled labor requiring at least two years training or experience not of a temporary or seasonal nature, for which qualified workers are unavailable in the United States. Relevant post-secondary education may be considered as training for the purposes of this classification.

Professional refers to a qualified foreign national who holds at least a United States baccalaureate degree or a foreign equivalent degree and who is a member of the professions.

Other Worker means a qualified alien who is capable, at the time of petitioning for this classification, of performing unskilled labor, requiring less than two years training or experience not of a temporary or seasonal nature, for which qualified workers are unavailable in the United States.

The third visa category has 40,000 visas allocated to it annually, plus any unused visas from the first two employment categories. However, the "other workers" section of this category are only allocated 10,000 visas per year, creating a substantial backlog in this particular classification. Therefore, wherever possible it is beneficial to petition as a skilled worker requiring two years of experience rather than as an "other worker" since more visas are available for skilled workers and the backlog, if any, is significantly shorter.

The third employment-based preference requires a job offer by an employer and an approved labor certification application (unless the position is a designated Schedule A occupation).

"Schedule A" is a list of occupations designated by the Department of Labor to be experiencing a shortage of able, willing, qualified and available U.S. workers. The benefit of Schedule A designation for a petitioner is the elimination of the need to obtain an approved individual labor certification from the DOL. Instead, the petitioner may submit Form ETA-750 directly to the INS along with the immigrant visa petition. Schedule A was formerly much more extensive, but now has been substantially scaled down by the Department of Labor. Currently, the only occupations certified as Schedule A are:

- Group I - Physical Therapists and Nurses
- Group II - Persons of Exceptional Ability in the Sciences and Non-Performing Arts.

However, the standard of proof for Group II persons of exceptional ability in the sciences and non-performing arts is just as high as for Persons of Extraordinary Ability in the EB-1-1 category. Thus, if an individual qualifies for Group II Schedule A classification the individual would probably qualify for EB-1-1 classification. EB-1-1 classification is more desirable because it eliminates the specific job offer requirement, generally priority dates remain current and there is little or no backlog. For a complete discussion of Schedule A, see Chapter Nine.

Every petition under EB-3 classification must be accompanied by an individual labor certification approved by the Department of Labor or by an application for Schedule A designation. The job offer portion of an individual labor certification or Schedule A application for a professional must demonstrate that the job requires the minimum of a baccalaureate degree.

Any requirements of training or experience for skilled workers, professionals, or other workers must be supported by letters from trainers or employers giving the name, address and title of the trainer or employer, and a description of the training received or the experience of the foreign national.

If the petition is for a **skilled worker**, the petition must be accompanied by evidence that the foreign national meets the educational, training, experience, or any other requirements of the individual labor certification or meets the requirements for Schedule A designation. The minimum requirements for this classification are at least **two years** of training or experience.

If the petition is for a **professional**, the petition must be accompanied by evidence that the foreign national holds a United States baccalaureate degree or a foreign equivalent degree and evidence that the foreign national is a member of the professions. Evidence of a baccalaureate degree may be in the form of an official college or university record showing the date the baccalaureate degree was awarded and the area of concentration of study. To show that the foreign national is a member of the professions, the petitioner must submit evidence showing that the **minimum** of a baccalaureate degree is required for entry into the occupation.

If the petition is for an unskilled or "other" worker (this category is also known as "E-W"), it must be accompanied by evidence that the foreign national meets any educational, training, experience, or other requirements of the particular labor certification application.

The determination of whether a worker is a skilled or other worker will be based on the requirements of training and/or experience placed on the job by the prospective employer, as certified by the Department of Labor.

For "skilled" or "other workers," the job offer requirement also requires that the employment being sponsored not be temporary or seasonal in nature, but rather that the job be a permanent job offer.

However, this does not prohibit the eventual dissolution of the permanent relationship by either the petitioner or the beneficiary. Provided that the relationship portrayed at the time of the filing was not a "sham" designed to confer permanent resident status on a foreign national where no permanent job offer actually existed at the time of filing, employment eventually may be terminated. There is no legal requirement that the employee remain in the same job once permanent residence is granted as long as there was no bad faith involved in the original hiring.

When structuring job offers and labor certifications, it is critical that the employers bear in mind the foreign national's qualifications and skills while not specifically tailoring the position to make the foreign national the only possible qualified applicant. Similarly, if the employer restricts the position in such a way as to minimize United States applicants, the labor certification and job offer may unintentionally exclude the foreign national as well. Therefore, in many instances, even though the employer might prefer to place a two year experience requirement in the Labor Certification application to avoid the "other worker" backlog, the Department of Labor will not approve the petition if the requirements are regarded as "restrictive" or beyond those normally required for the application. Consequently, many occupations, especially that of household workers are relegated to the unskilled, backlogged other worker category. See Chapter Nine for a more detailed discussion of the labor certification process.

SAMPLE FORM I-140

OMB #1115-0061
Immigrant Petition for Alien Worker

START HERE - Please Type or Print

Part 1. Information about the person or organization filing this petition.

If an individual is filing, use the top Name line. Organizations should use the second line.

Family Name	Given Name	Middle Initial

Company or Organization: Hong Kong Pharmaceuticals

Address - Attn:

Street Number and Name: 1 Corporate Drive	Room #:
City: Fort Lee	State or Province: New Jersey
Country: USA	Zip/Postal Code: 00010
IRS Tax #: 13-8888888	Social Security #: N/A

Part 2. Petition Type.

This petition is being filed for: (check one)

- a. ☐ An alien of extraordinary ability
- b. ☐ An outstanding professor or researcher
- c. ☒ A multinational executive or manager
- d. ☐ A member of the professions holding an advanced degree or an alien of exceptional ability
- e. ☐ A skilled worker (requiring at least two years of specialized training or experience) or professional
- f. ☐ An employee of the U.S. business operating in Hong Kong
- g. ☐ Any other worker (requiring less than two years of training or experience)

Part 3. Information about the person you are filing for.

Family Name: LAM	Given Name: Sidney	Middle Initial: Yi

Address - C/O

Street Number and Name: Chow Loon Alley 5	Apt. #: J
City:	State or Province:
Country: Hong Kong	Zip or Postal Code:
Date of Birth (month/day/year): 08/20/1955	Country of Birth: Hong Kong
Social Security # (if any): N/A	A# (if any): N/A
If in the U.S. — Date of Arrival (month/day/year): N/A	I-94#: N/A
If in the U.S. — Current Nonimmigrant Status:	Expires on (month/day/year):

Part 4. Processing Information.

Below give the U.S. consulate you want notified if this petition is approved and if any requested adjustment of status cannot be granted.

U.S. Consulate: City Hong Kong Country

FOR INS USE ONLY

Returned	Receipt
Resubmitted	
Reloc Sent	
Reloc Rec'd	
☐ Petitioner Interviewed ☐ Beneficiary Interviewed	

Classification
- ☐ 203 (b)(1)(A) Alien of Extraordinary Ability
- ☐ 203 (b)(1)(B) Outstanding Professor or Researcher
- ☐ 203 (b)(1)(C) Multi-national executive or manager
- ☐ 203 (b)(2) Member of professional w/adv. degree or of exceptional ability
- ☐ 203 (b)(3)(A)(i) Skilled worker
- ☐ 203 (b)(3)(A)(ii) Professional
- ☐ 203 (b)(3)(A)(iii) Other worker
- ☐ Sec. 124 IMMACT-Employee of U.S. business in Hong Kong

Priority Date	**Consulate**

Remarks

Action Block

To be completed by Attorney or Representative, if any

☐ **Fill in box if G-28 is attached to represent the petitioner**

VOLAG#

ATTY State License #

Continued on back

SAMPLE FORM I-140 (CONTINUED)

Part 4. Processing Information. (continued)

If you gave a U.S. address in part 3, print the person's foreign address below. If his/her native alphabet does not use Roman letters, print his/her name and foreign address in the native alphabet.

Name	Address
Sidney LAM	

Are you filing any other petitions or applications with this one?	☒ No	☐ yes, attach an explanation
Is the person you are filing for in exclusion or deportation proceedings?	☒ No	☐ yes, attach an explanation
Has an immigrant visa petition ever been filed by or on behalf of this person?	☒ No	☐ yes, attach an explanation

Part 5. Additional Information about the employer.

Type of petitioner (check one): ☐ Self ☐ Individual U.S. Citizen ☒ Company or organization ☐ Permanent Resident ☐ Other explain ________

If a company, give the following:
Type of business: Pharmaceutical Company

Date Established	Current # of employees	Gross Annual Income	Net Annual Income
1984	200		433,000,000.00

If an individual, give the following: Occupation	Annual Income

Part 6. Basic Information about proposed employment.

Job Title	Nontechnical Description of job
Director- Finance Manufacturing	Direct all manufacturing departments (see attached letter in support)

Address where person will work if different from address in part 1.

Is this a full-time position? ☒ yes ☐ No (hours per week ________) Wages per week $234,000 per y

Is this a permanent position? ☒ yes ☐ No | Is this a new position? ☐ yes ☒ No

Part 7. Information on spouse and all children you are filing for.

Provide an attachment listing the family members of the person you are filing for. Be sure to include their full name, relationship, date and country of birth, ar present address.

Part 8. Signature.

Read the information on the penalties in the instructions before completing this section.

I certify under penalty of perjury under the laws of the United States of America that this petition, and the evidence submitted with it, is all true and correct. I authorize the release of any information from my records which the Immigration and Naturalization Service needs to determine eligibility for the benefit I am seeking.

Signature Date

Please Note: If you do not completely fill this form, or fail to submit required documents listed in the instructions, you cannot be found eligible for the requested document and this application may be denied.

Part 9. Signature of person preparing form if other than above. (Sign below)

I declare that I prepared this form at the request of the above person and it is based on all information of which I have knowledge.

Signature Print Your Name Date

Firm Name and Address

PRACTICAL CONSIDERATIONS FOR COMPLETING FORM I-140

1. Part 2 - The petitioner must check one of the boxes.

2. Part 5 - Financial information concerning the employer relates to the continued economic viability of the petitioner and its ability to guarantee the beneficiary the wage indicated.

3. Part 6 - Write a brief job description followed by "see attached letter." The accompanying letter should give a complete job description.

In Labor Certification cases, the wage level shown should be consistent with the salary level indicated on the approved Labor Certification Application. This salary may be somewhat higher than that shown on the Labor Certification Application so long as it is consistent with normal salary movements. However, it should never be lower.

4. Part 7 - List the beneficiary's spouse and all children even if they will not accompany the beneficiary to the United States.

F. EB-4: FOURTH EMPLOYMENT-BASED IMMIGRANT CATEGORY

The fourth employment-based immigrant category is reserved for special immigrants. Special immigrants are defined by the INA as:

- Immigrants lawfully admitted for permanent residence that are returning from a temporary visit abroad. This is not really an employment based or immigrant category at all, but the technical classification in which people who have already immigrated to the United States are readmitted to the United States after a temporary trip abroad.

- Ministers of religion and other religious workers.

- Certain employees or retired employees of the U.S. government who have served abroad.

- Certain employees under the Panama Canal Act of 1979.

- Certain foreign medical graduates who entered the U.S. in H or J status before January 10, 1978.

- Certain officers and employees of international organizations who resided in the U.S. for requisite periods, and defined widows and widowers, and unmarried sons or daughters of such officers and employees.

- Certain persons declared dependent on a U.S. juvenile court or placed in state custody.

- Certain immigrants who have served in the U.S. armed forces.

Prior to the 1990 Act, special immigrants were not subject to numerical restrictions and did not have to file petitions with the INS. The 1990 Act created a cap of 10,000 visas per year available for special immigrants. Returning lawful permanent residents and certain former citizens entitled to regain citizenship are **excluded** from the fourth preference category and therefore are not subject to the cap. Most of the special immigrant categories were created to benefit a very small class of eligible individuals and in some cases there are no longer any individuals left to meet the requirements of some of the category. The minister and religious worker category is the most widely used category of special immigrants in the EB-4 preference.

Ministers and other Religious Workers

A foreign national, or any person on behalf of the foreign national, may file an I-360 visa petition for classification as a special immigrant religious worker. The petition may be filed by or for an alien, who (either abroad or in the United States), for at least the two years immediately preceding the filing of the petition, has been a member of a religious denomination which has a **bona fide** nonprofit religious organization in the United States.

The three types of religious workers that are eligible for EB-4 immigrant visas are:

- Ministers of the sponsoring religious denomination;

- Religious workers employed in a professional capacity in a religious vocation or occupation; and

- Religious workers employed in a non-professional capacity coming to work in a religious vocation or occupation either for the religious denomination or for a tax-exempt affiliate of the denomination.

In addition, the foreign national must be coming to the United States **solely** for the purpose of working as a minister, professional religious worker or non-professional religious worker. All three types of religious workers must have been performing the vocation, professional work, or other work continuously (either abroad or in the United States) for at least the two-year period immediately preceding the filing of the petition.

Congress, in the Immigration Act of 1990, limited the time to file petitions for religious workers and other workers to October 1, 1994. Congress has subsequently extended this time limit twice, initially to September 30, 1997 and currently, the program is set to "sunset" on September 30, 2000. Ministers in the EB-4 category are not subject to the sunset date of September 30, 2000. In addition, lay religious workers are limited to 5,000 of the 10,000 available visas. Currently, the 5,000 limit has created a backlog in the religious worker category.

One alternative for religious workers who wish to enter the United States is the R nonimmigrant category. The R nonimmigrant visa is a temporary visa that is available to ministers, professional workers, and other religious personnel who for the two years immediately prior to the petition have been a member of a religious denomination having a bona fide nonprofit, religious organization in the United States.

In comparison to the EB-4 category, an individual need only be a member of the religious denomination for the immediately preceeding two years to qualify as an R nonimmigrant, as opposed to the two year prior employment requirement in the EB-4 category. In addition, there is no limit on the number of individuals who may obtain R nonimmigrant classification and thus no backlog. However, the R visa is only a temporary visa that limits the visaholder's overall stay in the United States to five years and requires the visaholder to stay out of the U.S. for at least one year before reapplying for a new R visa. See Chapter Seven for a complete discussion of the R nonimmigrant visa category.

If an individual has an offer of employment in the United States in a religious capacity but does not have two years of prior employment that is required for EB-4 classification the individual may still be eligible to enter the U.S. as an R nonimmigrant. Once the R visaholder has worked in the U.S. for at least two years he or she may be eligible for EB-4 classification. As a practical consideration, the R visaholder should apply for EB-4 classification as soon as he or she becomes eligible to ensure an earlier priority date and avoid any possible backlog or delay. It is not advisable to delay applying for EB-4 classification during the R nonimmigrant's authorized period of stay because an R visaholder is limited to a five-year total period of stay in the United States. The R visaholder will not be able to remain in the U.S. or adjust status to that of a permanent lawful resident if he or she is out of status.

Definitions

A bona fide nonprofit religious organization in the United States means an organization exempt from taxation as described in section 501(c)(3) of the Internal Revenue Code of 1986 as it relates to religious organizations, or one that has never sought such exemption but establishes to the satisfaction of the Service that it would be eligible if it had applied for tax exempt status.

A bona fide organization which is affiliated with the religious denomination means an organization which is closely associated with the religious denomination and which is exempt from taxation as described in section 501(c) (e) of the Internal Revenue Code of 1986 as it relates to religious organizations.

Minister means an individual duly authorized by a recognized religious denomination to conduct religious worship and to perform other duties usually performed by authorized members of the clergy of that religion. In all cases, there must be a reasonable connection between the activities performed and the religious calling of the minister. The term does not include a lay preacher not authorized to perform such duties.

Professional capacity means an activity in a religious vocation or occupation for which the minimum of a United States baccalaureate degree or a foreign equivalent degree is required.

Religious denomination means a religious group or community of believers having some form of ecclesiastical government, a creed or statement of faith, some form of worship, a formal or informal code of doctrine and discipline, religious services and ceremonies, established places of religious worship, religious congregations, or comparable indicia of a bona fide religious denomination. For the purposes if this definition, an inter-denominational religious organization which is exempt from taxation pursuant to section 501 (c)(e) of the Internal Revenue Code of 1986 will be treated as a religious denomination.

Religious occupation means an activity that relates to a traditional religious function. Examples of individuals in religious occupations include, but are not limited to, liturgical workers, religious instructors, religious counselors, cantors, catechists, workers in religious hospitals or religious health care facilities, missionaries, religious translators, or religious broadcasters. This group **does not** include janitors, maintenance workers, clerks, fundraisers, or persons solely involved in the solicitation of donations.

Religious vocation means a calling to religious life evidenced by the demonstration of commitment practiced in the religious denomination, such as the taking of vows. Examples of individuals with a religious vocation include, but are not limited to, nuns, monks, and religious brothers and sisters.

Evidence Required for Religious Worker Petition

- Evidence that the organization qualifies as a nonprofit organization in the form of either documentation showing that the organization is exempt from taxation pursuant to the Internal Revenue Code as it relates to religious organizations or documentation that shows the organization would be eligible for exemption from taxation pursuant to the Internal Revenue Code.

- A letter from an authorized official of the religious organization in the United States that establishes the following:

- That immediately prior to the filing of the petition, the foreign national has the required two years of membership in the denomination and the required two years of experience in the religious vocation, professional religious work, or other religious work; and

- That if the foreign national is a religious professional, he or she has authorization to conduct religious worship and to perform other duties usually performed by authorized members of the clergy, including a detailed description of such authorized duties. A certificate of ordination may be requested when applicable; or

- That, if the foreign national is a religious professional, he or she has at least a United States baccalaureate or its foreign equivalent required for entry into the religious profession. In all professional cases, an official academic record showing that the foreign national has the required degree must be submitted; or

- That, if the foreign national is to work in another religious vocation or occupation, he or she is qualified in the religious vocation or occupation. Evidence of such qualification may include, but need not be limited to, evidence establishing that the foreign national is a nun, monk, or religious brother, or that the type of work to be done relates to a traditional religious function.

- If the foreign national is to work in a non-ministerial or non-professional capacity for a bona fide religious organization that is affiliated with the religious denomination, the letter from the authorized official must explain how the affiliation exists. The affiliate must provide the tax-exempt certificate issued by the IRS.

In addition to the evidentiary requirements listed above, the petition must contain a letter from the authorized official of the religious organization petitioning on behalf of the foreign national describing the details of the job offer. The letter should state how the beneficiary will carry on the vocation of a minister, including the terms of payment for services or other remuneration. If the beneficiary will work in a professional religious capacity or in other religious work the letter should also address the terms of payment for services or other remuneration. The letter should clearly indicate that the beneficiary **will not** be solely dependent on supplemental employment or solicitation of funds for support. Bank letters, recent audits, church membership figures, and other employment data may be submitted to the INS in borderline cases to bolster the letter in support.

G. EB-5: FIFTH EMPLOYMENT-BASED IMMIGRATION CATEGORY

The Immigration Act of 1990 created a new category designed to benefit foreign investors who invest at least $1,000,000 in the United States. The investment must be in a new commercial enterprise that will benefit the U.S. economy and create at least ten full-time jobs for qualifying workers. There is no labor certification requirement in this category and 10,000 immigrant visas are set aside per year for qualifying individuals. The purpose of this visa category was to infuse new capital and create new employment opportunities in the United States. To date, the category has been underutilized and the INS has narrowly construed many of the requirements for classification.

One of the many drawbacks for foreign investors is that by investing in the United States and applying for permanent resident status the individual's worldwide income becomes subject to United States tax laws. This is a situation that many foreign investors wish to avoid.

Another inconvenience of the EB-5 category is the lack of a pre-approval mechanism. These means a foreign national can not be granted an immigrant visa prior to actually making the investment, but rather must first make the investment and then apply for the visa. Further, there must be a demonstration that the funds involved were already put at risk. Finally, even if the funds put at risk otherwise qualify within the guidelines, there is still a condition placed on the resident status that must be reviewed after two years before full lawful resident status is granted. Consequently, if the business fails, the investor stands to lose not only the funds invested in the venture, but also may have his or her permanent resident status revoked.

If an individual is interested in investing and remaining in the United States, it may be possible for that individual to obtain an E-2 nonimmigrant investor visa. See Chapter Five for a complete discussion of the E visa category. The E-2 category may be an easier alternative to EB-5 classification. Given the definition "substantial investment", it may very well be less than $1,000,000 or $500,000 required for the immigrant investor visa. Although the E visa is a nonimmigrant visa, it offers the visaholder many of the advantages of permanent resident status provided that all factors remain the same, and possibly more favorable tax consequences. Therefore this is another option to consider when assessing a foreign national's best prospects and options.

Another possible option is to set up a subsidiary structure for a foreign parent organization, and then seek to petition as an L-1 managerial or executive transferee, and subsequently as an EB-3 immigrant. Again, the required investment may be considerably less than that required in the EB-5 category.

Petitions for Employment Creation Immigrants

A petition to classify a foreign national under the EB-5 this category must be filed on Form I-526, Immigrant Petition by Alien Entrepreneur. The individual may only file the petition for classification as an alien entrepreneur on his or her own behalf.

The **priority date** of a petition for classification as an alien entrepreneur is the date the petition is properly filed with the INS.

In order to obtain classification as an alien entrepreneur, a petition must be accompanied by evidence that the individual has invested or is actively in the process of investing lawfully obtained capital in a new commercial enterprise in the United States which will create positions for not fewer than 10 qualifying employees. The minimum amount of required capital is $1,000,000, except in certain designated low employment areas in which the minimum is lowered to $500,000.

Definitions of Terms

Capital means cash, equipment, inventory, other tangible property, cash equivalents, and indebtedness secured by assets owned by the alien entrepreneur, provided that the alien entrepreneur is personally and primarily liable and that the assets of the new commercial enterprise upon which the petition is based are not used to secure any of the indebtedness. All capital will be valued at fair market value in United States dollars. Assets acquired directly or indirectly by unlawful means (such as criminal activities) may not be considered capital for the purposes of this section.

Commercial Enterprise means any for-profit activity formed for the ongoing conduct of lawful business including, but not limited to, sole proprietorship, partnership (whether limited or general), holding company, joint venture, corporation, business trust, or other entity which may be publicly or privately owned. This definition includes a commercial enterprise consisting of a holding company and its wholly owned subsidiaries, provided that each subsidiary is engaged in a for-profit activity formed for the ongoing conduct of a lawful business. This definition does not include a noncommercial activity such as owning and operating a personal residence.

An **employee** is an individual who provides services or labor for the new commercial enterprise and who receives wages or other remuneration directly from the new commercial enterprise. Independent contractors are statutorily excluded from this definition.

Full-time employment means employment of a qualifying employee by the new commercial enterprise in a position that requires a minimum of 35 working hours per week. A job-sharing arrangement whereby two or more qualifying employees share a full-time position may count as full-time employment provided the hourly requirement per week is met. This definition does not include combinations of part-time positions even if, when combined, the positions meet the hourly requirement per week.

To **invest** means to contribute capital. The issuance of stock in exchange for a note, bond, convertible debt, obligation, or any other debt arrangement between the alien entrepreneur and the new commercial enterprise does not constitute a contribution of capital for the purposes of this part.

New means established after November 29, 1990.

Qualifying Employee means a United States citizen, a lawfully admitted permanent resident, or other immigrant lawfully authorized to be employed in the United States including, but not limited to, a conditional resident, a temporary resident, an asylee, a refugee, or an alien remaining in the United States under suspension of deportation. This definition does not include the alien entrepreneur, the alien entrepreneur's spouse, sons or daughters, or any nonimmigrant alien.

Rural Area means any area not within either a metropolitan statistical area or the outer boundary of any city or town having a population of 20,000 or more.

Targeted employment area is an area that, at the time of investment is a rural area or an area that has experienced unemployment of at least 150 percent of the national average rate. The qualifying investment in a targeted employment area is $500,000.

High Employment Area is a part of a metropolitan statistical area that at the time of the investment is not a targeted employment area, and is an area with an unemployment rate significantly below the national average unemployment rates. A qualifying investment in a high employment area within the United States is usually $1,000,000.

Troubled business means a business that has been in existence for at least two years, has incurred a net loss for accounting purposes during the twelve or twenty-four month period prior to the priority date on the alien entrepreneur's Form I-526, and the loss for such period is at least equal to twenty percent of the troubled business's net worth prior to the loss. For purposes of determining whether or not the troubled business has been in existence for two years, successors in interest to the troubled business will be deemed to have been in existence for the same time as the business they succeeded.

Multiple Investors - The establishment of a new commercial enterprise may be used as the basis of a petition for classification as an alien entrepreneur by more than one investor, provided each petitioning investor has invested or is actively in the process of investing the required amount for the area in which the new commercial enterprise is principally doing business, and provided each individual investor and contributor results in the creation of at least ten full-time positions for qualifying employees. For example, if there are two individuals seeking classification as alien investors under the EB-5 category and only one new commercial enterprise, each investor must separately contribute one million dollars and at least twenty full-time jobs must be created in the new enterprise.

The establishment of a new commercial enterprise may be used as the basis of a petition for classification as an alien entrepreneur even though there are several owners of the enterprise, including persons who arc not seeking classification under this section and non-natural persons, both foreign and domestic, provided that the sources of all capital invested is identified and all invested capital has been derived by lawful means.

Employment creation allocation - The total number of full-time positions created for qualifying employees is allocated solely to those alien entrepreneurs who have used the establishment of the new commercial enterprise as the basis of a petition on Form I-526. No allocation need be made among persons not seeking investor classification. The INS will recognize any reasonable agreement made among the alien entrepreneurs in regard to the identification and allocation of the qualifying positions.

What is a new commercial enterprise for the purposes of EB-5 classification?

A new commercial enterprise may consist of the following:

- The creation of an original business;

- The purchase of an existing business and simultaneous or subsequent restructuring or reorganization such that a new commercial enterprise results; or

- The expansion of an existing business through the investment of the required amount, so that a substantial change in the net worth or number of employees results from the investment of capital. Substantial change means a 40% increase either in net worth, or in the number of employees, so that the net worth or number of employees amounts to at least 140% of the pre-expansion net worth or number of employees.

Evidence Required to Show New Commercial Enterprise

To show that the petitioner has established a new commercial enterprise in the United States, the petition must be accompanied by the following items:

- As applicable, articles of incorporation, certificate of merger or consolidation, partnership agreement, certificate of limited partnership, joint venture agreement, business trust agreement, or other similar organizational document for new commercial enterprise.

- A certificate evidencing authority to do business in a state or municipality or, if the business does not require any certificate or the State or municipality does not issue such a certificate, a statement to that effect, or

- Evidence that as of a date after **November 29, 1990**, the required amount of capital for the area in which an enterprise is located has been transferred to an existing business, and that the investment has resulted in a substantial increase in the net worth or number of employees of the business to which the capital was transferred. This evidence must be in the form of stock purchase agreements, investment agreements, certified financial reports, payroll records, or any similar instruments, agreements, or documents evidencing the investment in the commercial enterprise and the resulting substantial change in the net worth and number of employees.

Funds must be placed "at risk"

In order to show that the petitioner has invested or is actively in the process of investing the required amount of capital, the petition must be accompanied by evidence that the petitioner has placed the required amount of capital at risk for the purpose of generating a return. Evidence of mere intent to invest, or of prospective investment arrangements entailing no present commitment will not suffice to show that the petitioner is actively in the process of investing. The foreign investor must show actual commitment of the required amount of capital. Such evidence may include, but need not be limited to:

- Bank statements showing amounts deposited in the United States business accounts for the enterprise;

- Evidence of assets which have been purchased for use in the United States enterprise, including invoices sales receipts, and purchase contracts containing sufficient information to identify such assets, their purchase, and purchasing entity;

- Evidence of property transferred from abroad for use in the United States enterprise, including United States customs Service commercial entry documents, bills of lading, and transit insurance policies containing ownership information and sufficient information to identify the property and to indicate the fair market value of such property;

- Evidence of monies transferred or committed to be transferred to the new commercial enterprise in exchange for shares of stock (voting or nonvoting, common or preferred). The purchase of stock may not include terms requiring the new commercial enterprise to redeem it at the holder's request; or

- Evidence of any loan or mortgage agreement, promissory note, security agreement, or other evidence of borrowing which is secured by assets of the petitioner, other than those of the new commercial enterprise, and for which the petitioner is personally and primarily liable.

Demonstration that the funds used for investment were obtained by "lawful means"

To show that the petitioner has invested, or is actively in the process of investing capital obtained through lawful means, the petition must be accompanied by:

- Foreign business registration records.

- Corporate, partnership and personal tax returns including income, franchise, property or any other tax returns of any kind filed within five years, within any taxing jurisdiction in or outside the United States by or on behalf of the petitioner;

- Evidence identifying any other source of capital; or

- Certified copies of any judgments or evidence of all pending governmental civil or criminal actions, governmental administrative proceedings, and any private civil actions involving monetary judgments against the petitioner from any court in or outside the United States within the past fifteen years.

Evidence that the new commercial enterprise will create jobs

To show that a new commercial enterprise will create not fewer than ten full-time positions for qualifying employees, the petition must be accompanied by:

- Documentation including copies of relevant tax records, **Form I-9** or other similar documents for ten qualifying employees, if such employees have already been hired following the establishment of the new commercial enterprise; or

- A copy of a comprehensive business plan showing that due to the nature and projected size of the new commercial enterprise, the need for not fewer than ten qualifying employees will result, including approximate dates, within the next two years, and when such employees will be hired.

Troubled Business

To show that a new commercial enterprise which has been established through a capital investment in a troubled business meets the statutory employment creation requirement, the petition must be accompanied by evidence that the number of existing employees is being or will be maintained at no less than the pre-investment level for a period of at least two years. Photocopies of tax records, Forms I-9, or other relevant documents for the qualifying employees and a comprehensive business plan shall be submitted in support of the petition.

Evidence that the petitioner will be involved in the management of new commercial enterprise

To show that the petitioner is or will be engaged in the management of the new commercial enterprise, either through the exercise of day-to-day managerial control or through policy formulation, as opposed to maintaining a purely passive role in regard to the investment, the petition must be accompanied by:

- A statement of the position title that the petitioner has or will have in the new enterprise and a complete description of the position's duties;

- Evidence that the petitioner is a corporate officer or a member of the corporate board of directors; or

- If the new enterprise is a partnership, either limited or general, evidence that the petitioner is engaged in either direct management or policy making activities. For purposes of this section, if the petitioner is a limited partner and the limited partnership agreement provides the petitioner with certain rights, powers, and duties normally granted to limited partners under the Uniform Limited Partnership Act, the petitioner will be considered sufficiently engaged in the management of the new commercial enterprise.

Evidence that the new commercial enterprise has created or will create employment in a targeted employment area

To show that the new commercial enterprise has created or will create employment in a targeted employment area, the petition must be accompanied by the following:

- In the case of a rural area: evidence that the new commercial enterprise is principally doing business within a civil jurisdiction not located within any standard metropolitan statistical area as designated by the Office of Management and Budget (OMB), or within any city or town having a population of 20,000 or more as based on the most recent decennial census of the United States; or

- In the case of a high unemployment area: evidence that the metropolitan statistical area, the specific county within a metropolitan statistical area, or the county in which a city or town with a population of 20,000 or more is located in which the new commercial enterprise is principally doing business has experienced an average unemployment rate of 150% of the national average rate; or

- A letter from an authorized body of the government of the state in which the new commercial enterprise is located which certifies that the geographic or political subdivision of the metropolitan statistical area or of the city or town with a population of 20,000 or more in which the enterprise is principally doing business has been designated a high unemployment area may also be submitted in lieu of other evidence.

Immigrant Investor Pilot Program

In 1992, Congress enacted the Immigrant Investor Pilot Program to stimulate greater interest in the basic investor program. Starting on October 1, 1993 and running for five consecutive fiscal years, the Pilot Program sets aside 300 visas per year out of the 10,000 available in the EB-5 category, for alien entrepreneurs (spouses and unmarried children) who make qualifying investments under the program. A qualifying investment is an investment that is made in a commercial enterprise located within a regional center. In 1997, Congress extended the Pilot Program and it is currently set to sunset in September 2000. In addition, Congress increased the number of visas to be set aside for the program to 3,000.

The relaxation of the job creation requirement is one major benefit of the Pilot Program. In comparison to the basic investor program, the alien entrepreneur is only required to use "reasonable methodologies" to demonstrate that ten or more jobs are actually created **indirectly** by the business. In the basic investor program, the alien entrepreneur is required to produce specific documentation that shows the direct creation of ten or more jobs (i.e. I-9 Forms, business plan). Reasonable methodologies may include multiplier tables, feasibility studies, analyses of foreign and domestic markets for goods or services to be exported, and other statistically valid forecasting devices which indicate the likelihood that the business will result in increased employment.

Definition of Terms

A **regional center** is any economic unit, public or private, which is involved with the promotion of economic growth, including increased export sales, improved regional productivity, job creation, and increased domestic capital investment.

The term **"exports"** for the purposes of the Pilot Program means services or goods that are produced directly or indirectly through revenues generated from a new commercial enterprise and which are transported out of the United States.

"Employee" for the purposes of the Pilot Program means an individual who provides services or labor in a job that has been created indirectly through investment in the new commercial enterprise.

"Full-time employment" for the purposes of the Pilot Program means employment of a qualifying employee in a position that has been created indirectly through revenues generated from increased exports from the Pilot Program that requires a minimum of 35 hours per week.

Qualified Regional Centers

To participate in the Pilot program a regional center must submit a proposal to the Assistant Commissioner for adjudications, that:

- Clearly describes how the regional center focuses on a geographical region of the United States, and how it will promote economic growth through increased export sales, improved regional productivity, job creation, and increased domestic capital investment;

- Provides in verbal detail how jobs will be created indirectly through increased exports;

- Provides a detailed statement regarding the amount and source of capital which has been committed to the regional center, as well as a description of the promotional efforts taken and planned by the supervisors of the regional center;

- Contains a detailed prediction regarding the manner in which the regional center will have a positive impact on the regional or national economy in general as reflected by such factors as increased household earnings, greater demand for business services, utilities, maintenance and repair, and construction both within and without the regional center; and

- Is supported by economically or statistically valid forecasting tools, including, but not limited to, feasibility studies, analyses of foreign and domestic markets for goods or services to be exported, and/or multiplier tables.

For a complete list of the participating regional centers see Appendix G.

To qualify as an alien entrepreneur under the Pilot Program, the individual must demonstrate the following:

- The applicant is making a qualifying investment with an approved regional center; and

- The investment will create jobs indirectly through revenue generated from increased exports resulting from the new commercial enterprise.

The petitioning process for an alien entrepreneur under the Pilot Program is the same as under the basic investor program, however, the petition under the Pilot Program must include a copy of the INS letter designating the regional center.

CAVEAT

Great caution must be exercised in dealing with pooled investment and limited partnership arrangements in which the investor is not required to invest the full $500,000 or $1,000,000 into the enterprise, or where the invested funds or a portion thereof will be held in escrow and not put into the business, or where there is a guaranteed buy-back of the investor's interest, or investments are made with funds borrowed without any security, or with borrowed funds secured only by the assets of the business. Although initially the INS was quite liberal in the types of qualifying investments, the INS has now disallowed many widely promoted pooled investment arrangements and even revoked conditional residence cases already approved.

SAMPLE INVESTOR LETTER

U.S. Department of Justice
Immigration & Naturalization Service
Vermont Service Center
St. Albans, Vermont

Re: **Kuang Park**
Immigrant Petition by Alien Entrepreneur

Dear Sir/Madam:

I am writing this letter on my own behalf to request that I be accorded an immigrant visa based on the investment which I have recently made in the United States which is over $1,000,000.

In support of my petition, I enclose the following documentation:

- Form I-526
- Filing Fee
- Certificate of Authority to do business in State of New York
- Payroll records for "Star Photo"
- Form I-9 records form employees of "Star Photo"
- Money Market Account # 6280659 Citibank, New York - "Kuang Park"
- Wire Transfer Record - From XYZ Bank, Seoul, South Korea to Citibank, NY in the amount of $1,000,000 US.
- Notarized and Translated Loan Agreement between XYZ Bank and Kuang Park - $750,000 US.
- Contract of Sale for Seoul Premises - $500,000 US received.
- Lease for "Photo Star" premises at 300 Broadway
- $500,000 between Kuang Park and Super Realty Inc.
- Business Plan - "Photo Star"
- South Korean Tax returns 1982-1997 - Kuang Park
- Certified letter from South Korean accountant re $1,000,000 US transfer.

As you will note from my petition, I initially invested $1,000,000 in "Star Photo", and have cumulatively invested $2,750,000 to date. This investment is to set up "Star Photo" a New York corporation which was organized in 1998, designed to build a state-of-the-art high-fashion photographic studio to be used by renowned artists and photographers around the world. (Please see the attached Certificate of Authority to do business in New York).

Equipped with superior hi-tech facilities including the latest in dark-room equipment, lighting fixtures and a professional on-site staff present to provide creative consulting, photographic assistance and administrative support, Star Photo is geared toward producing the best possible output on the market today. In pursuit of this goal, I have invested heavily in this business to insure that Star Photo has the most up-to-date equipment and accessories to serve our sophisticated clientele.

THE NATURE OF THE INVESTMENT AND HOW THE FUNDS WERE ACQUIRED

To date, I have invested $2,750,000 US to set up Star Photo. $500,000 of that investment was used to lease the six-story commercial building located at 300 Broadway, in which Star Photo is located. $1,000,000 is present in our United States bank account, as reserves needed to complete the construction of our penthouse floor. Additionally, we've transferred $500,000 worth of photographic equipment from my former Seoul-based studio. Finally, I have borrowed an additional $750,000 US from XYZ Bank in Seoul, which is set aside in my money market account in the United States for staff salaries, operating costs etc.

The $6,500,000 in funds listed above, has been acquired as follows:

- $1,000,000 - personal funds transferred from XYZ Bank in Seoul, to Citibank, New York. Funds earned from executive compensation over the past ten years as Executive Director of Star Photo, Seoul. (Please see certified letter and accompanying translation from South Korean accountant indicating the nature of these funds. Please also see copies of South Korean tax returns 1982-1997.)

- $500,000 - Used to lease the premises at 300 Broadway.
  These funds were acquired by the sale of Star Photo Studio in Seoul. (Please see enclosed contract of sale for that building and accompanying English translation).

- $500,000 - Assets transferred from Star Photo Seoul to Star Photo in New York.

- $750,000 secured loan from XYZ Bank, Seoul - security interest in the premises located at 300 Broadway, personal loan - Kuang Park. (Please see enclosed loan agreement, notarized and translated, and signed by XYZ Bank and myself).

EMPLOYMENT CREATION

At the time of initial investment, my plan was to hire approximately ten workers to fill the following positions in Star Photo:

1) Receptionist
2) Secretary
3) Lab Specialist
4) Marketing Representative
5) Stylist
6) Lighting Consultant
7) Photographers
8) Accountant
9) Interior Designer
10) Bookkeeper

** Please see attached business plan for further details.

However, our success has been even greater than initially envisioned and it appears that we will have two individuals working full-time in each of these listed positions. (Please note attached payroll records and Form I-9 records.) Therefore, we are now in the midst of hiring 10 additional workers to fill our unanticipated needs. Please note that these workers are in no way related to me and will be hired based solely upon their qualifications for the position in question.

Please further note that I have specifically set aside $1,000,000 in a separate bank account to cover all operating costs and salaries in the event that we experience any difficulties during the start-up period, so that our operations will in no way be jeopardized by a temporary lack of cash flow.

NATURE OF INVOLVEMENT IN STAR PHOTO

My proposed involvement in Star Photo as Director of this organization will be ongoing day-to-day supervision, subject to the approval of this immigrant visa petition. I have closed up my operations in South Korea where I previously ran a similar successful business and am eager to resume the activities of a Director of a photographic studio. Presently, Star Photo is being managed by an Interim Director who is a United States citizen, who is taking care of operations until I am authorized to work in the United States. However, upon approval of this immigrant petition, I will permanently move to the United States to manage and direct the policy and procedures of Star Photo including the management of personnel and the implementation of business plans.

Based upon the enclosed information and my qualification as an investor, I respectfully request that this immigrant visa petition be approved so that I may assume the position of Director of Star Photo Studio.

Very truly yours,

Kuang Park

SAMPLE I-526 PETITION FOR ALIEN INVESTOR

OMB No. 1115-0081
Immigrant Petition by Alien Entrepreneur

START HERE - Please Type or Print

FOR INS USE ONLY

Returned	Receipt
Resubmitted	
Reloc Sent	
Reloc Rec'd	
☐ Applicant Interviewed	

Action Block

Part 1. Information about you.

Family Name: Park	Given Name: Kuang	Middle Initial
Address - In Care of:		
Street # and Name		Apt. #
City or town: Seoul	State or Province	
Country: South Korea	Zip or Postal Code	
Date of Birth (month/day/year): 12/05/1957	Country of Birth: South Korea	
Social Security #: N/A	A#: N/A	
If in the U.S. — Date of Arrival (month/day/year)	I-94#	
If in the U.S. — Current Nonimmigrant Status	Expires on (month/day/year)	

Part 2. Application Type (check one).

a. ☒ This petition is based on an investment in a commercial enterprise in a targeted employment area for which the required amount of capital invested has been adjusted downward.

b. ☐ This petition is based on an investment in a commercial enterprise in an area for which the required amount of capital invested has been adjusted upward.

c. ☐ This petition is based on an investment in a commercial enterprise which is not in either a targeted area or in an upward adjustment area.

Part 3. Information about your investment.

Name of Commercial Enterprise Invested in: Star Photo	
Street Address: 300 Broadway, New York, New York 10021	
Phone #: 212-555-5555	Business Organized as (Corporation, partnership, etc...): Corporation
Kind of Business (*Example: Furniture Manufacturer*): Photographic Studio	
Date established (month/day/year): 01/01/1998	IRS Tax #: 13-5555555
Date of your initial Investment (month/day/year): 01/01/1998	Amount of your Initial Investment $: 1,000,000.00
Your total Capital Investment in Enterprise to date $: 2,750,000.00	% of Enterprise you own: 100%

If you are not the sole investor in the new commercial enterprise, list on separate paper the names of all other parties (natural and non-natural) who hold a percentage share of ownership of the new enterprise and indicate whether any of these parties is seeking classifications as an alien entrepreneur. Include the name, percentage of ownership and whether or not the person is seeking classification under section 203(b)(5).

If you indicated in Part 2 that the enterprise was in a targeted employment area or in an upward adjustment area, give the location at right.

County	State
New York	New York

To Be Completed by *Attorney or Representative,* if any
☐ Fill in box if G-28 is attached to represent the applicant

VOLAG#

ATTY State License #

Form I-526 (Rev. 12-2-91)

Continued on back

Part 4. Additional information about the enterprise.

Type of enterprise *(check one)*:

- ☒ new commercial enterprise resulting from the creation of a new business.
- ☐ new commercial enterprise resulting from the reorganization of an existing business.
- ☐ new commercial enterprise resulting from a capital investment in an existing business.

Assets:

Total amount in U.S. bank account	$ 1,000,000.00
Total value of all assets purchased for use in the enterprise	$ 3,000,000.00
Total value of all property transferred from abroad to the new enterprise	$ 1,500,000.00
Total of all debt financing	$ 1,000,000.00
Total stock purchases	$ 1,000,000.00
Other (explain on separate paper)	$
Total	$ 6,500,000.00

Income:	When you made investment	Gross	$ 20,000,000	Net	$ 4,000,000
	Now	Gross	$ 35,000,000	Net	$ 5,000,000
Net Worth:	When you made investment		$ 4,000,000	Now	$ 5,000,000

Part 5. Employment creation information.

# of full-time employees in Enterprise in U.S. (excluding you, spouse, sons & daughters)

When you made your initial investment 10 Now 20 Difference 10

How many of these new jobs were created by your investment? 10

How many additional new jobs will be created by your additional investment? 10

What is your position, office or title with the new commercial enterprise?

Director/Manager

Briefly describe your duties, activities and responsibilities.

Direct the financial, marketing and accounting functions of a state-of-the-art high fashion photography studio.

Your Salary 200,000 p.a. Cost of Benefits 10%

Part 6. Processing information.

Below give the U.S. Consulate you want notified if this petition is approved and if any requested adjustment of status cannot be granted.

American Consulate: **City** Seoul **Country** South Korea

If you gave a U.S. address in Part 1, print your foreign address below. If your native alphabet does not use Roman letters, print your name and foreign address in the native alphabet.

Name **Foreign Address**

Is an application for adjustment of status attached to this petition?	☐ yes	☒ no
Are you in exclusion or deportation proceedings?	☐ yes (If yes, explain on separate paper)	☒ no
Have you ever worked in the U.S. without permission?	☐ yes (explain on separate paper)	☒ no

Part 7. Signature.

Read the information on penalties in the instructions before completing this section.

I certify under penalty of perjury under the laws of the United States of America that this petition, and the evidence submitted with it, is all true and correct. I authorize the release of any information from my records which the Immigration and Naturalization Service needs to determine eligibility for the benefit I am seeking.

Signature Date

Please Note: *If you do not completely fill out this form, or fail to submit required documents listed in the instructions, you may not be found eligible for the requested document and this application may be denied.*

Part 8. Signature of person preparing form if other than above. *(Sign below)*

I declare that I prepared this application at the request of the above person and it is based on all information of which I have knowledge.

Signature Print Your Name Date

Firm Name and Address

Form I-526 (Rev. 12-2-91)

H. Removing the Conditions of Permanent Residence

Once the alien entrepreneur's petition for EB-5 classification has been approved and the alien entrepreneur's priority date is current, the alien entrepreneur and accompanying spouse or children will be eligible to obtain conditional permanent residence. Conditional permanent residence is in effect for two years at which time the entrepreneur must file Form I-829, Petition by Entrepreneur to Remove Conditions. The alien entrepreneur must file Form I-829 within the 90-day period proceeding the second anniversary of his or her admission to the U.S. as a conditional permanent resident. The entrepreneur's spouse and children should also be included in the petition to remove the conditions.

The petition to remove the conditions should be accompanied by the following evidence:

- Evidence that the foreign national established a commercial enterprise. Such evidence may include, but is not limited to, Federal Income tax returns;

- Evidence that the foreign national invested the requisite capital. Such evidence may include, but is not limited to, an audited financial statement or other probative evidence;

- Evidence that the foreign national met the requirements of EB-5 classification throughout the period of the foreign national's residence in the United States. The foreign national will be considered to have sustained the action required for removal of conditions if he or she has, in good faith, substantially met the capital investment requirement of the statute and continuously maintained his or her capital investment over the two years of conditional residence. Such evidence may include, but is not limited to, bank statements, invoices, receipts, contracts, business licenses, Federal or State income tax returns, and Federal or State quarterly tax statements; and

- Evidence that the foreign national has created and maintained ten full-time jobs for qualifying employees. In the case of a "troubled business" the foreign national entrepreneur must submit evidence that the commercial enterprise maintained the number of existing employees at no less than the pre-investment level period following his or her admission as a conditional permanent resident.

Form I-829 should be filed with the INS Service Center having jurisdiction over the location of the alien entrepreneur's commercial enterprise in the United States. The petition to remove the conditions of permanent residence may be filed even if the alien entrepreneur is not physically present in the United States, however, the alien and his or her family must return to the U.S. if the Service requests an interview in connection with the petition to remove the conditions.

If the alien entrepreneur fails to file Form I-829 within the 90-day period or fails to appear for a scheduled interview, the foreign national's permanent resident status will be automatically terminated and a notice to appear will be issued placing the foreign national under removal proceedings. Although the termination of permanent resident status may be appealed, it is crucial that an individual who obtains permanent residence in the EB-5 category keep track of the dates of approval and timely file Form I-829 within the ninety day period.

Contrary to expectations, the EB-5 program has been greatly under-utilized. The unpopularity of the EB-5 category has occurred for many reasons. Specifically, it may be because many potential investors do not wish to subject themselves to the tax consequences of U.S. permanent residence, do not wish to provide detailed accounting of the source of their investment funds, do not wish to subject themselves to the possibility of loss of both capital and resident status if their investment fails, and because there is often a less cumbersome and less expensive alternative through the EB-1-3 category (Intra-organization transfer).

Interestingly the EB-5 category peaked in the mid-1990's due to the advent of numerous leveraged pooled investment schemes. The subsequent disallowance of many such schemes by the INS has again stifled interest by foreign investors in this category. By and large the EB-5 category is often more suitable for individuals with no significant prior business experience and assets who have recently and legitimately acquired capital (through inheritance or otherwise) then it is for established foreign business persons who have either more direct ways of establishing permanent residence, or good reasons not to do so at all. There is also considerable Congressional and public resistance to the program that many perceive, albeit incorrectly, as "buying a green card."

FORM I-829 PETITION BY ENTREPRENEUR TO REMOVE THE CONDITIONS

U.S. Department of Justice
Immigration and Naturalization Service

OMB No. 1115-0190
Petition by Entrepreneur to Remove the Conditions

START HERE - Please Type or Print

FOR INS USE ONLY

Returned	Receipt
Resubmitted	
Reloc Sent	
Reloc Rec'd	
☐ Applicant Interviewed	
Remarks/Action	

To Be Completed by Attorney or Representative, if any
☐ Fill in box if G-28 is attached to represent the applicant
VOLAG#
ATTY State License #

Part 1. Information about you.

Family Name Park	Given Name Kuang	Middle Initial
Address - C/O		
Street Number and Name 50 Park Avenue		Apt. # 18 A
City New York	State or Province New York	
Country USA	ZIP/Postal Code 10013	
Date of Birth (Mo/Day/Yr) 12/05/1957	Country of Birth South Korea	
Social Security # 123-12-1234	A # N/A	
Conditional residence expires on (Mo/Day/Yr) 05/15/2001		
Mailing address if different from residence in C/O		
Street Number and Name		Apt. #
City	State or Province	
Country	ZIP/Postal Code	

Since becoming a conditional permanent resident, have you ever been arrested, cited, charged, indicted, convicted, fined or imprisoned for breaking or violating any law or ordinance (excluding traffic regulations), or committed any crime for which you were not arrested? ☐ **Yes** ☒ **No**

Part 2. Basis for petition. *(Check one)*

a. ☐ My conditional permanent residence is based on an investment in a commercial enterprise in a targeted employment area for which the required amount of capital invested has been adjusted downward.

b. ☒ My conditional permanent residence is based on an investment in a commercial enterprise in an area for which the required amount of capital invested has been adjusted upward.

c. ☐ My conditional permanent residence is based on an investment in a commercial enterprise which is not in either a targeted area or in an upward adjustment area.

d. ☐ I am a conditional permanent resident spouse or child of an entrepreneur, and I am unable to be included in a Petition by Entrepreneur to Remove Conditions (Form I-829) filed by my conditional resident spouse or parent.

e. ☐ I am a conditional permanent resident spouse or child of an entrepreneur who is deceased.

Part 3. Information about your spouse or children. *(List all your children. Attach another sheet if necessary.)*

Name	Date of Birth *(Mo/Day/Yr)*	If in U.S., give A#, current immigration status and U.S. Address
Hae Sook Kang	03/25/1959	Conditional Permanent Resident, 50 Park Avenue, 18A, NY, NY

Part 4. Information about your commercial enterprise.

Name of commercial enterprise in which you have invested:

Street Address 300 Broadway		City or Town New York	
State New York	ZIP/Postal Code 10021	Business Telephone #212-555-5555	IRS Tax # 13-5555555

Form I-829 (1-7-94)

FORM I-829 PETITION BY ENTREPRENEUR TO REMOVE THE CONDITIONS (CONTINUED)

Part 4. Continued.

Type of enterprise *(Check one)*:

- ☒ New commercial enterprise resulting from the creation of a new business.
- ☐ New commercial enterprise resulting from the reorganization of an existing business.
- ☐ New commercial enterprise resulting from a capital investment in an existing business.

Kind of Business *(Be as specific as possible.)* Photographic Studio

Date Business Established (Mo/Day/Yr) 01/01/1998	Amount of Initial Investment 1,000,000.00	Date of Initial Investment (Mo/Day/Yr.) 01/01/1998	% of Enterprise you Own 100%

List number of full-time employees in enterprise in U.S. (excluding you, spouse, sons and daughters):

At the time of your initial investment 10 Presently 20 Difference 10

How many of these new jobs were created by your investment? 10

Subsequent investment in the Enterprise

Date of Invest[illegible]	Amount of Investment	Type of Investment
01/01/1999		

Please provide the gross and net income generated annually by the commercial enterprise since your initial investment. Include all income gener[illegible] to date during the present year.

Year	G[illegible]	
1998		
1999		
2000	$1,950,000.00	$1,120,[illegible]

Has your commercial enterprise filed for bankruptcy, ceased business operations, or have any charges in its business organi[illegible] occurred since the date of your initial inv[illegible]

Has your commercial enterprise sold any corporate assets, [illegible]

☐ Yes (Explain on separate sheet)

Part 5. Signature. *(Read the information on penalties in the instructions [illegible])*

I certify, under penalty of perjury under the laws of the United States of America, that this petition and the evidence submitted with it, is all true and correct. I further certify that the investment was made in accordance with the laws of the United States and was not for the purpose of evading United States immigration laws. I also authorize the release of any information from my records which the Immigration and Naturalization Service needs to determine eligibility for the benefit being sought.

Signature of Applicant	Print Name Kuang Park	Date

Please note: If you do not completely fill out this form, or fail to submit any required documents listed in the instructions, you cannot be found eligible for the requested benefit, and this petition may be denied.

Part 6. Signature of person preparing form if other than above.

I declare that I prepared this petition at the request of the above person and it is based on all information of which I have knowledge.

Signature	Print Name	Date

Firm Name and Address

Chapter Nine
LABOR CERTIFICATION

A. INTRODUCTION

As contemplated by the immigration laws, there are two main avenues to obtaining permanent residence in the United States. A foreign national may obtain permanent residence through either an employment or family-based immigrant visa petition. In the employment-based visa process and in cases not involving priority workers, religious workers, or investors, labor certification is generally a prerequisite to immigrant visa and adjustment of status approval. Labor certifications are issued by the United States Department of Labor.

In this chapter we will discuss the requirements for obtaining labor certification from the Department of Labor, as well as strategies designed to facilitate this multi-tiered process.

In 1965, Congress introduced the modern labor certification requirement to the immigration laws in an attempt to protect U.S. citizens and permanent residents from competition from foreign workers in the U.S. labor market. Any foreign individual entering the U.S. to obtain employment on a permanent basis is inadmissible unless the Secretary of Labor issues a certification that the individual will not displace a United States citizen or permanent resident worker. Employment for the purposes of labor certification means permanent full-time work by an employee for an employer other than oneself.

When labor certification is a prerequisite for INS approval of an employment-based petition, the prospective employer must submit evidence to the Department of Labor (DOL) that the employment of the foreign national will not displace any U.S. citizen or permanent resident workers. The DOL, through regional and individual state offices, is responsible for verifying that there are no U.S. workers able, willing, qualified, and available for the position the employer wishes to fill. Further, the employer must demonstrate that the foreign national will be compensated at a rate in keeping with the prevailing wage for such employment in the United States. The employer is required to pay the foreign national the prevailing wage to ensure there will be no adverse effect upon the wages and working conditions of U.S. workers in similar positions.

All foreign nationals who wish to work permanently in the United States are subject to the labor certification requirement unless they meet the qualifications for some other path to permanent residence (e.g. family-based petitions, priority worker, investor, religious worker, asylees and refugees).

The following types of intending immigrants are **exempt from the labor certification requirement**:

Schedule A Occupations

Group I - Physical Therapists & Professional Nurses

Group II - Persons with Exceptional Ability in the Sciences and Non-performing Arts.

Employees in Schedule A occupations need not obtain labor certification from the U.S. Department of Labor, however, the Application for Alien Employment Certification (Forms ETA-750 Parts A and B) must be carefully completed and submitted directly to the Immigration and Naturalization Service together with the petition for Schedule A classification. The labor certification for Schedule A occupations being, in effect "pre-approved" as concerns its impact on the United States labor market. Schedule A occupations will be discussed in greater detail later in this chapter.

Priority Workers - First Employment-Based Immigrant Category

All foreign nationals who qualify for a visa petition under one of the categories in the first employment-based category are exempt from having to obtain labor certification. These include persons of extraordinary ability in the sciences, arts, education, business or athletics, outstanding professors and researchers, and multinational executives and managers of international companies. Please note that there is considerable overlap between Schedule A Group II, which is provided for in the Department of Labor's regulations and Priority Workers, added by statute in 1990. In practice, the Priority Worker category and regulations thereunder have supplanted reliance on Schedule A Group II.

National Interest Waiver: Second Employment-Based Category

A foreign national who possesses either exceptional ability in arts, sciences, or business, or an individual who holds an advanced degree in his/her profession and whose immigration to the United States "will substantially benefit prospectively the national economy, cultural or educational interests or welfare of the United States" may be eligible for a waiver of the labor certification requirement. There is no set formula to determine whether a foreign national's admission to the United States is in the national interest. The INS decides each waiver request on a case-by-case basis. However, over the past few years it has become increasingly difficult to obtain this type of waiver. For a discussion of national interest waivers see Chapter Eight.

Special Immigrants: Fourth Employment-Based Category

This category includes ministers of religion, other religious workers, and certain individuals designated by law to be "special immigrants."

Employment Creation Investors: Fifth Employment-Based Category

This category includes foreign investors who make a minimum investment of $1,000,000 or $500,000 in a new U.S. business or enterprise that will provide jobs for at least 10 U.S. workers.

Diversity Immigrants, Asylees and Refugees

Foreign nationals who qualify for the Diversity Visa Program, individuals granted asylum and individuals designated as refugees by the federal government are not subject to the labor certification requirement.

B. **<u>Overview of Labor Certification Processing</u>**

The Department of Labor certifies a given job offer only if it can be demonstrated that there are no qualified and willing United States workers to fill the position. The following is a synopsis of the process for acquiring labor certification.

Employers who wish to sponsor foreign nationals for permanent residence in the U.S. in categories that are not exempt from the labor certification requirement are obligated to submit the "Application for Alien Employment Certification" (Forms ETA-750 Parts A and B) to the Department of Labor prior to filing an employment-based visa petition with the INS. Part A of the labor certification application describes the employer's minimum requirements for the job offer, and Part B lists the foreign national's education and prior relevant experience.

An employer must develop a job description, including, but not limited to, job duties, <u>minimum</u> educational and experience requirements, and salary which is reflective of the position. The requirements will be embodied in the <u>"Offer of Employment"</u> which will eventually be advertised to the general public. The employer's offer of employment must contain a complete description of the job to be performed and the minimum education, training and experience the worker must possess to satisfactorily perform the job.

The job duties and requirements should be consistent with those defined for the job in the DOL's <u>Dictionary of Occupational Titles (DOT)</u> and those normally required for the job in the United States. Requirements may not be <u>unduly restrictive</u> or specifically tailored to the beneficiary of the labor certification application. Such job requirements, including proficiency in a language other than English, will be deemed unduly restrictive unless adequately documented as arising from a business necessity.

For example, if a foreign national has three years and three months of experience in nuclear engineering and the labor certification requires exactly the same amount of experience, it may appear to the DOL as if the employer is not making a bona fide effort to recruit United States workers. Similarly, if the employer imposes certain requirements such as knowledge of a foreign language, or knowledge of a particular product line, the employer may be asked to submit documentation evidencing that these requirements are actually required in order to perform the position specified in the labor certification application.

An employer may be eligible to file a "reduction in recruitment request" and avoid the recruitment efforts directed and administered by the State DOL consisting of formal job orders, if the employer has advertised for the position in question during the six months prior to the filing of the labor certification application.

When drafting a labor certification application, it is important to carefully draft the application to avoid attracting unqualified U.S. candidates for the position. Further, it is also important to carefully describe the job duties involved in the position, including as many details as possible.

Invariably, in cases where labor certification is filed, the employer will have already located a foreign national who he or she wishes to employ for the position. Before permanently hiring the foreign national, the employer must demonstrate that it has made a good faith effort to hire United States workers for the position. It is critical, therefore, that when an employer drafts a labor certification for a foreign worker, that it be neither over-inclusive nor under-inclusive. If the labor certification is too broad it will attract unqualified U.S. candidates, and if it is too narrow it will appear to be tailored to the exact qualifications of the foreign worker.

After the labor certification application has been thoughtfully drafted and all the necessary supporting documentation has been gathered, the employer will submit the entire package to the Department of Labor for processing. Due to substantial budget and personnel cuts over the last few years, the DOL is experiencing massive delays in the processing of labor certifications. Although the backlog at each regional and State DOL office varies, most offices are experiencing unprecedented delays.

The application is filed with the State Department of Labor that has jurisdiction over the foreign national's intended place of employment. The State office will review the application to confirm compliance with DOL occupational titles and other regulations. The State DOL office will then conduct a test of the U.S. labor market through the opening of a Job Order. This is done in an attempt to recruit U.S. workers that are ready, willing, able and qualified for the job being offered to the foreign national. The State DOL office will then direct the employer to place an advertisement for the position in a publication that is most likely to attract responses from qualified and willing United States workers. The advertisement directs interested parties to apply directly to the State DOL office, which then refers the applicant and his or her credentials to the employer.

The job order period lasts 30 days, although the State DOL office may and sometimes does, refer applicants to the employer until the time the labor certification is approved. At the close of the job order, the employer has a fixed amount of time to send a written report to the State DOL office outlining the results of their recruitment efforts.

Once the test of the labor market is complete and the results confirm that no qualified U.S. workers are identified for the position, the State DOL office will forward the application to the Regional Office of the Department of Labor for adjudication by a certifying officer (CO). The DOL Regional

Office is the only office that has the authority to grant or deny the labor certification application. There are ten DOL Regional Offices, each having jurisdiction over a number of State DOL offices. See Appendix H for a list of the ten Department of Labor Regional Offices

C. **IMPORTANT CONSIDERATIONS AND CONCEPTS:**

DRAFTING THE LABOR CERTIFICATION APPLICATION

Offer of Employment:

Job Description

The Department of Labor compares the information provided by the employer on Form ETA-750A, Question #9 (job title) and #13 (job description) to data contained in the Dictionary of Occupational Titles (DOT). The current DOT was developed in the 1930's and contains over 12,000 job descriptions and definitions for occupations in a wide array of industries. The DOT is available in both book and electronic format. The Department of Labor uses the DOT as a reference tool in determining whether the job and training requirements listed on the labor certification application are the actual minimum requirements for the specific job offer.

The DOT lists numerical designations and specific job duties to individual occupations and sets forth "Specific Vocational Preparation" (SVP) levels for each occupation listed. SVP levels are assigned from 1 to 9 and are defined by the DOL as the amount of lapsed time required by a typical worker to learn the techniques, acquire the information, and develop the facility needed for average performance in a specific job. Each occupation listed in the DOT has been assigned a numerical code, a job description, and a SVP level.

An employer must stay within the parameters of the SVP code for a specific position when drafting the minimum job, education and training requirements that appear on the labor certification application. The minimum requirements listed on the application may not exceed the SVP level listed in the DOT. If the minimum requirements exceed the SVP level for the occupation some or all of the job requirements will be classified as "unduly restrictive." An employer may be able to overcome this situation if it can be demonstrated that the industry wide standards for the occupation exceed the limits of the SVP level or that the employer has historically required more experience for this occupation.

In late 1998, the Department of Labor announced that the Dictionary of Occupational Titles would be slowly replaced with the Occupational Information Network (O*NET), an advanced technology database system. The O*NET database will be available to the public through work stations located in homes, schools, libraries, shopping centers, one-stop career centers, and at public and private companies. The O*NET database will include information concerning worker requirements, basic and cross functional skills, general knowledge, education, labor market information, occupational outlook and wages, skills, tasks, machines, tools and equipment, and experience requirements, including training, experience and licensing. "Job Zones" will eventually replace SVP levels. However, the O*NET database is not expected to be fully implemented for labor certification use until at least the year 2000.

Actual Minimum Requirements

Minimum requirements at which the employer has hired or intends to hire a worker in the job offered should be reflected in the offer of employment. The employer must document that it has not previously hired workers with less training or experience than what is required in the job offer and that it is not feasible to do so.

Experience with Petitioning Employer May not be Included in Labor Certification

When an employer has employed or currently

employs the foreign individual in the occupation for which certification is sought, the application for labor certification can not include as a job requirement experience gained by the individual in that position. This prohibition ensures that the individual was not previously hired for the position without possessing the skills that the employer is now certifying are the minimum requirements for the position.

There are some exceptions to this rule. If certification is sought in a different occupation from the one the individual currently holds or held with the employer, the employer may require the individual to have the skills that he or she gained with the employer. This will only be permitted if those skills are customarily required in that occupation. Occasionally, "on the job" training will be permitted as a requirement if it can be shown that the employer's situation has changed since the foreign worker was hired so that training of a U.S. worker would not be feasible. One example of this might be the retirement of the person who originally trained the foreign worker.

Restrictive Requirements: "Business Necessity"

When developing the minimum requirements for the position specified on the labor certification the employer must not include requirements that exceed the DOL's guidelines for the job title. Any requirements that exceed DOL guidelines or appear to be tailored to the foreign national's qualifications will be deemed to be "unduly restrictive." The DOL will categorize job requirements as "unduly restrictive" if they "demand skills, knowledge, abilities and conditions of employment which are not normally required to satisfactorily perform work in the occupation." The DOL automatically considers the following three types of requirements to be unduly restrictive: a foreign language requirement other than English, an unusual and non-customary combination of job duties, and a "live-at-work" requirement. When a job requirement is determined to be "unduly restrictive" the employer must justify the specific requirement on "business necessity" grounds. This usually involves submission of substantial evidence and documentation concerning the employer's operations.

The finding of restrictive requirements in a labor certification application will have an adverse effect on the processing time of the application. Under current DOL policy, all applications that list restrictive job requirements or requirements that did not exist before the individual was hired must be referred by the State DOL office to the regional level for review before processing can continue at the State DOL level. If the application is referred to the regional level at this stage, it will cause serious delays in the processing of the labor certification application. Therefore, it is crucial that the application be drafted in such a manner as to minimize the inclusion of requirements that may be deemed unduly restrictive. In addition, employers should be prepared at the time of filing the application to demonstrate business necessity for any requirements included in the application that do not conform to DOL guidelines.

To justify a requirement on business necessity grounds the job requirement must satisfy a three-prong test. The job requirement must bear a reasonable relationship to the position offered in the context of the employer's business, and the job requirements must be essential to perform, in a reasonable manner, the job duties as described by the employer. In addition, to meeting the reasonableness test the employer must show that either the position (including the restrictive requirements) predated the foreign worker or that the requirement is necessary because of a major change in the employer's business. For example, if an employer lists knowledge of French, German and Italian as requirements, the employer will need to show that it is a business necessity that the employee speak all of these languages in order to effectively communicate with the majority of the employer's clients.

Business necessity may be documented by the submission of third party letters, data from industry and academic periodicals, scientific reports, independent surveys, and other probative sources.

Conclusory statements made by the employer that are not supported by any additional documentation are not sufficient to establish business necessity. The employer must also provide the specific information requested by the Certifying Officer (CO) when responding to a charge that a job requirement is unduly restrictive. For example, a CO might request a client list and travel log to substantiate the employer's claim that fluency in Mandarin Chinese is a necessary job requirement because the position requires significant travel to China to service the majority of the employer's clients.

Determining the "Prevailing Wage"

Question #12 on Form ETA-750A requires the employer to specify the rate of pay for the position offered for labor certification. The stated rate of pay must be within five percent of the prevailing wage for the job offered as determined by the DOL unless the prevailing wage for the occupation is controlled by federal statutes. DOL regulations require the employer to pay the alien the prevailing wage for job offer to ensure that the employer is not underpaying the alien and thus adversely affecting the wages of U.S. workers. Once the labor certification application is filed the State DOL office is responsible for determining whether the employer is offering the prevailing wage.

In recent years, the Department of Labor has significantly revised its guidelines concerning prevailing wage determinations. Most notably in late 1997, the Department of Labor published its General Administration Letter 2-98 ("GAL 2-98") which reinforced the hierarchy contained in DOL regulations concerning the types of wage sources that may be used to calculate the prevailing wage for a specific job offer. If the position offered is an occupation for which a rate of pay has been established under the Davis-Bacon Act or the McNamara-O'Hara Service Control Act the wage rates under those statues are controlling. If the occupation is not covered by federal statute, the wage rate from an applicable union collective bargaining agreement will control. If the federal statutes or union wages do not apply, the State DOL must use wage information provided by the Bureau of Labor Statistic's occupational employment statistics (OES) database. An employer can challenge the wage rate computed by the OES system and may substitute the OES determination with a published or private wage rate survey if the survey meets the strict methodological standards set by the DOL.

If an employer wishes to substitute the OES wage information with a published or private survey the employer's survey must meet the following criteria:

- The data cannot be more than 2 years old.

- The survey must reflect the area of intended employment, unless there are not sufficient workers in the specific occupational classification relevant to the employer's job opportunity in the area of intended employment.

- The survey must reflect an arithmetic mean, not a median.

- The wage data contained in the survey must have been collected across industries that employ workers in the occupation.

- The survey must be based on sound statistical methods.

It is crucial that an employer meet the prevailing wage rate when setting the salary of the foreign national. If an employer submits an application to the State DOL office that lists a wage that does not meet the prevailing wage for the occupation, the office will contact the employer and request that the wage be revised to meet the appropriate level. If the employer refuses to amend the rate of pay, the State DOL office may refuse to authorize recruitment and will forward the application to the Regional DOL office for review by a certifying officer. This will cause significant delays in the processing time of the application. If the employer continues to refuse to amend the rate of pay, the labor certification application may ultimately be denied. In order to ensure compliance with the

DOL's prevailing wage data, prudent employers should use all the information available to them in developing the rate of pay for a specific job offer.

Quotas & Backlogs

A foreign national with an approved labor certification and an approved employment-based visa petition (Form I-140 Immigrant Petition for Alien Worker) remains subject to the worldwide immigration quota scheme at the time of visa processing. For immigrant visas that require labor certification, the priority date of the immigrant visa petition is the date the labor certification was accepted for filing at the State DOL office. An employer should carefully draft the labor certification in order to prevent inaccurately presenting the job requirements in such a manner as to place the offered position in the "other workers" category of the third employment-based category ("skilled workers," professionals without advanced degrees, and "other workers"). If the job requires at least two years training or experience it should be placed in the "skilled worker" category rather than the "unskilled worker" category. The unskilled worker category has traditionally experienced significant backlogs because this category is accorded only 10,000 visas per year, while the skilled workers category is accorded 30,000 visas per year plus any additional unused visas from the first and second employment-based visa categories.

D. REDUCTION IN RECRUITMENT

In late 1996, the DOL issued guidelines encouraging employers to test the labor market through prior recruitment before the filing of labor certification applications. The new guidelines were promulgated to increase efficiency and uniformity in the adjudication of applications that include evidence of prior recruitment and to reinvigorate use of the program. Labor certification applications that include evidence of prior recruitment are designated as "Reduction in Recruitment" (RIR) requests. If the RIR request is granted, the employer will not be subject to further supervised recruitment efforts by the State DOL office. In most cases this will dramatically reduce the overall time it takes to process the labor certification application.

The guidelines require the regional and State DOL offices to encourage RIR requests when applications include the following:

- Occupations for which there is little or no availability;
- No restrictive requirements;
- Do not include surplus occupations (see discussion of Schedule B occupations later in this chapter);
- Include at least the prevailing wage for the designated occupation; and
- The employer can document adequate recruitment for the position through sources normal to the occupation and industry within the previous 6 months.

The 1996 guidelines sanction the use of alternative methods of advertising (e.g. Internet advertising, job fairs, and university placement offices) as long as these sources are customary for the occupation and industry. In addition, the submission of at least one print ad is usually necessary although some certifying officers may require more. When employers submit evidence of prior recruitment over the previous six months they may use advertisements that do not include salary information. In the past, employers were not permitted to omit salary information in advertisements.

To file an RIR request an employer must submit the following documentation:

- Form ETA-750 Parts A & B, Application for Alien Employment Certification, in duplicate;
- Employer's letter in support of the request;
- Evidence of employer's recruitment efforts for the position during the previous 6 months;
- Notice of job posting at employer's place of business for 10 consecutive days;

- Information concerning the employer's effort to train U.S. workers, if applicable to the occupation and industry; and

- Documentation concerning the shortage of U.S. workers in the occupation and industry (if applicable to the position and if this information is not readily known by the DOL).

The employer's letter in support of the RIR request must also include a profile of the employer's business, detailed information about the job offer, a summary of the employer's recruitment efforts over the previous six months, a summary of the recruitment results of that effort, and a statement of the normal recruitment practices in the employer's industry.

Acceptable forms of documentation evidencing the employer's recruitment efforts over the previous six months include: copies of tear sheets for advertisements in newspapers and trade publications, hard copies of internet postings, and statements from employment referral agencies, university placement offices, and job fair sponsors.

Once an employer has gathered the requisite evidence and documentation for a RIR request, the entire package should be submitted to the State DOL office with jurisdiction over the intended location of employment. A request for reduction in recruitment should prominently appear on the cover letter submitted with the labor certification package. The State DOL office is responsible for expediting the review of RIR requests for completeness, prevailing wage compliance, and for the presence of restrictive job requirements.

If the State DOL office finds any deficiencies in the RIR request or if the State DOL believes that there are a surplus of U.S. workers for the occupation, the employer will be contacted and will be given the opportunity to withdraw the RIR request. If the employer chooses not to withdraw the RIR request the application will be sent to the Regional DOL office for review. The State DOL office must forward the RIR request, along with a report recommending or opposing the approval of the request, to the Regional DOL office for adjudication by a certifying officer (CO). The CO will either approve the request and certify the labor certification application, or if deficiencies are found in the employer's prior recruitment, the CO will send the application back to the State DOL office to undergo the usual recruitment program. If the CO contests the rate of pay or believes the job offer contains restrictive requirements the Regional DOL office will retain the application and eventually issue a Notice of Findings (NOF) to the employer. In either instance, if the RIR request is not approved at the regional level, the labor certification application will undergo the usual processing procedures and be subject to the same backlogs and waiting periods as non-RIR applications. Therefore, it is imperative that a RIR request be thoroughly researched and carefully prepared before being submitted to the DOL. As a practical matter the RIR request is a two-edged sword. If approved, it will substantially lessen the total processing time. However, if the RIR request is ultimately denied at the regional level, it will actually lengthen the process beyond the "normal" excessive waiting period.

E. <u>KICKBACKS</u>

Labor certification applications that are not designated for reduction in recruitment must undergo the usual review process at the State DOL level before advertising may commence through the opening of a job order. If the State DOL office finds prevailing wage deficiencies or restrictive requirements the employer will be contacted and given an opportunity to address those defects. Employers must provide information requested by the State office within 45 days of the date of the request. If complete information is not received within 45 days, the application will be returned. If the application is re-filed, it will be treated as a new application with the original date of receipt deleted and replaced with the re-filing date.

Since the acceptance date at the state level is used to establish the alien's priority date, State DOL offices are advised to request any information in writing and to advise the employer of the consequences of an untimely response. When the request is made by telephone and the application is being held in the State DOL office, a dated confirmation letter is sent to the employer with a copy placed in the application file.

The employer must provide complete information within 45 days in order to keep the original filing date. If the local office requests additional information, the employer will receive an additional 45 days to respond.

F. Standard Recruitment Program

If the employer has not conducted prior recruitment before the submission of the labor certification application and the State DOL office has found no prevailing wage deficiencies or restrictive requirements, the employer will be authorized to begin recruitment. At this point, the State DOL office will open a Job Order, commencing the thirty-day recruitment period. During this period, the employer must fulfill the recruitment requirement, which is a three-part process including the opening of the job order, advertising to the general public, and the posting of a job notice.

G. ADVERTISING

To comply with the advertising requirement, the employer must place an advertisement for the job opportunity in a newspaper of general circulation or in a professional, trade or ethnic publication, whichever is appropriate to the occupation and most likely to elicit responses from qualified United States workers. The employer may request the local office's assistance in drafting the text and in many instances the State DOL office will require the employer to submit a draft of the advertisement with the initial filing or any subsequent revisions of the labor certification. The advertisement must:

- Direct applicants to report or send resumes, as appropriate for the occupation to the State DOL office for referral to the employer;
- Include a State office I.D. # and the complete address or telephone number of the State office, but do not identify the employer;
- Describe the job opportunity with particularity;
- State the rate of pay, which may not be below the prevailing wage for the occupation;
- Offer prevailing conditions;
- State the employer's minimum job requirements.
- Offer training if employers normally provide training for this position.
- Offer wages, terms and conditions of employment that are no less favorable than those offered to the foreign national.
- If published in a newspaper of general circulation, be published for at least three consecutive days; or if published in a professional, trade or ethnic publication, be published in the next published edition.

Based on the job opportunity described in the application, the State DOL office will recommend the type of media most appropriate for advertising and advise the employer to place the advertisement in those areas.

Appropriate media may be a trade or professional journal or ethnic publication, a daily newspaper of general circulation in the nearest urban area or even in another urban area or wherever advertisements for the occupation customarily appear. The intent is that the advertising appears in a publication most likely to elicit responses from United States workers.

Posting Requirement

The posting requirement is intended to encourage word-of-mouth publicity about the job opportunity and thereby publicize the position to a certain segment of the labor market. It is aimed at qualified employees within an organization, as well as to non-employees who may learn of the job opportunity from employees. Employees of and visitors to the employer who are not interested or qualified for the job may know of United States workers who are interested and qualified for the position.

Appropriate locations for posting job opportunity notices are bulletin boards near wage, hour, occupational safety, and health notices or where other notices of interest to all employees are posted. The posted notice need only appear where the job opportunity is located. However, employers should be encouraged to seek United States workers by posting notice of the job at all of the employer's locations.

The DOL does not regulate the specific size of posted notice as long as it is made to be conspicuous and clearly visible. Posting practices such as placing actual size copies of newspaper advertisements on crowded bulletin boards are unacceptable.

The employer must post the job opportunity after the filing of the labor certification application and during the 30-day recruitment period. The notice must be posted for 10 consecutive business days.

The posting must include the following information:

- A description of the job opportunity with particularity;
- The rate of pay, that is not below the prevailing wage for the occupation;
- Wage conditions;
- The employer's minimum job requirements;
- An offer of training if employers normally offer training for this position;
- Offer wages, terms and conditions of employment that are no less favorable than those offered to the foreign national; and
- Direct applicants to report to the employer.

Department of Labor regulations require, in addition to the posting requirement, certain groups be provided with notice of the filing of the labor certification application on behalf of a foreign worker. Since 1990, the posting notice requirement has served to fill the notice of filing requirement and employers are not required to provide separate notice. The posting notice must inform third parties that they have the ability to submit information relating to the labor certification application to the Department of Labor. This may include other employees, applicants and other individuals who are likely to be adversely affected by the hiring of the foreign national listed in the labor certification application.

Rejection of United States Workers

The employer's advertisement directs applicants to submit applications to the DOL, who in turn forwards the resumes of potential applicants to the employer. Often the resumes forwarded to the employer are not carefully screened, and the DOL may in fact send resumes that do not fit the minimum requirements set forth in the labor certification application. The employer bears the burden of screening the resumes and conducting interviews, when appropriate. When the employer has either rejected the resumes, or rejected the applicants who interviewed for the position, it is the employer's responsibility to explain the reason behind each rejection. If United States workers have applied for the job opportunity the employer must document that they were rejected solely for lawful job-related reasons.

The employer must state specific reasons for rejecting each United States worker who applied in response to advertisements, the posted notice, the job order, or other sources of recruitment. Resumes of applicants, if available, should be submitted with the application to support the employer's statement.

The employer should screen applicants against the stated requirements in the job offer and should not impose additional requirements during interviews with U.S. workers. To be regarded as qualified, U.S. workers must make it known during interviews or on their resumes that they meet the employer's stated minimum requirements for the job opportunity. It is not acceptable for an employer to reject United States workers who may be "overqualified," but are willing to accept the job at the wage and conditions offered.

Employers should screen each applicant unless the applicant's resume conclusively demonstrates that he or she is not qualified for the position. If an employer can not conclusively reject an applicant on the basis of his or her resume, the employer must interview the applicant, thereby assuring conformity with DOL regulations.

Examples of job-related types of reasons for which United States workers may be rejected for a job opportunity are:

- The applicant does not have the training and experience required by the employer.
- The applicant is not willing to accept the stated salary or work hours as posted.

Reasons for rejecting United States workers that are non job-related and invalid:

- Personal situations, such as an applicant's marital status and religious affiliations.
- Factors that can only be determined from actual job performance (e.g. initiative and interest in the work).
- The employer feels the foreign worker is more qualified for the position than the U.S. applicant.
- The employer does not "like" the applicant

H. RECRUITMENT RESULTS

After the recruitment period has ended the employer is required to submit a written report to the State DOL office reporting the results of the test of the U.S. labor market. The report must be submitted to the State DOL within the time allotted. The report of recruitment results must:

- Identify each recruitment source by name;
- State the number of U.S. workers responding to the employer's recruitment;
- State the names, addresses, and provide resumes (if any) of the U.S. workers interviewed for the job opportunity and job title of the person who interviewed each worker; and
- Explain, with specificity, the lawful job-related reasons for not hiring each U.S. worker interviewed.

I. FINAL PROCESSING:

Once the State DOL office has received the employer's recruitment report the employer's recruitment procedures will be reviewed for compliance with DOL regulations. The 1996 DOL guidelines permit the State DOL office to designate applications for "fast-track" adjudication at the regional level if there are no irregularities found in the employer's recruitment procedures. Applications chosen for fast-track review are labeled "Limited Review" (LP) by the State office.

Limited Review Processing

Although procedures for designating applications for limited review processing vary at each State office, generally the application must meet some or all of the following criteria in order to be appropriately designated "limited review":

- The prevailing wage was offered;
- There were no unusual job requirements;
- The application did not contain uncommon job duties to the occupation;

- The required education and experience for the position did not exceed the SVP level; and

- Only a few U.S. applicants applied but they were clearly unqualified for the position.

Applications designated for limited review processing are transmitted to the regional level for expedited approval and are to undergo only limited scrutiny by the certifying officer. The goal of the limited review processing procedures is to increase efficiency and reduce the backlog at the regional level. However, the effectiveness of this program is limited because limited review procedures are not uniformly administered at all State DOL offices. The DOL should strive in the future to standardize the criteria for limited review processing to ensure that the program is successfully utilized in all jurisdictions.

If the State DOL office does find irregularities in the employer's recruitment procedures the employer application will be sent to the Regional DOL office for review.

J. FINAL DETERMINATION:

If the complete labor certification application package is not designated for limited review processing the package is forwarded by the State DOL office to the Regional DOL office with jurisdiction over that State office. Each complete labor certification application package must include a report from the State DOL office either recommending or opposing the approval of the labor certification application. Although not determinative, an unfavorable State DOL report will nonetheless be persuasive evidence that the employer has not complied with some or all of the DOL's requirements. A positive determination will be issued if the CO finds that qualified U.S. workers are unavailable and that the terms of the employment will not adversely affect the wages and working conditions of workers in the United States similarly employed.

If the CO intends to deny an application, a Notice of Findings (NOF) indicating the basis for denial is forwarded to the employer who will then have an opportunity to rebut the reasons for the potential denial or amend the application to overcome the inadequacies of the application.

If the rebuttal is not submitted within 35 days, the deficiencies outlined in the NOF are considered to be valid and the denial takes effect. Employers will only be permitted one extension of the time limit to respond to the NOF. If the CO rejects the reply rebutting the NOF, a Notice of Final Determination denying the application for certification will be issued to the employer. The employer then has the right to appeal the denial to an Administrative Law Judge with final recourse to the Board of Alien Labor Certification Appeals (BALCA).

K. Substitution of Aliens on Labor Certification Form

Employers who frequently sponsor foreign nationals for permanent employment in the U.S., such as computer consulting firms, are often faced with a rapidly changing workforce. If an employer has filed or obtained a labor certification for one individual, but the individual has subsequently left the employer's company, the employer may substitute another individual for the position. However, the new applicant must have been qualified for the position at the time the original labor certification was filed. If an employer wishes to substitute another foreign national, a new ETA-750 A & B Forms, in duplicate, must be filed with the INS if the underlying labor certification has already been approved by the DOL. If the labor certification application in question is still pending the new ETA-750 A & B should be sent to the DOL.

L. SPECIAL TYPES OF LABOR CERTIFICATION APPLICATIONS:

Schedule "A" Occupations

Historically, DOL regulations have contained a list of occupations that are "pre-certified" as having a known shortage of qualified U.S. workers in the U.S. labor market. In practice, DOL precertification means that an employer does not have to file an individual labor certification application for the position.

Over the years, the DOL has made various revisions to the Schedule A list of precertified occupations. Currently, there are only two groups of occupations designated for Schedule A precertification. Group I includes Physical Therapists and Professional Nurses and Group II includes Persons with Exceptional Ability in the Sciences and Non-performing Arts.

Group I: Physical Therapists

A physical therapist, for the purposes of precertification, is defined by DOL regulations as "a person who applies the art and science of physical therapy to the treatment of patients with disabilities, disorders and injuries to relieve pain, develop or restore function, and maintain performance, using physical means, such as exercise, massage, heat, water, light, electricity, as prescribed by a physician or surgeon."

To file for Schedule A precertification on behalf of a physical therapist, the employer must submit ETA-750 Parts A & B, in duplicate, clearly evidencing the existence of prearranged employment. In addition, the employer must submit evidence that a notice of filing of the application was provided to the bargaining representative or to the employer's current employees. Most importantly, the application must include a letter or statement signed by an authorized state physical therapy licensing official in the State of intended employment, evidencing or corroborating that the foreign national is qualified to take the State's licensing examination for physical therapists.

Professional Nurses

A professional nurse, for the purposes of Schedule A precertification, is defined by DOL regulations as a person who applies the art and science of nursing, which reflects comprehension of principles derived from physical, biological, and behavioral sciences. Professional nursing generally includes the making of clinical judgements concerning the observation, care, and counsel of persons requiring nursing care, the administering of medicines and treatments prescribed by the physician or dentist, and the participation in activities for the promotion of health and the prevention of illness in others.

An employer seeking a Schedule A labor certification on behalf of a professional nurse must file the labor certification application, notice of filing, and documentation that:

- Demonstrates that the foreign nurse has passed the Commission on Graduates of Foreign Nursing Schools (CGFN) Examination; or

- The foreign nurse holds a full and unrestricted (permanent) license to practice nursing in the State of intended employment.

Group II: Persons with Exceptional Ability in the Sciences & Performing Arts

An employer filing a Schedule A precertification application on behalf of persons under Group II must also file ETA-750 Parts A & B, in duplicate, and the notice of filing. In addition, the employer must provide documentation testifying to the widespread acclaim and international recognition accorded the beneficiary by recognized experts in his or her field. The employer must also present evidence that the beneficiary's work in the field during the past year and the intended employment require exceptional ability.

DOL regulations require the application to be supported by <u>two</u> out of the following seven types of documentation:

- Documentation of the foreign national's receipt of internationally recognized prizes or awards for excellence in the field for which certification is sought.

- Documentation of the foreign national's membership in international associations, in the field for which certification is sought, which requires outstanding achievement of their members, as judged by recognized international experts in their disciplines or fields.

- Published material in professional publications about the foreign national, relating to the foreign national's work in the field for which certification is sought, that includes the title, date, and author of such published material.

- Evidence of the foreign national's participation on a panel, or individually, as a judge of the work of others in the same or an allied field of specialization for which certification is sought.

- Evidence of the foreign national's original scientific or scholarly research contributions of major significance in the field for which certification is sought.

- Evidence of the foreign national's authorship of published scientific or scholarly articles in the field for which certification is sought, in international professional journals or professional journals with an international circulation.

- Evidence of the display of the foreign national's work, in the field for which certification is sought, at artistic exhibitions in more than one country.

It is important to note that the requirements for Group II precertification are very similar to the requirements for special handling of labor certification applications for persons with exceptional ability in the performing arts (see discussion below) and the first employment-based category for persons with extraordinary ability in the arts, sciences, business, education and athletics. A foreign national who qualifies for Group II designation will most likely qualify for classification in the first preference employment based category. As previously noted, the first employment based category for persons with extraordinary ability and distinguished professors and researchers provides total exemption from labor certification that is remarkably similar to Schedule A Group II. Accordingly, most individuals who qualify for Schedule A Group II, file under the EB-1-1 or EB-1-2 categories. It's noted that in either instance (Priority worker or Schedule A Group II) the initial and sole filing for petition approval is with the INS on Form I-140.

Prior to filing a Schedule A labor certification application, the employer should thoroughly research the applicant's education and experience and carefully consider whether the applicant is eligible in a different category. For example, if the foreign national is eligible for classification as a priority worker in the first employment preference category he or she is exempt from the labor certification requirement.

All Schedule A labor certification applications are filed with the INS Service Center having jurisdiction over the foreign national's intended place of employment and **not** with the Department of Labor. The INS is responsible for reviewing the application and supporting documentation and may request an advisory opinion from the Division of Foreign Labor Certifications. The INS is solely responsible for making the final determination concerning the approval or denial of the application. INS decisions may not be appealed.

L. **Schedule "B" Occupations:**

The Department of Labor has compiled a list of occupations for which foreign nationals may not receive labor certification. Located in DOL regulations, Schedule B is list of occupations the DOL has designated as having a surplus of U.S. workers available or easily trained. In addition, the DOL holds that if foreign nationals are hired to fill Schedule B occupations, the wages and working conditions of U.S. workers similarly employed will be adversely affected.

For the most part, occupations listed in Schedule B require workers to have little or no education or experience. Some occupations listed in Schedule B include: parking lot attendants, bartenders, elevator operators, receptionists, hotel cleaners, short order cooks and domestic household workers. For a complete list of Schedule B occupations see Appendix F.

If an employer wishes to sponsor a foreign national in an occupation that appears on Schedule B, the employer must file a waiver request along with the labor certification application and required supporting documentation. The waiver request should be addressed to the certifying officer at the regional level, but the initial filing of the application should be made to the State DOL office. The CO will only review the waiver request after the employer has participated in the usual recruitment procedures at the local level.

N. Occupations designated for Special Handling

Congress amended the Immigration and Naturalization Act in 1990 to permit the "special handling" of two types of labor certification applications. The DOL, through its implementing regulations, has designated college and university professors and persons with exceptional ability in the performing arts for special handling. Employers, who wish to sponsor foreign workers to fill these types of positions, need only prove that there are no U.S. workers equally qualified to the foreign worker. In a standard labor certification application the employer must prove that there are no U.S. workers available who meet the minimum qualifications of the job offer. There are different evidentiary and recruitment requirements for the two types of occupations that are designated for special handling.

College and University Professors:

Colleges and Universities who wish to sponsor foreign nationals for teaching positions must submit the following documentation:

- Form ETA-750 Parts A & B, in duplicate; including a statement of the qualifications of the applicant and a full description of the job offer;

- Evidence that the employer selected the foreign national for the position pursuant to a competitive recruitment and selection process, and that the foreign national was deemed to be more qualified than any U.S. workers who applied for the job opportunity;

- A signed statement from the official at the college or university with hiring authority, describing the employer's recruitment procedure, and summarizing the recruitment results;

- An official report from the employer recommending the selection of the foreign national at the end of the recruitment and selection process;

- A copy of at least one advertisement for the job offer placed in a national professional journal, that included the job title, duties, and requirements and evidence of all other recruitment sources utilized; and

- A separate statement of the foreign national's education or professional qualifications and academic achievements.

Applications for special handling for college and university teachers must be submitted to the DOL within eighteen months after the employer has ended the competitive recruitment process for the position it wishes to fill with the foreign national. In addition, colleges and universities are subject to the same posting requirements as other employers and must provide a notice of filing to the collective bargaining representative in the occupational classification. If there is no collective bargaining representative, the employer must conspicuously post the notice of filing at the place of employment for ten consecutive days.

Labor certification applications for non-teaching positions at colleges and universities in positions such as researchers, librarians, and other administrative staff, are not eligible for special handling and must undergo the standard labor certification process.

Labor certification applications on behalf of college and university professors must be sent to the State DOL for review. The State DOL office will review the application for compliance and then forward it to the Regional DOL office for adjudication by a certifying officer. Labor certification applications designated for special handling must be expeditiously reviewed at both the state and regional levels.

Persons of Exceptional Ability in the Performing Arts:

Employers who wish to sponsor foreign nationals for positions that require exceptional ability in the performing arts must submit the following:

- Form ETA-750 Parts A & B, in duplicate; including a statement of the qualifications of the applicant and a full description of the job offer;

- Documentation that the foreign national's work experience during the past 12 months required exceptional ability, and that the foreign national's intended work in the U.S. will require exceptional ability;

- A copy of at least one advertisement placed in a national publication appropriate to the occupation, describing the job opportunity with particularity;

- A statement of the results of recruitment; and

- Documentation that unions, if customarily used as a recruitment source in the area or industry, were unable to refer equally qualified U.S. workers.

The employer must demonstrate the foreign national's exceptional ability in the performing arts through the submission of the following types of materials:

- Documents attesting to the current widespread acclaim and international recognition accorded to the individual, and receipt of internationally recognized prizes or awards for excellence;

- Published material by or about the individual, such as critical reviews or articles in major newspapers, periodicals, and/or trade journals;

- Evidence of earnings commensurate with the claimed level of ability;

- Playbills and starbillings;

- Materials attesting to the outstanding reputation of theaters, concert halls, night clubs, and other establishments in which the individual has appeared, or is scheduled to appear; and/or

- Materials attesting to the outstanding reputation of repertory companies, ballet troupes, orchestra, or other organizations in which or with which the individual has performed during the past year in a leading or starring capacity.

The DOL's requirements for persons with exceptional ability in the performing arts appear quite similar to the INS' regulations concerning persons with extraordinary ability in the first preference employment-based category. However, the DOL has made a policy decision to retain special handling for labor certification applications for these types of occupations because it believes there are instances where the foreign national may only qualify for special handling labor certification, but not for total exemption from the labor certification as a priority worker.

Labor certification applications on behalf of persons with exceptional ability in the performing arts are filed directly with National DOL office for special handling.

O. CONCLUSIONS

The labor certification process is unquestionably a difficult and time-consuming "gauntlet." However, for a substantial percentage of immigrants it is the only way to proceed, and can not be avoided. Perhaps the most common error made by foreign workers who wish to permanently remain in the United States is waiting too long before starting the labor certification process. It is especially important for those individuals who are already working under temporary nonimmigrant status (H-1B, L-1B) to start the labor certification process early, in order to avoid falling out of status and/or using up their overall authorized period of stay. Often in such cases labor certification can not be completed before the individual must leave the United States, resulting in substantial disruption of individual and corporate plans. We can not emphasize too strongly the need for advance consideration and planning of immigration strategies.

SAMPLE LABOR CERTIFICATION FORMS ETA-750 PARTS A & B

OMB Approval No. 44-R1301

U.S. DEPARTMENT OF LABOR
Employment and Training Administration

APPLICATION
FOR
ALIEN EMPLOYMENT CERTIFICATION

IMPORTANT: READ CAREFULLY BEFORE COMPLETING THIS FORM

PRINT legibly in ink or use a typewriter. If you need more space to answer questions in this form, use a separate sheet. Identify each answer with the number of the corresponding question. SIGN AND DATE each sheet in original signature.

To knowingly furnish any false information in the preparation of this form and any supplement thereto or to aid, abet, or counsel another to do so is a felony punishable by $10,000 fine or 5 years in the penitentiary, or both (18 U.S.C. 1001)

PART A. OFFER OF EMPLOYMENT

1. Name of Alien (Family name in capital letter, First, Middle, Maiden)
PATEL Khan

2. Present Address of Alien (Number, Street, City and Town, State ZIP code or Province, Country)
1 Business Park Drive
Elizabeth New Jersey 01010

3. Type of Visa (If in U.S.)
H-1B

The following information is submitted as an offer of employment.

4. Name of Employer (Full name of Organization)
Computers Inc.

5. Telephone
(732) 555-555

6. Address (Number, Street, City and Town, State ZIP code)
1 Business Park Drive
Elizabeth New Jersey 01010

7. Address Where Alien Will Work (if different from item 6)

8. Nature of Employer's Business Activity	9. Name of Job Title	10. Total Hours Per Week a. Basic	10. b. Overtime	11. Work Schedule (Hourly)	12. Rate of Pay a. Basic	12. b. Overtime
Computer Consulting & Training	Software Engineer	40		9:00 a.m. 6:00 p.m.	$ 65,000 per year	$ N/A per hour

13. Describe Fully the job to be Performed (Duties)

Design and develop software applications for financial institutions using PowerBuilder, Sybase, Java, HTML, Object Oriented Programming & C++

14. State in detail the MINIMUM education, training, and experience for a worker to perform satisfactorily the job duties described in item 13 above.

	Grade School	High School	College	College Degree Required (specify)
EDUCATION (Enter number of years)				Master**
				Major Field of Study: Computer Science, Electronic Engineering or related filed

	No. Yrs.	No. Mos.	Type of Training
TRAINING			

	Job Offered Yrs.	Job Offered Mos.	Related Occupation Yrs.	Related Occupation Mos.	Related Occupation (specify)
EXPERIENCE (Number)	2**	or	2**		Software development

15. Other Special Requirements
** In lieu of masters and two years experience , will accept Bachelor's degree in Computer Science, Electronic Engineering or related field & five years experience in job offered or in Software Development

16. Occupational Title of Person Who Will Be Alien's Immediate Supervisor ➤ ➤ Project Manager

17. Number of Employees Alien Will Supervise ➤ 2

ENDORSEMENTS (Make no entry in section - for Government use only)

Date Forms Received	
L.O.	S.O.
R.O.	N.O.
Ind. Code	Occ. Code
Occ. Title	

Replaces MA 7-50A, B and C (Apr. 1970 edition) which is obsolete.

ETA 750 (Oct. 1979)

SAMPLE LABOR CERTIFICATION (CONTINUED)

18. COMPLETE ITEMS ONLY IF JOB IS TEMPORARY			19. IF JOB IS UNIONIZED (Complete)	
a. No. of Openings To Be Filled By Aliens Under Job Offer	b. Exact Dates You Expect To Employ Alien		a. Number of Local	b. Name of Local
	From	To		c. City and State

20. STATEMENT FOR LIVE-AT-WORK JOB OFFERS (Complete for Private Household ONLY)						
a. Description of Residence		b. No. Persons residing at Place of Employment				c. Will free board and private room not shared with any-one be provided? ("X" one) ☐ YES ☐ NO
("X" one) ☐ House ☐ Apartment	Number of Rooms	Adults		Children	Ages	
			BOYS			
			GIRLS			

21. DESCRIBE EFFORTS TO RECRUIT U.S. WORKERS AND THE RESULTS. (Specify Sources of Recruitment by Name)

-Posted notices on premises and on electronic job data bank.
-Advertisements in local newspapers
-Word of mouth

22. Applications require various types of documentation. Please read Part II of the instructions to assure that appropriate supporting documentation is included with your application.

23. EMPLOYER CERTIFICATIONS

By virtue of my signature below, I HEREBY CERTIFY the following conditions of employment.

a. I have enough funds available to pay the wage or salary offered the alien.

b. The wage offered equals or exceeds the prevailing wage and I guarantee that, if a labor certification is granted, the wage paid to the alien when the alien begins work will equal or exceed the prevailing wage which is applicable at the time the alien begins work.

c. The wage offered is not based on commissions, bonuses, or other incentives, unless I guarantee a wage paid on a weekly, bi-weekly, or monthly basis.

d. I will be able to place the alien on the payroll on or before the date of the alien's proposed entrance into the United States.

e. The job opportunity does not involve unlawful discrimination by race, creed, color, national origin, age, sex, religion, handicap, or citizenship.

f. The job opportunity is not:

(1) Vacant because the former occupant is on strike or is being locked out in the course of a labor dispute involving a work stoppage.

(2) At issue in a labor dispute involving a work stoppage.

g. The job opportunity's terms, conditions and occupational environment are not contrary to Federal, State or local law.

h. The job opportunity has been and is clearly open to any qualified U.S. worker.

24. DECLARATIONS

DECLARATION OF EMPLOYER ➤ Pursuant to 28 U.S.C. 1746, I declare under penalty of perjury the foregoing is true and correct.

SIGNATURE	DATE
NAME (Type or Print) John Smith	TITLE President

AUTHORIZATION OF AGENT OF EMPLOYER ➤ I HEREBY DESIGNATE the agent below to represent me for the purposes of labor certification and I TAKE FULL RESPONSIBILITY for accuracy of any representations made by my agent.

SIGNATURE OF EMPLOYER	DATE
NAME OF AGENT (Type or Print)	ADDRESS OF AGENT (Number, Street, City, State, ZIP code)

SAMPLE LABOR CERTIFICATION (CONTINUED)

PART B. STATEMENT OF QUALIFICATIONS OF ALIEN

FOR ADVICE CONCERNING REQUIREMENTS FOR ALIEN EMPLOYMENT CERTIFICATION: If alien is in the U.S., contact nearest office of Immigration and Naturalization Service. If alien is outside U.S., contact nearest U.S. Consulate.

IMPORTANT: READ ATTACHED INSTRUCTIONS BEFORE COMPLETING THIS FORM.

Print legibly in ink or use a typewriter. If you need more space to fully answer any questions on this form, use a separate sheet. Identify each answer with the number of the corresponding question. Sign and date each sheet.

1. Name of Alien (Family name in capital letters)	First name	Middle name	Maiden name
PATEL	Khan		

2. Present Address (No., Street, City or Town, State or Province and ZIP code)	Country	3. Type of Visa (If in U.S.)
1 Business Park Drive Elizabeth New Jersey 01010		H-1B

4. Alien's Birthdate (Month, Day, Year)	5. Birthplace (City or Town, State or Province)	Country	6. Present Nationality or Citizenship (Country)
11/10/70	Chinnamandem Andrha Pradesh	India	India

7. Address in United States Where Alien Will Reside

1 Business Park Drive
Elizabeth, New Jersey 01010

8. Name and Address of Prospective Employer if Alien has job offer in U.S.	9. Occupation in which Alien is Seeking Work
Computers Inc. 1 Business Park Drive Elizabeth New Jersey 01010	Software Engineer

10. "X" the appropriate box below and furnish the information required for the box marked

		City in Foreign Country	Foreign Country
a.	☐ Alien will apply for a visa abroad at the American Consulate in →		
		City	**State**
b.	☒ Alien is in the United States and will apply for adjustment of status to that of a lawful permanent resident in the office of the Immigration and Naturalization Service at →	New York, New York	

11. Names and Addresses of Schools, Colleges and Universities Attended (Include trade or vocational training facilities)	Field of Study	FROM Month	FROM Year	TO Month	TO Year	Degrees or Certificates Received
Banaglore University, India	Computer Science	06-88		08-92		Bachelor's Degree

SPECIAL QUALIFICATIONS AND SKILLS

12. Additional Qualifications and Skills Alien Possesses and Proficiency in the use of Tools, Machines or Equipment Which Would Help Establish if Alien Meets Requirements for Occupation in Item 9.

Certified PowerBuilder Developer Associate; Sun Certified JAVA programmer; Diploma in RDMS from Software Solution

13. List Licenses (Professional, journeyman, etc.)

14. List Documents Attached Which are Submitted as Evidence that Alien Possesses the Education, Training, Experience, and Abilities Represented

Endorsements	DATE REC. DOL
(Make no entry in this section - FOR Government Agency USE ONLY)	O.T. & C.

(Items continued on next page)

SAMPLE LABOR CERTIFICATION (CONTINUED)

15. WORK EXPERIENCE. List all jobs held during the last three (3) years. Also, list any other jobs related to the occupation for which the alien is seeking certification as indicated in item 9.

a. NAME AND ADDRESS OF EMPLOYER
Computer Incorporated
1 Business Park Drive, Elizabeth, New Jersey 01010

NAME OF JOB	DATE STARTED Month Year	DATE LEFT Month Year	KIND OF BUSINESS
Software Engineer	12/99	Present	Computer Consulting & Training

DESCRIBE IN DETAIL THE DUTIES PERFORMED, INCLUDING THE USE OF TOOLS, MACHINES OR EQUIPMENT — NO. OF HOURS PER WEEK: 40

System study, design & development of Quantitative Estimations Tool (QUEST). For the financial services industry, involved in design & development of Server application that executes calculations, & generates the data to publish over Internet, decision making & other statistical purposes. Tools used: PowerBuilder, Sybase SQL Server, C++, DB-Library, Java, HTML, Javascript, Microsoft IIS, Windows NT, Sun Solaris, TCP/IP, Object Oriented Programming, & PowerSoft Foundation Class libraries.

b. NAME AND ADDRESS OF EMPLOYER
Computer Designs Corporation
8 South Fredricksburg, Margate, New Jersey 08405

NAME OF JOB	DATE STARTED Month Year	DATE LEFT Month Year	KIND OF BUSINESS
Analyst/Programmer	10/97	11/99	Software Development & Consulting

DESCRIBE IN DETAIL THE DUTIES PERFORMED, INCLUDING THE USE OF TOOLS, MACHINES OR EQUIPMENT — NO. OF HOURS PER WEEK: 40

Involved in system study, design, development & implementation of applications. Designed & developed the Cash Module in TRS. Tools and technology used for development include PowerBuilder, Sybase SQL Server, PowerLock/PowerTool class libraries, Windows 95 & NT, Novell Netware, HP UNIX, & Object Oriented Programming. Data window Technology was used to develop the client/server part of the application. JAVA, HTML, JAVA Script, TCP/IP, Microsoft IIS were used to enable the application for the Internet.

c. NAME AND ADDRESS OF EMPLOYER
Data Check, Inc.
909 Long Valley Road, Long Valley, New Jersey 09990

NAME OF JOB	DATE STARTED Month Year	DATE LEFT Month Year	KIND OF BUSINESS
Software Engineer	09/92	09/97	Software Development & Consulting

DESCRIBE IN DETAIL THE DUTIES PERFORMED, INCLUDING THE USE OF TOOLS, MACHINES OR EQUIPMENT — NO. OF HOURS PER WEEK: 40

Involved in the design and development of various applications for the financial services industry. Tools used for the development & design were PowerBuilder, C, C++, Sybase SQL Server, Object Oriented features, SunOS, PowerSoft Foundation, HTML, & API.

16. DECLARATIONS

DECLARATION OF ALIEN ➤ ➤ Pursuant to 28 U.S.C. 1746, I declare under penalty of perjury the foregoing is true and correct.

SIGNATURE OF ALIEN	DATE
Khan PATEL	

AUTHORIZATION OF AGENT OF ALIEN ➤ ➤ I hereby designate the agent below to represent me for the purposes of labor certification and I take full responsibility for accuracy of any representations made by my agent.

SIGNATURE OF ALIEN	DATE

NAME OF AGENT (Type or print)	ADDRESS OF AGENT (No., Street, City, State, ZIP code)

SAMPLE ADVERTISEMENT REQUIRED IN THE LABOR CERTIFICATION PROCESS

ENGINEER, ELECTRONIC DESIGN – Melville, NY - Design, develop, modify and evaluate electronic parts, components and integrated circuitry for PWM resonant power supply equipment; conduct experimental tests and evaluate results; investigate and conduct studies analyzing existing topologies; specify doc for power supply products and verify accuracy thereof; interface w/tech wire, breadboard, debug and test new equipment. $38,014.25/yr. 40hrs/wk. - M.S. in Electrical Engin'g. 6 mos exp. or 6 mos related Lab Instructor &/or Graduate Teaching Assistant. Through ed. or work exp. must know: SPICE, MTHCAD, CIRCAD, Digital Storage Oscilloscopes, Gain-Phase Analyzers & design of power stage control loop for both PWM & Resonant Power Supplies & State-Space Averaging. Send resumes in dupl. to: BA#7, P.O. Box 703, New York, N.Y. 10014-0703.

Chapter Ten
FAMILY-BASED IMMIGRATION

A. INTRODUCTION

Historically, one of the most important goals of United States immigration policy has been family unification. In furtherance of this goal, Congress has structured the family-based immigrant categories to provide for the unification of many different types of family members.

The immigration laws provide for two main paths to obtaining permanent residence in the United States. Qualified foreign nationals may be the beneficiaries of either an employment-based immigrant visa petition or a family-sponsored immigrant visa petition. In this chapter, we will discuss the different types of family relationships that are provided for by the immigration laws and the procedures for obtaining and maintaining lawful permanent residence.

In order for an individual to obtain permanent resident status based upon a family relationship, the petition and supporting documentation submitted to the INS must corroborate that a statutorily approved relationship exists between the petitioner and the beneficiary.

Immediate Relatives

Spouses, minor unmarried children and parents of United States citizens are classified as "Immediate Relatives" under the Immigration and Nationality Act. Widows and widowers are also included in the Immediate Relative category.

There is no limit to the number of immediate relatives on whose behalf immigrant petitions may be submitted. In addition, immediate relatives are not subject to quotas. However, among the 480,000 visas which are set aside for family sponsored immigration, 226,000 of these visas are set aside for the four preference categories. The remaining visas are to be allocated to individuals who qualify as immediate relatives. Although there is no limit on the number of immediate relatives who may acquire visas the initial number of visas for immediate relatives must be taken from the overall numbers allotted to the family-based categories.

The allocation of visas are merely an accounting mechanism designed to fulfill the intentions of Congress in standardizing United States immigration policy. Even if the family-based visas are exhausted, immediate relatives will not be affected since there is no limit on the number of immediate relatives who may immigrate to the United States based on a valid immediate relative petition.

Family Preference Categories - 226,000 visas allocated on an annual basis.

First Preference - Unmarried adult sons and daughters of United States citizens.

23,400 Visas allocated per year in addition to any unused visas from the Fourth Family Preference Category.

Second Preference – Spouses, and minor unmarried children of lawful permanent residents.

Adult unmarried sons and daughters of lawful permanent residents.

114,200 Visas allocated per year plus any unused visas from First Family Preference Category.

Third Preference - Married sons and daughters of United States citizens.

23,400 allocated per year plus any unused visas from the top two preference categories.

Fourth Preference - Brothers and sisters of United States citizens.

65,000 visas allocated per year plus any unused visas from the first three preference categories.

Visa Numbers

The allocation of immigrant visa numbers is a rather complex system which takes into account the overall immigrant visa numbers allocated per year, the countries to whom they are chargeable, as well as the allocation by family-based immigrant category.

Visa numbers are an integral part of the immigration process since approval of an immigrant visa petition does not in and of itself authorize a foreign national to remain in the United States. Rather, upon approval of an immigrant visa petition the individual must verify whether there is a visa number currently available from his or her country of birth. The country of birth governs the visa availability, therefore it is important to ascertain the individual's place of birth before embarking on the visa petition process.

Derivative Status for Spouse and Children of Each Family-Based Category

For each of the family-based immigrant categories there is derivative status available for the spouse and unmarried minor children of the beneficiary of the immigrant petition. For example, if a United States citizen is petitioning on behalf of her married daughter under the third family-based preference category, the daughter's spouse would be able to obtain derivative immigrant status on the basis of his or her marriage to the beneficiary of the principal petition.

There is, however, no derivative status available to foreign nationals in the Immediate Relative category. In practice, this means that if a woman obtained immigrant status based upon her marriage to a United States citizen she cannot bring her children to the United States as derivatives of her status. The alternative option is often to have the United States citizen husband petition on the children's behalf as his stepchildren (see definition below). Another option is to wait until the wife obtains permanent resident status and then she can petition for the children under the second family preference category for unmarried sons and daughters of permanent residents. However, the quota delays associated with this category make this solution impractical.

Derivative Status for Spouse and Children Following to Join

Another caveat in this regard is that a spouse and children in existence at the time a foreign national is immigrating to the United States may derive status and priority date from the principal beneficiary even if the spouse or children do not immigrate at the same time as the principal beneficiary. Spouses and children may follow to join at a later date as long as they continue to qualify as spouses or children under the immigration laws.

Since the definition of each of the family relationships are critical to qualification as a beneficiary of one of the four family categories listed above, or as an immediate relative, it is important to be familiar with the statutory definitions of the major family relationships.

B. DEFINITIONS

Spouse - The term "spouse", "wife" or "husband" does not include a spouse, wife or husband by reason of any marriage ceremony where the contracting parties are not physically present in the presence of each other, unless the marriage has been consummated.

Child - The term child encompasses a range of different familial relationships.

"Child" means an unmarried person under twenty-one years of age who is:

- a **child born in wedlock**

- a **stepchild**, whether or not born out of wedlock, provided that the child had not reached the age of eighteen years at the time the marriage creating the status of stepchild occurred.

Note that a stepchild continues to be entitled to immigration benefits from the marriage creating the stepparent/stepchild relationship, even though the relationship between the natural parent and stepparent was terminated at a later date, provided the marriage was a valid marriage and a family relationship continued to exist as a matter of fact between the stepparent and stepchild.

- a child **legitimated** under the law of the child's residence or domicile or under the law of the father's residence or domicile, whether in or outside the United States, if the legitimization takes place before the child reaches the age of eighteen years and the child is in the legal custody of the legitimating parent or parents at the time of such legitimization.

- A **child born out of wedlock**, by, through whom or on whose behalf, a status, privilege, or benefit is sought by virtue of the relationship of the child to its natural mother or to its natural father, if the father has or had a bona fide parent-child relationship with the child.

- a child **adopted** while under the age of sixteen years if the child has been in the legal custody of, and has resided with the adopting parent or parents for at least two years, provided that no natural parent of any adopted child, will thereafter, by virtue of that parentage be accorded any right, privilege or status under the Immigration and Nationality Act;

- A child who is an **orphan** because of the death or disappearance of, abandonment or desertion by, or separation or loss from, both parents or for whom the sole or surviving parent is incapable of providing the proper care and has in writing irrevocably released the child for emigration and adoption. A United States citizen must adopt the child before the child reaches the age of 16 in order to meet the requirements for classification as an immediate relative. A United States citizen who is married must adopt the child jointly with his or her spouse. If the U.S. citizen is unmarried, he or she must be at least twenty-five years of age.

Parent - The term "parent," "father," or "mother" for the purposes of immediate relative classification, means a parent, father or mother as long as the relationship exists on the basis of any one of the relationships enumerated under the heading of child defined in the INA. In order for a parent to be eligible for classification as an Immediate Relative, the United States citizen child petitioning on his or her behalf must be over the age of twenty-one.

Widow/Widower - Widows and widowers are eligible for classification as Immediate Relatives if they meet the following requirements:

- The widow/widower had been married to the U.S. citizen for at least two years prior to the citizen's death. The U.S. citizen is not required to have had the status of U.S. citizen for the entire two-year period, but must have been an U.S. citizen at the time of death.

- The petition is filed within two years of the citizen spouse's death.

- The couple was not legally separated at the time of death.

- The widow/widower has not remarried at the time the petition is filed.

C. EVIDENCE REQUIRED TO PROVE FAMILY RELATIONSHIP

The burden is on the petitioner to establish the existence of the family relationship required in each of the family-based categories. The nature of the evidence may vary from country to country, however, the best type of evidence is usually original documents consisting of birth certificates, marriage certificates and other identity documents. For various reasons, certain countries do not have primary evidence available to prove family relationships. Therefore, secondary evidence is acceptable in some situations. The Department of State maintains a record of document availability in various countries around the world. This information is contained in the Foreign Affairs Manual (FAM) published by the Department of State.

Immigrant petitions filed with INS Service Centers do not have to include original documents. The INS will accept certified copies of original documents. Foreign language documents must be translated in English and certified by a competent translator.

Primary Evidence to Prove Family Relationship Between Petitioner and Beneficiary

A petition submitted on behalf of a spouse must include evidence of the United States citizenship or lawful permanent residence of the petitioner and evidence of the claimed relationship. A petition submitted on behalf of a spouse must be accompanied by a certificate of marriage issued by civil authorities, and proof of the legal termination of all previous marriages of both the petitioner and the beneficiary. As will be discussed in greater detail in this chapter the petition must also include evidence that the marriage is a bona fide marriage, which was not entered into for the purposes of evading the immigration laws.

A petition submitted by a mother on behalf of a child born in or out of wedlock (regardless of age) must include the birth certificate of the child, which shows the name of the mother. If the mother's name on the birth certificate is different from her name on the petition, evidence of the name change must also be submitted.

A petition submitted by a father on behalf of a child born in wedlock (regardless of age) must include the birth certificate of the child, the marriage certificate of the parents, and proof of legal termination of the parent's prior marriages, if any, issued by civil authorities.

A petition submitted by the purported father on behalf of a child born out of wedlock must show that the petitioner is the natural father of the beneficiary and a bona fide parent-child relationship was established when the child was unmarried and under twenty-one years of age. Primary evidence to establish that the petitioner is the child's natural father is the beneficiary's birth certificate, issued by civil authorities and showing the father's name. If the father's name has been legally changed, evidence of the name change must also accompany the petition.

Evidence of a parent/child relationship should establish more than a mere biological relationship. Emotional and/or financial ties or a genuine concern and interest by the father for the child's support, instruction, and general welfare must also be demonstrated.

The following types of evidence may be used to document the father's relationship with an out of wedlock child: money order receipts or canceled checks showing the father's financial support of the beneficiary; the father's income tax returns; the fathers' medical or insurance records which include the beneficiary as a dependent; school records for the beneficiary; correspondence between the parties; or, notarized affidavits of friends, neighbors, school officials, or other associates knowledgeable about the relationship.

A petition submitted by a parent on behalf of a stepchild must include the stepchild's birth certificate, issued by civil authorities and showing the name of the beneficiary's parent to whom the petitioner is married, a marriage certificate issued by civil authorities which shows that the petitioner and the child's natural parent were married before the stepchild reached the age of eighteen, and evidence of the termination of any prior marriages of the petitioner and the natural parent of the stepchild.

A petition submitted on behalf of a brother or sister must include the petitioner's own birth certificate and the birth certificate of the beneficiary showing a common mother. If the sibling petition is being submitted on the basis of a common father, the petition must also include the petitioner's and the beneficiary's birth certificates, the marriage certificate of the parents and proof of legal termination of the any prior marriages of the parents.

A petition submitted by a child (born in or out of wedlock) on behalf of a mother must include the birth certificate of the petitioner showing the mother's name. If the mother's name on the birth certificate is different from her name on the petition, evidence of the name change must also be submitted.

A petition submitted by a child (born in wedlock) on behalf of a father must include the birth certificate of the child, the marriage certificate of the parents, and proof of legal termination of the parent's prior marriages, if any issued by civil authorities. If the petitioner was born out of wedlock the petition must include the same evidence required in a petition submitted by a father on behalf of a child born out of wedlock.

Petitions submitted on the basis of a family relationship created by adoption may only be filed if the adoption took place before the child reached the age of sixteen; the child was in the legal custody of the adopting parent(s) for at least two years; and the child resided with the parent(s) for at least two years. In addition, a copy of the adoption decree must be submitted with the petition.

Secondary Evidence to Prove Family Relationship Between Petitioner and Beneficiary

- Baptismal Certificate - A certificate under the seal of the church where the baptism occurred within two months after birth, showing the date and place of the child's birth, date of baptism and the names of the child's parents.

- School Records - A letter from the school authorities having jurisdiction over the school attended (preferably the first school), showing the date of admission to the school, child's date of birth or age at that time, place of birth, and the names and places of birth of parents, if shown in the school records.

- Census Records - State of federal census record showing the names and places of birth and dates of birth or ages of the persons listed.

- Affidavits - Written statements sworn to or affirmed by two persons who were living at the time, and who have personal knowledge, of the event you are trying to prove, for example, the date and place of birth, marriage or death. The persons making the affidavits may be relatives and need not be citizens of the United States. Each affidavit should contain the following information regarding the person making the affidavit: his or her full name and address; date and place of birth, relationship to the beneficiary of petitioner, if any; full information concerning the event; and complete details concerning how he or she acquired knowledge of the event.

BATTERED SPOUSES AND CHILDREN

In 1994, Congress passed the Violent Crime Control and Law Enforcement Act (1994 Crime Bill) which included the Violence Against Women Act. The 1994 Act added new provisions to the INA permitting "battered" alien spouses and children of U.S. citizens and lawful permanent residents to self-petition as immediate relatives or under the second family-based preference category.

An abused spouse or a parent of an abused child may file a self-petition if the following requirements are met:

- The spouse of the battered spouse is a U.S. citizen or lawful permanent resident;

- The battered spouse is eligible for immigrant classification either as an immediate relative or under the second preference category;

- The battered spouse resides in the United States at the time the petition is filed;

- The battered spouse resided in the United States with the U.S. citizen or lawful permanent resident;

- The spouse was battered by, or has been the subject of extreme cruelty perpetrated by, the qualifying spouse during the marriage, or is the parent of a child who has been the subject of the abuse by the qualifying relative during the marriage;

- The battered spouse is a person of good moral character;

- The battered spouse entered into the marriage to the citizen or lawful permanent resident in good faith; and

- The battered spouse is a person whose removal would result in extreme hardship to himself, herself, or his or her child.

The self-petitioning spouse/parent must be legally married to the batterer when the petition is filed with the INS. After the petition is filed, the termination of the marriage will not have an adverse effect on the decision made on the self-petition. However, the self-petitioner may not remarry while the self-petition is pending with the INS. The abusive spouse must be a citizen of the United States or a lawful permanent resident when the self-petition is filed and when it is approved. Changes in the abuser's citizenship or lawful permanent resident status after approval will have no effect on the self-petition.

The INS defines "battered by or was the subject of extreme cruelty" as including, but not limited to, being the victim of any act or threatened act of violence, including any forceful detention, which results or threatens to result in physical or mental injury. Psychological or sexual abuse or exploitation, including rape, molestation, incest (if the victim is a minor), or forced prostitution are considered to be acts of violence. Other abusive actions may be acts of violence under certain circumstances, including acts that, in and of themselves may not initially appear violent but are part of an overall pattern of violence. The abuse must have been committed by the U.S. citizen or lawful permanent resident spouse against the self-petitioner or the self-petitioner's child, and must have taken place during the marriage.

For the purposes of self-petitions submitted by spouses and children, the INS will consider all credible evidence of extreme hardship submitted with the self-petition, including evidence of hardship arising from circumstances surrounding the abuse. Extreme hardship claims are evaluated on a case-by-case basis after a review of all the evidence in the case.

Self-petitioning spouses/parents must submit evidence of the citizenship of the abusive spouse or proof of the spouse's lawful permanent residence. The self-petitioning spouse must also submit evidence of the marital relationship including the marriage certificate and proof of the termination of all prior marriages, if any, of both the self-petitioner and the abuser. In addition, the self-petitioning spouse must include documents that demonstrate he or she resided with the abuser in the United States, and that the self-petitioner is currently residing in the United States. Employment records, utility receipts, school records, hospital or medical records, birth certificates of children born in the U.S., deeds, mortgages, rental records, insurance policies, affidavits or any other type of credible evidence of residency may be submitted.

Evidence of the abuse committed by the U.S. citizen or lawful permanent resident must also be submitted with the petition. Evidence of abuse may include, but is not limited to, reports and affidavits from police, judges and other court officials, medical personnel, school officials, clergy, social workers, and other social service agency personnel. Any other forms of credible relevant evidence will also be considered. Evidence of the self-petitioner's good moral character must also be submitted with the petition.

Battered Children

Although the eligibility and evidentiary requirements for self-petitions filed by abused children are generally the same as for self-petitions filed by abused spouses, there are a few notable differences.

An abused child may file a self-petition if the following requirements are met:

- The child must be a child of a citizen or lawful permanent resident of the United States;

- The child must be eligible to file an immediate relative or second preference immigrant visa petition;

- The child is residing in the United States at the time the petition is filed;

- The child resided in the United States with the U.S. citizen or lawful permanent resident parent;

- The child has been battered by, or has been the subject of extreme cruelty perpetrated by the U.S. citizen or lawful permanent resident parent while residing with him or her;

- The child is a person of good moral character; and

- The child would be subject to extreme hardship if he or she were removed.

At the time of the petition the abused child must be unmarried, less than twenty-one years of age, and otherwise qualify as the abuser's child under the definition of child discussed earlier in this chapter. Termination of the abuser's parental rights or a change in legal custody does not alter the self-petitioning relationship as long as the abused child meets the definition of child. A self-petitioning child must submit evidence of the qualifying parental relationship (e.g. birth certificates, marriage and divorce certificates, or adoption decrees), the abusive parent's citizenship or immigration status as a lawful permanent resident, evidence of the child's good moral character, evidence of the abuse and evidence that demonstrates the abused child would suffer extreme hardship if her or she is removed.

D. AFFIDAVITS OF SUPPORT

Any foreign national who, in the opinion of the Attorney General at the time of application for admission or adjustment of status, is likely at any time to become a public charge is inadmissible to the United States. Prior to the 1996 Act, visa applicants were required to submit evidence of financial viability in order to overcome this ground of inadmissibility. Congress, in the 1996 Act imposed stricter sponsorship requirements for filing family-based immigrant visa petitions. The 1996 Act requires a legally enforceable affidavit of support (Form I-864) be submitted with all family-based visa petitions and in some employment-based visa petitions to overcome the public charge ground of inadmissibility. The sponsor must execute and file an affidavit of support for each beneficiary listed on the visa petition including any aliens accompanying or following to join the principal beneficiary.

Sponsors must be:

- At least eighteen years of age;
- Domiciled in the U.S. or any territory or possession of the U.S.; and
- A citizen of the U.S. or a foreign national lawfully admitted for permanent residence.

Execution of the affidavit of support creates a contract between the sponsor and the U.S. government for the benefit of the intending immigrant, and any Federal, State, or local government agency or private entity that provides any means-tested benefit to the intending immigrant.

The sponsor's obligation to the intending immigrant is terminated by operation of law when the intending immigrant:

- Becomes a citizen of the United States;
- Has worked, or can be credited with 40 qualifying quarters of work;
- Ceases to hold the status of an alien lawfully admitted for permanent residence and has left the U.S.; or
- The intending immigrant or the sponsor dies.

In order for the intending immigrant to overcome the public charge ground of inadmissibility, the sponsor must demonstrate the means to maintain an annual income of at least 125% of the Federal poverty line. The federal poverty line means a level of income equal to the poverty guidelines issued by the Secretary of Health and Human Services. The poverty guidelines include income information for households of various sizes. For example, the 1998 poverty guidelines require a household of six to demonstrate an income of $22,050 to be considered living above the poverty line. A household of six, however, must demonstrate an income of $31,062 (125%) to meet the affidavit of support requirements created in the 1996 Act. The poverty guidelines are updated annually and must be consulted before executing an affidavit of support on behalf of an intending immigrant.

If the sponsor is on active duty in the Armed Forces of the United States and the intending immigrant is the sponsor's spouse or child, the sponsor's income must be equal to at least 100% of the Federal poverty line.

In order to demonstrate that the sponsor meets the income requirements, the sponsor must submit his or her Federal tax return for each of the three most recent taxable years along with the affidavit of support. The sponsor is only required to attach his or her tax returns if the sponsor is required to file a federal tax return under the tax laws of the United States. If the sponsor is not required to file tax returns, he or she must submit comparable evidence demonstrating his or her annual income or assets.

The sponsor does not have to meet the minimum income requirements on his or her own. The income of the members of the sponsor's household may also be included. Household members include:

- The sponsor;
- Individuals related to the sponsor by birth, marriage, or adoption who have been living in the sponsor' residence for the previous six months; and
- All persons listed as dependents on the sponsor's most recent federal tax regardless of the dependent's residence.

The income of the intending immigrant may also be included as long as the beneficiary of the immigrant visa petition has been living in the sponsor's residence for at least six months at the time the affidavit is filed. The ability to include the intending immigrant's income is especially important in cases where the intending immigrant is the primary wage earner. The sponsor is only able to include the income of his or her spouse or other household members if they agree in writing to make their income available.

If other members of the sponsor's household agree to be jointly and severally liable for any reimbursement obligations the sponsor may incur a Form I-864A, Contract between Sponsor and Household Member must be executed. If the intending immigrant is making his or her income available Form I-864A does not have to be filed.

If the sponsor can not show sufficient income, he or she can submit proof of significant assets to meet the financial means requirement. The sponsor, other household members, or the intending immigrant may own the assets in question. To be a significant asset the value of the asset must be at least five times the difference between the sponsor's total household income and the federal poverty guideline. In addition, the asset must be easily convertible into cash within one year.

Assets that may be used include: savings in a bank or other financial institution; stock, bonds, and certificates of deposit, life insurance policies, real estate and personal property. The sponsor must establish the location and ownership of each asset listed on the affidavit of support.

If the sponsor can not meet the minimum income requirements either through proof of household income or assets, a co-sponsor may file a separate affidavit of support on behalf of the intending immigrant. Each co-sponsor must file a separate I-

864 and independently satisfy the income or asset requirements. The petitioner and the co-sponsor can not combine their income or assets to reach the minimum requirements. Each co-sponsor is jointly and severally liable for the support of the intending immigrant. There is no limit on the number of co-sponsors that may be used, but each co-sponsor must meet the age, domicile and alienage requirements.

The mandatory affidavit requirement does not apply to widows or widowers self-petitioning for lawful permanent residence based on a marriage to a deceased U.S. citizen. In addition, the mandatory affidavit requirement does not apply to battered spouses and children filing self-petitions. Refugees and asylees submitting applications for adjustment of status are also exempt from the mandatory affidavit of support requirement because foreign nationals under these categories are not subject to the public charge ground of inadmissibility.

The affidavit of support must contain an original signature and be notarized by a notary public or signed before an Immigration or Consular Officer.

E. PROCEDURE FOR FILING FAMILY-BASED IMMIGRANT PETITION

If the beneficiary is not in the United States or the beneficiary wishes to process the immigrant visa petition at a U.S. Consulate abroad, the petition and supporting documents should be filed with the INS Service Center that has jurisdiction over the petitioner's place of residence. See Appendix A for the address and jurisdiction of the four INS Service Centers.

If the petitioner resides in Austria, Germany, Greece, Hong Kong, India, Italy, Kenya, Korea, Mexico, Philippines, Singapore, Thailand and the United Kingdom, the petition must be filed with the INS office located in that country. The beneficiary of the petition does not have to reside in the same jurisdiction as the petitioner for the INS overseas office to accept the petition. An overseas INS office may accept a petition filed by a petitioner who does not reside within the office's jurisdiction when it is established that emergent or humanitarian reasons for acceptance exist or when it is in the national interest. Overseas INS offices are not permitted to accept self-petitions.

However, it is also important to note that the sponsor indicated on the affidavit of support must be domiciled in the United States or any territory of the United States. Domicile for the purposes of filing an affidavit of support means the place where a sponsor has a residence, with the intention to maintain that residence for the foreseeable future. Lawful permanent residents who have applied for preservation of status while living abroad and U.S. citizens living temporarily abroad because of employment obligations to U.S. companies are considered to be domiciled in the United States for affidavit of support purposes.

Form I-130, Petition for Alien Relative, should be filed in most of the family-based categories. Form I-360, Petition for Amerasian, Widow or Special Immigrant, should be used for self-petitions filed by Widows, Battered Spouses, and Battered Children. Both Form I-130 and Form I-360 clearly delineate the different relationships that may serve as the basis for each petition.

SAMPLE FORM I-864 AFFIDAVIT OF SUPPORT

U.S. Department of Justice
Immigration and Naturalization Service

OMB #1115-0214

Affidavit of Support under Section 213A of the Act

START HERE - Please Type or Print

Part 1. Information on Sponsor (You)

Last Name	First Name	Middle Name	
AUSTIN	Herbert	A.	
Mailing Address *(Street Number and Name)* 8 Ryebrook Lane		Apt/Suite Number	
City Ryebrook		State or Province NY	
Country USA		Zip/Postal Code 11111	Telephone Number 914 555-5555

Place of Residence if different from above *(Street Number and Name)*		Apt/Suite Number
City		State or Province
Country	Zip/Postal Code	Telephone Number
Date of Birth *(Month, Day, Year)* 8/10/33	Place of Birth *(City, State, Country)* NY, NY	Are you a U.S. Citizen? ☒ Yes ☐ No
Social Security Number 101-01-1001	A-Number *(If any)*	

FOR AGENCY USE ONLY

This Affidavit	Receipt
[ ] Meets [ ] Does not meet Requirements of Section 213A Officer's Signature Location Date	

Part 2. Basis for Filing Affidavit of Support

I am filing this affidavit of support because *(check one):*

a. ☒ I filed/am filing the alien relative petition.

b. ☐ I filed/am filing an alien worker petition on behalf of the intending immigrant, who is related to me as my __________ *(relationship)*.

c. ☐ I have ownership interest of at least 5% of __________ *(name of entity which filed visa petition)* which filed an alien worker petition on behalf of the intending immigrant, who is related to me as my __________ *(relationship)*.

d. ☐ I am a joint sponsor willing to accept the legal obligations with any other sponsor(s).

Part 3. Information on the Immigrant(s) You Are Sponsoring

Last Name		First Name	Middle Name
AUSTIN		rita	S.
Date of Birth *(Month,Day,Year)* 04/04/1937		Sex: ☐ Male ☒ Female	Social Security Number *(If any)* 111-10-1111
Country of Citizenship Russia		A-Number *(If any)*	
Current Address *(Street Number and Name)* 8 Ryebrook Lane		Apt/Suite Number	City Ryebrook
State/Province NY	Country USA	Zip/Postal Code 11111	Telephone Number 914 555-5555

List any spouse and/or children immigrating with the immigrant named above in this Part: *(Use additional sheet of paper if necessary.)*

Name	A-Number *(If any)*	Social Security Number *(If any)*

Part 4. Eligibility to Sponsor

To be a sponsor you must be U.S. citizen or national or lawful permanent resident. If you are not the petitioning relative, you must provide proof of status. To prove status, U.S. citizens or nationals must attach a copy of a document proving status, such as a U.S. passport, birth certificate, or certificate of naturalization, and lawful permanent residents must attach a copy of both sides of their Alien Registration Card (Form I-551).

The determination of your eligibility to sponsor an immigrant will be based on an evaluation of your demonstrated ability to maintain an annual income at or above 125 percent of the Federal poverty line (100 percent if you are a petitioner sponsoring your spouse or child and you are on active duty in the U.S. Armed Forces). The assessment of your ability to maintain an adequate income will include your current employment, household size, and household income as shown on the Federal income tax returns for the 3 most recent tax years. Assets that are readily converted to cash and that can be made available for the support of sponsored immigrants if necessary, including any such assets of the immigrant(s) you are sponsoring, may also be considered.

The greatest weight in determining eligibility will be placed on current employment and household income. If a petitioner is unable to demonstrate ability to meet the stated income and asset requirements, a joint sponsor who *can* meet the income and asset requirements is needed. Failure to provide adequate evidence of income and/or assets or an affidavit of support completed by a joint sponsor will result in denial of the immigrant's application for an immigrant visa or adjustment to permanent resident status.

A. Sponsor's Employment

I am: 1. ☐ Employed by ______________________ *(Provide evidence of employment)*
Annual salary __________ *or* hourly wage $ __________ *(for* _____ *hours per week)*
2. ☒ Self employed ______________________ *(Name of business)*
Nature of employment or business Accountant
3. ☐ Unemployed or retired since ______________________

B. Use of Benefits

Have you or anyone related to you by birth, marriage, or adoption living in your household or listed as a dependent on your most recent income tax return received any type of means-tested public benefit in the past 3 years?

☐ Yes ☒ No *(If yes, provide details, including programs and dates, on a separate sheet of paper)*

C. Sponsor's Household Size

		Number
1.	Number of persons (related to you by birth, marriage, or adoption) living in your residence, including yourself. *(Do NOT include persons being sponsored in this affidavit.)*	1
2.	Number of immigrants being sponsored in this affidavit *(Include all persons in Part 3.)*	1
3.	Number of immigrants **NOT** living in your household whom you are still obligated to support under a previously signed affidavit of support using Form I-864.	0
4.	Number of persons who are otherwise dependent on you, as claimed in your tax return for the most recent tax year.	0
5.	Total household size. ***(Add lines 1 through 4.)*** **Total**	2

List persons below who are included in lines 1 or 3 for whom you previously have submitted INS Form I-864, *if your support obligation has not terminated.*

(If additional space is needed, use additional paper)

Name	A-Number	Date Affidavit of Support Signed	Relationship
N/A			

Part 4. Eligibility to Sponsor *(Continued)*

D. Sponsor's Annual Household Income

Enter total unadjusted income from your Federal income tax return for the most recent tax year below. If you last filed a joint income tax return but are using only your *own* income to qualify, list total earnings from your W-2 Forms, or, *if* necessary to reach the required income for your household size, include income from other sources listed on your tax return. If your *individual* income does not meet the income requirement for your household size, you may also list total income for anyone related to you by birth, marriage, or adoption currently living with you in your residence if they have lived in your residence for the previous 6 months, or any person shown as a dependent on your Federal income tax return for the most recent tax year, even if not living in the household. For their income to be considered, household members or dependents must be willing to make their income available for support of the sponsored immigrant(s) and to complete and sign Form I-864A, Contract Between Sponsor and Household Member. A sponsored immigrant/household member only need complete Form I-864A if his or her income will be used to determine your ability to support a spouse and/or children immigrating with him or her.

You must attach evidence of current employment and copies of income tax returns as filed with the IRS for the most recent 3 tax years for yourself and all persons whose income is listed below. See "Required Evidence" in Instructions. Income from all 3 years will be considered in determining your ability to support the immigrant(s) you are sponsoring.

- ☐ I filed a single/separate tax return for the most recent tax year.
- ☒ I filed a joint return for the most recent tax year which includes only my own income.
- ☐ I filed a joint return for the most recent tax year which includes income for my spouse and myself.
  - ☒ I am submitting documentation of my individual income (Form W-2 and 1099).
  - ☐ I am qualifying using my spouse's income; my spouse is submitting a Form I-864A.

Indicate most recent tax year 1998 *(tax year)*

Sponsor's individual income $ 65,000

or

Sponsor and spouse's combined income $______
(If joint tax return filed; spouse must submit Form I-864A.)

Income of other qualifying persons.
(List names; include spouse if applicable. Each person must complete Form I-864A.)

______ $______

______ $______

______ $______

Total Household Income $ 65,000

Explain on separate sheet of paper if you or any of the above listed individuals are submitting Federal income tax returns for fewer than 3 years, or if other explanation of income, employment, or evidence is necessary.

E. Determination of Eligibility Based on Income

1. ☐ I am subject to the 125 percent of poverty line requirement for sponsors.
   ☐ I am subject to the 100 percent of poverty line requirement for sponsors on active duty in the U.S. Armed Forces sponsoring their spouse or child.
2. Sponsor's total household size, from Part 4.C., line 5 2.
3. Minimum income requirement from the Poverty Guidelines chart for the year of 2 *(year)* is $ 13,562 for this household size.

If you are currently employed and your household income for your household size is equal to or greater than the applicable poverty line requirement (from line E.3.), you do not need to list assets (Part 4.F. and 5) or have a joint sponsor (Part 6) unless you are requested to do so by a Consular or Immigration Officer You may skip to Part 7, Use of the Affidavit of Support to Overcome Public Charge Ground of Admissibility. **Otherwise, you should continue with Part 4.F.**

Part 4. Eligibility to Sponsor *(Continued)*

F. Sponsor's Assets and Liabilities

Your assets and those of your qualifying household members and dependents may be used to demonstrate ability to maintain an income at or above 125 percent (or 100 percent, if applicable) of the poverty line *if* they are available for the support of the sponsored immigrant(s) and can readily be converted into cash within 1 year. The household member, other than the immigrant(s) you are sponsoring, must complete and sign Form I-864A, Contract Between Sponsor and Household Member. List the cash value of each asset *after* any debts or liens are subtracted. Supporting evidence must be attached to establish location, ownership, date of acquisition, and value of each asset listed, including any liens and liabilities related to each asset listed. See "Evidence of Assets" in Instructions.

Type of Asset	**Cash Value of Assets** *(Subtract any debts)*
Saving deposits	$
Stocks, bonds, certificates of deposit	$
Life insurance cash value	$
Real estate	$
Other *(specify)*	$
Total Cash Value of Assets	$_______________

Part 5. Immigrant's Assets and Offsetting Liabilities

The sponsored immigrant's assets may also be used in support of your ability to maintain income at or above 125 percent of the poverty line *if* the assets are or will be available in the United States for the support of the sponsored immigrant(s) and can readily be converted into cash within 1 year.

The sponsored immigrant should provide information on his or her assets in a format similar to part 4.F. above. Supporting evidence must be attached to establish location, ownership, and value of each asset listed, including any liens and liabilities for each asset listed. See "Evidence of Assets" in Instructions.

Part 6. Joint Sponsors

If household income and assets do not meet the appropriate poverty line for your household size, a joint sponsor is required. There may be more than one joint sponsor, but each joint sponsor must individually meet the 125 percent of poverty line requirement based on his or her household income and/or assets, including any assets of the sponsored immigrant. By submitting a separate Affidavit of Support under Section 213A of the Act (Form I-864), a joint sponsor accepts joint responsibility with the petitioner for the sponsored immigrant(s) until they become U.S. citizens, can be credited with 40 quarters of work, leave the United States permanently, or die.

Part 7. Use of the Affidavit of Support to Overcome Public Charge Ground of Inadmissibility

Section 212(a)(4)(C) of the Immigration and Nationality Act provides that an alien seeking permanent residence as an immediate relative (including an orphan), as a family-sponsored immigrant, or as an alien who will accompany or follow to join another alien is considered to be likely to become a public charge and is inadmissible to the United States unless a sponsor submits a legally enforceable affidavit of support on behalf of the alien. Section 212(a)(4)(D) imposes the same requirement on employment-based immigrant, and those aliens who accompany or follow to join the employment-based immigrant, if the employment-based immigrant will be employed by a relative, or by a firm in which a relative owns a significant interest. Separate affidavits of support are required for family members at the time they immigrate if they are not included on this affidavit of support or do not apply for an immigrant visa or adjustment of status within 6 months of the date this affidavit of support is originally signed. The sponsor must provide the sponsored immigrant(s) whatever support is necessary to maintain them at an income that is at least 125 percent of the Federal poverty guidelines.

I submit this affidavit of support in consideration of the sponsored immigrant(s) not being found inadmissible to the United States under section 212(a)(4)(C) (or 212(a)(4)(D) for an employment-based immigrant) and to enable the sponsored immigrant(s) to overcome this ground of inadmissibility. I agree to provide the sponsored immigrant(s) whatever support is necessary to maintain the sponsored immigrant(s) at an income that is at least 125 percent of the Federal poverty guidelines. I understand that my obligation will continue until my death or the sponsored immigrant(s) have become U.S. citizens, can be credited with 40 quarters of work, depart the United States permanently, or die.

Part 7. Use of the Affidavit of Support to Overcome Public Charge Grounds *(Continued)*

Notice of Change of Address.

Sponsors are required to provide written notice of any change of address within 30 days of the change in address until the sponsored immigrant(s) have become U.S. citizens, can be credited with 40 quarters of work, depart the United States permanently, or die. To comply with this requirement, the sponsor must complete INS Form I-865. Failure to give this notice may subject the sponsor to the civil penalty established under section 213A(d)(2) which ranges from $250 to $2,000, unless the failure to report occurred with the knowledge that the sponsored immigrant(s) had received means-tested public benefits, in which case the penalty ranges from $2,000 to $5,000.

If my address changes for any reason before my obligations under this affidavit of support terminate, I will complete and file INS Form I-865, Sponsor's Notice of Change of Address, Within 30 days of the change of address. I understand that failure to give this notice may subject me to civil penalties.

Means-tested Public Benefit Prohibitions and Exceptions.

Under section 403(a) of Public Law 104-193 (Welfare Reform Act), aliens lawfully admitted for permanent residence in the United States, with certain exceptions, are ineligible for most Federally-funded means-tested public benefits during their first 5 years in the United States. This provision does not apply to public benefits specified in section 403(c) of the Welfare Reform Act or to State public benefits, including emergency Medicaid; short-term, non-cash emergency relief; services provided under the National School Lunch and Child Nutrition Acts; immunizations and testing and treatment for communicable diseases; student assistance under the Higher Education Act and the Public Health Service Act; certain forms of foster-care or adoption assistance under the Social Security Act; Head Start programs; means-tested programs under the Elementary and Secondary Education Act; and Job Training Partnership Act programs.

Consideration of Sponsor's Income in Determining Eligibility for Benefits.

If a permanent resident alien is no longer statutorily barred from a Federally-funded means-tested public benefit program and applies for such a benefit, the income and resources of the sponsor and the sponsor's spouse will be considered (or deemed) to be the income and resources of the sponsored immigrant in determining the immigrant's eligibility for Federal means-tested public benefits. Any State or local government may also choose to consider (or deem) the income and resources of the sponsor and the sponsor's spouse to be the income and resources of the immigrant for the purposes of determining eligibility for their means-tested public benefits. The attribution of the income and resources of the sponsor and the sponsor's spouse to the immigrant will continue until the immigrant becomes a U.S. citizen or has worked or can be credited with 40 qualifying quarters of work, provided that the immigrant or the worker crediting the quarters to the immigrant has not received any Federal means-tested public benefit during any creditable quarter for any period after December 31, 1996.

I understand that, under section 213A of the Immigration and Nationality Act (the Act), as amended, this affidavit of support constitutes a contract between me and the U.S. Government. This contract is designed to protect the United States Government, and State and local government agencies or private entities that provide means-tested public benefits, from having to pay benefits to or on behalf of the sponsored immigrant(s), for as long as I am obligated to support them under this affidavit of support. I understand that the sponsored immigrants, or any Federal, State, local, or private entity that pays any means-tested benefit to or on behalf of the sponsored immigrant(s), are entitled to sue me if I fail to meet my obligations under this affidavit of support, as defined by section 213A and INS regulations.

Civil Action to Enforce.

If the immigrant on whose behalf this affidavit of support is executed receives any Federal, State, or local means-tested public benefit before this obligation terminates, the Federal, State, or local agency or private entity may request reimbursement from the sponsor who signed this affidavit. If the sponsor fails to honor the request for reimbursement, the agency may sue the sponsor in any U.S. District Court or any State court with jurisdiction of civil actions for breach of contract. INS will provide names, addresses, and Social Security account numbers of sponsors to benefit-providing agencies for this purpose. Sponsors may also be liable for paying the costs of collection, including legal fees.

Part 7. Use of the Affidavit of Support to Overcome Public Charge Grounds *(Continued)*

I acknowledge that section 213A(a)(1)(B) of the Act grants the sponsored immigrant(s) and any Federal, State, local, or private agency that pays any means-tested public benefit to or on behalf of the sponsored immigrant(s) standing to sue me for failing to meet my obligations under this affidavit of support. I agree to submit to the personal jurisdiction of any court of the United States or of any State, territory, or possession of the United States if the court has subject matter jurisdiction of a civil lawsuit to enforce this affidavit of support. I agree that no lawsuit to enforce this affidavit of support shall be barred by any statute of limitations that might otherwise apply, so long as the plaintiff initiates the civil lawsuit no later than ten (10) years after the date on which a sponsored immigrant last received any means-tested public benefits.

Collection of Judgment.

I acknowledge that a plaintiff may seek specific performance of my support obligation. Furthermore, any money judgment against me based on this affidavit of support may be collected through the use of a judgment lien under 28 U.S.C. 3201, a writ of execution under 28 U.S.C. 3203, a judicial installment payment order under 28 U.S.C. 3204, garnishment under 28 U.S.C. 3205, or through the use of any corresponding remedy under State law. I may also be held liable for costs of collection, including attorney fees.

Concluding Provisions.

I, Herbert Austin______________________________, *certify under penalty of perjury under the laws of the United States that:*

(a) I know the contents of this affidavit of support signed by me;
(b) All the statements in this affidavit of support are true and correct;
(c) I make this affidavit of support for the consideration stated in Part 7, freely, and without any mental reservation or purpose of evasion;
(d) Income tax returns submitted in support of this affidavit are true copies of the returns filed with the Internal Revenue Service; and
(e) Any other evidence submitted is true and correct.

______________________________ ____________________
(Sponsor's Signature) *(Date)*

Subscribed and sworn to *(or affirmed)* before me this

________ day of ____________ *(Month)*, ________ *(Year)*

at ____________________________,

My commission expires on ____________

____
(Signature of Notary Public or Officer Administering Oath)

____
(Title)

Part 8. If someone other than the sponsor prepared this affidavit of support, that person must complete the following:

I certify under penalty of perjury under the laws of the United States that I prepared this affidavit of support at the sponsor's request, and that this affidavit of support is based on all information of which I have knowledge.

Signature	Print Your Name	Date	Daytime Telephone Number

Firm Name and Address

SAMPLE FORM I-130 PETITION FOR ALIEN RELATIVE

U.S. Department of Justice
Immigration and Naturalization Service (INS)

OMB # 1115-0054

Petition for Alien Relative

DO NOT WRITE IN THIS BLOCK - FOR EXAMINING OFFICE USE ONLY

Action Stamp

Fee Stamp

Section of Law:
☐ 201 (b) spouse ☐ 203 (a)(1)
☐ 201 (b) child ☐ 203 (a)(2)
☐ 201 (b) parent ☐ 203 (a)(4)
☐ 203 (a)(5)
AM CON: ________

Petition was filed on ______________ (priority date)
☐ Personal Interview ☐ Previously Forwarded
☐ Pet. ☐ Ben. "A" File Reviewed ☐ Stateside Criteria
☐ Field Investigations ☐ I-485 Simultaneously
☐ 204 (a)(2)(A) Resolved ☐ 204 (h) Resolved

Remarks:

A. Relationship

1. The alien relative is my
☒ Husband/Wife ☐ Parent ☐ Brother/Sister ☐ Child

2. Are you related by adoption?
☐ Yes ☒ No

3. Did you gain residence through adoption?
☐ Yes ☒ No

B. Information about you

1. Name (Family Name in CAPS) (First) (Middle)
FINN Paul L.

2. Address (Number and Street) (Apartment Number)
26-28 115th Street
(Town or City) (State/Country) (ZIP/Postal Code)
Queens NY 10000

3. Place of Birth (Town or City) (State/Country)
Queens NY

4. Date of Birth (Mo/Day/Yr)
5/15/61

5. Sex
☒ Male ☐ Female

4. Marital Status
☒ Married ☐ Single ☐ Widowed ☐ Divorced

7. Other Names Used (including maiden name)
None

8. Date and Place of Present Marriage (if married)
8/18/98 New York, NY

9. Social Security Number
000-00-0001

10. Alien Registration Number (if any)
N/A

11. Names of Prior Husbands/Wives
None N/A

12. Date(s) Marriage(s) Ended
N/A

13. If you are a U.S. citizen, complete the following:
My citizenship was acquired through (check one)
☒ Birth in the U.S.
☐ Naturalization (Give number of certificate, date and place it was issued)
☐ Parents
Have you obtained a certificate of citizenship in your own name?
☐ Yes ☐ No
If "Yes", give number of certificate, date and place it was issued

14a. If you are a lawful permanent resident alien, complete the following:
Date and place of admission for, or adjustment to, lawful permanent residence, and class of admission:

14b. Did you gain permanent residence status through marriage to a United States citizen or lawful permanent resident? ☐ Yes ☐ No

C. Information about your alien relative

1. Name (Family Name in CAPS) (First) (Middle)
FINN Leslie

2. Address (Number and Street) (Apartment Number)
26-28 115th Street
(Town or City) (State/Country) (ZIP/Postal Code)
Queens NY 10000

3. Place of Birth (Town or City) (State/Country)
Manchester U.K.

4. Date of Birth (Mo/Day/Yr)
10/19/1961

5. Sex
☐ Male ☒ Female

4. Marital Status
☒ Married ☐ Single ☐ Widowed ☐ Divorced

7. Other Names Used (including maiden name)
Leslie Spencer

8. Date and Place of Present Marriage (if married)
8/18/98 New York, NY

9. Social Security Number
111-11-1111

10. Alien Registration Number (if any)
N/A

11. Names of Prior Husbands/Wives
Charles Windsor

12. Date(s) Marriage(s) Ended
4/4/96 London, UK

13. Has your relative ever been in the U.S.?
☒ Yes ☐ No

14. If your relative is currently in the U.S., complete the following: He or she last arrived as a (visitor, student, stowaway, without inspection, etc.)
H-1B

Arrival/Departure Record (I-94) Number
123-1234567

Date Arrived (Month/Day/Year)
1/15/97

Date authorized stay expired, or will expire as shown on Form I-94 or I-95
1/14/2000

15. Name and Address of Present Employer (if any)
Computer Inc.

Date this employment began (Month/Day/Year)
1/18/97

16. Has your relative ever been under immigration proceedings?
☐ Yes ☒ No Where __________ When __________
☐ Exclusion ☐ Deportation ☐ Rescission ☐ Judicial Proceedings

INITIAL RECEIPT	RESUBMITTED	RELOCATED		COMPLETED		
		Rec'd	Sent	Approved	Denied	Returned

Form I-130 (Rev. 4/11/91) Y

(CONTINUED)

(continued) Information about your alien relative

... wife and all children of your relative (if your relative is your husband/wife, list only his or her children).

(Country of Birth)

U.K.

Daughter 10/3/00 U.S.A.

... United States where your relative intends to live

(Town or City) (State)

NY

(Province) (Country) (Phone Number)

London England U.K.

... native alphabet is other than Roman letters, write his or her name and address abroad in the native alphabet:

(Town or City) (Province) (Country)

(Country) (Month) (Year) To (Month) (Year)

... 115th Street Queens NY 8/1/98 Present

21. Check the appropriate box below and give the information required for the box you checked:

☐ Your relative will apply for a visa abroad at the American Consulate in ______ (City) (Country)

☒ Your relative is in the United States and will apply for adjustment of status to that of a lawful permanent resident in the office of the Immigration and Naturalization Service at New York, NY (City) (State) If your relative is not eligible for adjustment of status, he or she will apply for a visa abroad at the American Consulate in ______ (City) (Country)

(Designation of a consulate outside the country of your relative's last residence does not guarantee acceptance for processing by that consulate. Acceptance is at the discretion of the designated consulate.)

D. Other Information

1. If separate petitions are also being submitted for other relatives, give names of each and relationship.

None

2. Have you ever filed a petition for this or any other alien before? ☐ Yes ☒ No

If "Yes", give name, place and date of filing, and result.

Warning: The INS investigates claimed relationships and verifies the validity of documents. The INS seeks criminal prosecutions when family relationships are falsified to obtain visas.

Penalties: You may, by law be imprisoned for not more than five years, or fined $250,000, or both, for entering into a marriage contract for the purpose of evading any provision of the immigration laws and you may be fined up to $10,000 or imprisoned up to five years or both, for knowingly and willfully falsifying or concealing a material fact or using any false documents in submitting this petition.

Your Certification: I certify, under penalty of perjury under the laws of the United States of America, that the foregoing is true and correct. Furthermore, I authorize the release of any information from my records which the Immigration and Naturalization Service needs to determine eligibility for the benefit that I am seeking.

(Signature) ______ (Date) ______ (Phone Number) 718 555-5555

Signature of Person Preparing Form if Other than Above

I declare that I prepared this document at the request of the person above and that it is based on all information if which I have any knowledge.

Print Name ______ (Address) ______ (Signature) ______ (Date) ______

G-28 ID Number ______

Volag Number ______

SAMPLE FORM I-360 PETITION FOR AMERASIAN, WIDOW, OR SPECIAL IMMIGRANT

U.S. Department of Justice
Immigration and Naturalization Service

OMB No. 1115-01
Petition for Amerasian, Widow or Special Immigra

START HERE - Please Type or Print

Part 1. Information about person or organization filing this petition.

(Individuals should use the top name line; organizations should use the second line.) If you are a self-petitioning spouse or child and do not want INS to send notices about this petition to your home, you may show an alternate mailing address here. If you are filing for yourself and do not want to use an alternate mailing address, skip to part 2.

Family Name LOPEZ	Given Name Maria	Middle Initial
Company or Organization Name		
Address - C/O		
Street Number and Name 2500 Wilshire Blvd		Apt. #
City LA	State or Province CA	
Country USA		ZIP/Postal Code 25617
U.S. Social Security # 111-11-1100	A # 56 566 566	IRS Tax # *(if any)*

Part 2. Classification Requested (check one):

a. ☐ Amerasian
b. ☐ Widow(er) of a U.S. citizen who died within the past 2 years
c. ☐ Special Immigrant Juvenile
d. ☐ Special Immigrant Religious Worker
e. ☐ Special Immigrant based on employment with the Panama Canal Company, Canal Zone, Government or U.S. Government in the Canal Zone
f. ☐ Special Immigrant Physician
g. ☐ Special Immigrant International Organization Employee or family member
h. ☐ Special Immigrant Armed Forces Member
i. ☒ Self-Petitioning Spouse of Abusive U.S. Citizen or Lawful Permanent Resident
j. ☐ Self-Petitioning Child of Abusive U.S. Citizen or Lawful Permanent Resident
k. ☐ Other, Explain: ______________________

Part 3. Information about the person this petition is for.

Family Name LOPEZ	Given Name Maria	Middle Initial
Address - C/O		
Street Number and Name 2500 Wilshire Blvd.		Apt. #
City LA	State or Province CA	
Country USA		ZIP/Postal Code 25617
Date of Birth *(Month/Day/Year)* 06/04/1970	Country of Birth Mexico	
U.S. Social Security # *(if any)* 111-11-1100	A # *(if any)* 56-566-566	

Marital Status: ☐ Single ☐ Married ☒ Divorced ☐ Widowed

Complete the items below if this person is in the United States:

Date of Arrival *(Month/Day/Year)* 6/15/94	I-94# # N/A 326
Current Nonimmigrant Status EWI	Expires on *(Month/Day/Year)* N/A

FOR INS USE ONLY

Returned	Receipt
Resubmitted	
Reloc Sent	
Reloc Rec'd	
☐ Petitioner/ Applicant Interviewed	
☐ Beneficiary Interviewed	

☐ I-485 Filed Concurrently
☐ Bene "A" File Reviewed

Classification

Consulate

Priority Date

Remarks:

Action Block

To be completed by Attorney or Representative, if any

☐ Fill in box if G-28 is attached to represent the applicant

VOLAG #

ATTY State License #

SAMPLE FORM I-360 PETITION FOR AMERASIAN, WIDOW, OR SPECIAL IMMIGRANT (CONTINUED)

Part 4. Processing Information.

Below give the United States Consulate you want notified if this petition is approved and if any requested adjustment of status cannot be granted.

American Consulate: City Mexico City	Country Mexico

If you gave a United States address in Part 3, print the person's foreign address below. If his/her native alphabet does not use Roman letters, print his/her name and foreign address in the native alphabet.

Name	Address

Sex of the person this petition is for.	☐ Male	☒ Female
Are you filing any other petitions or application with this one?	☒ No	☐ Yes (How many? ______)
Is the person this petition is for in exclusion of deportation proceedings?	☒ No	☐ Yes (Explain on a separate sheet of paper)
Has the person this petition is for ever worked in the U.S. without permission?	☒ No	☐ Yes (Explain on a separate sheet of paper)
Is an application for adjustment of status attached to this petition?	☒ No	☐ Yes

Part 5. Complete only if filing for an Amerasian.

Section A. Information about the mother of the Amerasian.

Family Name	Given Name	Middle Initial

Living? ☐ No (Give date of death ______) ☐ Yes (Complete address line below) ☐ Unknown (attach a full explanation)

Address

Section B. Information about the father of the Amerasian. If possible, attach a notarized statement from the father regarding parentage. Explain on separate paper any question you cannot fully answer in the space provided on this form.

Family Name	Given Name	Middle Initial
Date of Birth (Month/Day/Year)	Country of Birth	

Living? ☐ No (Give date of death ______) ☐ Yes (Complete address line below) ☐ Unknown (attach a full explanation)

Home Address

Home Phone #	Work Phone #

At the time the Amerasian was conceived:

☐ The father was in the military (indicated branch of service below - and give service number here): ______

☐ Army ☐ Air Force ☐ Navy ☐ Marine Corps ☐ Coast Guard

☐ The father was a civilian employee abroad. Attach a list of names and addresses of the organizations which employed him at that time.

☐ The father was not in the military, and was not a civilian employed abroad. *(Attach a full explanation of the circumstances.)*

Part 6. Complete only if filing for a Special Immigrant Juvenile Court Dependent.

Section A. Information about the Juvenile.

List any other names used.

Answer the following questions regarding the person this petition is for. If you answer "no" explain on a separate sheet of paper.

Is he or she still dependent upon the juvenile court or still legally committed to or under the custody of an agency or department of a state?	☐ No	☐ Yes
Does he/she continue to be eligible for long term foster care?	☐ No	☐ Yes

Continued on next page.

Part 7. Complete only if filing as a Widow/Widower, a Self-petitioning Spouse of an Abuser, or as a Self-petitioning Child of an Abuser

Section A. Information about the U.S. citizen husband or wife who died or about the U.S. citizen or lawful permanent resident abuser.

Family Name LOPEZ	Given Name Juan	Middle Initial
Date of Birth *(Month/Day/Year)* 15/5/69	Country of Birth USA	Date of Death *(Month/Day/Year)*

He or she is now, or was at time of death on *(check one)*

- ☒ U.S. Citizen born in the United States.
- ☐ U.S. Citizen born abroad to U.S. citizen parents.
- ☐ U.S. Citizen through Naturalization *(Show A #)* ______
- ☐ U.S. lawful permanent resident *(Show A #)* ______
- ☐ Other, explain ______

Section B. Additional Information about you.

How many times have you been married?	How many times was the person in Section A married?	Give the date and place you and person in section A were married. *(If you are a self-petitioning child, write: "N/A")*
1	1	9/7/98

When did you live with the person named in Section A? From *(Month/Year)* 12/15/97 until *(Month/Year)* 8/5/99

If you are filing as a widow/widower, were you legally separated at the time of the U.S. citizens's death? ☐ No ☐ Yes, *(attach explanation).*

Give the last address at which you lived together with the person named in Section A, and show the last date you lived together with that person at that address:

100 Beverly Place LA, CA 6/5/99

If you are filing as a self-petitioning spouse, have any of your children filed separate self-petitions? ☒ No ☐ Yes *(show child(ren)'s full names):*

Part 8. Information about the children and spouse of the person this petition is for.

A widow/widower or a self-petitioning spouse of an abusive citizen or lawful permanent resident should also list the children of the deceased spouse or of the abuser.

A. Family Name	Given Name	Middle Initial	Date of Birth (Month/Day/Year)
Country of Birth	Relationship ☐ Spouse ☐ Child		A #
B. Family Name	Given Name	Middle Initial	Date of Birth (Month/Day/Year)
Country of Birth	Relationship ☐ Child		A #
C. Family Name	Given Name	Middle Initial	Date of Birth (Month/Day/Year)
Country of Birth	Relationship ☐ Child		A #
D. Family Name	Given Name	Middle Initial	Date of Birth (Month/Day/Year)
Country of Birth	Relationship ☐ Child		A #
E. Family Name	Given Name	Middle Initial	Date of Birth (Month/Day/Year)
Country of Birth	Relationship ☐ Child		A #
F. Family Name	Given Name	Middle Initial	Date of Birth (Month/Day/Year)
Country of Birth	Relationship ☐ Child		A #

SAMPLE FORM I-360 PETITION FOR AMERASIAN, WIDOW, OR SPECIAL IMMIGRANT (CONTINUED)

G. Family Name	Given Name	Middle Initial	Date of Birth (Month/Day/Year)
Country of Birth	Relationship ☐ Child		A #
H. Family Name	Given Name	Middle Initial	Date of Birth (Month/Day/Year)
Country of Birth	Relationship ☐ Child		A #

Part 9. Signature. *Read the information on penalties in the instructions before completing this part. If you are going to file this petition at an INS office in the United States, sign below. If you are going to file it at a U.S. consulate or INS office overseas, sign in front of a U.S. INS or consular official.*

I certify, or, if outside the United States, I swear or affirm, under penalty of perjury under the laws of the United States of America, that this petition, and the evidence submitted with it, is all true and correct. If filing this on behalf of an organization, I certify that I am empowered to do so by that organization. I authorize the release of any information from my records, or from the petitioning organization's records, which the Immigration and Naturalization Service needs to determine eligibility for the benefit being sought.

Signature Maria LOPEZ		Date
Signature of INS or Consular Official	Print Name	Date

Please Note: If you do not completely fill out this form, or fail to submit required documentation listed in the instructions, then the person(s) filed for may not be found eligible for a requested benefit, and it may have to be denied.

Part 10. Signature of person preparing form if other than above. (sign below)

I declare that I prepared this application at the request of the above person and it is based on all information of which I have knowledge.

Signature	Print Your Name	Date
Firm Name and Address		

F. IMMIGRATION MARRIAGE FRAUD AMENDMENTS OF 1986

As a result of what had been perceived as widespread fraud in the area of "sham marriages" designed to confer immigration benefits upon foreign nationals, regulations were formulated to address these concerns and make sure that marriages were in fact legitimate ones. Prior to these regulations, a widespread practice in the United States took place whereby foreign nationals contracted with United States citizens to enter into "sham marriages" designed exclusively to confer immigration benefits upon the foreign national seeking permanent residence. This type of fraud is a criminal offense in the United States. Therefore, in order to obtain permanent resident status based upon marriage to a United States citizen or a Lawful Permanent Resident, the foreign national and his or her spouse must provide evidence that their marriage is legitimate and was not entered into for the purpose of obtaining immigration benefits.

It is also worth noting that a foreign national spouse is not initially granted resident status of a permanent nature in the United States upon the filing of an immediate relative petition. Rather, upon proof of the spousal relationship, a foreign national will be granted **Conditional** Permanent Resident Status. The rights, privileges, responsibilities and duties that apply to all other permanent residents apply equally to conditional permanent residents. A conditional permanent resident is eligible to file petitions on behalf of qualifying relatives and to reside permanently in the United States in accordance with the immigration laws.

To become a **Permanent Resident** of the United States free from any conditions, the foreign national must remain married for two years, and a joint petition to remove the condition must be filed by the conditional resident and his or her United States citizen or legal permanent resident spouse. The petition to remove the conditions must be filed within the ninety days before the second anniversary of foreign national's grant of conditional resident status. The petition to remove the conditions may only be filed after the ninety-day period if the foreign national establishes to the satisfaction of the INS that there was good cause for failure to file or the foreign national is requesting a waiver of the joint filing requirement. The waiver of the joint filing requirement will be discussed in detail later in this chapter.

Marriages Deemed Proper

Marriages between parties related by blood are restricted. Similarly, marriages that cannot be upheld because an impediment stands in the way of their formation are also invalid. For example, this occurs when an individual has not secured a valid divorce decree prior to remarriage. Homosexual and incestuous marriages are not recognized for immigration purposes.

Common Law Marriages

If the marriage which is the basis for the immediate relative petition took place in the United States, the validity of the marriage will be considered under the appropriate State law (of one of the fifty states in the United States) where the marriage was entered into and where both parties where present. Therefore, common law marriages are acceptable for immigration purposes if they were valid under the state law where the marriage took place and recognized as being fully equivalent in every respect to a traditional legal marriage, i.e. it bestows all of the same legal rights and duties as a traditional marriage. An official verification or a legal briefing verifying full marital rights, including inheritance rights, is acceptable proof of the validity of such marriage.

A foreign national is a "spouse " for immigration purposes if the marriage has not been terminated, even though the parties are separated. In order for a marriage to be considered valid, the finality of the beneficiary's or petitioner's prior divorce must be valid. If, however, the divorce decree is issued after the marriage with the petitioner, the marriage will not be upheld, since it preceded the divorce.

Types of Proof Needed to Prove Marriage not a Sham Marriage Entered into for Immigration Benefits

- Wedding pictures or other family photos;
- Evidence of property owned together;
- Lease;
- Tax Returns;
- Letters from employers listing spouse as beneficiary of life insurance policies;
- Mortgage for Home;
- Joint Consumer Loans;
- Joint Credit Cards;
- Joint Checking and/or Savings Account; and
- Any other comparable evidence.

G. PETITION TO REMOVE CONDITIONS OF RESIDENCE

A foreign national granted conditional permanent resident status through marriage to a United States citizen or permanent resident must file the "Petition to Remove the Conditions on Residence" (Form I-751) within ninety days of the second anniversary of the date the conditional resident status was granted. The petition to remove the conditions must be filed jointly by the conditional permanent resident and his or her spouse through whom the conditional status was acquired by marriage. The joint filing requirement may be waived in certain circumstances that will be discussed later in this chapter.

The petition to remove the conditions must be filed within the ninety day time period regardless of the amount of physical presence the conditional permanent resident spouse has accumulated in the United States. The petition may also be filed even if the conditional permanent resident is not present in the United States at the time of filing. Regulations require the conditional permanent resident to be present in the United States if the INS requests an interview in connection with the petition to remove the conditions.

Initial Evidence Required for Petition

Alien Registration Card

The petition to remove the conditions on residence must be filed with a copy of the foreign national's alien registration card, and with a copy of the alien registration card of any of the conditional resident children included in the petition.

In order to have the conditional status removed the conditional permanent resident must prove that the marriage upon which status is based was entered into in "good faith" and was not entered into for the purposes of circumventing immigration laws. The documentation required to demonstrate the "good faith" of the marriage may include as much evidence as possible detailing the circumstances of the relationship from the date of the marriage to the date the petition to remove the conditions is filed. If the marriage has ended prior to the filing of the petition to remove the conditions evidence should be submitted detailing the circumstances surrounding the end of the marriage. The documents should cover as much of the time period that has elapsed since the inception of the marriage.

Documents to Prove the Relationship Necessary to Remove Conditional Resident Status

- Documentation showing joint ownership of property;
- Lease showing joint tenancy of a common residence;
- Documentation showing commingling of financial resources;
- Birth certificates of children born to the marriage;
- Affidavits of third parties having knowledge of the bona fides of the marital relationship; or
- Other documentation establishing that the marriage was not entered into in order to evade the immigration laws of the United States.

Waiver of Joint Filing Requirement

If a spouse seeks a waiver of the joint filing requirements he or she may file the petition to remove the conditions at any time before the second anniversary of obtaining conditional status. In addition, he or she may apply after the two-year anniversary date has passed but before Immigration Judge enters a final order of removal.

A waiver of the joint filing requirements is available when:

- The petitioning spouse is deceased.

- The removal of the conditional permanent resident would result in **extreme hardship** to himself or herself, to a dependent child, or to any subsequent non-U.S. citizen spouse. The conditional permanent resident filing for the waiver bears the burden of establishing extreme hardship.

- The marriage upon which his or her status was based was entered into good faith by the conditional permanent resident but the marriage was terminated by divorce or annulment, and the conditional permanent resident was not at fault in failing to file a timely petition. The conditional permanent resident must prove that the marriage has ended either through divorce or annulment.

- The qualifying marriage was entered into in good faith by the conditional resident but during the marriage the foreign national spouse or child was battered by or subject to extreme cruelty committed by the citizen or permanent resident spouse or parent. The definition of battery and extreme cruelty for this provision is the same for self-petitions discussed earlier in this chapter. However, a conditional permanent resident may apply for a waiver of the joint filing requirement under this provision regardless of whether he or she is still married to the battering U.S. citizen of lawful permanent resident spouse.

Death of Spouse

If the conditional permanent resident is seeking a waiver of the joint filing requirement based upon the death of the petitioning spouse, a copy of the death certificate must also be submitted with the petition.

Termination of Marriage

If the conditional permanent resident is filing a waiver of the joint filing requirement because the marriage has been terminated, the petition must also include a copy of the divorce decree or other document terminating or annulling the marriage.

Battering or Extreme Mental Cruelty

A conditional permanent resident filing for a waiver of the joint filing requirement because he or she, or the conditional resident child was battered or subjected to extreme mental cruelty, should submit the following documentation with the petition:

- Evidence of the physical abuse, such as expert testimony in the form of reports and affidavits from police, judges, medical personnel, school officials and social service agency personnel, and original affidavits.

- Evidence of the extreme mental cruelty, and an original evaluation by a professional recognized by the INS as an expert in the filed. These experts include clinical social workers, psychologists and psychiatrists. A clinical social worker who is not licensed only because the State in which he or she practices does not provide for licensing, is considered a licensed professional recognized by the INS if he or she is included in the Register of Clinical Social Workers published by the National Association of Social Workers or is certified by the American Board of Examiners in Clinical Social Work. Each evaluation must contain the professional's full name, professional address and license number. The evaluation must also identify the licensing, certifying or registering authority.

- A copy of the divorce decree if the marriage was terminated by divorce on grounds of physical abuse or mental cruelty.

SAMPLE FORM I-751, PETITION TO REMOVE THE CONDITIONS ON RESIDENCE

U.S. Department of Justice
Immigration and Naturalization Service

OMB No. 1115-0145
Petition to Remove the Conditions on Residence

START HERE - Please Type or Print

Part 1. Information about you.

Family Name FINN	Given Name Leslie	Middle Initial

Address - C/O:

Street Number and Name 26-28 115th Street	Apt. #
City Queens	State or Province NY
Country USA	Zip/Postal Code 10000
Date of Birth (month/day/year) 10/19/1961	Country of Birth U.K.
Social Security # 111-11-1111	A # N/A
Conditional residence expires on (month/day/year) 12/1/01	

Mailing address if different from residence in C/O:

Street Number and Name	Apt. #
City	State or Province
Country	Zip/Postal Code

Part 2. Basis for Petition (check one).

a. ☒ My conditional residence is based on my marriage to a U.S. citizen or permanent resident, and we are filing this petition together.

b. ☐ I am a child who entered as conditional permanent resident and I am unable to be included in a Joint Petition to Remove the Conditional Basis of Alien's Permanent Residence (Form I-751) filed by my parents.

My conditional residence is based on my marriage to a U.S. citizen or permanent resident, but I am unable to file a joint petition and I request a waiver because: (check one)

c. ☐ My spouse is deceased.

d. ☐ I entered into the marriage in good faith, but the marriage was terminated through divorce/annulment.

e. ☐ I am a conditional resident spouse who entered into the marriage in good faith, or I am a conditional resident child, who has been battered or subject to extreme mental cruelty by my citizen or permanent resident spouse or parent.

f. ☐ The termination of my status and deportation from the United States would result in an extreme hardship.

Part 3. Additional Information about you.

Other names used (including maiden name): Leslie Spencer	Telephone # 718 555-5555
Date of Marriage 8/18/98	Place of Marriage New York, NY

If your spouse is deceased, give the date of death (month/day/year)

Are you in deportation or exclusion proceedings? ☐ Yes ☒ No

Was a fee paid to anyone other than an attorney in connection with this petition? ☐ Yes ☒ No

FOR INS USE ONLY

Returned	Receipt
Resubmitted	
Reloc Sent	
Reloc Rec'd	
☐ Applicant Interviewed	

Remarks

Action

To be completed by Attorney or Representative, if any

☐ Fill in box if G-28 is attached to represent the applicant

VOLAG#

ATTY State License #

 Continued on back.

Part 3. Additional Information about you. (cont'd)

Since becoming a conditional resident, have you ever been arrested, cited, charged, indicted, convicted, fined or imprisoned for breaking or violating any law or ordinance (excluding traffic regulations), or committed any crime for which you were not arrested?	☐ Yes ☒ No
If you are married, is this a different marriage than the one through which conditional residence status was obtained?	☐ Yes ☒ No
Have you resided at any other address since you became a permanent resident?	☐ Yes ☒ No (If yes attach a list of all addresses and dates.)
Is your spouse currently serving or employed by the U.S. government and serving outside the U.S.?	☐ Yes ☒ No

Part 4. Information about the spouse or parent through whom you gained your conditional residence.

Family Name FINN	Given Name Paul	Middle Initial L.	Phone Number 718 555-5555
Address 26-28 115th Street	Queens	NY	10000
Date of Birth (month/day/year) 5/15/61	Social Security # 000-00-0001	A# N/A	

Part 5. Information about your children. *List all your children. Attach another sheet if necessary*

	Name	Date of Birth (month/day/year)	If in U.S., give A#, current immigration status and U.S. Address	Living with you?
1	Windsor Caitlin	7/31/87	CPR same as parent	☒ Yes ☐ No
2	Windsor Patrick	9/21/89	CPR same as parent	☒ Yes ☐ No
3	Windsor Katie	10/3/00	U.S. Citizen	☒ Yes ☐ No
4				☐ Yes ☐ No

Part 6. Complete if you are requesting a waiver of the joint filing petition requirement based on extreme mental cruelty.

Evaluator's ID Number: State: ☐☐ Number: ☐☐☐☐☐☐☐☐	Expires on (month/day/year)	Occupation
Last Name	First Name	Address

Part 7. Signature. *Read the information on penalties in the instructions before completing this section. If you checked block "a" in Part 2 your spouse must also sign below.*

I certify under penalty of perjury under the laws of the United States of America, that this petition, and the evidence submitted with it, is all true and correct. If conditional residence was based on a marriage, I further certify that the marriage was entered in accordance with the laws of the place where the marriage took place, and was not for the purpose of procuring an immigration benefit. I also authorize the release of any information from my records which the Immigration and Naturalization Service needs to determine eligibility for the benefit being sought.

Signature	Print Name Leslie FINN	Date
Signature of spouse	Print Name Paul FINN	Date

Please note: If you do not completely fill out this form, or fail to submit any required documents listed in the instructions, then you cannot be found eligible for the requested benefit, and this petition may be denied.

Part 8. Signature of person preparing form if other than above.

I declare that I prepared this form at the request of the above person and it is based on all information of which I have knowledge.

Signature	Print Name	Date
Firm Name and Address		

Form I-751 (Rev. 12-4-91)

PRACTICE POINTERS FOR COMPLETING FORM I-751

Petitioners should be aware that any statements made on Form I-751 that might be construed as inconsistent with a bona fide marriage might result in the INS requesting an interview.

Part 1: The conditional resident's address provided in this Part should be the same as the spouse's address provided in Part 4. If there is a legitimate reason why the spouses live separately (such as work related reasons) an explanation should be attached to the Petition.

Part 2: Box (a) should be checked if the couple is filing a joint petition.

Any child who was either admitted into the United States more than ninety days after his or her parents, or whose parents have died should check box (b).

Box (c), (d), (e) or (f) should be checked if the conditional resident is unable to file a joint petition and is requesting a waiver of that requirement. All pertinent documents regarding the waiver request should be attached to the Petition. Part 6 provides an additional waiver on grounds of "extreme mental cruelty." In that case, the conditional resident must provide an evaluation by a professional and attached the evaluation to the petition.

Failure to File Petition to Remove the Conditions

Failure to file the petition to remove the conditions within the ninety-day period will result in the automatic termination of conditional permanent resident status and the INS may initiate removal proceedings against the individual.

Effect of Filing Form I-751

Upon the receipt of a properly filed petition to remove the conditions the conditional permanent resident's status is extended until the INS adjudicates the petition. Upon filing the petition, the alien will receive a filing receipt that should be carried along with their alien registration card. If travel outside the United States is required during this time period, the presentation of the alien registration card along with the filing receipt will allow the alien to be readmitted. This filing receipt enables the alien to travel outside the United States and be readmitted for the period of status extension.

H. Family-Based or Employment-Based Immigrant Visa Petitions

As we have stressed throughout the course of this book, the best course of action to take when dealing with the INS is the path of least resistance. Therefore, when deciding how best to obtain permanent resident status in the United States, it is important to bear this factor in mind, as well as take into account the visa numbers available under each category.

For example, a foreign national may be eligible to immigrate to the United States on the basis of either an employment or a family relationship. If a foreign national is eligible to petition as an immediate relative spouse or as a priority worker under the first employment category, it might be more advantageous to petition on the basis of the employment-based visa. By choosing the latter course of action, and assuming visa number availability, the foreign national will enjoy the benefit of permanent residence without the condition that is attached when petitioning on the basis of a marriage to a United States citizen or permanent resident.

Alternatively, if the foreign national chooses to petition on the basis of his or her spousal relationship, he or she will be granted conditional permanent residence whose conditional nature will be removed only upon the filing of a "Petition to Remove the Conditions on Residence" Form I-751, two years after the initial grant of status.

Another point worth considering is that sons and daughters of foreign nationals granted conditional residence on the basis of marriage will be granted conditional derivative residence contingent upon the parent's status. Therefore, again it may be advisable to petition through the employment based immigrant process if this is a possible option.

I. **CONCLUSION**

The benefit of filing a family-based immigrant petition is that it allows the beneficiary to obtain permanent residence without the need to go through the labor certification process, as in some of the employment-based categories. This may ultimately save the potential immigrant time that he or she would otherwise have to wait while applying for labor certification. However, there are other backlogs for certain categories such as the second family-based category for spouses and children of legal permanent residents. Therefore, it is important to weigh the different immigration options available and consider which avenue will prove to be the most expedient.

Chapter Eleven
PENALTIES, BARS & RESTRICTIONS

A. INTRODUCTION

The Illegal Immigration Reform and Immigrant Responsibility Act of 1996 (IIRIRA) created startling and unprecedented new penalties for foreign nationals unlawfully present in the United States, and for nonimmigrants who overstay their authorized period of admission to the United States. In addition to creating new penalties, the 1996 Act toughened penalties and bars to admission already in existence in the immigration laws. These new and enhanced penalties have far-reaching consequences and in many cases create permanent bars to admission to the United States.

B. NONIMMIGRANT VISA OVERSTAYS

One of the most important changes made to the INA by the 1996 Act was the creation of section 222(g), popularly referred to as the "anti-consulate shopping" provision. Congress created section 222(g) in an effort to punish and deter foreign nationals from overstaying their authorized period of nonimmigrant stay in the United States.

A nonimmigrant is subject to section 222(g) if he or she remains in the United States past the authorized period of stay stamped on the I-94 card received at the time of last admission to the United States, or any extension of such status granted by the INS. This means, if a nonimmigrant overstays their period of authorized admission <u>even by one day</u>, the visa the nonimmigrant used to gain admission to the United States is automatically invalidated and void, and he or she will have to apply for a new visa in their home country. The statute does not differentiate between inadvertent and purposeful overstays. For the purposes of section 222(g) it does not matter why or how the nonimmigrant overstayed the period of authorized admission.

The foreign national may not be readmitted to the U.S. as a nonimmigrant unless he or she obtains a new visa in a consular office located in the country of the foreign national's nationality. If there is no consular office located in the foreign national's country of nationality the Secretary of State may designate another consular office to accept the nonimmigrant visa petition. All other foreign nationals subject to 222(g) may only obtain a new visa in a third country when the Department of State grants a waiver based on extraordinary circumstances.

<u>Who is Subject to Section 222(g)?</u>

Section 222(g) became effective on September 30, 1996 and applies to any foreign national seeking admission on or after that date. The statute voids visas issued before, on, or after September 30, 1996, regardless of whether the nonimmigrant remained in the United States beyond the period of stay authorized by the Attorney General before or after the enactment date of the statute.

For example, a foreign national issued a multiple, indefinite B-2 visa in 1994, is admitted to the United States for six months in 1995. During the 1995 trip, the foreign national remained in the United States beyond his I-94 expiration date. That foreign national is now subject to section 222(g) if he seeks to be readmitted with that B-2 visa on or after September 30, 1996, even though the period of overstay took place before the enactment date of 222(g). The harsh effects of section 222(g) apply to any nonimmigrant who the INS determines has overstayed any period of authorized admission, even if the period of overstay took place years before section 222(g) was enacted.

There are, however, certain individuals who are not subject to the draconian consequences of section 222(g) by virtue of the type of status and admission they have in the United States. In addition, certain nonimmigrants are not subject to 222(g) until the INS or an Immigration Judge officially finds that they have violated nonimmigrant status.

The following classes of foreign nationals are **not subject** to Section 222(g) by virtue of the type of status they hold in the United States:

Participants in the Visa Waiver Pilot Program are not subject to section 222(g) because they have not entered the United States with visas. Foreign nationals who are eligible to participate in the visa waiver program may be admitted to the United States at ports of entry as visitors for business (B-1) or visitors for pleasure (B-2). Eligible foreign nationals may be admitted to the U.S. for up to ninety days without having to first obtain a nonimmigrant visa at an U.S. consular post. See Chapter Two for a more detailed discussion of the Visa Waiver Program and a list of participating countries.

Entrants under other waiver provisions are also not subject to section 222(g) by virtue of the fact that they have been admitted to the United States without having to present a valid visa. If there is no underlying visa, the consequences of section 222(g) can not be triggered. For example, Canadian nationals seeking to enter the U.S. under most nonimmigrant categories do not have to obtain a visa prior to seeking admission to the United States.

Individuals who enter the U.S. without inspection (EWI) are not subject to section 222(g) because they do not possess a valid visa and they have not been admitted to the United States for a date certain. Individuals who enter without inspection have actually bypassed the official process of admission and are deemed to be unlawfully present in the United States. Individuals who are unlawfully present in the U.S. are subject to other penalty provisions of the INA that will be discussed in greater detail later in this chapter.

Individuals who fall out of status for some other reason other than an overstay violation, such as unauthorized employment, do not trigger the effects of section 222(g) because they do not meet the statutory definition. In order to trigger section 222(g) the nonimmigrant must overstay the period of authorized admission stamped on the I-94 card. Status violators will begin to accrue periods of unlawful presence from the date of status violation but they are not subject to section 222(g) until they overstay the period of authorized admission.

Nonimmigrants admitted to the United States under Duration of Status (D/S) status (e.g. I, F, M, J) are not subject to section 222(g) because they have not been admitted until a specific date. Nonimmigrants admitted under D/S status are instead authorized to remain until the completion of the authorized activity. Nonimmigrants admitted under D/S status will not be subject to section 222(g) unless the INS or an Immigration Judge officially finds a violation of status has occurred.

In addition to the class of individuals described above, foreign government officials and representatives of international organizations applying for the following nonimmigrant visas are **not subject** to section 222(g) by operation of law: A-1, A-2; C-2, C-3; G-1, G-2, G-3, G-4; NATO-1, NATO-2, NATO-3, NATO-4, NATO-5, and NATO-6.

Foreign Nationals in Possession of More than one Nonimmigrant Visa

When a foreign national is in possession of more than one nonimmigrant visa, the nonimmigrant visa under which the foreign national was admitted and overstayed becomes automatically void and is cancelled pursuant to section 222(g). The foreign national may only be readmitted to the United States on a visa issued in his or her country of nationality, unless an extraordinary circumstances exception is granted. While the other nonimmigrant visa in the foreign national's possession does not become automatically void, it may not be used for admission if it was not issued in the foreign national's country of nationality. Therefore, if the other nonimmigrant visa was not issued in the country of the alien's nationality it will also be automatically voided.

Strategies for Avoiding Section 222(g)

The best strategy for nonimmigrants to employ to avoid the harsh consequences of section 222(g) is to be constantly aware of the date stamped on the I-94 card received at the time of each and every admission to the United States. For nonimmigrants who travel frequently and even for those who do not, it is critical that they do not to overstay the date stamped on the I-94 card, even by one day. Nonimmigrants who travel frequently have the advantage of receiving a new period of admission at the time of each re-entry. However, if they do not keep track of each new period of admission they may inadvertently overstay. Nonimmigrants who rarely travel abroad often unintentionally stay past their date of authorized admission because they do not keep track of the dated stamped on the I-94 card. For instance, the accompanying spouse and children of an E nonimmigrant may unintentionally stay past the authorized period of admission because they confuse the date stamped on the I-94 card with the date of visa expiration.

To avoid triggering section 222(g), all non-exempt nonimmigrants and their accompanying spouses and children should timely file for extensions of stay or leave by the last day of authorized stay. If the individual's underlying visa remains valid, he or she may travel outside the United States before the period of admission ends and receive a I-94 card with a new period of admission at United States port of entry.

Who is Eligible for a Waiver of Section 222(g)?

All individuals subject to section 222(g), who leave the United States and seek new nonimmigrant visas, must apply for nonimmigrant visas at the American Consulate located in the country of their nationality. If there is no American Consulate in the country of nationality, individuals subject to section 222(g) may make nonimmigrant visa applications at a consulate designated by the Secretary of State. The State Department has also ruled that foreign nationals with dual nationality subject to section 222(g) must apply in the country of residence.

Certain other individuals subject to 222(g) are eligible to apply for new nonimmigrant visas at a third country consulate if the Secretary of State finds extraordinary circumstances exist.

Extraordinary Circumstances

The Secretary of State is authorized to permit an individual subject to section 222(g) to apply at third country consular post for a new nonimmigrant visa if she finds that "extraordinary circumstances" exist. A request for an extraordinary circumstance exemption must be made to the adjudicating consular officer in the third country. If the consular officer accepts the waiver request, the request will be forwarded to the Visa Office for final determination. Individual waiver requests based on extraordinary circumstances are decided on a case-by-case basis.

Department of State regulations provide that extraordinary circumstances may be found where compelling humanitarian or national interests exist or where necessary for the effective administration of the immigration laws. Extraordinary circumstances will not be found upon the basis of convenience or financial burden to the foreign national, the foreign national's relative, or the foreign national's employer.

In addition to individual waiver requests, the Secretary of State may also grant blanket waivers to foreign nationals subject to 222(g) based on extraordinary circumstance if they can meet pre-established requirements.

The Department of State has ruled a foreign national whose current residence is in a foreign country other than the country of their nationality is eligible for a blanket waiver if he or she applies for a new visa in the country of residence and not in some other third country.

Additionally, certain foreign medical graduates who receive a waiver of the two year foreign residence requirement (see Chapter Seven) are eligible for a blanket exception if the waiver is sought by an interested U.S. government agency or a State Department of Public Health in connection with an application for an H-1B visa.

Finally, applicants for A-1, A-2, C-2, C-3, G-1, G-2, G-3, G-4, NATO-1, NATO-2, NATO-3, NATO-4, NATO-5, and NATO-6 are eligible for the blanket extraordinary circumstance exemption.

Nonimmigrant Visa Waiver From the INS

Foreign nationals who arrive at U.S. ports of entry with a visa that has become automatically void under section 222(g) may apply to the INS for a waiver under section 212(d)(4) of the Immigration and Nationality Act. This waiver is available for foreign nationals who seek admission to the United States who do not possess valid nonimmigrant visas. This waiver may only be used in limited circumstances to ameliorate the effects of section 222(g).

To be eligible for this waiver the Attorney General and the Secretary of State must act jointly when the following circumstances exist:

- Unforeseen emergency in individual cases;
- Reciprocity with respect to nationals of foreign contiguous territory of adjacent islands and residents having a common nationality with those nationals; or
- In the case of individuals proceeding in immediate and continuous transit through the United States under contracts authorized under the immigration laws.

Waiver applications are accepted and reviewed on a case-by-case basis at the discretion of the inspecting officer. To apply for a waiver, the foreign national must file Form I-193 (Application for a Waiver of Passport and/or Visa), with a designated officer, and pay the required fee. If a foreign national is not eligible for a waiver at the time of admission or the waiver request is denied, he or she will be subject to expedited removal. The foreign national may be given the opportunity to withdraw the application for admission before he or she is officially placed under expedited removal proceedings.

C. THREE AND TEN YEAR BARS OF ADMISSIBILITY:

"UNLAWFUL PRESENCE"

Congress, in the 1996 Act created new bars to admissibility for foreign nationals who remain "unlawfully present" in the United States for specified periods of time. The bars for unlawful presence are popularly referred to as the three and ten year bars to admissibility. The unlawful presence provisions went into effect on April 1, 1997. No time spent in unlawful presence before April 1, 1997 may be used to trigger the three and ten year bars.

A foreign national unlawfully present in the United States for a period of more than 180 days but less than one year, who voluntarily departed the United States is ineligible for readmission to the U.S. for three years from the date of departure.

A foreign national unlawfully present in the United States for one year or more, who departs or is removed from the U.S. is inadmissible for 10 years from the date of departure or removal.

For purposes of the ten-year bar it does not matter whether the individual departed voluntarily from the United States or was deported or removed after formal proceedings. Individuals who are unlawfully present in the United States are not subject to the three and ten year bars until they depart the United States and attempt to return before the statutory period of inadmissibility has expired.

A foreign national is statutorily defined as "unlawfully present" if the individual is present in the United states after the expiration of the period of stay authorized by the Attorney General or is present in the United States without being admitted or paroled.

Generally, three categories of foreign nationals are subject to the penalties stemming from unlawful presence in the United States:

- Individuals who enter without inspection (EWI);
- Individuals who overstay the date on the I-94 card (visa overstays); and
- Individuals who are determined by the INS or an Immigration Judge to have violated the terms of stay (status violators).

Statutory Exceptions to Three and Ten Year Bars

The following classes of foreign nationals are statutorily exempt from acquiring periods of unlawful presence for purposes of the three and ten year bars:

- **Minors:** Any time spent in unlawful presence under the age of 18 does not count toward calculation of the three and ten year bars.

- **Lawful Permanent Residents:** are not subject to the three and ten year bars.

- **Asylees:** no period of time in which an individual has a bona fide application for asylum pending may be taken into account in calculating periods of unlawful presence, unless the applicant for asylum engaged in unauthorized employment.

- **Battered Women and Children:** Battered women and children are not subject to the three-year bar if they meet the statutory definition of a battered wife or child. (See Chapter Ten for a full discussion of battered spouse and children provisions.)

- **Nonimmigrants Admitted Under Duration of Stay (D/S) Status**: unlawful presence does not accrue for nonimmigrants admitted under D/S Status until the INS or an Immigration Judge makes a determination that the nonimmigrant has violated status.

Tolling of Unlawful Presence

One of the three major classes of individuals subject to the bar of admissibility based on unlawful presence are individuals who overstay the date of admission stamped on the I-94 card. Visa overstays, as discussed earlier in this chapter, are subject to the penalties of section 222(g). In addition, foreign nationals who overstay the period of admission also begin to accrue unlawful presence and may trigger the three and ten year bars after departure from the United States. However, for purposes of the three year bar, individuals who are admitted or paroled may suspend the period of unlawful presence for up to 120 days pending a timely "nonfrivilous" application for change or extension of status. Foreign nationals are only eligible for the suspension of unlawful presence if they have not engaged in unauthorized employment. The application for extension or change of status must be made prior to the expiration of status. Tolling is only available for suspension of the three-year bar and has no effect on accrual of time against the ten-year bar of admissibility.

Waiver of the Three and Ten Year Bar:

Extreme Hardship

A foreign national may apply for a waiver of the three and ten-year bars if he or she is the spouse or child of a United States citizen or lawful permanent resident (LPR) and the refusal of the foreign national's admission would result in extreme hardship to the qualifying U.S. citizen or LPR relative. The 1996 Act does not define extreme hardship, however, the term "extreme hardship" can be found in other immigration contexts.

To apply for a waiver based on extreme hardship the foreign national must file Form I-601 (Application for Waiver of Grounds of Excludability) and the applicable fee. The waiver can not be filed while the individual is in the United States because the unlawful presence bar is not triggered until the individual departs the United States. Waiver requests are decided on a case-by-case basis and are subject to the complete discretion of the Attorney General. The Attorney General's decision is not subject to judicial review and may not be appealed.

Nonimmigrants subject to the exclusion based on unlawful presence are eligible to apply for a discretionary waiver of inadmissibility pursuant section 212(d)(3) of the Immigration and Nationality Act.

U.S. Department of Justice
Immigration and Naturalization Service

OMB No. 1115-0048

Application for Waiver of Grounds of Excludability

DO NOT WRITE IN THIS BLOCK

☐ 212 (a) (1) ☐ 212 (a) (10) Fee Stamp
☐ 212 (a) (3) ☐ 212 (a) (12)
☐ 212 (a) (6) ☐ 212 (a) (19)
☐ 212 (a) (9) ☐ 212 (a) (23)

A. Information about applicant -

1. Family Name(Surname in CAPS) (First) (Middle)
JAMES Sarah

2. Address (Number and Street) (Apartment Number)
19 Lily Valley Road

3.(Town or City) (State/Country) (ZIP/Postal Code)
Huntington New York 11743

4. Date of Birth *(month/Day/Year)* 5.I&N File Number
09/18/1960 A-22 222 222

6. City of Birth 7. Country of Birth
Liverpool England

8. Date of visa application 9. Visa applied for at:
5/12/99 London, England

10. **Applicant was declared inadmissible to the United States for the following reasons:** (List acts, convictions, or physical or mental conditions. If applicant has active or suspected tuberculosis, the reverse of this page must be fully completed.)

212 (a)(9)(b)(v)

Unlawful Presence

11. Applicant was previously in the United States, as follows:

City & State	From(Date)	To(Date)	I&NS Status
Huntington, NY	12/1/98	5/10/99	Proceeding
New York, NY	3/5/94	11/15/98	Overstay

12. Social Security Number
123-12-1234

B. Information about relative, through whom applicant claims eligibility for a waiver -

1. Family Name(Surname in CAPS) (First) (Middle)
JAMES Andrew M.

2. Address(Number and Street) (Apartment Number)
19 Lily Valley Road

3. (Town or City) (State/Country) (ZIP/Postal Code)
Huntington New York 11743

4. Relationship to applicant 5. I&NS Status
Husband U.S. Citizen

C. Information about applicant's other relatives in the U.S. ***(List only U.S. citizens and permanent residents)***

1. Family Name(Surname in CAPS) (First) (Middle)
JAMES Ethan I.

2. Address (Number and Street) (Apartment Number)
19 Lily Valley Road

3.(Town or City) (State/Country) (ZIP/Postal Code)
Huntington New York 11743

4. Relationship to applicant 5. I&NS Status
Son

1. Family Name(Surname in CAPS) (First) (Middle)
JAMES Hunter A.

2. Address (Number and Street) (Apartment Number)
19 Lily Valley Road

3.(Town or City) (State/Country) (ZIP/Postal Code)
Huntington New York 11743

4. Relationship to applicant 5. I&NS Status
Daughter

1. Family Name(Surname in CAPS) (First) (Middle)

2. Address (Number and Street) (Apartment Number)

3.(Town or City) (State/Country) (ZIP/Postal Code)

4. Relationship to applicant 5. I&NS Status

Signature *(of applicant or petitioning relative)*

Relationship to applicant *Date*

Signature *(of person preparing application, if not the applicant or petitioning relative)* ***I declare that this document was prepared by me at the request of the applicant, or petitioning relative, and is based on all information of which I have any knowledge.***

Signature

Address *Date*

Initial receipt	Resubmitted	Relocated		Completed		
		Received	Sent	Approved	Denied	Returned
	343					

D. Student Visa Abusers ("Parachute Kids")

The 1996 Act also created a new penalty for "student visa abusers." If a foreign student obtains F-1 status in order to pursue a course of study at a private elementary or secondary school or in a language training program that is not publicly funded and then abandons or terminates study at the private school to attend a public elementary or secondary school or a publicly funded adult education language program, the student will be deemed to be a "student visa abuser."

The student will be considered to have violated his or her status and the underlying F nonimmigrant visa will be voided. In addition, the student will be excludable from the United States for a period of five years from the date of the violation. Congress created this provision to punish those children, popularly referred to as "parachute kids," who jump from private school to public school upon admission to the United States in F-1 status. A foreign student will not be subject to the student visa abuser penalty if he or she transfers to a public secondary school from a private secondary school, only attends the public school for up to twelve months, and reimburses the local school for the per capita cost of education at the particular school. The INS must approve the change of school.

E. Additional Grounds of Inadmissibility Under the Immigration and Nationality Act

In addition to the bars of admissibility discussed earlier in this chapter, applicants for immigrant and nonimmigrant admission to the United States may also be subject to other grounds of inadmissibility contained in the Immigration and Nationality Act. The INA contains ten major areas of inadmissibility and there are waivers available in many of the categories. Although a number of the grounds of inadmissibility contained in the INA relate to crimes, smuggling and other areas outside the scope of this book, the following is a brief summary of some of those grounds that may affect even law-abiding business entrants.

Health-Related Grounds: Foreign nationals who seek to enter the United States may not be admitted if they are identified by the Secretary of Health and Human Services as having a communicable disease of public health significance. AIDS is a communicable disease of public health significance by operation of law. A waiver of this ground of inadmissibility is available for spouses, sons and daughters of U.S. citizens and lawful permanent residents.

Vaccinations: Immigrants seeking admission and/or adjustment of status as lawful permanent residents must present evidence of having received vaccinations against vaccine-preventable diseases. These include mumps, measles, rubella, polio, tetanus and diphtheria toxoids, pertussis, influenza type B and hepatitis B, and any other vaccinations for vaccine-preventable diseases recommended by the Advisory Committee for Immunization Practices. If the applicant can not document that he or she has received the appropriate vaccinations, the applicant is inadmissible. There is a waiver available for this ground of inadmissibility.

Drug abusers and addicts: Foreign nationals determined to be present drug abusers or addicts under regulations issued by the Secretary of Health and Human Resources are inadmissible to the United States. There is no waiver of this ground of inadmissibility.

Uncertified foreign health-care workers: Foreign nationals coming to the United States as non-physician workers are inadmissible unless they present a certificate from the Commission on Graduates of Foreign Nursing Schools, or an equivalent approved certificate. Foreign nurses must meet certain licensing and education requirements, and must also be competent in oral and written English before they can be admitted to work in the United States.

Failure to attend removal proceedings: Any foreign national who without reasonable cause fails or refuses to attend or remain in attendance at a hearing to determine the individual's inadmissibility or removability is inadmissible for five years from their date of departure or removal from the United States.

Misrepresentation: Any foreign national who, by fraud or willfully misrepresenting a material fact, seeks to procure (or has sought to procure or has procured), a visa, other documentation, or admission into the United or other any other benefit under the INA, is inadmissible. Arriving foreign nationals charged with this ground of inadmissibility are subject to expedited removal and may be expelled without any hearing or judicial proceeding.

A waiver of this ground of inadmissibility is available for spouses, sons, or daughter of U.S. citizens and lawful permanent residents. The waiver may be granted in the sole discretion of the Attorney General if it can be demonstrated that the refusal of the foreign national's admission would result in extreme hardship to the citizen or lawfully resident spouse or parent. There is no judicial review of a denial of a waiver request under this provision.

False claim to United States citizenship: Any foreign national who falsely claims to be a U.S. citizen for any purpose or benefit under the immigration laws, or any Federal or State statue is inadmissible. This ground of inadmissibility was introduced in the 1996 Act and is only applicable to violations made on or after September 30, 1996. There is no waiver available for this ground of inadmissibility.

Unlawful Voters: Any foreign national who has voted in violation of any Federal, State, or local constitutional provision, statute, ordinance, or regulation is inadmissible. There is no waiver for this ground of inadmissibility.

Former citizens who renounced citizenship to avoid taxation: Any former citizen of the United States whom the Attorney General determines renounced citizenship for the purpose of avoiding taxation by the Federal government is inadmissible. This provision is applicable to former citizens who renounced their citizenship on or after September 30, 1996.

Document fraud violations: Foreign nationals subject to final orders for violations of the document fraud provisions of the Immigration and Nationality Act (section 274C) are inadmissible. A waiver is available for this ground of inadmissibility under the same conditions as those for smugglers. However, in the case of a foreign national seeking admission or adjustment of status additional conditions apply.

Foreign nationals previously removed: Any foreign national who has been removed after arrival (expedited removal) or at the end of removal proceedings initiated after their arrival in the United States, is inadmissible for five years from the date of removal. If the foreign national is subject to a second order of removal he or she is inadmissible for twenty years. Foreign nationals who are removed pursuant to a conviction for an aggravated felony are permanently barred from the United States.

Any other foreign national not subject to the above-mentioned ground of inadmissibility who has been ordered removed or who has departed the United States while an order of removal was outstanding is inadmissible for ten years. If the Attorney General consents to the foreign national's application for readmission this ground of inadmissibility will not apply.

F. **Conclusion**

The consequences of unlawful presence and status overstay are unquestionably harsh, and often present traps for the unwary. It is therefore more important than ever to vigilantly maintain proper status, and to be familiar with INS procedures and legal requirements. It is essential when applying for an immigrant or nonimmigrant visa at any Embassy or Consulate to be fully prepared to prove with documents the lawfulness of periods of presence in the United States.

One commentator pointed out in referring to the new bars and penalties, "not only has the bridge been made narrower but the river below has been filled with poisonous snakes and crocodiles." While this statement may seem extreme, the effect of the 1996 Act is now being felt by thousands of otherwise qualified immigrant and nonimmigrant visa applicants who leave the United States only to be told they are not eligible to return for a decade. Hopefully, Congress will be persuaded to ameliorate these harsh provisions.

Chapter Twelve
CONCLUSIONS AND OBSERVATIONS

CONCLUSIONS AND OBSERVATIONS

United States Immigration Law is unquestionably the most complex in the world. While the immigration laws of other countries may be stricter in many ways, they are by no means as complex, and their governmental authorities usually do not have total discretion with no right of appeal. On the other hand, the United States has a constantly changing web of statutes, regulations, operation instructions, and administrative and judicial decisions, with an important role played by private attorneys on behalf of applicants and their sponsors. In fact, many observers feel that United States Immigration Law is even more complex than United States Tax Law, United States Securities Law and United States Trade Law.

United States Immigration Law was not always this complex. In fact, for the first hundred years of our existence (1776-1876) there was virtually no restriction on immigration, as the country needed the plentiful labor provided by new immigrants in order to grow. As the country expanded westward to the Pacific Ocean, and as the industrial cities in the East and the Mid-West developed, millions of immigrants were encouraged to resettle in the United States and to provide the population for a growing country.

The first major Immigration Acts were enacted in 1875 and 1882 and provided mainly for exclusion of those thought to be undesirable, such as convicts, prostitutes, lunatics, and those likely to become public charges. The 1882 Act also provided for the exclusion of persons from China, and was a reaction to the large number of Chinese immigrants who had been admitted to the United States in order to build the transcontinental railroad, which was completed in the latter part of the Nineteenth Century.

The statutes of 1885 and 1887 sought to bar cheap foreign labor in areas in which the Government believed such employment would depress the domestic labor market. This was the beginning of the concept of protecting the American labor market, a principle that has been carried forward to the present and is reflected in the labor certification requirement for many immigrants. However, at that time, its application was much more limited.

The laws enacted in 1891, 1903, and 1907 broadened the exclusion of "undesirables," and excluded aliens with contagious diseases, those who were convicted of crimes involving moral turpitude, paupers, polygamists, epileptics, beggars, anarchists, insane persons, and the like. However, plentiful labor and increased population were still needed, and no quota on immigration was imposed, except for the continued exclusion of Chinese nationals. Even this restriction was often avoided by natives of China whose fathers had acquired United States citizenship by naturalization while working in the United States, and who, therefore, had a claim to derivative United States citizenship. These individuals were allowed to immigrate with their families.

The first quota system, enacted in 1917, set limits according to country of national origin and barred immigration from Asia altogether, with the exception of the Japanese. A literacy requirement for new immigrants was also established at that time. In 1921, after the end of the First World War, there was a general fear that Southern Europeans fleeing their ravished countries would overrun the United States. In response, Congress enacted the National Origins Quota System, which set an annual quota for each country at a specified percentage of the number of natives of that country counted in the census of 1910. The National Origins Quota System in various forms remained in effect until 1965. The so-called Asiatic Barred Zone remained in effect until 1952.

The establishment of quotas in 1917 recognized that the United States could not continue to accept all those who sought to live here. It had also reflected the growing trend toward "isolationism" and outright fear of foreigners, and the desire to maintain the "stability" of America. Of course, this attitude lost sight of the fact that immigration had built the United States and that in less than a century America, through its new immigrants, had transformed an almost totally undeveloped continent into one of the most powerful nations in the world. It is also significant that, although quotas were then being imposed, they were almost totally nonselective, except for the grounds of exclusion previously mentioned. This reflected our continuing need for a source of plentiful unskilled labor to fuel our growing industrial economy during the relatively prosperous times which followed the First World War (1917-1929).

Interestingly enough, there were no new major restrictions placed on immigration during the so-called Great Depression (1929-1942). This was because the United States ceased to be an economic magnet during the period of the Depression, and recent studies have shown that there was even a reverse immigration, with many immigrants and their families returning to Europe where they could return to family farms and former trades.

During the Second World War, immigration from belligerent countries at war with the United States was completely eliminated, and immigration from countries under military occupation became impossible. During the War itself, no provision was made for acceptance of refugees or displaced persons outside of the normal quota, and boat loads of refugees seeking to land in the United States were turned away.

Following the Second World War, emergency legislation was passed for expedited admission of displaced persons, and for the "War Brides" of United States Servicemen. However, these measures were regarded as providing temporary relief only, and did not represent any change in basic United States immigration philosophy.

A fundamental change did occur in 1952 with the passage of the McCarran-Walter Act, which was enacted after a two-year study by the United States Senate. This important statute established the general format of modern United States immigration law.

The 1952 Act kept the National Origins Quota System, but dropped the percentage to one-sixth of one percent of the 1920 Census for each country. The previous percentage was two percent of the number for each country. The Act established racial quotas for Asia and provided detailed deportation and exclusion grounds and procedures. Most important of all, the Act established preferences within each quota for aliens with special skills, creating for the first time a selective element to United States Immigration Law.

In 1965, as a result of efforts by the Kennedy Administration, major amendments to the Immigration Act were enacted. Racial and National Origin quotas were totally eliminated, and a 20,000 per year quota cap was placed on each Eastern Hemisphere country. A quota of 120,000 from the Western Hemisphere and 180,000 immigrants from the Eastern Hemisphere was established. Definitions of the Preference Categories based on skills, and family relationships were also modified. The amendments also introduced the important concept of Labor Certification wherein the Department of Labor had to certify that each primary immigrant (with the exception of those immigrating on the basis of close relatives) would not displace a United States worker. The law also provided for the admission of refugees seeking political asylum.

Subsequent legislation in 1976 and 1980 equalized the quotas for the Eastern and Western Hemispheres and added many additional numbers for refugees. The 1952 and 1965 Acts, and subsequent legislation also regularized and defined various categories for the admission of non-immigrants on "working visas," such as H, L, J, etc., and placed a great distinction in the law between immigrant and nonimmigrant. In fact, everyone was presumed to be an immigrant (and therefore excludable without an immigrant visa) unless he or she could establish bona fide nonimmigrant intent.

The next sweeping change took place in 1986. For the first time, Congress established Criminal and Civil penalties for employers hiring aliens not authorized to work in the United States, and also established various legalization (amnesty) programs for aliens who had been illegally in the United States for specified periods of time. These philosophically opposite measures were enacted as a part of a legislative compromise on how to deal with the estimated millions of aliens who had entered or remained in the United States without lawful status.

Following the Immigration Reform and Control Act of 1986, the pace of legislation in the immigration area greatly accelerated. Literally scores of proposed immigration statutes were introduced in both Houses of Congress and sent to Committee, and many have been enacted into law. Examples are the Marriage Fraud Amendments of 1986, the Anti-Drug Abuse Act of 1986 and 1988, The Nursing Relief Act of 1989, and numerous Technical Corrections Acts and portions of non-immigration statutes containing immigration provisions.

The present system, which this book primarily addresses, was created by the Immigration Act of 1990, passed on November 29, 1990. This Act greatly altered the selection system, increased the quotas for highly skilled and needed individuals, provided a category for the first time for immigrant investors, created many new nonimmigrant categories such as R, O, P, and Q, and redefined some of the old ones (H & L). In so doing, Congress added a dimension of complexity unprecedented in American Immigration Law. Subsequently, in 1996, with the passage of the Illegal Immigration Reform and Immigrant Responsibility Act (IIRAIRA), Congress added unprecedented harsh provisions to the statute. The list of deportable offenses was greatly expanded, with a commensurate curtailment or complete elimination of discretionary relief from deportation and judicial review. Additionally, draconian consequences and bars were added for both long-term and short-term status violators, and simple overstays.

In reviewing the pattern of the United States immigration regulation, we can see a definite trend moving from completely open immigration to a very selective and regulated system. To a great extent, this is reflective of the change in the American economy which, over our more than 200 year history has gone from a rapidly expanding and growing one, to a more mature and static economy. Additionally, many of the more onerous changes in American Immigration laws, many of which impose severe criminal penalties and enhanced grounds for removal, stem from a reaction by the American Government to an influx of illegal immigration to the United States which began in the 1960's and 1970's, and which continues to this day.

The trends in United States Immigration law are clear, but often conflicting. They can be summarized as follows:

(A) Overwhelming complexity that leads to delay and uncertainty. This is enhanced by the complex rules and procedures of the several different Government agencies which administer the Immigration process, including the Department of State, the Department of Labor, The Immigration & Naturalization Service, the Executive Office of Immigration Review and the Federal Courts;

(B) Rapid Change. The United States Congress now frequently modifies and "tinkers" with parts of the Immigration system, usually at the behest of private interest groups seeking benefits. Such groups have included fashion models, nurses, farm workers, international advertising agencies, United States Labor unions, and national groups such as Cubans, Haitians, Nicaraguans, Hondurans, and nationals of the former Soviet Republic. All of these groups have been the beneficiaries of special legislation passed at their behest;

(C) Increasing selectivity within complex categories based on perceived benefit to the country, and the desire to assist particular national groups.

(D) Stricter grounds for removal of aliens with elimination of many procedural rights to immigration law violators, drug offenders, and "aggravated felons;"

(E) Increased judicial involvement, with many public interest groups and voluntary agencies bringing individual actions in Federal Court in order to have laws or policies invalidated or changed;

(F) Special legislation and special programs designed to admit or provide status to large groups of individuals who are fleeing, or who claim to be fleeing persecution in their home country. This policy is often inconsistent with the stated legislative goals of selectivity and family re-unification, which have been in effect since 1952.

Against this background, it has become more important than ever for individuals and businesses to carefully study and follow changes in United States Immigration law and policy. One must understand not only the explicit and often conflicting provisions of the statutes, regulations and procedures of the various agencies administering immigration law, but also the temperament and attitude of the individuals who administer the law. As the initial point of contact is usually with an immigration inspector at the airport, or an immigration examiner reviewing applications at one of the four INS Service Centers, or perhaps with an Immigration investigator at one's place of business, it is essential that all submissions and presentations be geared to these individuals, as well as to the substance of the law.

It is hoped that this book will provide the user with a powerful tool in making immigration decisions and applications. However, we must again point out that the area of United States Immigration Law is changing faster than any other area of law in America, and material contained in this book will necessarily have to be updated on a regular basis. Additionally, this book should not be construed as providing specific legal advice on individual cases, and the opinion of an attorney specializing in immigration law should be sought before individual decisions are implemented. The editors and publishers believe that this book is the most useful of its kind in print today.

APPENDIX A

IMMIGRATION AND NATURALIZATION SERVICE HEADQUARTERS

425 Eye Street, N. W.
Washington, D.C. 20536
(202) 514-2000

IMMIGRATION AND NATURALIZATION SERVICE REGIONAL OFFICES

EASTERN OPERATIONS REGIONAL OFFICE
70 Kimball Avenue
South Burlington, VT 05403-6813
(802) 660-5000
Fax: (802) 660-5114
Regional Director – William R. Yates

CENTRAL OPERATIONS REGIONAL OFFICE
7701 N. Stemmons Freeway
Dallas, TX 75247
(214) 767-7600
Fax: (214) 767-7475
Regional Director – Mark K. Reed

WESTERN OPERATIONS REGIONAL OFFICE
24000 Avila Road
P.O. Box 30080
Laguna Niguel, CA 92607
(949) 360-2995
Fax: (949) 360-3081
Regional Director - Johnny N. Williams

IMMIGRATION AND NATURALIZATION SERVICE
SERVICE CENTERS

VERMONT SERVICE CENTER
P.O. Box 9589
St. Albans, VT 05479-9589
75 Lower Weldon St.
St. Albans, VT 05479-0001
(802) 527-3160
Fax: (802) 527-3252

Jurisdiction:
CT, DE, DC, ME, MD, MA, NH, NJ, NY, PA, PR, RI, VT, VA, WV

NEBRASKA SERVICE CENTER
850 "S" Street
Lincoln, NE 68501
(402) 437-5218
(402) 437-5958

Jurisdiction:
AK, CO, ID, IL, IN, IA, KS, MI, MN, MO, MT, NE, ND, OH, OR, SD, UT, WA, WI, WY

TEXAS SERVICE CENTER
P.O. Box 8511488
Mesquite, TX, 75185-1488
4141 St. Augustine Rd.
Dallas, TX, 75227

(214) 381-1423
Fax: (214) 767- 7412

Jurisdiction:
AL, AR, FL, GA, KY, LA, MS, NM, NC, OK, SC, TN, TX

CALIFORNIA SERVICE CENTER
P.O. Box 10589
Laguna Niguel, CA 92607-0589
2400 Avila Rd.
Laguna Niguel, CA 92607

(714) 360-2769; - 2733
Fax: (714) 643-1583

Jurisdiction:
AZ, CA, HI, NV

APPENDIX B

AMERICAN IMMIGRATION LAWYERS ASSOCIATION

1400 Eye Street, N.W. Suite 1200
Washington, DC 20005
(202) 216-2400
Fax: (202) 371-9449
Web site: http://www.aila.org

APPENDIX C

TREATIES CONTAINING TREATY TRADER AND TREATY INVESTOR PROVISIONS IN EFFECT BETWEEN THE UNITED STATES AND OTHER COUNTRIES 9 FAM §41.51, Exhibit 1

Treaties marked with one asterisk (*) contains only treaty investor provisions and allow only E-2 issuance, not E-1. Treaties marked with two asterisks (**) contain only treaty trader provisions and allow only E-1 issuance, not E-2.

ARGENTINA
Treaty of Friendship, Commerce and Navigation. (Article II)
Entered into force December 20, 1854.
10 Stat. 1005; TS 4; Bevans 61

Bilateral Investment Treaty
Entered into force October 20, 1994
S. Treaty Doc. No. 2
103d Cong., 1st Sess. (1993)

ARMENIA**
Bilateral Investment Treaty
Entered into force March 29, 1996.

AUSTRALIA
Immigration Act of 1990, §204
Treaty trader provisions entered into force December 16, 1991
Treaty investor provisions entered into force December 27, 1991

AUSTRIA
Treaty of Friendship, Commerce and Consular Rights (Article I)
Entered into force May 27, 1931
47 Stat. 1876; TS 838; 5 Bevans 341; 118 UNTS 241

BANGLADESH**
Bilateral Investment Treaty (Article II)
Entered into force July 25, 1989
S. Treaty Doc. No. 23
99th Cong., 2d Sess. (1986)

BELGIUM
Treaty of Friendship, Establishment and Navigation. (Article II)
Entered into force October 3, 1963
(Treaty of 1875 in force prior to this date)
214 UST 1284; TIAS 5432; 480 UNTS 149

BOLIVIA**
Treaty of Peace, Friendship, Commerce and Navigation. (Article III)
Entered into force November 9, 1862
12 Stat. 1003; TS 32; 5 Bevans 721.

BOSNIA-HERZEGOVINA
Based on Treaty with Former Yugoslavia. Treaty of Commerce
Entered into force November 15, 1882
22 Stat. 963; TS 319; 12 Bevans 1227

BRUNEI*
Treaty of Peace, Friendship, Commerce and Navigation. (Article II)
Entered into force July 11, 1853
10 Stat. 909; TS 33; Bevans 1080

BULGARIA**
Bilateral Investment Treaty
Entered into force June 2, 1994
S Treaty Doc. No. 3
103d Cong. 1st Sess. (1993)

CAMEROON**
Bilateral Investment Treaty (Article II)
Entered into force April 6, 1989
S. Treaty Doc. No. 22
99th Cong. 2d Sess. (1986)

CANADA
On September 28, 1988, the President signed Pub.L. 100-49 which implements the provision of the United States-Canada Free Trade Agreement. Section 307(a) of the law made INA §101(a)(15)(E) applicable to Canadian citizens. The agreement and the implementing provisions became effective January 1, 1989.
102 Stat. 1851; Pub.L. 100-449.

CHINA (Taiwan)
Treaty of Friendship, Commerce and Navigation. (Article II)
Entered into force November 30, 1948
63 Stat. 1299; TIAS 1871; 6 Bevans 761; 25 UNTS 69

COLOMBIA
Treaty of Peace, Amity, Navigation and Commerce (Article III)
Entered into force June 10, 1848
9 Stat. 881; TS54; 6 Bevans 868

CONGO, DEMOCRATIC REPUBLIC OF ** (formerly Zaire)
Bilateral Investment Treaty (Article II)
Entered into force July 28, 1989
S. Treaty Doc. No. 17
99th Cong., 2d Sess. (1986)

CONGO, REPUBLIC OF**
Bilateral Investment Treaty
Entered into force August 13, 1994

COSTA RICA
Treaty of Friendship, Commerce and Navigation. (Article II)
Entered into force May 26, 1852
10 Stat. 916; TS 62; 6 Bevans 1013

CZECH REPUBLIC**
Bilateral Investment Treaty
Entered into force December 19, 1992
S. Treaty Doc. No. 31
102nd Cong., 2d Sess. (1992)

DENMARK
Treaty of Friendship, Commerce and Navigation. (Article II)
Entered into force July 30, 1961
(Convention of 1826 was in force prior to this date)
12 UST 908; TIAS 4797; 421 UNTS 105

ECUADOR**
Bilateral Investment Treaty
Entered into force May 11, 1997.

EGYPT**
Bilateral Investment Treaty
Entered into force June 27, 1992

ESTONIA
Treaty of Friendship, Commerce and Consular Rights (Article I)
Entered into force May 22, 1926
44 Stat. 2379; TS 736; 7 Bevans 620; 50 LNTS 13
Bilateral Investment Treaty
Entered into force February 16, 1997.

ETHIOPIA
Treaty of Amity and Economic Relations (Article VI)
Entered into force October 8, 1953
4 USTS 2134; TIAS 2864; 206 UNTS 41

FINLAND
Treaty of Friendship, Commerce and Consular Rights. (Article I)
Entered into force August 10, 1934
49 Stat. 2659; TS 868; 7 Bevans 718; 152 LNTS 45
Protocol Amending Treaty to allow E-2s
Entered into force December 11, 1992.

FRANCE
Convention of Establishment (Article II)
Entered into force December 21, 1960.
11 UST 2398; TIAS 4625; 401 UNTIS 75

GEORGIA
Bilateral Investment Treaty
Entered into force August 17, 1997

GERMANY (FRG)
Treaty of Friendship, Commerce and Navigation.
Entered into force July 14, 1956
7 UST 1839; TIAS 3593 273 UNTS 3

GREECE*
Treaty of Friendship, Commerce and Navigation. (Article II)
Entered into force October 13, 1954
5 UST 1829; TIAS 3057; 224 UNTS 279

GRENADA**
Bilateral Treaty Investment
Entered into force March 3, 1989
S. Treaty Doc. No. 25
99th Cong., 2d Sess. (1986)

HONDURAS
Treaty of Friendship, Commerce and Consular Rights. (Article I)
Entered into force July 19, 1928
45 Stat. 2618; TS 764; 8 Bevans 905; 87 LNTS 421

IRAN
Treaty of Amity, Economic Relations and Consular Rights (Article II)
Entered into force June 16, 1957
8 UST 899; TIAS 3853; 284 UNTS 93
Note: Treaty inoperative because of Executive Order preventing trade with Iran.

IRELAND
Treaty of Friendship, Commerce and Navigation. (Article I)
Entered into force September 14, 1950
1 UST 785; TIAS 2155; 206 UNTS 269
Protocol Amending Treaty to allow E-2s
Entered into force November 18, 1992

ISRAEL *
Treaty of Friendship, Commerce and Navigation. (Article II)
Entered into force April 3, 1954
5 UST 550; TIAS 2948; 219 UNTS 237

ITALY
Treaty of Friendship, Commerce and Navigation
(Article I and Article XXIV, ¶7)
Entered into force July 26, 1949
63 Stat. 2255; TIAS 1965; 9 Bevans 261; 79 UNTS 171

JAMAICA
Bilateral Investment Treaty
Entered into force May 7, 1997

JAPAN
Treaty of Friendship, Commerce and Navigation. (Article I)
Entered into force October 30, 1953
4 UST 2063; TIAS 2863; 206 UNTS 143

KAZAKHSTAN*
Bilateral Treaty Investment
Entered into force January 12, 1994
S. Treaty Doc. No. 12
103d Cong., 1st Sess. (1993)

KOREA
Treaty of Friendship, Commerce and Navigation. (Article II)
Entered into force November 7, 1957
8 UST 2217; TIAS 3947; 302 UNTS 281

KYRGYZSTAN**
Bilateral Investment Treaty
Entered into force January 12, 1994
S. Treaty Doc. No. 13
103d Cong., 1st Sess. (1993)

LATVIA*
Treaty of Friendship, Commerce and Consular Rights. (Article I)
Entered into force July 25, 1928
45 Stat. 2641; TS 765; 9 Bevans 531; 80 LNTS 35
Bilateral Investment Treaty
Entered into force December 26, 1996

LIBERIA
Treaty of Friendship, Commerce and Navigation. (Article I)
Entered into force November 21, 1939
54 Stat. 1739; TS 956; 9 Bevans 595; 201 LNTS 163

LUXEMBOURG
Treaty of Friendship, Establishment and Navigation. (Article II)
Entered into force March 28, 1963
14 UST 251; TIAS 5306; 474 UNTS 3

MEXICO
On December 8, 1992 the President signed Public Law No. 103-182 which implements the North American Free Trade Agreement. Section 341 of the law made INA §101(a)(15)(E) applicable to Mexican citizens. The Agreement and the implementing provisions became effective January 1, 1994.
Pub. L. No. 103-182, 107 Stat. 2057.

MOLDOVA**
Bilateral Investment Treaty
Entered into force November 25, 1994.

MONGOLIA**
Bilateral Investment Treaty
Entered into force January 1, 1997.

MOROCCO*
Bilateral Investment Treaty
Entered into force May 29, 1991

NETHERLANDS
Treaty of Friendship, Commerce and Navigation. (Article II)
Entered into force December 5, 1957
8UST 2043; TIAS 3942; 285 UNTS 231
(The Treaty which entered into force in 1957 applies to
Aruba and the Netherlands Antilles).

NORWAY
Treaty of Commerce and Navigation. (Article I)
Entered into force January 18, 1828
8 Stat. 346; TS 348; 11 Bevans 876

Treaty of Friendship, Commerce and Consular Rights
Entered into force September 13, 1932
47 Stat. 2135; TS 852; 10 Bevans 481; 134 LNTS 81

OMAN
Treaty of Amity, Economic Relations and Consular Rights (Article II)
Entered into force June 11, 1960
11 UST 1835; TIAS 4630; 380 UNTS 181

PAKISTAN
Treaty of Friendship and Commerce
Entered into force February 12, 1961
12 UST 110; TIAS 4683; 404 UNTS 259

PANAMA**
Bilateral Investment Treaty
Entered into force May 30, 1991

PARAGUAY
Treaty of Friendship, Commerce and Navigation. (Article II)
Entered into force March 7, 1860
12 Stat. 1091; TS 272; 10 Bevans 888

PHILIPPINES
On September 6, 1955, pursuant to Article V of the revised Trade Agreement between the United States and the Philippines, notes were exchanged between the two governments implementing the provisions of the Act of June 18, 1954 thereby rendering INA §101(a)(15)(E) applicable to Philippine nationals. There is no commercial treaty in force between the two countries.
Entered into force September 6, 1955
6 UST 3030; TIAS 3349; 238 UNTS 109

POLAND*
Bilateral Investment Treaty
Entered into force August 6, 1994.*

ROMANIA**
Bilateral Investment Treaty
Entered into force January 15, 1994
S. Treaty Doc. No. 36
103d Cong., 1st Sess. (1993)

SENEGAL*
Bilateral Investment Treaty
Entered into force October 25, 1990

SLOVAK REPUBLIC
Bilateral Investment Treaty
Entered into force December 19, 1992
S. Treaty Doc. No. 31
102d Cong., 2d Sess. (1992)

SPAIN
Treaty of Friendship and General Relations (Article II)
Entered into force April 14, 1903
33 Stat. 2105; TS 422; 11 Bevans 628

SRI LANKA
Bilateral Investment Treaty
Entered into force May 1, 1993
S. Treaty Doc. No. 25
102d Cong., 2d Sess. (1992)

SURINAME
Treaty of Friendship, Commerce and Navigation. (Article II)
Entered into force December 5, 1957
8 UST 2043; TIAS 3942; 285 UNTS 231

SWEDEN
Immigration Act of 1990, §204
Entered into force February 20, 1992

SWITZERLAND
Treaty of Friendship, Commerce and Extradition. (Article I)
Entered into force November 8, 1855
11 Stat. 587; TS 353; 11 Bevans 894

THAILAND
Treaty of Amity and Economic Relations
Entered into force June 8, 1968
19 UST5843; TIAS 6540; 652 UNTS 253

TOGO
Treaty of Amity and Economic Relations
Entered into force February 5, 1967
18 UST 1; TIAS 6193; 680 UNTS 159

TRINIDAD & TOBAGO**
Bilateral Investment Treaty
Entered into force December 26, 1996

TUNISIA**
Bilateral Investment Treaty (Article II)
Entered into force February 7, 1933
S. Treaty Doc. No. 6
102d Cong., 2d Sess. (1992)

TURKEY
Treaty of Establishment and Sojourn (Article I)
Entered into force February 15, 1933
47 Sta. 2432; TS 859; 11 Bevans 1127; 138 LNTS 345

Bilateral Investment Treaty
Entered into force May 18, 1990
S. Treaty Doc. No. 19
99th Cong., 2d Sess. (1986)

UKRAINE**
Bilateral Investment Treaty
Entered into force November 16, 1996

UNITED KINGDOM
Convention to Regulate Commerce (Article I)
Entered into force July 3, 1815
8 Stat. 228; TS 110; 12 Bevans 49.
The Convention which entered into force in 1815 applies only to British territory in Europe the British Isles [except Republic of Ireland], the Channel Islands and Gibraltar and to 'inhabitants' of such territory. This term, as used in the Convention means "one who resides actually and permanently in a given place, and has his domicile there." Also in order to qualify for treaty trader or treaty investor status under this Treaty, the alien must be a national of the United Kingdom. Individuals having the nationality of the Commonwealth other than the United Kingdom do not qualify for treaty trader or treaty investor status under this Treaty.

YOGUSLAVIA
Treaty of Commerce (Article I)
Entered into force November 15, 1882
22 Stat. 963; TS 319; 12 Bevans 1227
(Although we do not recognize Serbia-Montenegro and Macedonia, we consider them to be successor entities that are bound by the treaty rights and obligations.)

ZAIRE
Bilateral Investment Treaty (Article II)
Entered into force July 28, 1989
S. Treaty Doc. No. 17, 99th Cong., 2d. Sess. (1986)

APPENDIX D

IMMIGRATION AND NATURALIZATION SERVICE DISTRICT OFFICES

Albany Suboffice
James T. Foley Federal Court House
445 Broadway, Rm. 227
Albany, NY 12207
(518) 431-0330
Fax: (518) 431-0329

Albuquerque Suboffice
517 Gold Ave. SW, Rm. 1010
Albuquerque, NM 87103
(505) 248-7351

Atlanta District Office
Dr, Martin Luther King, Jr., BLDG.
77 Forsythe Street, SW
Atlanta, GA 30303-0253
Fax: (404) 331-5158

Anchorage District Office
620 East 10th Ave., Suite 102
(907) 271-4953

Baltimore District Office
Nations Bank Center
100 South Charles, 12th Floor
Baltimore, MD 21201
(410) 962-2120
Fax: (410) 962-7555

Boston District Office
John F. Kennedy Federal Bldg.
Government Center, Rm. E.160
Boston, MA 02203
(617) 565 -3879
Fax: (617) 565-3097

Buffalo District Office
Federal Center
130 Delaware Avenue
Buffalo, NY 14202
(716) 849-6760

Charleston Suboffice
Federal Bldg., Rm. 110
334 Meeting Street
Charleston, SC 29403
(843) 767-7083

Charlotte Suboffice
210 East Woodlawn Rd.
Suite 138, Bldg. 6
Charlotte, NC 28217
(704) 523-1704

Charlotte Amalie Suboffice
5500 Veterans Dr.
Federal BLDG.
St. Thomas
Virgin Islands 00802
(340) 774-1390
Mailing Address:
P.O. BOX610
Charlotte Amalie
St. Thomas, VI 00804

Chicago District Office
10 West Jackson Blvd., Suite 218
Chicago, IL 60604
(312) 353-7334
Fax: (312) 886-8188

Cincinnati Suboffice
J. W. Peck Federal Bldg.
550 Main Street, Rm. 8511
Cincinnati, OH 45202
(513) 287-6080

Cleveland District Office
Celebreeze Federal Office Bldg., Rm. 1917
1240 East 9th Street
Cleveland, OH 44199
(216) 522-4766
Fax: (216) 522-7039

Dallas District Office
8101 N. Stemmons Freeway
Dallas, TX 75247
(214) 655-5384

Denver District Office
Albrook Center
4730 Paris Street
Denver, CO 80239
(303) 371-3041

Detroit District Office
Federal Building
333 Mount Elliot Street, 1st Floor
Detroit, MI 48207
(313) 259-8560

El Paso District Office
1545 Hawkins Blvd.,
El Paso, TX 79925
(915) 225-1941

Fresno Suboffice
856 Fulton Mall
Fresno, CA 93721
(539) 487-5091
Fax: (209) 487-5939

Guam Suboffice
801 Pacific News BLDG., Rm. 801
238 O'Hara St
Agana, GU 96910
(671) 472-7349

Halingen District Office
2102 Teege Avenue.
Harlingen, TX 78550
(956) 425-7333

Hartford Suboffice
Ribicoff Federal Bldg.
450 Main Street
Hartford, CT 06103-3060
(860) 240- 1984

Helena District Office
2800 Skyway Drive
Helena, MT 59602-1230
(406) 449-5288
Fax: (406) 449-5082

Honolulu District Office
595 Ala Moana Blvd.
P.O. Box 461
Honolulu, HI 96813
(808) 532-3721

Houston District Office
126 North Point
Houston, TX 77060
(281) 774-4611
Fax: (281) 774-5987

Indianapolis Suboffice
Gateway Plaza
950 N. Meridian, Suite 400
Indianapolis, IN 46204
(317) 226-6009

Jacksonville Suboffice
400 W. Bay Street
Room G-18
Jacksonville, FL 32202
(904) 232-2624

Kansas City District Office
9747 Northwest Conant Avenue
Kansas City, MO 64153
(816) 891-0603

Las Vegas Suboffice
3373 Pepper Lane
Las Vegas, NV 89120
(702) 451-3597

Louisville Suboffice
Gene Snyder Federal BLDG.
601 West Broadway, Rm. 601
Louisville, KY 40202
(502) 582-6375

Los Angeles District Office
300 North Los Angeles Street
Los Angeles, CA 90012
(213) 526-7647

Memphis Suboffice
1341 Sycamore View, Suite 100
Memphis, TN 38134
(901) 544-0264

Miami District Office
7880 Biscayne Blvd., Rm. 100
Miami, FL 33138
(305) 536-5741

Milwaukee Suboffice
517 East Wisconsin Avenue
1st Floor, Room 186
Milwaukee, WI 53202
(414) 297-3565

Newark District Office
Peter Rodino Federal Bldg.
970 Broad Street, Rm. 136
Newark, NJ 07102
(973) 645-4400

New Orleans District Office
Postal Service Bldg., Rm. T-8011
701 Loyola Avenue
New Orleans, LA 70113
(504) 589- 6533

New York District Office
26 Federal Plaza
New York, NY 10278
(212) 264-5650

Norfolk Suboffice
5280 Henneman Drive
Ground Level
Norfolk, VA 23513
(757) 858-6292

Oklahoma City Suboffice
West Park Business Center
4149 Highline Blvd., Suite 300
Oklahoma City, OK 73108
(405) 942-8670

Omaha District Office
3736 South 132nd Street
Omaha, NE 68144
(402) 697-9155

Philadelphia District Office
1600 Callowhill St., Rm. 100
Philadelphia, PA 19130
(215) 656-7144

Phoenix District Office
Federal Building
2035 North Central Avenue
Phoenix, AZ 85004
(602) 379-3122

Pittsburgh Suboffice
2130 Federal Building
1000 Liberty Avenue
Pittsburgh, PA 15222
(412) 395-4456

Portland, OR District Office
Federal BLDG.
511 Northwest Broadway
(503) 326-3006

Portland, ME District Office
176 Garnett Dr.
(207) 780-3352

Providence Suboffice
200 Dyre Street
Providence, RI 02903

Reno Suboffice
1351 Corporate Blvd.
Reno, NV 89502
(702) 784-5427

St. Albans Suboffice
Federal Bldg., P.O. Box 328
St. Albans, VT 05478
(802) 527-3292

St. Croix District Office
1468 Kingshill
(340) 778-6559

St. Louis Suboffice
1222 Spruce Street
Rm. 1100
St. Louis, MO 63103-2815
(314) 539-2532

Sacramento Suboffice
711 Jay Street
Sacramento, CA 95814
(916) 498-6450

St. Paul District Office
2901 Metro Drive,
Bloomington, MN 55425
(612) 854- 7754

San Antonio District Office
U.S. Federal Bldg.
8940 Four Winds Drive
San Antonio, TX 78239
(210) 967-7065

Salt Lake City Suboffice
5272 So. College Drive
Suite 100
Salt Lake City, UT 84123
(801) 265 - 8678

San Diego District Office
U.S. Federal Bldg.
880 Front Street
San Diego, CA 92188
(619) 557-5570

San Francisco District Office
630 Sansome Street, Rm. 200
San Francisco, CA 94111
(415) 705-4411

San Jose Suboffice
280 South First St. Rm. 1150
San Jose, CA 95112
(787) 766-5329

San Juan District Office
Federal BLDG
Chardon St. Rm. 380
Hato Ray, P.R. 00919
(787) 766-5280

Seattle District Office
815 Airport Way, South
Seattle, WA 98134
(206) 553-5956

Spokane Suboffice
U.S. Federal Courthouse Bldg.
West 920 Riverside Ave., Rm.691
Spokane, WA 99201
(509) 353-2129

Tampa Suboffice
5522 West Cypress
Tampa, FL 33609
(813) 288-1217

Tucson Suboffice
6431 South Country Club Road
Tucson, AZ 85701
(520) 670- 4624

Washington, D.C. District Office
4420 N. Fairfax Drive, Rm. 210
Arlington, VA 22203
(202) 307-1501

APPENDIX E

ASYLUM OFFICES

Arlington, VA (ZAR)
1500 Wilson Blvd.
Lobby Level
Arlington, VA 22209
(703) 525-8141
Fax: (703) 812-8455
Director - Marla J. Belvedere

Jurisdiction:
DC, PA (western), MD, VA,
WV, NC, GA, AL, SC

Houston, TX (ZHN)
Mailing address:
P.O. Box 67026
Houston, TX 77267-0262

Street address:
126 Northpoint Dr.
Houston, TX 77060
(281) 774-4830
Fax: (281) 774-5992
Director - Marie Hummert

Jurisdiction:
AK, CO, LA, MS, NM, OK
TN, TX, UT, WY

Miami, FL (ZMI)
77 S. E. 5th St., 3rd Fl.
Miami, FL 33131
(201) 530-6074 x310
Fax: (305) 530-6070
Director - Erich Cauller

Jurisdiction:
FL, Puerto Rico,
U.S. Virgin Islands

Chicago, IL (ZCH)
401 S. LaSalle St., 8th Fl.
Chicago, IL 60605
(312) 353-9607
Fax: (312) 886-0204
Director - Robert Esbrook

Jurisdiction:
IL, IN, MI, WI, MN, ND, SD, KS,
MO, OH, IA, NE, MT, ID, KY

Los Angeles, CA
Mailing address:
P.O. Box 65015
Anaheim, CA 92815-5015

Street address:
290 S. Anaheim Blvd., Rm. 101
Anaheim, CA 92805
(714) 635-0126
Fax: (714) 635-8707
Acting Director – Irene Martin

Jurisdiction:
AZ, CA (southern), NV (southern)

Newark, NJ (ZNK)
1200 Wall St. West, 4th Fl.
Lyndhurst, NJ 07071
(201) 531-0555
Fax: (201) 531-1877
Director - Susan Dibbins

Jurisdiction:
ME, MA, NH, NJ, CT, DE
Most of NY, PA, RI, VT.

Rosedale, NY (ZNY)
One Cross Island Plaza, Rm. 3413
Rosedale, NY 11422
(718) 723-5954
Fax: (718) 723-1121
Director - Patricia Trubiano

Jurisdiction:
NY (within boroughs of Queens, Brooklyn, Staten Island).

San Francisco, CA (ZSF)
Mailing address:
P.O. Box 77530
San Francisco, CA 94107

Street Address:
75 Hawthorne St.
3rd Floor, South Wing
San Francisco, CA 94105
415) 741-8411
Fax: (415) 744-8409
Director - Lawrence Crider

Jurisdiction:
CA (northern), NV (only areas under Reno suboffice jurisdiction), OR, WA, AK, HI, Guam

APPENDIX F

SCHEDULE B OCCUPATIONS

(1) Assemblers
(2) Attendants, Parking Lot
(3) Attendants (Service Workers such as Personal Service Attendants, Amusement and Recreation Service Attendants)
(4) Automobile Service Station Attendants
(5) Bartenders
(6) Bookkeepers II
(7) Caretakers
(8) Cashiers
(9) Charworkers and Cleaners
(10) Chauffeurs and Taxicab Drivers
(11) Cleaners, Hotel and Motel
(12) Clerks, General
(13) Clerks, Hotel
(14) Clerks and Checkers, Grocery Stores
(15) Clerk Typists
(16) Cooks, Short Order
(17) Counter and Fountain Workers
(18) Dining Room Attendants
(19) Electric Truck Operators
(20) Elevator Operators
(21) Floorworkers
(22) Groundskeepers
(23) Guards
(24) Helpers, any industry
(25) Hotel Cleaners
(26) Household Domestic Service Workers
(27) Housekeepers
(28) Janitors
(29) Key Punch Operators
(30) Kitchen Workers
(31) Laborers, Common
(32) Laborers, Farm
(33) Laborers, Mine
(34) Loopers and Toppers
(35) Material Handlers
(36) Nurses' Aides and Orderlies
(37) Packers, Markers, Bottlers and Related
(38) Porters
(39) Receptionists
(40) Sailors and Deck Hands
(41) Sales Clerks, General

(42) Sewing Machine Operators and Handstitchers
(43) Stock Room and Warehouse Workers
(44) Streetcar and Bus Conductors
(45) Telephone Operators
(46) Truck Drivers and Tractor Drivers
(47) Typists, Lesser Skilled
(48) Ushers, Recreation and Amusement
(49) Yard Workers

Descriptions of Schedule B occupations-

1) "Assemblers" perform one or more repetitive tasks to assemble components and subassemblies using hand or power tools to mass-produce a variety of components, products or equipment. They perform such activities as riveting, drilling, filing, bolting, soldering, spot welding, cementing, gluing, cutting and fitting. They may use clamps or other work aids to hold parts during assembly, inspect or test components, or tend previously set-up or automatic machines.

2) "Attendants, Parking Lot" park automobiles for customers in parking lots or garages and may collect fees based on time span of parking.

3) "Attendants (Service Workers such as Personal Service Attendants, Amusement and Recreation Service Attendants)" perform a variety of routine tasks attending to the personal needs of customers at such places as amusement parks, bath houses, clothing check-rooms, and dressing rooms, including such tasks as taking and issuing tickets, checking and issuing clothing and supplies, cleaning premises and equipment, answering inquiries, checking lists, and maintaining simple records.

4) "Automobile Service Station Attendants" service automotive vehicles with fuel, lubricants, and automotive accessories at drive-in service facilities; may also compute charges and collect fees from customers.

5) "Bartenders" prepare, mix, and dispense alcoholic beverages for consumption by bar customers, and compute and collect charges for drinks.

6) "Bookkeepers II" keep records of one facet of an establishment's financial transactions by maintaining one set of books; specialize in such areas as accounts-payable, accounts-receivable, or interest accrued rather than a complete set of records.

7) "Caretakers" perform a combination of duties to keep a private home clean and in good condition such as cleaning and dusting furniture and furnishings, hallways and lavatories; beating, vacuuming, and scrubbing rugs; washing windows, waxing and polishing floors; removing and hanging draperies; cleaning and oiling furnaces and other equipment; repairing mechanical and electrical appliances; and painting.

8) "Cashiers" receive payments made by customers for goods or services, make change, give receipts, operate cash registers, balance cash accounts, prepare bank deposits and perform other related duties.

9) "Charworkers and Cleaners" keep the premises of commercial establishments, office buildings, or

apartment houses in clean and orderly condition by performing, according to a set routine, such tasks as mopping and sweeping floors, dusting and polishing furniture and fixtures, and vacuuming rugs.

10) "Chauffeurs and Taxicab Drivers" drive automobiles to convey passengers according to the passengers' instructions.

11) "Cleaners, Hotel and Motel" clean hotel rooms and halls, sweep and mop floors, dust furniture, empty wastebaskets, and make beds.

12) "Clerks, General" perform a variety of routine clerical tasks not requiring knowledge of systems or procedures such as copying and posting data, proofreading records or forms, counting, weighing, or measuring material, routing correspondence, answering telephones, conveying messages, and running errands.

13) "Clerks, Hotel" perform a variety of routine tasks to serve hotel guests such as registering guests, dispensing keys, distributing mail, collecting payments, and adjusting complaints.

14) "Clerks and Checkers, Grocery Stores" itemize, total, and receive payments for purchases in grocery stores, usually using cash registers; often assist customers in locating items, stock shelves, and keep stock-control and sales-transaction records.

15) "Clerk Typists" perform general clerical work which, for the majority of duties, requires the use of typewriters: perform such activities as typing reports, bills, application forms, shipping tickets, and other matters from clerical records, filing records and reports, posting information to records, sorting and distributing mail, answering phones and similar duties.

16) "Cooks-Short Order" prepare and cook to order all kinds of short-preparation-time foods; may perform such activities as carving meats, filling orders from a steamtable, preparing sandwiches, salads and beverages, and serving meals over a counter.

17) "Counter and Fountain Workers" serve food to patrons at lunchroom counters, cafeterias, soda fountains, or similar public eating places; take orders from customers and frequently prepare simple items, such as desert dishes; itemize and total checks; receive payment and make change; clean work areas and equipment.

18) "Dining Room Attendants" facilitate food service in eating-places by performing such tasks as removing dirty dishes, replenishing linen and silver supplies, serving water and butter to patrons, and cleaning and polishing equipment.

19) "Electric Truck Operators" drive gasoline- or electric-powered industrial trucks or tractors equipped with forklift, elevating platform, or trailer hitch to move and stack equipment and materials in a warehouse, storage yard, or factory.

20) "Elevator Operators" operate elevators to transport passengers and freight between building floors.

21) "Floorworkers" perform a variety of routine tasks in support of other workers in and around such work sites as factory floors and service areas, frequently at the beck and call of others; perform such tasks as cleaning floors, materials and equipment, distributing materials and tools to workers, running errands, delivering messages, emptying containers, and removing materials from work areas to storage or shipping areas.

22) "Groundskeepers" maintain grounds of industrial, commercial, or public property in good condition by performing such tasks as cutting lawns, trimming hedges, pruning trees, repairing fences, planting flowers, and shoveling snow.

23) "Guards" guard and patrol premises of industrial or business establishments or similar types of property to prevent theft and other crimes and prevent possible injury to others.

24) "Helpers (any industry)" perform a variety of duties to assist other workers who are usually of a higher level of competency of expertness by furnishing such workers with materials, tools, and supplies, cleaning work areas, machines and equipment, feeding or offbearing machines, and/or holding materials or tools.

25) "Hotel Cleaners" perform routine tasks to keep hotel premises neat and clean such as cleaning rugs, washing walls, ceilings and windows, moving furniture, mopping and waxing floors, and polishing metalwork.

26) "Household Domestic Service Workers" perform a variety of tasks in private households, such as cleaning, dusting, washing, ironing, making beds, maintaining clothes, marketing, cooking, serving food, and caring for children or disabled persons. This definition, however, applies only to workers who have had less than one year of documented full-time paid experience in the tasks to be performed, working on a live-in or live-out basis in private households or in public or private institutions or establishments where the worker has performed tasks equivalent to tasks normally associated with the maintenance of a private household. This definition does not include household workers who primarily provide health or instructional services.

27) "Housekeepers" supervise workers engaged in maintaining interiors of commercial residential buildings in a clean and orderly fashion, assign duties to cleaners (hotel and motel), charworkers, and hotel cleaners, inspect finished work, and maintain supplies of equipment and materials.

28) "Janitors" keep hotels, office buildings, apartment houses, or similar buildings in clean and orderly condition, and tend furnaces and boilers to provide heat and hot water; perform such tasks as sweeping and mopping floors, emptying trash containers, and doing minor painting and plumbing repairs; often maintain their residence at their places of work.

29) "Keypunch Operators", using machines similar in action to typewriters, punch holes in cards in such a position that each hole can be identified as representing a specific item of information. These punched cards may be used with electronic computers or tabulating machines.

30) "Kitchen Workers" perform routine tasks in the kitchens of restaurants. Their primary responsibility is to maintain work areas and equipment in a clean and orderly fashion by performing such tasks as mopping floors, removing trash, washing pots and pans, transferring supplies and equipment, and washing and peeling vegetables.

31) "Laborers, Common" perform routine tasks, upon instructions and according to set routine, in an industrial, construction or manufacturing environment such as loading and moving equipment and supplies, cleaning work areas, and distributing tools.

32) "Laborers, Farm" plant, cultivate, and harvest farm products, following the instructions of supervisors, often working as members of a team. Their typical tasks are watering and feeding livestock, picking fruit and vegetables, and cleaning storage areas and equipment.

33) "Laborers, Mine" perform routine tasks in underground or surface mines, pits, or quarries, or at tipples, mills, or preparation plants such as cleaning work areas, shoveling coal onto conveyors, pushing mine cars from working faces to haulage roads, and loading or sorting material onto wheelbarrows.

34) "Loopers and Toppers" tend machines that shear nap, loose threads, and knots from cloth surfaces to give uniform finish and texture, (ii) operate looping machines to close openings in the toes of seamless hose or join knitted garment parts, (iii) loop stitches or ribbed garment parts on the points of transfer bars to facilitate the transfer of garment parts to the needles of knitting machines.

35) "Material Handlers" load, unload, and convey materials within or near plants, yards, or worksites under specific instructions.

36) "Nurses' Aides and Orderlies" assist in the care of hospital patients by performing such activities as bathing, dressing and undressing patients and giving alcohol rubs, serving and collecting food trays, cleaning and shaving hair from the skin areas of operative cases, lifting patients onto and from beds, transporting patients to treatment units, changing bed linens, running errands, and directing visitors.

37) "Packers, Markers, Bottlers, and Related" pack products into containers, such as cartons or crates, mark identifying information on articles, insure that filled bottles are properly sealed and marked, often working in teams on or at end of assembly lines.

38) "Porters" carry baggage by hand or handtruck for airline, railroad or bus passengers, and perform related personal services in and around public transportation environments. Keep building premises, working areas in production departments of industrial organizations, or similar sites in clean and orderly condition.

39) "Receptionists" receive clients or customers coming into establishments, ascertain their wants, and direct them accordingly; perform such activities as arranging appointments, directing callers to their destinations, recording names, times, nature of business and persons seen and answering phones.

40) "Sailors and Deck Hands" stand deck watches and perform a variety of tasks to preserve painted surfaces of ships and to maintain lines, running gear, and cargo handling gear in safe operating condition; perform such tasks as mopping decks, chipping rust, painting chipped areas, and splicing rope.

41) "Sales Clerks, General" receive payment for merchandise in retail establishments, wrap or bag merchandise, and keep shelves stocked.

42) "Sewing Machine Operators and Hand-Stitchers" operate single- or multiple-needle sewing machines to join parts in the manufacture of such products as awnings, carpets, and gloves; specialize in one type of sewing machine limited to joining operations. Join and reinforce parts of articles such as garments and curtains, sew buttonholes and attach fasteners to such articles, or sew decorative trimmings on such articles, using needles and threads.

43) "Stock Room and Warehouse Workers" receive, store, ship, and distribute materials, tools, equipment, and products within establishments as directed by others.

44) "Streetcar and Bus Conductors" collect fares or tickets from passengers, issue transfers, open and close doors, announce stops, answer questions, and signal operators to start or stop.

45) "Telephone Operators" operate telephone switchboards to relay incoming and internal calls to phones in an establishment, and make connections with external lines for outgoing calls; often take messages, supply information and keep records of calls and charges; often are involved primarily in establishing, or aiding telephone users in establishing, local or long distance telephone connections.

46) "Truck Drivers and Tractor Drivers" drive trucks to transport materials, merchandise, equipment or people to and from specified destinations, such as plants, railroad stations, and offices. Drive tractors to move materials, draw implements, pull out objects imbedded in the ground, or pull cables of winches to raise, lower, or load heavy materials or equipment.

47) "Typists, Lesser Skilled" type straight-copy material, such as letters, reports, stencils, and addresses, from drafts or corrected copies. They are not required to prepare materials involving the understanding of complicated technical terminology, the arrangement and setting of complex tabular detail or similar items. Their typing speed in English does not exceed 52 words per minute on a manual typewriter and/or 60 words per minute on an electric typewriter and their error rate is 12 or more errors per 5 minute typing period on representative business correspondence.

48) "Ushers (Recreation and Amusement)" assist patrons at entertainment events to find seats, search for lost articles, and locate facilities.

49) "Yard Workers" maintain the grounds of private residences in good order by performing such tasks as mowing and watering lawns, planting flowers and shrubs, and repairing and painting fences. They work on the instructions of private employers.

APPENDIX G

AUTHORIZED EB-5 PILOT PROGRAM PARTICIPANTS

World Trade Center/Greenville-Spartenburg Inc.
315 Old Boiling Springs Road
Greer, SC, 29650

Beacon U.S. Studios Inc.
5610 Sanderling Way
Blaine, WA, 98230

City of New Orleans
Mayor's Economic Development Department
1300 Perdido Street, Suite 8E10
New Orleans, LA, 70112

North Country Alliance
One Lincoln Boulevard
Rouses Point, NY, 12979

Aero-Space Port International Group
512 Strander Boulevard
Tukwila, WA, 98188

North Texas Commission
P.O. Box 610246
DFW Airport, TX, 75261

CMB Export LLC
Corona Professional Center
400 S. Ramona Avenue, Suite 212AA
Corona, CA, 91719

Legacy Project
1100 Spring Street, Suite 600
Atlanta, GA, 30309

Abacacus Advisors, Inc.
195 Boston Post Road
Weston, MA, 02193

American Export Partners
10 State Street
Charleston, SC, 29401

Danou Enterprises
World Trade Center Detroit/Windsor
1251 Fort Street
Trenton, MI, 48183

Pueblo Economic Development Corporation
P.O. Box 5807
Pueblo, CO, 81002

GV Development
7525 W. Highway 68
P. O. Box 10430
Golden Valley, AZ, 86410-2430

Unibex Global Corporation
1201 Eleanor Avenue
Las Vegas, NV, 89106

State of Hawaii Department of Business
Economic Development & Tourism
P.O. Box 2359
Honolulu, HI, 96804

Atlanta International Center for Academics and Athletics
1131 Alpharetta Street
Roswell, GA, 30075

The Gateway Freedom Fund (Golden Rainbow Freedom Fund)
18034 13th Street
Seattle, WA, 98177

West Rand Gold Trust
P.O. Box 2222
Ridgecrest, CA, 93556

Miami Chinese Community Center, Ltd.
331 NE 18th Street
Miami, FL, 33132

CKS Western Inc. World Trade Center
602 W. Graham Drive
Lake Elsinore, CA, 92530

Empirical Entertainment
6255 Sunset Boulevard, Suite 2000
Hollywood, CA, 90028

State of Vermont
Agency of Commerce and Community Development
109 State Street
Montpellier, VT, 05609-0501

Trading Partners International of California LLC
2677 N. Main Street, Suite 930
Santa Ana, CA, 92705

APPENDIX H

Department of Labor Regional Offices

REGION I

Regional Certifying Officer
U. S. Department of Labor
E.T.A./Alien Labor Certification
Boston, MA, 00203
(617) 565- 2264; - 4446
Fax: (617) 565- 2158

REGION II

Regional Certifying Officer
U. S. Department of Labor
E. T .A.
201 Varick Street Rm. 775
New York, NY, 10014
(212) 337-2185; -2193; - 2184; - 2387
Fax: (212) 337-1342

REGION III

Regional Certifying Officer
U.S. Department of Labor
E. T .A.
(215) 596-6363; - 5033
Fax: (215) 596-0480

Mailing Address:
P. O. Box 8796
Philadelphia, PA, 19101 – 8796

Delivery Address:
3535 Market St. Rm. 13450
Philadelphia, PA, 19104 - 8796

REGION IV

Regional Certifying Officer
U.S. Department of Labor
E. T .A.
Atlanta Federal Center Rm. 6M12
61 Forsyth St., SW
Atlanta, GA, 30303
(404) 562- 2092

REGION V

Regional Certifying Officer
U.S. Department of Labor
E. T .A.
230 S. Dearborn St. Rm. 605
Chicago, IL, 60604
(312) 353-1059; - 1550; - 4703; - 8145; - 8927
(312) 793 - 7950
Fax: (312) 353-1509

REGION VI

Regional Certifying Officer
U.S. Department of Labor
E. T .A.
525 Griffin Street Suite 311
Dallas, TX, 75202
(214) 767- 4989; - 4976
Fax: (214) 767-4788

REGION VII

Regional Certifying Officer
U.S. Department of Labor
E. T .A.
City Center Square
1100 Main St., Suite. 1050
Kansas, MI, 64105
(816) 426-1650
Fax: (816) 426 – 2729

REGION VIII

Regional Certifying Officer
U.S. Department of Labor
E. T .A.
1999 Broadway, Ste. 1780
Denver, CO, 80202
(303) 844-1650
Fax: (303) 884-1685

REGION IX

Regional Certifying Officer
U.S. Department of Labor
E. T .A.
71 Stevenson Street
P.O. Box 193767
San Francisco, CA, 94119-3767
(415) 975- 4601
Fax: (415) 975-4660

REGION X

Regional Certifying Officer
U.S. Department of Labor
E. T .A.
1111 Third Avenue, Suite 900
Seattle, WA, 98101-2069
(206) 553-5297
Fax: (206) 553-2069

APPENDIX I

IMMIGRATION WEB SITES*

UNITED STATES IMMIGRATION AND NATURALIZATION SERVICE
http://www.ins.usdoj.gov/

DEPARTMENT OF JUSTICE
http://www.usdoj.gov/

EXECUTIVE OFFICE OF IMMIGRATION REVIEW
http://www.usdoj.gov/eoir

BOARD OF IMMIGRATION APPEALS
http://www.usdoj.gov/eoir/eoirmain.htm#BIA

DEPARTMENT OF LABOR
http://www.dol.gov/

EMPLOYMENT TRAINING ADMINISTRATION
http://www.doleta.gov/

OFFICE OF ADMINISTRATIVE LAW JUDGES
http://www.oalj.dol.gov/libina.htm

OCCUPATIONAL EMPLOYMENT STATISTICS
http://stats.bls.gov/oeshome.htm

DICTIONARY OF OCCUPATIONAL TITLES
http://www.oalj.dol.gov/libdot.htm

OCCUPATIONAL OUTLOOK HANDBOOK
http://stats.bls.gov/ochome.htm

DEPARTMENT OF STATE
http://www.state.gov/

DEPARTMENT OF STATE, BUREAU OF CONSULAR AFFAIRS
http://travel.state.gov

VISA BULLETIN
http://travel.state.gov/visa.bulletin.html

DEMOCRACY, HUMAN RIGHTS AND LABOR
http://www.state.gov/www/global/human_rights/index.html

UNITED STATES INFORMATION AGENCY
http://www.usia.gov/

EXCHANGE VISITOR ("J") SKILLS LIST
http://www.usia.gov/abtusia/leagl/gc/cfrs/514/skills.txt

EXCHANGE VISITOR PROGRAM REGULATIONS
http://www.usia.gov/abtusia/legal/gc/cfrs/514/514.htm

RESPONSIBLE OFFICER PROGRAM MANUAL
http://www.usia.gov/abtusia/legal/gc/cfrs/514/rom.htm

FEDERAL REGISTER
http://www.gpo.gov/su_docs/aces/aces140.html

AMNESTY INTERNATIONAL
http://www.amnesty.org

* Please note that web site addresses are subject to change

UNITED STATES IMMIGRATION LAWS:
Working, Living, and Studying in America

SECOND EDITION

BARST & MUKAMAL LLP

STEVEN S. MUKAMAL
AND
MARTIN L. ROTHSTEIN

William S. HEIN & Co., Inc.

CHAPTER FOUR - THE L VISA CATEGORY

CHAPTER ELEVEN – PENALTIES, BARS & RESTRICTIONS

